———————————— ∞ · ∞ · ∞ ————————————

"Tim Bartik has written a thoughtful book on the value of a local approach to financing and creating early interventions to foster child development. The economic case for supplementing the early environments of disadvantaged children is compelling. Annual rates of return of 7–10 percent per annum have been estimated—higher than the return on stocks over the period 1945–2008. Yet there are substantial barriers to the adoption of these programs, which Bartik documents. Bartik makes a valuable argument for engaging governments and private organizations at the local level to design and finance these programs. He presents evidence that there are substantial benefits from early childhood programs that accrue to localities. This book shows that a decentralized approach to early childhood development will encourage experimentation and will adapt the programs to local needs. In an era of stringent federal budgets, Bartik offers a plan for raising the support needed to put effective programs into place."
—*James Heckman, Nobel Prize–winning economist, University of Chicago*

"Timothy Bartik takes us on an expertly narrated tour of that middle ground between what theory says ought to happen and what the real world actually presents. His disciplined fidelity to the evidence makes this, like every Bartik book, a guidepost for policy."
—*John D. Donahue, Harvard Kennedy School; former Assistant Secretary of Labor*

"Building a strong workforce—one that will drive the economic growth and prosperity of the future—requires the strong foundation that quality preschool provides. Tim Bartik delivers an important message—one that both employers and policymakers should heed. Our Chamber continues to advocate that local and state economies are strengthened by investments in both quality pre-K programs and business incentives. It cannot be a matter of choosing one over the other."
—*Dave Adkisson, President and CEO, Kentucky Chamber of Commerce*

"Tim Bartik's book makes an excellent case that increasing our investment in a continuum of early childhood programs pays off when examined from a business and economic perspective. This work includes an important contribution by quantifying how specific improvements in program design of early childhood programs will increase economic benefits. It's past the time to expand our early childhood program investments within the context of a commitment to quality and accountability. This would be a good book for business leaders and others who should focus on an economic rationale for public investment in early childhood learning."
—*Harriet Dichter, former Secretary, Pennsylvania Department of Public Welfare*

———————————— ∞ · ∞ · ∞ ————————————

"Bartik's new book is a comprehensive and compelling argument for a one-two economic development punch: how state and local governments need to combine both tax incentives for businesses and investments in early childhood education. Once again, Bartik shows why he is the 'go-to guy' on the economics of local economic development."
—*Michael Mandel, former Chief Economist at* BusinessWeek

"When oxygen is literally being sucked out of state and federal budgets, we can't afford to assume that what we're doing with taxpayer dollars works, in spite of the growing evidence that it doesn't. State and local economic development officials need new strategies, ones backed by fact and evidence. Tim Bartik provides exactly this in his powerfully researched book that documents the link between economic development and investing in young children in ways never done before. Now business leaders and development officials have a sober, fact-based framework for increasing personal incomes, local and state workforce competitiveness, and national fiscal strength. This is a framework for getting our country back on its feet and keeping it there."
—*Robert Dugger, founder and Managing Partner, Hanover Investment Group; Chairman of the Advisory Board, Partnership for America's Economic Success*

"Whenever a new book, report, or article appears with Tim Bartik as the author, I take notice and make time for reading. I know that it will be lucidly written and ably argued. Tim has a knack for picking a real problem on which to work and a good feel for what's the level of rigor that is needed. Many economists do not. Lastly, Tim understands that an economy grows on the basis of lots of forces and events. Not all of them are narrowly economic. Tim's work on investments in early childhood development is an excellent example."
—*William Schweke, Senior Fellow, Corporation for Enterprise Development*

"The case for treating early childhood development as economic development is long overdue. Timothy Bartik's book is the first to take a comprehensive and in-depth look at this issue. Examining both economic development and early childhood development from a local perspective, Bartik makes a convincing argument that early childhood investments are an important but often overlooked form of economic development. Indeed, he also makes a strong case that from a national perspective we are underinvesting in our children, especially in our most at-risk children. Bartik's book has much to offer those working in the field of economic development and gives much-needed support to early childhood educators and their profession."
—*Arthur Rolnick, former Senior Vice President and Director of Research, Federal Reserve Bank of Minneapolis*

"States will continue to need to make harder choices as fiscal realities change. The good news is that those choices will increasingly be based on evidence of what works, a change that is long overdue. The other good news is that children should finally come out on top—the evidence is on their side. I have pushed for years to invest more in our youngest citizens, and I am delighted to have new ammunition for that fight in the form of this new book from Tim Bartik."

—Barbara O'Brien, Lieutenant Governor, State of Colorado

"The disastrous consequences of short-term decision making in economics and policy are more evident today than ever. Timothy Bartik is an exponent of the view that there is no short term. His latest book is a must read for everyone concerned with setting priorities for government spending and our children's futures."

—W. Steven Barnett, Codirector, National Institute for Early Education Research

"For too long, supports for young children have been seen as a feel-good issue that mainly concerns families, and not one that affects all of us as a nation. In this book, Tim Bartik uses solid economic evidence of benefits not just from "hothouse" early childhood programs but from a large-scale Chicago program currently in existence to demonstrate the critical need for policymakers to pay attention. Leaders in the early childhood community are delighted to have this new tool, and we hope it helps put to rest any lingering doubts that our collective future depends on investing wisely in our children and in their futures."

—William H. Bentley, President and CEO, Voices for America's Children

"Timothy Bartik is that rare economist who is deeply committed to making his work accessible to policymakers while maintaining the highest technical standards and let-ting empirical research drive his recommendations. Here he has created an invaluable framework for comparing the cost-effectiveness of business incentives and strategic investments in human capital as alternative strategies for promoting the economic well-being of states and their residents. This book should be required reading for every governor's chief policy advisor and every state legislator who serves on a tax, economic development, or education committee."

—Michael Mazerov, Senior Fellow, State Fiscal Project, Center on Budget and Policy Priorities

"The future of America is no longer dependent on our natural resources or geographic location; it is our people. More importantly it is our ability to produce bright, intuitive lifelong learners. Bartik has crafted a must read for those who truly care about com-munity and economic sustainability."

—Ron Kitchens, CEO, Southwest Michigan First

Investing in Kids

Investing in Kids

Early Childhood Programs and Local Economic Development

Timothy J. Bartik

2011

W.E. Upjohn Institute for Employment Research
Kalamazoo, Michigan

Library of Congress Cataloging-in-Publication Data

Bartik, Timothy J.
  Investing in kids : early childhood programs and local economic development /
Timothy J. Bartik.
     p. cm.
  Includes bibliographical references and index.
  ISBN-13: 978-0-88099-372-2 (pbk. : alk. paper)
  ISBN-10: 0-88099-372-3 (pbk. : alk. paper)
  ISBN-13: 978-0-88099-373-9 (hardcover : alk. paper)
  ISBN-10: 0-88099-373-1 (hardcover : alk. paper)
1. Economic development—United States. 2. Early childhood education—United
States. I. Title.
  HC79.E47B37 2010
  338.973—dc22
                                  2010049422

The facts presented in this study and the observations and viewpoints expressed are
the sole responsibility of the author. They do not necessarily represent positions of
the W.E. Upjohn Institute for Employment Research.

Cover design by Alcorn Publication Design.
Index prepared by Diane Worden.
Printed in the United States of America.
Printed on recycled paper.

To my mother, Jean Jennings Bartik, with love, and in recognition of a life of determination and integrity.

Contents

Tables

Figures

Acknowledgments

I appreciate the financial support of the Upjohn Institute and the Pew Charitable Trusts for the research for and writing of this book. In addition, I appreciate the financial support of the Upjohn Institute and the Pew Charitable Trusts, along with that of the Committee for Economic Development, for the research that led up to this book. The findings and opinions expressed in this book are mine, and do not necessarily reflect the views of the Upjohn Institute, the Committee for Economic Development, or the Pew Charitable Trusts.

At the Upjohn Institute, I appreciate the support of the Institute's president, Randy Eberts. I also appreciate research assistance from Wei-Jang Huang, and assistance with the manuscript's many complexities from Claire Black. Linda Richer and the entire Upjohn Institute library staff also assisted in tracking down various references, for which I thank them. Comments on the manuscript and manuscript plans were received at various stages from Kevin Hollenbeck, Michelle Miller-Adams, Rich Wyrwa, Ben Jones, and George Erickcek. The manuscript was edited by Ben Jones.

At the Pew Charitable Trusts, I appreciate the support of Sara Watson and Elaine Weiss. I also received helpful comments from Elaine Weiss and Rob Krupicka at Pew, and from Albert Wat at Pre-K Now.

Additionally, I received helpful comments from two anonymous outside reviewers. These comments led to some significant revisions in the draft manuscript.

I have learned from the opportunity to present versions of this research to different early childhood audiences. I appreciate opportunities to make such presentations provided by Diane Neighbors of the Vanderbilt Child and Family Study Center in Tennessee; the Louisiana Family Impact Seminar; Diane Halstead of the Pennsylvania Early Learning Investment Commission, the Pennsylvania Early Learning Keys to Quality; Rob Dugger of the Invest in Kids Working Group; and Judy Samelson of the Michigan Early Childhood Investment Corporation.

I have also benefited from the opportunity to present versions of this research to economic development audiences. I appreciate such opportunities provided by Karen Bogenschneider of the Wisconsin Family Impact Seminar, the Milken Institute, George Fulton of the Research Seminar in Quantitative Economics, Hillary Eley of the Branch County Area Chamber of Commerce, and Dana Rothstein of the International Economic Development Council.

In Kalamazoo, I have learned from my work with the Early Childhood Committee of the community organizing group ISAAC, and with the Kalamazoo County Committee for Early Childhood Education. I have learned from many individuals in these groups, but I wanted in particular to acknowledge Denise Hartsough, Rachael Tanner, and Rochelle Habeck-Hunt.

1
Introduction

This book presents arguments for the following propositions: Local[1] economic development strategies in the United States should include extensive investments in high-quality early childhood programs, such as prekindergarten (pre-K) education,[2] child care, and parenting assistance. Economic development policies should also include reforms in business tax incentives. But economic development benefits—higher earnings per capita in the local community—can be better achieved if business incentives are complemented by early childhood programs. Economic development benefits can play an important role in motivating a grassroots movement for investing in our kids.

I first became involved with early childhood policy in May of 2005, when I was contacted by a vice president for the Committee for Economic Development (CED). CED is a national organization of business executives and university presidents that sponsors research and takes positions on policy issues. CED tends to take "centrist" positions.

As I was to discover later, CED's work on early childhood issues was largely funded by the Pew Charitable Trusts, a large national foundation headquartered in Philadelphia. Pew had decided to get involved in promoting the greater availability of high-quality pre-K education in the fall of 2001. Pew soon moved into a national leadership role in promoting pre-K expansion. As David Kirp, professor of public policy at the University of California, Berkeley, says in his book *The Sandbox Investment*, "Ever since the Pew Charitable Trusts made preschool a priority, the foundation has largely masterminded the national early education agenda" (Kirp 2007, pp. 174–175). Pew has provided much of the funding for the National Institute for Early Education Research at Rutgers University, and for the advocacy group Pre-K Now. After several years of focusing its efforts on pre-K education, Pew has expanded to encompass a broader set of early childhood programs.

According to Pew staff, political support for early childhood programs is enhanced by evidence that these programs provide business or economic benefits: "One very successful part of the early education message that resonates with a variety of important audiences," say Pew staff Urahn and Watson (2006), "has been the macroeconomic benefits prekindergarten offers to the communities and states that invest in early education. This message has generated substantial interest from advocates, policymakers, and business leaders, helping them understand the value of early education in a new light." Therefore, Pew has funded research that explores different ways of measuring the economic or business return to pre-K education. In the past several years, Pew has also funded research on the economic returns to other early childhood programs. This Pew research funding includes my 2005–2006 research on the economic development effects of universal pre-K education, my 2007–2008 research on the economic development effects of other early childhood programs, and now this book, which summarizes and expands on this earlier work.[3]

When I was contacted in 2005, CED's request was to "compare the net benefits/rate of return to prekindergarten programs with alternative state and local economic development investments (such as sports stadiums, business parks, facilities relocation, and the like)." The committee mentioned that it had contacted me because "much of your work focuses on economic development." My previous work in this area includes a 1991 book on the distributional effects of economic development programs, and research publications on the effects of taxes and public services on business location decisions, and on how to evaluate local economic development programs.

As I reflected on CED's request, I decided it made more sense if modified. This research seeks to be relevant to the concerns of political and business leaders interested in local economic development. To achieve this relevance, we need to consider effects of prekindergarten programs that are similar in character to the effects of economic development programs. For example, one of the most important benefits of some high-quality pre-K programs is the resulting reduction in crime when the children get older. Crime reduction is of interest to police chiefs and to voters in general. But crime reduction is not the primary goal of economic development programs. Rather, these programs seek to create jobs and earnings for local residents. If there is any case to be made for pre-K programs as "economic development programs," then pre-K programs need to provide "economic development benefits." These benefits are increased jobs or earnings for local residents.

Ironically, my modification of the CED/Pew request was inspired by a research publication that focused on crime reduction. In 1996 (updated in 1998), the RAND Corporation published *Diverting Children from a Life of Crime* (Greenwood et al. 1998). This publication compared the anticrime effects of California's "three strikes" law, which mandates long prison sentences for repeat offenders, with the anticrime effects of four social programs. These four social programs include 1) home visits, 2) parenting training and therapy, 3) high school graduation incentives, and 4) early supervision of delinquent high school youth. Greenwood et al. compared these four social programs with the "three strikes" law in terms of the serious crimes averted per million dollars spent.

I admired this RAND publication because it directly addressed concerns about crime. The publication says that if your goal is reduced crime, here is what various programs can do for you. RAND accepted the legitimacy of concerns about crime rather than belittling those concerns. RAND tried to provide objective evidence on what is the best means of achieving anticrime goals.

My thought was that something similar could be done for economic development goals. As is developed further in this book, there are good reasons to think that economic development goals are important. But what is the best strategy for achieving those goals? Could pre-K play an important role in achieving economic development goals? These are questions that could benefit, it seemed to me, from some objective investigation.

CLARIFYING PREVIOUS THINKING

My 2005 research was not the first research on what early childhood programs can do for local economies. Much of the recent interest in the economic development benefits of pre-K education was sparked by a March 2003 article by Rolnick and Grunewald, "Early Childhood Development: Economic Development with a High Public Return." Art Rolnick was director of research at the Federal Reserve Bank of Minneapolis until 2010. Rolnick is a well-known participant in debates related to Minnesota and Twin Cities economic development. Rob Grunewald is a regional economic analyst at the Minneapolis Fed. This article was quickly shared within the early childhood community. The article was also quickly used to advocate for more funding for high-quality pre-K education. As Rolnick (2008) said, because of this article, "our phones have been ringing off the hook."

In this article, Rolnick and Grunewald (2003) argue for pre-K because "we estimate the real internal rate of return for the Perry School program at 16 percent . . . about 80 percent of the benefits went to the general public (students were less disruptive in class and went on to commit fewer crimes), yielding over a 12 percent internal rate of return for society in general . . . The returns to [early childhood development programs] are especially high when placed next to other spending by governments made in the name of economic development. Yet [early childhood development] is rarely considered as an economic development measure." (For those unfamiliar with the research on pre-K, the Perry Preschool program of the 1960s is the pre-K program with the best research evidence for long-term benefits after age 25. Participants in Perry Preschool have been compared with a randomly chosen control group up through age 40.[4] This comparison includes employment, earnings, education, welfare receipt, and involvement with crime.)

My concern about the Rolnick/Grunewald argument is that the authors treat "economic development benefits" as being the same as "economic benefits." But "economic development benefits" form a category of economic benefits that has a special importance. In arguing for the superiority of early childhood development over business incentives, Rolnick and Grunewald include all benefits. For the Perry Preschool program, they include the benefits from crime reduction, which are at least half of the benefits of this program.[5] However, reduced crime is not the same as better employment opportunities. Economic development practitioners are trying to improve employment opportunities for local residents. Are early childhood programs a good "economic development investment" if we only consider effects on employment opportunities for local residents?

An emphasis on "economic development benefits" only makes sense if such benefits are especially important. As this book will argue, improved employment opportunities for local residents do have special importance. There is something different about local jobs for local residents as an economic good. There is also a special political importance attached to these kinds of economic development benefits.

Prior to my 2005 research, there also existed research on what early childhood programs provide in "economic multiplier" benefits. Key contributors to this research have been Professor Mildred Warner at Cornell, and the Insight Center for Community Economic Development. This research estimates the economic impacts of more government spending on early childhood programs. The extra spending will lead to multiplier effects: early childhood programs will buy local supplies; pre-K teachers or other employees of early childhood programs will buy local goods and services.

Multiplier effects have a political appeal: the economic benefits are immediate. However, a state or local government that expands spending on early childhood programs must also raise taxes, unless federal or other outside funding is available. As is developed in this book, once one accounts for both taxes and spending, multiplier effects of early childhood programs are modest.

The most important economic development benefit of early childhood programs comes from their effects on their child participants. When they become adults, these former child participants have improved job skills and job attitudes. Quality has improved for their labor supply. Better local labor supply will increase local earnings. (There also are some effects on the labor supply of the parents. But for most programs, parental effects are smaller than effects on former child participants.)

Obviously, pre-K programs for four-year-olds are not sending kids into the workforce at age five. The economic development benefits of early childhood programs are mostly long-term. These economic development benefits do not begin to take off until former child participants enter the labor force, and they are not fully realized until these former child participants enter their prime earnings years. The long-term nature of economic development benefits of early childhood programs is a political handicap, because politicians often have a short-term perspective. Advocates for early childhood programs must consider how to make these long-term benefits more salient. Policy analysts must also consider that the "local" economic development benefits of early childhood programs will depend on how many former childhood participants stay in the local economy.

A BALANCED ECONOMIC DEVELOPMENT STRATEGY:
BOTH LABOR DEMAND AND LABOR SUPPLY POLICIES

Local economic development practitioners in the United States have traditionally relied on business incentives. By "business incentives," I mean policies that provide discretionary tax breaks or special services to individual employers. These discretionary tax breaks or services may be for varied purposes: encouraging new branch plants, business expansions, and new small businesses; or discouraging business closings or contractions. The bulk of these incentives are in the form of special tax breaks for new or expanding businesses, or to save and retain jobs in existing businesses. A good example of a business incentive is a property tax abatement for a new manufacturing branch plant, under which the new plant's property taxes are reduced.

Some advocates for early childhood programs are categorically opposed to business incentives for local economic development. For example, Rolnick and Grunewald (2003) argue that business incentives to encourage economic development are "fundamentally flawed."[6]

The position taken in this book is not as unfavorable to business incentives. Both business incentives and early childhood programs can promote economic development. Economic development benefits— higher earnings per capita for the residents of a state or local area—can be produced by boosts to the quantity and quality of local labor supply or labor demand. More and better jobs can result from early childhood programs that boost the quality of the local labor supply. This boost to labor supply will indirectly entice employers to create more and better jobs. But more and better jobs can also result from business incentive programs that boost the quantity or quality of local labor demand. Tax breaks or special services to individual employers may cause them to boost the number or quality of jobs.

Hence, both early childhood programs and business incentive programs may boost state or local earnings per capita. For both early childhood programs and business incentive programs, the issue is "bang for the buck." Per dollar of resources, what boost to state or local earnings per capita is provided? How does this vary with different designs of early childhood programs, or of business incentive programs? How does this vary in different local circumstances?

THE ADVANTAGES OF THINKING AND ACTING LOCALLY

Focusing on local economic development benefits is not simply a strategy for gaining support for early childhood programs from state and local business leaders and policymakers. Early childhood programs are a policy area in which it makes sense to have state and local governments take a strong role. As this book will show, many of the economic development benefits of early childhood programs are local. State and local early childhood programs may also be more innovative, effective, and flexible than a top-down federal program. The federal government should support state and local initiatives to improve early childhood program quality, data, and accountability. Well-run early childhood programs serve not only local interests, but also the national interest, so some federal financial support for early childhood programs is justified. But any federal intervention should be designed to allow for considerable local flexibility.

Conversely, some federal restrictions may be needed in order to ensure that business incentives advance national interests. As this book will show, for some business incentives, a state's pursuit of its own interests may take jobs away from other states and sizably damage the national interest. However, other business incentives may provide a greater boost to economic productivity and thus serve the national interest.

WHY CONSIDER EARLY CHILDHOOD PROGRAMS AND BUSINESS INCENTIVES TOGETHER?

This book is addressed to two audiences: 1) the early childhood policy and research community, and 2) the economic development policy and research community. Both communities, I would argue, need to understand the other community's problems and programs. The book is designed so that a reader could read only the early childhood sections or only the business incentive sections. But I think readers in both the early childhood and the economic development communities will benefit from both topics.

The economic development community needs to understand the drawbacks of traditional business incentives. There are several drawbacks: the benefits of such incentives are sensitive to good design, the possible benefits of incentives are uncertain, the incentives do not have a particularly favorable effect on income distribution, the incentives have much lower benefits in local economies that already have enough job growth, and the benefits of many incentives are lower from a national perspective. But beyond that, economic development policymakers also need to understand the economic development case for early childhood programs: early childhood programs can complement business incentives by offering more benefits for lower income groups and more clear-cut national benefits.

The other side of the coin is that the early childhood community, too, needs to understand the economic development case for early childhood programs. Proponents of early childhood programs must understand this case to effectively argue for their programs to the business community and state and local policymakers. To understand the economic development case, the early childhood community needs to understand why the economic development benefits of more local job opportunities are so valuable. Moreover, the early childhood community needs to appreciate how well-designed business incentive programs may make sense from a local perspective and even a national perspective. Advocating for a balanced economic development strategy, which includes both early childhood programs and reformed business incentives, makes more sense than trying to abolish business incentives and replace them with early childhood programs.

Business incentives and early childhood programs should be considered together because they complement each other in a balanced economic development strategy. Programs to directly create jobs via business incentives should be complemented by helping local residents obtain the skills needed for those jobs, via policies such as early childhood programs. Some local economies may need more of a boost to labor demand, whereas other local economies may need more of a boost to labor supply. But most local and national economies will benefit considerably from strengthening both labor demand and supply.

A ROAD MAP FOR THIS BOOK[7]

Chapter 2 explains why the benefits of local economic development are so important. Chapter 3 presents estimates that well-designed business incentive programs may, for each dollar invested, produce more than a $3 increase in state earnings per capita.

Chapter 4 considers the economic development benefits of pre-K education, high-quality child care and early education, and nurse home-visitation programs for disadvantaged first-time mothers. The chapter presents estimates that such high-quality early childhood programs may, for each dollar invested, produce a $2 to $3 increase in state earnings per capita.

Chapter 5 considers what constitutes "good design" for business incentives and early childhood programs. How do various features affect these programs' economic development benefits? For both business incentives and early childhood programs, the cost-effectiveness of these programs varies greatly with program design. Chapter 6 considers the implications of uncertainty: we don't know for certain the benefits of either a new business incentive or an early childhood program. How can we reconcile the need for more research with the potential benefits from near-term expansions and reforms of early childhood programs and business incentives?

Chapter 7 considers the political problem posed because the benefits of early childhood programs are mostly long-term, whereas elections occur every two years. How can the benefits of early childhood programs be made more relevant to policymakers with a short-term perspective?

Chapter 8 considers the effects of business incentives and early childhood programs on families at different income levels. Will early childhood programs have greater social benefits and political attractiveness if they are targeted at low-income families, or made accessible universally? Based on current evidence, the chapter concludes that universally accessible pre-K education, compared to pre-K education targeted at low-income families, offers greater economic as well as political benefits.

Chapter 9 shows that the benefits of business incentives and early childhood programs differ greatly across local economies of different sizes and different previous growth trends. Chapter 10 considers how the national perspective on a state's business incentives and early childhood programs may differ from the state's perspective. Under what circumstances do the spillover effects of one state's programs on other states justify federal intervention? The national perspective points to the need to regulate business incentives and promote early childhood programs.

Chapter 11 analyzes the ethical issues raised by business incentive programs and early childhood programs. Do these programs' interventions with individual businesses and families violate ethical principles? Chapter 12 shows how the approach used in this book to analyze early childhood programs can be used to estimate the economic development benefits of other human capital improvements. These other human capital improvements include better school test scores, increases in educational attainment, improved public health, and crime reduction.

Chapter 13 explains why the book's arguments and evidence make a case for a broad grassroots movement to improve early childhood programs. During the nineteenth and twentieth centuries in the United States, local economic development benefits were frequently invoked as arguments for creating graded common schools for all students and creating high schools that all students were expected to attend. History and research suggest that local economic development benefits can help support a new grassroots movement for early childhood programs.

Notes

1. In referring to "local economic development," I sometimes use that term as shorthand for "state and local economic development." States are one type of location that can experience local economic development.

2. In this book, I refer to part-time or full-time programs for three- and four-year-olds that have a predominantly educational focus as "pre-K programs" or "pre-K education," where "pre-K" is short for "prekindergarten." Some of the quotations I use refer to such programs as "pre-K" programs, whereas other quotations refer to such programs as "preschool." I avoid "preschool" because it seems a strange way to refer to a program that is predominantly educational in focus, and that in many cases is run by the public school system.

3. In writing this book, I have double-checked the numbers and simulations, and updated some numbers. Therefore, some of these new and improved detailed numbers differ modestly from results presented in my previous reports (Bartik 2006, 2008). However, these differences are modest enough that none of the previous qualitative findings of these reports must be altered. Even so, the numbers in this book should be regarded as more up-to-date and definitive estimates.

4. The Perry study has followed the lives of 123 high-risk children from African American families who lived near the Perry Elementary School in Ypsilanti, Michigan, in the 1960s.

5. In the benefit-cost analysis of the Perry Preschool program by Schweinhart et al. (2005, Table 7.8, errata-corrected version), 48 percent of the public benefits from the program are due to crime reduction. The percentage of the benefits from crime reduction would be even greater if nonmonetary costs to victims of crime were included.

6. From interviews with Art Rolnick, it is clear that his involvement in early childhood programs originally grew out of his opposition to business incentives. Opposing business incentives leads to the logical question of whether there is any alternative. When asked "How does a person in your position . . . come to focus on children?" Rolnick (2008) replied as follows: "It was an accident . . . Much of my work over the last dozen years has raised questions about . . . local economic development initiatives . . . We argued that these types of economic development programs do not create jobs, they just move them around . . . The work we were doing on the economic bidding war led us to ask the question, 'What would be the best way to promote local economic development?'"

7. In addition to the book text, there are appendices that provide additional theoretical and empirical detail on this book's arguments and estimates. These appendices are available on-line from the Upjohn Institute at http://www.upjohn.org/investinginkids/appendices.html, or via e-mail from the author. On request, a hard-copy version of these appendices is also available.

2

The Nature and Importance
of Local Economic Development
Benefits, and How They Are
Affected by Labor Demand
and Labor Supply

What is local economic development in the United States? Should we care about local economic development? Why? What are local economic development's benefits? Which of these benefits is most important? What public policies best provide these benefits? By addressing these questions, this chapter provides a conceptual framework used throughout this book.

To analyze local economic development, we must first define it. In the United States, state and local policymakers often define economic development as growth of employment, output, or population.[1]

For reasons I will give in a moment, a better definition of local economic development is growth in local per capita income. Most such growth is due to growth in local earnings per capita. The increase in local earnings per capita will be this book's definition of local economic development benefits.

Growth in local earnings per capita depends upon using local labor more productively. Unemployed labor can become employed, or employed labor can become employed in better jobs.

Why focus on per capita income or earnings rather than total income or earnings? This focus makes sense because increases in per capita income or earnings are more reliable than increases in total income or earnings in delivering a variety of economic and social benefits. First, increases in per capita income or earnings correspond to some persons gaining income. Increases in total income or earnings that are due to population growth alone, with no per capita income or earnings growth, do not necessarily correspond to any individual person gaining income. A society that has per capita income growth is more likely to be a society that offers expanded economic opportunity to a wide variety of its members.

Second, increases in per capita income are more likely than increases in total income to improve the fiscal situation of state and local governments. The evidence suggests that most state and local public services are, in the long run, produced and delivered at the same average costs per person regardless of local population, beyond some minimum population (Fisher 1996; Inman 1979). Increasing population by itself provides few long-run fiscal benefits to state and local governments. Increasing per capita income allows an improvement in the state and local fiscal situation. The same public services can be financed with a lower ratio of state and local taxes to income, or higher levels of public services can be financed with the same ratio of state and local taxes to income. As will be discussed later in this chapter, fiscal benefits are not the largest benefit from improving local economic development. But they are a benefit.

Third, increases in per capita income are more likely than increases in population alone to improve the quality of life in a local community. Higher-population communities are different from lower-population communities. Whether they are better is a matter of opinion. Higher per capita income is a more reliable way of improving the amenities of a local community. Crime is likely to be lower. Private as well as public services are likely to be better. Problems such as homelessness and poverty will be alleviated.

Fourth, growth in per capita income is likely to improve the quality of political life in a community. As argued by Harvard economist Benjamin Friedman (2005), a community or nation with better growth in per capita income is more likely to be tolerant of different groups. Per capita income growth encourages more generosity toward the disadvantaged. It also encourages more support of environmental protection. Finally, growth in per capita income may encourage greater support for the democratic process.

For all these reasons, increases in per capita income or earnings are a far better measure of economic success than increases in overall income or earnings. Such increases in per capita income and earnings can be accomplished by increases in the productivity with which local resources are used.

Of course, increases in local job growth may cause increases in per capita income or earnings, since increases in local job growth may raise local employment-to-population ratios (local employment rates) or raise local wages. These possibilities are explored further later in this chapter.

WHAT IS LOCAL ECONOMIC DEVELOPMENT POLICY?

If local economic development is increasing local per capita income or increasing the productivity with which local resources are used, almost any local policy affects economic development.

But what is usually called local economic development policy is a narrower set of policies. These policies are carried out by state or local economic development organizations. Such organizations are sometimes government agencies, but in many cases are quasipublic or even private organizations. Private economic development organizations often have some government funding.

These economic development organizations typically provide "business incentives." The goal of these business incentives is to affect business job growth or the types of jobs provided by business. The rationale is that such job growth will boost local standards of living and the local fiscal situation.

These business incentives take the form of assistance to individual businesses that is provided on a somewhat discretionary basis. The assistance is targeted at a particular type of business or customized to the particular business. This assistance may be in the form of a tax abatement or tax incentive that forgives all or a portion of the normal taxes paid by the business. Business incentives also include services that are customized to the needs of individual businesses.

Chapter 3 will review the various types of business incentives in more detail. For this chapter, a good example of a tax incentive to keep in mind is property tax abatements. Under property tax abatements, a new branch plant, or a plant expansion, pays lower than normal property tax rates on the new or expanded plant. The abatement is typically approved by some unit of local government, under rules decided by the state government. Property tax abatements may be targeted by the local government toward business expansions that are thought to offer particularly large economic development benefits—for example, businesses that pay higher wages. Other tax incentives include various discretionary state corporate income tax credits, tax increment financing, and enterprise zones.

A good example of a business incentive that is a customized business service is customized job training. Under customized job training, state or local governments pay for the training provided to workers at a specific business. The training is adapted to the business's specific training needs. The training may be tied to the business locating a new facility in the state or expanding its operations. Training is typically provided by local community colleges. Other customized business services include subsidized or free infrastructure or land, industrial extension services, entrepreneurial training, small business advice, business incubators, research and development grants, help in dealing with state and local business regulations, and help in finding a site for a new or expanded business.

In dollar magnitude, more business incentives take the form of tax incentives than customized services. Among all tax incentives, property tax abatements are probably the largest.

It is difficult to draw a definite line between business incentives on the one hand and more general tax breaks for business or services to business on the other. For example, a property tax abatement for expanding manufacturers is similar to providing a credit under the state corporate income tax to offset additional property taxes for expanding manufacturers. If community colleges design training programs to meet the needs of local businesses, and these training programs are heavily subsidized by the state, this is quite similar to a generous program of customized training grants.

THE IMPORTANCE OF LOCAL ECONOMIC DEVELOPMENT

The budget resources devoted to business incentives are a small part of state and local government. For example, it has been estimated that business incentives amount to $30 billion per year (Bartik 2001, p.

251). From many perspectives, $30 billion is a lot of money. However, it is less than 2 percent of the $1.9 trillion in annual own-source state and local government revenue (U.S. Census Bureau [2007]; figures come from the 2007 Census of Governments.) Economic development programs are larger if we include tax breaks for businesses that are written into state and tax law as entitlements, such as investment tax credits. With such tax breaks included, the total resources devoted to state and local economic development might be over $50 billion per year (Fisher and Peters 2004; Thomas 2000). This amount is still small compared to total state and local revenue or expenditure. Other state and local government functions, such as education, are far larger. For example, state and local governments spend about $535 billion annually on elementary and secondary education, and $205 billion on higher education.[2]

However, state and local economic development is an overriding goal of state and local government. It affects whether the local community survives and thrives. Local economic development efforts to keep local productivity high are critical for a community's future. If local productivity is low, then the community will lose jobs and people. If the productivity is too low, then the community will not survive. In contrast, if local productivity grows, then the community survives and living standards improve.

Economic development is an overriding goal in that other goals of state and local government must be reconcilable to the economic development goal. State and local governments provide education, public safety, transportation and other infrastructure, and so on. Each of these programs has specific goals. But if a local community is to survive and thrive, these other goals must be pursued in a way that either helps economic development, or at least does not hurt too much. Taxes must be raised to support these programs. But the tax structure must minimize adverse effects on local economic development.

This argument is not unique to me. For example, political scientist Paul Peterson, in his classic 1981 book *City Limits*, argues the following:

> In sum, cities, like private firms, compete with one another so as to maximize their economic position. To achieve this objective, the city must use the resources its land area provides by attracting as much capital and as high a quality labor force as is possible. Like a private firm, the city must entice labor and capital resources by offering appropriate inducements. Unlike the nation-state, the

American city does not have regulatory powers to control labor and capital flows. The lack thereof sharply limits what cities can do to control their economic development, but at the same time the attempt by cities to maximize their interests within these limits shapes policy choices . . .

Local government leaders are likely to be sensitive to the economic interests of their communities. First, economic prosperity is necessary for protecting the fiscal base of a local government . . . Second, good government is good politics . . . Few policies are more popular than economic growth and prosperity. Third, and most important, local officials usually have a sense of community responsibility. They know that, unless the economic well-being of the community can be maintained, local business will suffer, workers will lose employment opportunities, cultural life will decline, and city land values will fall. To avoid such a dismal future, public officials try to develop policies that assist the prosperity of their community—or, at the very least, that do not seriously detract from it . . . It is quite reasonable to posit that local governments are primarily interested in maintaining the economic vitality of the area for which they are responsible. (Peterson 1981, p. 29)

This obsession of state and local governments with local economic development can be given a negative spin. Some local economic development policies might primarily benefit a few wealthy local residents with political influence. Few other residents might benefit. Sociologist Harvey Molotch's classic article "The City as a Growth Machine" stated in its abstract summarizing this article the following:

A city and, more generally, any locality, is conceived [in this article] as the areal expression of the interests of some land-based elite. Such an elite is seen to profit through the increasing intensification of the land use of the area in which its members hold a common interest. An elite competes with other land-based elites in an effort to have growth-inducing resources invested within its own area as opposed to that of another. Governmental authority, at the local and nonlocal levels, is utilized to assist in achieving this growth at the expense of competing localities. Conditions of community life are largely a consequence of the social, economic, and political forces embodied in this growth machine. (Molotch 1976, p. 309)

Molotch goes on to say in the body of the article that

> I speculate that the political and economic essence of virtually any given locality, in the present American context, is *growth*. I further argue that the desire for growth provides the key operative motivation toward consensus for members of politically mobilized local elites, however split they might be on other issues, and that a common interest in growth is the overriding commonality among important people in a given locale—at least insofar as they have any important local goals at all. Further, this growth imperative is the most important constraint upon available options for local initiative in social and economic reform. It is thus that I argue that the very essence of a locality is its operation as a growth machine. (Molotch 1976, pp. 309–310)

The concern of state and local leaders with local economic development goes back to the beginning of the American republic. Many American cities and towns were developed by local boosters. Success often depended upon finding some magnet for local growth: a canal, a rail line, a state university, the state capital.

ECONOMIC DEVELOPMENT: WHAT IS IT GOOD FOR? ABSOLUTELY NOTHING EXCEPT LAND VALUES?

However, there are powerful arguments that economic development, when it focuses on local job growth, only benefits landowners. I will argue that the evidence refutes these arguments. The argument and refutation are worth going into for several reasons. First, there are many policy analysts who accept these arguments against economic development. Second, the refutation helps further reveal the nature of economic development benefits and how they are obtained. A better understanding of the goals of economic development helps make better policy.

The argument that local job growth only affects land values goes as follows: There is a large volume of migration of people among local economies. For example, during a typical year, 4 percent of persons move into or out of a typical metropolitan area.[3] Even a sizable shift in job growth in a metropolitan area can be offset with modest shifts in labor migration. We would expect such shifts in migration if an area's growth makes it more desirable. Such migration would continue until local unemployment, wages, and prices have adjusted to offset any initial advantages from higher local wages or better employment opportunities. The most likely adjustment would be a return to the original unemployment rate, an increase in local nominal wages, and an increase in local land prices sufficient that increased local housing prices offset the increase in nominal wages. Real wages (wages controlling for local prices) would be unchanged. Land prices would be expected to increase because of the in-migration of businesses and households, which increases local land demand relative to local land supply.[4] Only landowners would benefit from the increase in local growth. Workers would not benefit from these adjustments except to the extent that they were also landowners. Given the ease in shifting migration, one would expect these local adjustments to take place relatively quickly.

This argument can be described as the "capitalization argument." Any benefit temporarily offered to workers by local job growth will be quickly offset by migration. This migration offsets the initial labor market advantages by increasing local land prices. This argument has been advanced by academics on both the right and the left. Among conservatives, economist Steven Marston has argued that "workers move rationally enough to take advantage of and so eliminate gains in migration between areas of the United States" (Marston 1985, p. 75). In Marston's view, the ease of migration eliminates the prime justification for "programs that 'target' government funds to 'depressed areas' with the intention of reducing unemployment there" (p. 58). On the left, Molotch's "Growth Machine" article and his subsequent work (Logan and Molotch 1987) argue that local growth mainly benefits land-owning elites, and not the general public. Specifically, because of worker migration, Molotch (1976) argues that job creation does not benefit local workers or the local unemployed much: "As jobs develop in a fast-growing area, the unemployed will be attracted from other areas in sufficient numbers not only to fill those developing vacancies but also to form a work-force sector that is continuously unemployed. Thus, just as local growth does not affect aggregate employment, it likely has very little long-term impact upon the local rate of unemployment" (pp. 320–321).

Of course, land value increases are still benefits. Even if local job growth does not benefit workers, it still benefits landowners. If the costs of the economic development policy were less than the resulting land value increases, then the policy would have benefits greater than costs. However, the benefits of this policy would be regressive. The value of land owned by households increases with household income. It increases sufficiently that the ratio of the value of land owned to household income increases with household income. Therefore, upper-income households would on average get a greater percentage boost to income from land value increases than would lower-income households. Furthermore, if all the benefits of local job growth accrue to landowners, shouldn't the costs of local economic development policies be borne by landowners? Why should economic development programs be paid for by workers?

HYSTERESIS: AN ARGUMENT FOR WHY LOCAL JOB GROWTH DEVELOPMENT MIGHT HELP WORKERS

One argument for why local job growth might help workers is that job experience provides benefits in a world with imperfect mobility. I advanced this argument in my 1991 book (Bartik 1991a). This argument is based in part on previous writings of Nobel Prize–winning economist Edmund Phelps. The argument is that in the short run, local job growth may provide residents with employment opportunities they otherwise would not have obtained. The resulting extra employment experience increases their long-run equilibrium employment rates and wage rates. Such labor market effects are labeled "hysteresis effects." The "hysteresis" term is borrowed from physics and engineering. "Hysteresis" refers to a system whose equilibrium depends upon the history of the system. In this case, the equilibrium of local employment rates and wage rates depends on the history of employment shocks to that local economy. This theory was eloquently advanced by Phelps in 1972:

> Of [the changes caused by a boom], job experience, with its opportunities for learning by doing and on-the-job training, is possibly the most important. When people are engaged in sustained work of a kind with which they have not had any similar experience, they become different for it in a number of ways that are relevant for the equilibrium unemployment rate. Getting to work on time is just

about the most important habit a worker can have in nearly every kind of job . . . For many of the people who comprise the hard-core, most frequently unemployed group, getting to be "reliable" and learning to work with other people are necessary attributes for continuation in the job.

For other people, the opportunity to acquire skills at more demand-ing jobs in the skill hierarchy than they could ordinarily qualify for under normal always-equilibrium aggregate demand behavior may be the more important aspect . . . The upgrading of many workers that results from a disequilibrating rise of aggregate demand may gradually lead to a true upgrading in the average quality of the labor force. (Phelps 1972, p. 79)

Here is how Phelps's theory can be applied to local labor markets. Workers are not instantly mobile. If local job opportunities increase, the current residents have some advantage in obtaining those jobs. Obtain-ing a job, compared to being unemployed, provides extra job experi-ence. Obtaining a better job, compared to working at a worse job, pro-vides better job experience. More or better job experience increases the individual's job skills. It may also improve the individual's self-concept. Finally, more or better job experience may improve a worker's reputa-tion with employers. All of these effects may result in a worker with permanently higher employment rates and wage rates. The temporary advantages of the local economy's new and better jobs become long-lasting advantages for some of the local economy's original residents.

BUT WHY ARE JOBS SAID TO OFFER "BENEFITS"? IS THERE "SOMETHING SPECIAL" ABOUT JOBS?

This discussion might seem strange to many economists. Why is obtaining a job a benefit? Workers provide time in exchange for wages. The value of their time is a cost of working. In economics jargon, the value that an individual places on his time is his "reservation wage"—that is, the lowest wage at which he would agree to accept a job. Sup-pose the labor market is such that labor supply and labor demand are always equal. Wages fluctuate to equate labor supply and demand. All job seekers easily obtain jobs. In such an economy, an increase in labor demand results in hiring some additional workers who were not previously working. These workers chose not to work because their reservation wage was more than the previous wage rate. The additional labor demand increases the wage rate enough that now they are willing to work. These workers do gain slightly. Their gain is equal to the difference between the new market wage and their reservation wage. But we would expect the increase in wages to be slight, so the gain per worker hired should not be great. The "benefit" from the additional employment should be far less than the wages paid.

This common view among economists probably seems strange to most noneconomists. As noted by economist Paul Courant, "Economists view labor as a cost . . . Mayors, undergraduates, presidents, union officials, and (other?) folks in bars *say* that they view labor (or, at least, jobs) as benefits. They count as benefits of public programs (and location-specific capital subsidies) the added employment, sometimes as jobs, sometimes as increased payroll" (Courant 1994, p. 875). As Courant muses, there does seem to be "something special about jobs" to the public.

One way to reconcile the public's view with the economist's view is to assume some involuntary unemployment. Wages might be such that labor supply exceeds labor demand. This also implies that there are many people who are willing to work at reservation wages that are quite a bit less than the market wage.

What economic model might explain persistent involuntary unemployment? One such model would be "efficiency wage" models of the labor market.[5] In efficiency wage models, it is assumed that individual employers find that increasing wages above the market-clearing level is in the employer's interest. The higher wage may increase worker productivity enough to justify the wage increase. Productivity may increase because at the market-clearing wage, workers have no incentive to avoid shirking on the job, since they can easily get another job. Productivity may also increase because firms find that at the market-clearing wage there is too much employee turnover, which increases a firm's costs for hiring and training new workers. Finally, workers may have some notion of a "fair wage." When the economy is booming, and unemployment is so low that we can think of the labor market as "clearing," workers may have a notion of a fair wage that exceeds that market-clearing wage. A perceived "unfair wage" may reduce worker morale and productivity. For all of these reasons, an individual employer may find it in the firm's interest to increase its wages above the market-clearing wage. And if one employer finds it in its interest, so will others. As many employers increase wages, unemployment will increase. The higher unemployment will reduce shirking and worker turnover, and restrain demands for a fair wage. This higher unemployment substitutes for the impossible desire of all employers to pay more than the market wage. A new equilibrium is reached when higher wages have induced enough unemployment that all employers are willing to pay the same market wage. This new equilibrium market wage exceeds the market-clearing wage. The new equilibrium includes an equilibrium level of involuntary unemployment.

With involuntary unemployment, and wages exceeding reservation wages, there may be significant benefits to the increase in jobs resulting from local economic development. The gap between a newly hired worker's wage and his or her "reservation wage" may be large. We would expect this gap to be higher in local labor markets with high unemployment.

This argument also helps explain why there can be gains from worker upgrading to better jobs. When an economy booms, individuals are able to obtain better jobs than they otherwise would have obtained. Often, these upwardly mobile individuals are quite productive in the new jobs. This raises the question of why employers didn't hire these individuals before at lower wages. An efficiency wage model might explain this. Employers in some industries or occupations may find that it increases productivity to set wages higher than the next best alternative for some qualified job seekers. This can explain why market wages might allow similar individuals to get different-quality jobs.

An even more radical notion of why jobs are "special" is the social meaning of jobs and wages. My reservation wage may exaggerate my true cost of obtaining a job. I may place a great value on being employed. But part of the value of being employed is receiving a wage that I regard as a "fair wage." If I become employed in a job at the minimum fair wage at which my self-respect would allow me to take the job, I may experience a significant gain. By becoming employed, I become a socially valued member of the community. However, that significant gain does not mean that I would take the job for a lower wage.

I would perceive that lower wage as damaging to my self-respect and my happiness.

This argument is consistent with research on how unemployment affects human happiness. For example, Blanchflower and Oswald have found that "to 'compensate' men exactly for unemployment would take a rise in income of [approximately] $60,000 per annum [in 1990s dollars]" (Blanchflower and Oswald 2004, p. 1373). This compensation is derived by measuring how much unemployment affects reported happiness compared to how much income affects reported happiness. This figure logically implies reservation wages for being employed that are close to zero or even negative. But no one thinks the unemployed are willing to take a job for zero wages.

Why are jobs so important to happiness, and why is unemployment so stigmatizing? A review of the "happiness determinants" literature by economists Bruno Frey and Alois Stutzer concludes the following:

> Numerous studies have established . . . that the unemployed are in worse mental (and physical) health than working people. As a result, they are subject to a higher death rate, more often commit suicide and are more prone to consuming large quantities of alcohol. Their personal relationships are also more strained . . . Being unemployed has a stigma attached to it, particularly in a world in which one's work essentially defines one's position in life . . . An estimation across Swiss communities shows that the stronger the social norm to live off one's own income, the lower the unemployed people's reported satisfaction with life. (Frey and Stutzer 2002, pp. 420, 421)

The norm of work may be encouraged by modern capitalism. Our society stresses the connection between an individual's work and economic and social success. In a society committed to egalitarian values, one's success is supposed to depend on one's work, and not on other unmerited factors (e.g., who one's parents are). Such a society may look down on those who do not work. Tocqueville commented on this over 175 years ago in *Democracy in America*:

> In democratic peoples, where there is no hereditary wealth, everyone works to live or has worked, or was born of people who worked. The idea of work as a necessary, natural, and honest condition of humanity is therefore offered to the human mind on every side.

> Not only is work not held in dishonor among these peoples, but it is held in honor; the prejudice is not against it but for it. In the United States, a rich man believes that he owes it to public opinion to devote his leisure to some operation of industry or commerce or to some public duty. He would deem himself disreputable if he used his life only for living. It is to escape this obligation of work that so many rich Americans come to Europe; there they find the debris of aristocratic societies among whom idleness is still honored.
>
> Equality not only rehabilitates the idea of work, it uplifts the idea of working to procure lucre. (Tocqueville 2000, p. 525).

Unemployment thus has a large individual cost to the unemployed. But unemployment also may have a social cost to the employed. Studies have shown that the happiness of everyone is affected by the overall unemployment rate as well as by whether one is personally unemployed (Tella, MacCulloch, and Oswald 2001). The effect of a 1-point rise in unemployment in reducing life satisfaction is greater per person for the unemployed than for the employed, by about 15 times as much. But because there are so many more employed persons than unemployed, the aggregate "social cost" of a rise in unemployment is much greater than the loss to the unemployed. Calculations suggest that the social costs of a rise in unemployment are probably six times the loss to the unemployed.

Why do the employed suffer a reduction in life satisfaction from a rise in unemployment? An increase in unemployment increases the employed's perceived risk of becoming unemployed. Also, the employed's happiness may be affected by the unemployment of friends and relatives. Finally, the employed may care about the unemployment of persons they do not know but whom they regard as fellow members of society.

Therefore, there may be significant social benefits to increasing employment rates. These social benefits may even exceed the earnings increase due to these increased employment rates.

BUT WHY ARE LOCAL JOBS SO IMPORTANT? AFTER ALL, I COULD GET THOSE SAME JOB OPPORTUNITIES ELSEWHERE

But why would *local* jobs present special opportunities for local residents? Local residents might be able to obtain similar opportunities elsewhere.

The problem is that these "similar opportunities" are outside the home community. Leaving the home community involves costs. Some of these costs are financial moving costs. But the more important costs are the "psychological moving costs" of weakening ties to familiar places and people. These ties are valuable in and of themselves; they are part of what makes life worth living. These ties are also valuable for instrumental purposes: Familiarity with one's home can help in obtaining a new job or finding new housing. If one is down on one's luck, friends and family can provide assistance. As Paul Courant put it, "Having a place in the local community, and knowing how to function there, is a valuable asset" (Courant 1994, p. 876).

Another way to put it is that staying in one's home community maintains the advantages of "a sense of place." This sense of place is a type of social capital. Abandoning it is not without costs. Regional economist Roger Bolton describes the value of a sense of place:

> In some established places there is a sense of community. This sense of community is also capital. It is intangible, and regional economists do not talk much about it, but it *is* capital; it is productive, and residents of a place that has a strong sense of place certainly know it and appreciate it. Their appreciation of it is evidenced by the one bit of evidence that ought to make economists notice: people are willing to pay for it.
>
> . . . A "sense of place" [is] a concept widely used by geographers, architects, and planners. It refers to a complex of intangible characteristics of a place that make it attractive to actual and potential residents and influence their behavior in observable ways. Both the "setting" of the place and the social interactions of the community are important, and setting includes natural, cultural, and historical characteristics . . .

> . . . Public investments in local economic development . . . are especially important in declining or stagnant places . . . They are motivated at times by a felt need to attract new stable employment opportunities and tax bases, which are essential to prevent the out-migration that would destroy the sense of place . . .
>
> The returns to the sense-of-place asset are a general measure of security—security of stable expectations, and security of being able to operate in a familiar environment and to trust other citizens, merchants, workers, etc. . . . There is also a basic feeling of plea-sure at living in a community, or knowing that others live in such a community, that has been created by a combination of social inter-actions in a particular setting. (Bolton 1992, pp. 192, 193, 194)

For all these reasons, job opportunities available in one's home area are superior to those available in some strange place. Furthermore, because of local ties, local residents have an advantage in getting access to additional or better jobs. Therefore, moving up to improved employ-ment opportunities or a better job is easier as well as more desirable in one's home community.

OTHER POSSIBLE BENEFITS OF LOCAL JOB GROWTH

So far, I have identified two possible benefits of local job growth: 1) increased land values, and 2) increased real earnings of local residents. What are the other possible benefits (or costs) of local job growth?

Local Businesses

Local businesses may benefit because of the increased local demand brought about by local economic growth. Local businesses may lose because of the increased wages and local costs brought about by local economic growth. In addition, the changing scale of the local economy may have advantages or disadvantages for different types of local busi-nesses. For example, a weekly newspaper or corner hardware store may do better in a smaller community. A more specialized retailer may do better in a larger community.

Whatever the effects on local businesses, we would expect these benefits and costs to largely be captured in local land values. Capital is mobile in response to changes in profits. Any temporary increase in profits will attract capital that will compete and bring profit rates back down to a normal level. However, if growth causes a net increase in overall demand for land, then the value of business real estate will increase along with housing real estate.

State and Local Governments

The effect of local job growth on the state and local fiscal situation is likely positive. As mentioned previously, local population and employment growth that is *not* accompanied by increased earnings per capita will probably on average have neutral effects on the state and local fiscal situation.[6] But local job growth will increase per capita earnings and income. This increased per capita income is likely to positively affect the state and local fiscal situation. Increased per capita income may allow lower spending per capita on income support programs. Higher employment rates and wages may reduce need for welfare and Medicaid. Higher per capita income will also increase revenue from state and local income, sales, and property taxes.

In-Migrants

Some of the jobs brought about by local job growth will go to in-migrants to the local economy. By "in-migrants" I mean anyone who moves into the local economy. This includes those moving in from other local areas in the United States.

As I have argued in the past (Bartik 1991a), the benefits from local economic development for in-migrants are slight. In-migrants could have moved to any one of a number of local economies. From the perspective of in-migrants, this local economy is not unique. Whatever a local economy offers to in-migrants is available elsewhere.

There is an asymmetry here between the original local residents and in-migrants. The original local residents view the additional jobs provided in their home as unique: they provide opportunities that preserve valuable ties to the place. In addition, the original local residents may obtain superior opportunities here, because of local connections. On the other hand, in-migrants must view jobs provided in this place as similar to jobs provided in other places. It is hard to believe that some extra jobs provided in, for example, Kalamazoo, make much difference in the opportunities available to a potential in-migrant located elsewhere in the United States. If these jobs had not been created in Kalamazoo, this in-migrant would not have been much worse off. He or she could have moved elsewhere.

Environmental Effects

Local economic development may produce environmental effects. The most obvious environmental effects are environmental costs. Pollution of air, water, and land may increase because of more households and businesses. Congestion may increase. Local economic development may also cause various changes in the character of the community. Some of these changes may be undesirable. For example, growth may cause a loss of some sense of intimacy. On the other hand, some changes may be desirable: economic change may shake up the political power structure and open it to broader participation.

WHERE THE RUBBER HITS THE ROAD: EMPIRICAL EVIDENCE ON THE EFFECTS OF INCREASES IN LOCAL LABOR DEMAND

In sum, increases in local job growth may increase local property values, increase local real earnings, provide some net benefits to local government, and have some environmental effects. Which of these effects is most important? What does empirical evidence show?

Much of my research career has been spent trying to answer that question. The research is largely based on studies of what has happened to different metropolitan areas over time.

One recent publication of mine tried to summarize this evidence (Bartik 2005).[7] This summary found that a local labor demand shock that increased a metropolitan area's employment would have persistent effects on annual real earnings, property values, and the state and local government's fiscal situation. The labor demand shock considered would increase the long-run level of employment in the metro area by 1 percent. The effects on annual real earnings, property values, and the state and local government's fiscal situation are stated as a percentage of the metropolitan area's annual personal income. (A 10 percent interest rate is used to convert increases in property values into their equivalent in terms of annual flows of income.)[8] These calculations, based on a variety of previous studies, are for effects in the medium run (say, five years after the employment increase). (Although these effects are "medium-run," they would be expected to persist at much the same level for some time.) The calculations are as follows:

- Increase in real earnings of original local residents: 0.28 percent of annual local-area personal income.

- State and local government increase in fiscal surplus: 0.05 percent of annual local-area personal income.

- Annual flow value of increase in local property values (adjusted for taxes): 0.07 percent of annual local-area personal income.

- Total measured effects (sum of these three effects): 0.40 percent.

These earnings increases are due to local residents' experiencing increased employment rates and moving up to better-paying occupations. The empirical evidence suggests that roughly half of the earnings increase is due to higher employment rates, and roughly half is due to occupational upgrading. Empirical estimates also suggest that real wages for a given occupation are not changed because of local employment growth; rather, real wage increases for individuals are due to moving up to better-paying occupations (Bartik 1991a).

These higher employment rates are consistent with estimates that suggest that only one-fifth of the new jobs created by higher local labor demand result in increased employment rates for local residents.[9] The remaining jobs are filled by changes in migration.[10] In these estimates of medium-run effects, the increased employment rates of local residents are entirely due to increases in labor force participation rates. In the short run, there is also some reduction in local unemployment rates, but this disappears after three or four years.

Therefore, the conclusion is that most of the local benefits of growth are increases in the real earnings of the original local residents. State and local governments also gain more in taxes than they must pay in public service expenditures. But fiscal gains are modest compared to the earnings gains. Property value gains are also modest compared to the earnings gains.

What is the intuition behind this conclusion? Part of the intuition is that more businesses and households in a metropolitan area can be accommodated with relatively modest land price increases. The supply of developed land is responsive to increases in demand. In addition, to the extent that there is some fiscal surplus, it is probably due to higher earnings per capita. The fiscal surplus is thus considerably less than the earnings gains, as state and local fiscal systems only have modest tax rates as a percentage of total earnings.

In contrast, the labor earnings associated with new jobs are large compared to the employment increase. A 1 percent increase in local employment increases local earnings by about 1 percent. This 1 percent increase in real earnings includes earnings of new residents as well as increased earnings of the original residents. A sizable portion of the increase in total earnings goes to the original residents. About one-fifth of the new jobs go to increasing the employment rates of the residents. From this employment rate increase alone, the percentage increase in the original residents' earnings will be one-fifth of the 1 percent increase in employment. Furthermore, the occupational upgrading effects of stronger local labor demand are about as big as the earnings effects of higher employment rates. It is much easier for local residents to get and keep jobs in better-paying occupations if local demand conditions are favorable. Therefore, local residents are able to capture close to 40 percent of the increased earnings that are due to growth.[11]

As mentioned above, there will also be environmental effects of this increase in employment. However, the magnitude of such environmental effects is likely to be specific to the local economy and the character of the growth. Environmental effects may be positive or negative.

These estimated effects are for an average increase in local employment growth in a typical local economy. Effects could vary for many reasons. For example, effects on the state and local fiscal situation would depend on whether there was excess capacity in local infrastructure. If there is such excess capacity, then the fiscal effects on state and local government may be more favorable.

Chapter 9 will consider how effects may vary in local economies of different sizes or growth rates.[12]

Estimated effects may vary with the types of jobs. Estimates suggest that the wage mix of jobs matters. Empirical estimates suggest that an area that attracts higher-wage industries will have higher earnings per local resident. (By "higher-wage," I mean wages that are high compared to worker skills.) Other local industries in such areas will be forced to pay higher wages by the higher wage mix. In addition, the higher local wage structure increases local residents' participation rates in the labor market. Chapter 5 considers how the wages of new jobs affect calculations of benefits. The effects are considerable.

Estimated employment-rate effects and earnings effects of labor-demand increases may also be greater if efforts are made to improve the likelihood of good employment matches between these new job openings and local nonemployed residents. This issue will also be addressed when the design of local economic development policies is discussed in Chapter 5.

All of these estimates are for effects in the "medium run," about five years after the employment increase. However, these effects persist for much longer. For example, the empirical studies suggest effects on the employment rates of local residents that do not decline much for at least 17 years after the initial employment increase. This persistence is consistent with hysteresis theories of the long-run effects of labor market experience. Local residents are able to use better job opportunities in the short run to achieve a persistently better position in the labor market.

NOT EVERYONE AGREES: THE BLANCHARD-KATZ PERSPECTIVE AND ITS POLICY IMPLICATIONS

Many economists believe that the above discussion is incorrect. They believe that local labor markets quickly and fully adjust through migration to some shock to local labor demand. This belief is largely based on an influential paper by Olivier Blanchard of MIT and Lawrence Katz of Harvard: "Regional Evolutions," published in 1992 in *Brookings Papers on Economic Activity*.

According to Blanchard and Katz's (1992) article, "The effects [of employment shocks] on unemployment and [labor force] participation [rates] steadily decline and disappear after five to seven years . . . By five to seven years, the employment response consists entirely of the migration of workers" (p. 34). I agree with Blanchard and Katz that employment shocks yield a large migration response. I also agree that after five to seven years, the effects on unemployment disappear. But in contrast to Blanchard and Katz, I conclude that employment shocks have effects on labor force participation rates that are quite persistent.[13] In addition, local labor demand changes have persistent effects on occupational attainment.

Blanchard and Katz's article has been influential on both scholarship and policy attitudes. The article has been cited more than 300 times since its publication.[14]

Former *New York Times* reporter Peter Passell used Blanchard and Katz's research to argue that manufacturing-plant closings or military-base closings had few persistent effects on local labor markets: "History suggests that local economic shocks—in this case, base and plant closings—dissipate quickly," writes Passell (1992). "Lawrence Katz of Harvard and Olivier Blanchard of the Massachusetts Institute of Technology estimate that, on average, regional differences in unemployment have been eliminated within five years." Blanchard and Katz's results have been cited by European government bodies interested in the consequences of greater labor mobility in the European Union (Rowthorn and Glyn 2006).

If Blanchard and Katz's results are correct, then local economic development would have few persistent effects on labor markets. The major beneficiaries of local economic development would not be local workers, but rather local landowners or local government.

Blanchard and Katz's model suffers from some econometric problems.[15] The intuitive argument is that Blanchard and Katz's results are biased by errors in measuring local labor force participation rates and unemployment rates. Blanchard and Katz base their conclusion in part on how measured labor force participation rates or unemployment rates adjust to observed shocks to their past values. Blanchard and Katz's estimates are biased because there is so much noise in the available measures of these local rates. Shocks to statistical noise of course *do* quickly dissipate. Measurement error will have little correlation over time.[16] This makes it appear that shocks to employment rates quickly dissipate.

Blanchard and Katz's results also contradict previous literature on the long-run effects of employment growth (Bartik 1993a). Furthermore, at least three studies since 1992 suggest that Blanchard and Katz's results are incorrect. These studies attribute the problems in their results to measurement error. My 1993 study takes Blanchard and Katz's data and reestimates using a model that directly allows for longer-term effects of employment growth, which corrects for the measurement error problem. According to this reestimation, the effects of local labor demand on labor force participation rates persist for at least 17 years (Bartik 1993a). Rowthorn and Glyn (2006) correct for measurement error in several different ways and find that shocks to local employment rates (employment-to-population ratios) in the United States tend to dissipate by 1 percent per year. This implies that it would take on the order of a century for a shock's effects on local employment rates to completely disappear. Partridge and Rickman (2006) use an estimating framework that relies on variables that are less subject to measurement error. They also have more flexible assumptions about long-run effects of local labor demand shocks on migration. Their results are similar to my 1991 and 1993 results for the short-run and long-run effects of shocks to local labor demand on local employment-to-population ratios. In the short run, about three-fifths of the new jobs are reflected in higher employment-to-population ratios of local residents. In the long-run equilibrium, about one-fifth of the new jobs are reflected in higher employment-to-population ratios of local residents. This long-run equilibrium is reached in about eight years.

How can the reader who doesn't specialize in econometrics judge the merits of this dispute? Consider the following thought experiment. Jobs created in a local economy must *ultimately* be reflected in one of two ways: 1) employment for local residents who would otherwise be nonemployed and 2) local employment for persons who otherwise would have lived elsewhere. (Of course, created jobs can *immediately* go to local residents who otherwise would have been employed elsewhere in the local economy. However, job-to-job mobility of local residents would then create job openings elsewhere in the local economy. Ultimately, the chain of job openings can only be filled by local nonemployed people or nonresidents.) Blanchard and Katz's estimates agree with the research consensus on job creation's effects in the short run. If 1,000 new jobs are created in a local economy, then the short-run effect is that at least 600 go to local residents who otherwise would be nonemployed. Only 400 go to persons who otherwise would have lived elsewhere. Therefore, 600 local residents gain valuable job experience that they otherwise would not have obtained. Blanchard and Katz do not dispute this research consensus.

This job experience builds skills, self-confidence, and reputation with other local employers. It also means that these 600 local residents have the advantages of being insiders in the labor market. Their current employers know their performance. The employers avoid the costs of hiring and training by retaining these employees. Is it plausible that *none* of these 600 local residents is able to use these advantages of employment experience to remain employed seven years later? The complete disappearance of these initial advantages is the implication of Blanchard and Katz's estimates. On the other hand, the estimates obtained by me (Bartik 1993a) and by Partridge and Rickman (2006) imply that perhaps 200 of these 600 local residents are able to use their extra employment experience to persistently increase their odds of being employed. This two-thirds dissipation of the initial advantages of gaining a job seems more plausible than a complete dissipation.

THE ZERO-SUM-GAME ARGUMENT: WHY CARE ABOUT LOCAL BENEFITS WHEN WHAT COUNT ARE NATIONAL BENEFITS?

Some critics of local economic development policies may find this entire discussion irrelevant. If local job growth does not raise national economic development in some way, then local economic development policies are a zero-sum game. Any gains to attracting jobs to this one local area are offset by losses to other local areas.

The zero-sum-game argument is not always correct. As discussed in Chapter 10, there are several conditions under which local economic development policies might promote the national interest. Local economic competition might promote the national interest if more distressed local areas offer more business incentives. Local economic competition might also promote the national interest if these business incentives include services that increase productivity.

On the other hand, under some conditions, local economic competition may not promote the national interest. Business tax incentives offered by affluent areas offer few net national social benefits. As discussed in Chapter 10, a social cost of such competition is the resulting redistribution of income to some business owners.

However, local benefits are still of great importance, for several reasons. First, local benefits are important to state and local policymakers and voters. These policymakers and voters want to know what local economic development policy can do for them. This is a legitimate question that deserves a reasonable answer.

Second, we need to understand the local perspective to decide how the nation should best intervene in local economic development policies. We need to know the relationship between local benefits and national benefits. If local benefits from business incentives exceed national benefits, then state and local policymakers may overexpand business incentives. Some national policy to constrain incentives might be warranted. If local benefits are less than national benefits for early childhood programs, then state and local policymakers may underinvest in early childhood programs. Some national policy to encourage more activity in that area could be justified.

Third, national benefits are ultimately the sum of local benefits. Therefore, understanding how to measure local benefits is one way to better measure national benefits.

Fourth, there are better estimates of local effects than of national effects of business incentives. Estimated effects of local economic development can rely on observations from many local areas over many years. Local areas can provide true "laboratories of democracy." National benefits in the end have only one laboratory. Policies may change the national economy over time. But at the national level, it is difficult to separate out the influence of economic policies from other forces. Local data provide more extensive information for sorting out the effects of policy versus other forces.

Fifth, given the great demands on federal resources in the future, what state and local governments choose to do is likely to be crucial to many domestic policy areas. This includes the domestic policy areas of business incentives and early childhood programs. The federal government faces large fiscal demands in such policy areas as Social Security, health care, and national defense. Whether the federal government has the budgetary resources or political will to play the lead role in dealing with many other important domestic policy areas is questionable. We need to understand how state and local policymakers should view benefits. Their perceptions of the benefits of local economic development policies are likely to play a key role in shaping many important domestic policies.

IF GROWTH PROVIDES BENEFITS, WHY WORRY ABOUT THE DETAILS?

Some economic developers, or state and local policymakers, may regard this chapter's analysis as too nitpicky. As long as local economic growth produces local benefits, what difference does their exact nature make? Shouldn't state and local policymakers just care about total local benefits? Does it really make a difference whether these benefits take the form of earnings increases, land value increases, or fiscal surpluses?

Perhaps local economic developers should focus on just obtaining growth. Others can worry about who actually benefits from local economic growth and what to do about it. Figuring out what policies will work to increase local growth is complicated enough. Adding the extra goal of increasing the benefits from a given amount of growth complicates policymaking. Perhaps local economic developers would be more effective if they specialized in promoting growth.

Herbert Rubin's well-known 1988 article, "Shoot Anything That Flies; Claim Anything That Falls: Conversations with Economic Developers," describes the difficulties of local economic development in the United States, as viewed by economic development practitioners. As Rubin (1988) describes it, "[The] work environment [of economic developers] is complex and undefined and involved an uncertain technology . . . Many of the practitioners were frustrated because they and their fellow citizens had little, if any, control over decisions that affected their local economies . . . They saw only a weak relationship between their efforts and resulting changes . . . Even trying to find out whether tactics are working can prove frustrating" (pp. 237, 239).

One of Rubin's economic developer interviewees said that the most frustrating part of his job was "the uncontrollable factors that you work with. For example, the downturn in the economy. We couldn't do anything about it. We lost one of our major manufacturers." Other economic developers also said that success was frequently outside their control. "You can be just great because . . . the Illinois Department of Transportation makes some decision," one said.

Therefore, local economic developers face great challenges: they must increase local economic development with only limited tools, while large forces affect the local economy. If it is hard to affect any local growth, it is tempting to make the task easier by not worrying about the type of growth. If it is hard to ever see success, it is tempting to claim any local growth as a success, regardless of who obtains the jobs. The title of Rubin's article comes from a quotation from one local economic developer, who said, "There is a phrase that many people won't admit to, but [they operate by]: 'Shoot anything that flies; claim anything that falls.'"

Why then worry about the benefits from growth? First, analyzing the benefits of local growth suggests that different approaches to local economic development policy may differ dramatically in benefit-cost ratios. For example, if the earnings of local residents are the key benefit, it makes a great deal of difference who gets the jobs and what those jobs pay. This may affect which jobs should be targeted by local economic developers. It may also suggest that local economic development should be linked with local workforce development and placement programs. This may require redefining the nature of the economic developer's job. I will follow up on this discussion in Chapter 5, which considers what signifies high-quality design in local economic development policies.

Second, if the benefits of business incentives are largely increased employment rates and higher wage rates of local residents, then a natural question is whether there are alternatives to business incentives for achieving these benefits. The answer to this question is yes. We can adopt policies to increase the quality or quantity of local labor supply. Exploring this alternative is this book's central task.

WHAT ARE THE LABOR SUPPLY POLICIES THAT AFFECT THE QUANTITY OR QUALITY OF LABOR SUPPLY IN A STATE OR LOCAL AREA?

The labor supply policies analyzed in this book result in two types of increases in labor supply.[17] A single program may yield both types. First, there are increases in the local area's labor supply due to increased labor force participation rates of local residents. Labor force participation rates increase because local residents become more willing and able to be employed. Second, there are increases in the local area's labor supply due to increased skills of local residents. As a result of better skills, local residents become more qualified for better-paying jobs.

Several labor supply policies might increase labor force participation rates or skills of local residents. Such policies include promoting the following: pre-K education and other early childhood programs, K–12 education, local community colleges or local universities, job training programs, and welfare-to-work programs. The special focus for most of this book is on early childhood programs. This focus is in part due to the greater empirical evidence on early childhood programs. In addition, early childhood programs may have greater effect per additional dollar spent than some of these other programs. However, Chapter 12 will consider how the analysis can be extended to other programs that increase the quantity or quality of the labor supply of local residents.

WHAT ARE THE KEY ISSUES IN HOW EARLY CHILDHOOD AND OTHER LABOR SUPPLY PROGRAMS AFFECT LOCAL ECONOMIC DEVELOPMENT BENEFITS?

As I have discussed, the benefits of stronger labor demand are primarily the increase in employment rates and earnings of local residents. Policies such as business incentives can deliver these benefits. However, employment rates and earnings can also be increased by labor supply policies that increase local residents' labor force participation rates or labor skills. To analyze the effectiveness of these labor supply policies in increasing earnings, I will consider the following four questions:

1) Should we count the increased earnings and employment rates of local residents whose labor force participation or labor skills are increased by a policy, but who then move out of their local area? How should local policymakers view such benefits? How should national policymakers view them?

2) Of the local residents who participate in these labor supply programs, what percentage will stay in the local area? Is there much reason for a local area to invest in these programs if everyone moves out?

3) If local participants in labor supply programs stay in the local economy, what will be the overall effect on local employment rates and earnings rates? Even if the employment rates and earnings of local participants increase, will total employment and earnings in the local economy increase? Suppose that after the program participants had entered the local labor force, there was no change in overall local employment rates and earnings rates. Under that supposition, any gain for local program participants must have been offset by displacing other local residents from jobs and earning opportunities. The magnitude of such displacement depends in part on how employers respond to the increase in labor force participation and job skills of some local residents. Overall employment and earnings must respond to labor supply programs if these programs are not to have 100 percent displacement effects.

4) If local participants in labor supply programs move out of the local area, analogous questions about net impact can be asked at the national level: Will this increase in the labor force participation and job skills of some persons lead to a net increase in jobs and earnings in the national economy? Will any increase for former participants in jobs and earnings be offset by the displacement of other persons in the national economy from jobs and earnings opportunities? Or, will employers at the national level respond by creating additional jobs and higher earnings opportunities?

Here, in this chapter, I provide some general answers to these questions. Chapter 4 and other chapters provide specific estimates for specific programs.

An additional overriding question for pre-K or any other early childhood program is whether it successfully raises labor force participation and skills among participants. This issue will be considered when we get to specific early childhood programs in Chapter 4.

TWO PERSPECTIVES ON THE BENEFITS TO OUT-MOVERS

Should benefits to "out-movers" be counted? I assume that from a local policy perspective, these benefits should not be counted. Local policymakers want to see their policies reflected in increased employment rates and earnings rates in their local economy.

This local perspective seems analogous to the local perspective on business incentives. The local perspective does not include the losses to other local areas if business incentives take jobs away from these areas.

On the other hand, I do not count against a program the loss of out-migrants to other areas. If a program leads some individuals to move elsewhere, I do not consider the loss of their earnings to be a true loss. The out-mover is presumably no worse off because of the move. The focus in analyzing the benefits of public policies should be on the gains or losses to individuals from those policies. The relevant issue is simply which gains or losses count. I focus on individuals who increase their employment rates or earnings rates. The question is which individuals should count in this calculation. From a local perspective, it seems reasonable to only count individuals who remain in the local area.

The earnings gains of those who stay will increase local per-capita earnings and local per-capita income. As discussed previously in this chapter, this increase in per-capita income will improve the local community in several ways. These ways include local improvements in fiscal conditions, quality of life, and the political climate.

In Chapter 10, I consider the national perspective. From a national perspective, I also focus on gains in employment rates and earnings rates. However, now these gains are counted regardless of where someone lives. This is the same approach used when taking a national perspective on the increased employment rates and earnings rates resulting from business incentives.

HOW MOBILE IS THE U.S. POPULATION?

From a local perspective, one argument against labor supply programs is that former program participants will move out of the local area. But the U.S. population is less mobile than people think.

Of course, many Americans move into or out of a typical state or local area in a given year. But many more do not. Some of those who do move are repeated movers. And some of those who move out later move back.

Figure 2.1 presents an attempt I made with two different data sets to roughly determine average mobility and how it varies with age. One line in the figure shows with U.S. census data (the Public Use Microdata Sample, or PUMS, data from the 2000 census) what percentage of Americans live in their state of birth by age. The other line in the figure uses data from the Panel Survey of Income Dynamics (PSID) to show what percentage of Americans live in the same state they lived in at age four. The PSID has the advantage of following the same individuals over time. The PUMS data are inferring behavior over time from observations on individuals at the same time but of different ages. The PSID data also examine mobility since age four, which is the age at which pre-K education investments would be made. The PUMS data are looking at mobility since birth, which is prior to early-childhood investments (with the exception of prenatal interventions). However, the PUMS data have much larger sample sizes. Furthermore, the PUMS data can provide suggestive estimates of mobility behavior for much older ages. The PSID data have not been around long enough to follow individuals for much more than 30 years.

What this figure shows is that a surprisingly high percentage of Americans stay in their "home state" (birth state or state at age four) or return to their home state. Overall, it appears that at least three-fifths of all Americans spend the bulk of their working career in their home state.

Further explorations show that the percentage staying in their home state is lower for more educated Americans. However, even among Americans with a college degree, at least 45 percent probably stay in their home state for most of their working career (Bartik 2009b). It is important to recall that even among younger cohorts, most Ameri-

Figure 2.1 Percentage of U.S. Adults Living in Same State as at Birth or in Early Childhood

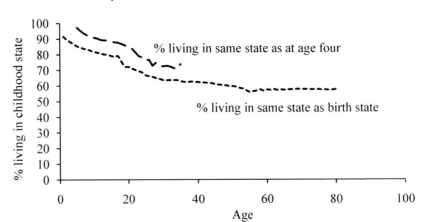

NOTE: Data on percentages living in birth state are calculated by the author from the Public Use Microdata Samples (PUMS), 2000 census. Note that these figures are biased downward, probably about 6 percent, because of households listing location of hospital as state of birth, not residential location of mother at time of birth. Data on percentages living in same state as at age four are calculated by the author from the Panel Survey of Income Dynamics (PSID), Geocode version. More information on these data is available in Bartik (2009b). Note that these percentages do not require continuous residence in same state. Those who return to a state are also included in percentages living in same state.

cans do *not* get a bachelor's degree. For example, among the age 25–29 cohort, about 70 percent of Americans have not received a bachelor's degree.[18]

The percentage staying in their home metropolitan area is lower than the percentage staying in their home state. However, at least half of all Americans appear to spend most of their working career in the metropolitan area they lived in at age four (Bartik 2009b). I will explore the implications of a metropolitan-area perspective versus a state perspective in Chapter 9.

The percentage of individuals who remain in their home area probably varies in different local areas. For example, it would be expected that larger metropolitan areas or faster-growing metropolitan areas would retain a larger proportion of persons who benefited from early childhood investments. Chapter 9 will explore how the economic development benefits from early childhood investments vary with local area size and growth.

State and local policies that invest in early childhood programs are not doomed to fail to help local economic development because everyone leaves. This is confirmed by real-world early childhood programs. For example, in the famous Perry Preschool program, 82 percent of the former program participants still lived in the state of Michigan as of age 40 (Schweinhart et al. 2005, p. 40).

HOW WILL A STATE OR LOCAL AREA'S EMPLOYERS RESPOND TO A LOCAL INCREASE IN LABOR FORCE PARTICIPATION OR JOB SKILLS?

Suppose every child in Michigan, beginning forty-two years ago, had enjoyed the same beneficial preschool experience as the fortunate sixty or so in the Ypsilanti study [of the Perry Preschool program]. Suppose further that the sequence of economic catastrophes visited on Michigan—and especially on its African American labor force—had been exactly the same: the rising challenge of Japanese competition in the automobile industry in the 1970s, the near collapse of the Chrysler Corporation in 1979, the devastating Rust Belt recessions of the early 1980s. How much would these economic outcomes have been changed by universal preschool? Not at all—except to the tiny extent that the spending on preschool itself created new, publicly funded teaching jobs in the affected communities.

Under these conditions, what would the Ypsilanti study, capturing a fair sample of preschoolers, have shown? The answer is clear: economic outcomes for the African American community would have been exactly what they actually were. But now every job, every case of joblessness—and every prison cell—would be filled by someone who went through preschool . . . [It is] a false inference that because something works for an individual, it will also change outcomes for the entire population.

—James Galbraith (2008, pp. 155–156)

Even if former early childhood program participants increase their education and labor force participation and remain in the same local area, overall employment rates and wage rates in that area need not increase. For employment rates and wage rates to change, employers would have to respond to the change in labor supply by adding more and different jobs. If employers do not respond, then any additional jobs or better jobs attained by former program participants will come from displacing other local residents from jobs. This is the essence of Galbraith's argument given above. If overall employment is fixed, then an expansion of high-quality early childhood programs will only affect who gets the jobs.

However, most labor economists would probably disagree, believing that in the long run, the quantity of labor demanded will come close to fully adjusting to changes in the quantity or quality of labor supplied. This assumption is based on the belief, backed by some empirical evidence, that labor supply does not respond much to wages. If labor supply does not respond much to wages, but labor demand does respond to wages, then in the long run the quantity of labor demanded must adjust to match labor supply. A minority of economists would agree with Galbraith that employment is largely set by labor demand. Under these assumptions, natural or policy-induced changes in labor supply will not have much effect on the overall quantity of labor demanded.

Which side has the better of this debate? Much less is known about how local labor markets respond to labor supply shocks than about how they respond to labor demand shocks. It is easy to find measurable variables that cause large, independent changes in labor demand.[19] For example, the national growth of an area's specialized export-base industries is strongly associated with local area growth and is a good proxy for a labor demand shock. In contrast, it is hard to find large changes in local labor force participation and worker skills that occur independently of changes in local labor demand.

My empirical estimates suggest a considerable long-run response of local labor demand to a supply shock.[20] However, this response is less than 100 percent. The detailed results vary depending upon what labor demand estimates are used. Consider a labor supply shock that increases some group's participation rate in the local labor market by an amount sufficient to equal x percent of the local labor market's employment. Then the empirical estimates suggest that local employment-to-population ratios, or earnings per capita, will increase by somewhere in the range of 47 to 89 percent of that x percent. The implied displacement effects are 11 percent (100 percent − 89 percent) to 53 percent of the original labor supply shock.

In other words, displacement effects may be significant, as they can be as great as one-half. However, in most cases displacement is not as great as one-half. And even one-half displacement leaves the glass half full. Local labor demand is responsive enough that local labor supply increases can make a difference.

Therefore, the truth lies somewhere between the traditional view of labor economists and the view of more demand-oriented economists such as Galbraith. There are some displacement effects that result from increases in labor supply. But this displacement is not close to complete.

For Chapter 4's baseline calculations of the labor market effects of early childhood programs, I assume displacement effects of one-third. If early childhood programs have effects on labor supply of y percent, I assume that the net local labor market effects on local employment and earnings are two-thirds of y percent. This assumption is in the range of plausible estimates of displacement effects and net local labor market effects of labor supply shocks. I also consider in Chapter 6 the implications of uncertainty about these net labor market effects.

Estimates done by Bound et al. (2004) are roughly consistent with these displacement effect estimates. They consider the labor market effects of an increase in a state's college graduates. Based on their estimates, an increase in a state's flow of college graduates is associated with a long-run increase in a state's stock of college graduates of 30 percent as much as the increase in flow. As mentioned above, slightly fewer than half of college graduates stay in their home state during their working life. This suggests that, out of a state's college graduates who stay, the net effect on the state's stock of college graduates is about 60 percent.

These assumptions about displacement are consistent with research that has been done on the displacement effects of welfare reform. Welfare reform induced an increase in the labor force participation of single mothers. The research literature has not reached a consensus about whether increased employment of former welfare recipients came at the expense of other workers. Nevertheless, the empirical evidence does suggest that overall employment rates did increase in response to welfare reform, not just the employment rates of single mothers (Bartik 2002). However, there are some signs that this increase in labor supply did have some short-run and medium-run depressing effects on overall wages (Bartik 2002), although this finding is disputed (Lerman and Ratcliffe 2001; Lubotsky 2004).

WHAT ABOUT THE RESPONSE AT THE NATIONAL LEVEL?

The national responses depend on how national labor supply and labor demand respond to wages and unemployment. These national changes in labor supply and demand will not include interstate migration of population or business.

My empirical estimates imply that the net national labor market response to a labor supply shock of x percent will be 85 percent of x percent for employment and 68 percent of x percent for earnings.[21] In other words, displacement will plausibly be about 32 percent for earnings, and only 15 percent for employment.

In Chapter 10, which considers the national perspective, I assume national displacement of one-third for both employment and earnings. I did not want to inflate the national estimates of the effects of pre-K and other early childhood programs by assuming lower displacement.

I should note that my displacement assumptions are conservative assumptions compared to those of most labor economists. Most economic analyses of programs that increase labor force participation or education levels assume that 100 percent of the increased labor supply is absorbed by labor demand. In contrast, I make assumptions that scale back the benefits of early childhood programs by one-third.

Of course, my assumptions are not conservative compared to economists such as Galbraith who assume that labor market outcomes are demand-determined. However, the empirical evidence suggests that displacement is not 100 percent.

CONCLUSION

Providing good jobs for all is a crucial issue. Providing such jobs is more beneficial if those jobs can be provided locally. More and better local jobs help preserve a valuable sense of place, a type of local social capital. More and better jobs improve local earnings per capita. Increased local earnings per capita improve local quality of life, the local political climate, and the local fiscal situation.

A business incentive policy is one way of providing good jobs for all. An increase in local earnings is by far the most important benefit provided by business incentives. Business incentives should be viewed as a part of local labor market policy. These business incentives improve the demand side of the local labor market.

But increased local employment rates and earnings rates can also be provided by increasing local residents' employability and skills. Programs that do so are working on the labor supply side. This increase in labor supply will lead to significant increases in the quantity and quality of local labor demanded.

This chapter has outlined how these different policies affect local employment and earnings. The estimates provided here, however, are only general estimates of how labor supply or labor demand affects local outcomes. Chapters 3 and 4 provide estimated labor market impacts for specific programs. Subsequent chapters will explore other issues related to these estimates. These other issues include how effects vary with program quality, and national effects.

Notes

1. Consider a recent summary for the National Governors Association of governors' state of the state addresses (Institute for the Study of Knowledge Management in Education 2008). This summary was for governors' speeches in 2008, before the full extent of the recession that started in December 2007 was apparent. The author of this summary counted a speech as addressing economic development if it mentioned economic growth. Ninety-three percent of governors' speeches in 2008 included proposals to boost state economic growth.
2. Dollar figures in this book will generally be stated in 2007 dollars. However, the dollar figures for government expenditures and revenue for different purposes are stated in fiscal year 2007 dollars here. The $30 billion figure given by Bartik

(2001) is a rough figure, perhaps best interpreted as late 1990s dollars. State and local resources today devoted to business incentives are probably still best estimated by a rough estimate of $30 billion in nominal dollars.

3. Data on this can be derived from published tabulations of the Annual Social and Economic Supplement to the Current Population Survey (CPS), available from the Census Bureau, in a set of tables labeled Geographic Mobility. The latest statistics, from 2007–2008, show annual gross in-migration to metropolitan areas of persons aged one and above of 3.4 percent (U.S. Census Bureau 2009). This is a little below some past figures. For example, the figure from 1996–1997 for gross metro in-migration was 4.4 percent (Bartik 2001, p. 64).

4. The implicit model is a Roback-style model (Roback 1982) with unemployment added and a wage curve model (Blanchflower and Oswald 1994) added that relates the level of real wages to the level of unemployment. A model of this sort is presented in Bartik (2001, Appendix 1). All workers and businesses are assumed to be identical. In long-run equilibrium, worker utility is equalized across local areas, and business profit rates are equalized across local areas. The employment growth is assumed to be brought about by a shock to some location-specific amenity that affects employer profitability, not anything that affects worker mobility. The new real wage and unemployment rate must be such that worker utility is again equalized to the national average. In a model with unemployment, the wage curve relationship between unemployment and the real wage is assumed to mean that any permanently lower unemployment must raise real wages. Yet we can't have permanently lower unemployment and higher real wages, as this would increase worker utility in the metro area above its national level. Therefore real wages and unemployment must be restored to their original levels.

5. There is a vast literature on efficiency wage models of the labor market. See, for some examples, Akerlof and Yellen (1986); Blanchflower and Oswald (1994); Davidson (1990); Layard, Nickell, and Jackman (1991); and Solow (1990).

6. The neutral fiscal effects of growth by itself apply to the average local area. Of course, there may be deviations from these averages in different local areas. For example, if there is underutilized local infrastructure, the required spending increases from growth may be reduced. This makes a fiscal surplus from growth more likely. On the other hand, in other local economies the required infrastructure improvements may be quite costly. Growth may cause net fiscal costs.

7. Appendix 2A (available, as noted in Chapter 1, on-line from the Upjohn Institute or via e-mail from the author) reproduces the calculations from Bartik (2005).

8. This 10 percent interest rate is much higher than the appropriate social discount rates. However, it may be closer to how individuals subjectively value property-value increases versus income increases. If we use some of the recommended discount rates in Chapter 7, which are based on how people behave in the housing market, we would get interest rates of between 3 and 10 percent, and the annual value of property-value increases would be even lower than stated here.

9. Bartik (2005) explains the derivation of these estimates in some detail. These calculations are reproduced in Appendix 2A. These estimates are derived from estimates of how employment-growth shocks affect employment rates and occupa-

tional upgrading, from Bartik (1991a). Intuitively, a shock of 1 percent to employment raises employment rates by about one-fifth of 1 percent. This raises earnings by one-fifth of 1 percent. There is a similar-sized boost to earnings from increases in occupational attainment—that is, from individuals' moving to better-paying occupations. As a result, overall earnings increase by about two-fifths of 1 percent. The numbers reported in this chapter and in Bartik (2005) for labor market effects as a percentage of income are lower than 0.4 percent for two reasons. First, the numbers are reported as a percentage of personal income. Earnings are a little less than three-fourths of personal income. Second, the numbers are adjusted downward for state and local sales and income taxes. Therefore, we end up with labor market effects of 0.28 percent of income rather than in the range of 0.4 percent.

10. Should we add an additional negative cost to business incentives because they increase in-migration? Business incentives might seem to increase the real costs of relocation for people. However, this is an incorrect analysis. First, it is not clear that business incentives increase the overall volume of migration. For example, business incentives in economically distressed areas may reduce the volume of out-migration. Second, given whatever policies are adopted, the model used here assumes that migration responses are optimal. The existence of strong ties to place explains why providing additional job opportunities in my home region may provide special benefits. However, holding constant whatever pattern of labor demand exists across locations, the resulting migration decisions that promote the interests of each individual also promote the overall interests of society.

11. That is, because one-fifth of the new jobs go to local residents, the earnings per capita of local residents go up by 20 percent of the total local earnings increases, simply because of increases in local employment-to-population ratios. Occupational upgrading due to local job growth has about the same effect on local earnings per capita as is caused by higher employment-to-population ratios. Therefore, occupational upgrading effects increase local earnings per capita by about 20 percent of the increase in total local earnings. Combining these two effects, local earnings per capita increase by about 40 percent of the increase in total local earnings.

12. Note that I assume that effects in a metropolitan area are similar to effects for a state. The reasons for this assumption are discussed in Chapter 9.

13. Why is there a difference between the long-run effects of job growth on unemployment and its effects on labor force participation? This is a conclusion from empirical research, so it's true in practice, but why is it true in theory? One possibility is that unemployment that differs from some equilibrium level may bring about changes in job growth and labor force participation that bring unemployment back to that equilibrium level. Labor force participation represents a change in labor supply, so one would not expect the same sort of equilibrating reactions.

14. To be exact, the Social Sciences Citation Index finds 371 citations to Blanchard and Katz (1992).

15. Specifically, the dynamic effects of Blanchard and Katz's model are derived by regressing a U.S. state's unemployment rates and labor force participation rates on lagged unemployment rates and labor force participation rates as well as on

state employment growth. Long-run effects will depend upon the coefficients on the lagged dependent variables. But state unemployment rates and labor force participation rates for a given year are measured with considerable error. This will bias the coefficients on the lagged dependent variables toward zero. This bias toward zero will tend to reduce long-run effects. Furthermore, the model assumes that the effects of shocks to the lagged dependent variables from all causes will be the same as shocks to the lagged dependent variables from job growth. These econometric issues are further discussed in Bartik (1993a) and Rowthorn and Glyn (2006).

16. For CPS measures of local unemployment rates and labor force participation rates, there will be some year-to-year correlation in measurement error because half of the sampled housing units will be in the survey the same month of adjacent years. However, measurement error should be uncorrelated over two years.

17. I do not focus in this book on two other local labor supply policies: 1) policies to attract or repel foreign immigrants and 2) policies to attract or repel domestic in-migrants. These policies are potentially important. There is much controversy about immigration. There have also been some recent suggestions that state and local policy should attract highly educated and entrepreneurial in-migrants, the so-called creative class. (See, for example, the series of books and speeches published by Richard Florida, starting with Florida [2002]).

I omit these immigrant and domestic-migrant policies because these policies probably have quite different local economic development benefits than policies to increase local residents' labor force participation or job skills. Immigrants or in-migrants bring with them considerable additional assets, and this affects local purchases. Immigrants or in-migrants also stimulate the local housing construction sector. Research by Greenwood and Hunt (1995) has established that these "demand effects" of immigration are crucial to determining the effects of immigration on local wages. Considering these effects of immigration and domestic in-migration would overextend this book's scope.

18. According to the U.S. Department of Education (2008, Table 8), based on the March 2008 CPS, only 30.8 percent of persons ages 25 to 29 had obtained a bachelor's degree.

19. By "independent," I mean exogenous to local labor market variables. For instance, in the past I have used national industry growth shocks to instrument for local job growth (Bartik 1991a).

20. In Appendix 2B, I consider what local labor market responses to labor supply shocks are plausible. This appendix is based on models of how local labor markets work, and on empirical estimates of the responsiveness of labor demand and supply.

21. These empirical estimates are also available in Appendix 2B.

3
Estimated Economic Development Effects of Well-Designed Business Incentive Programs

This chapter provides estimates of a state's economic development benefits from a well-designed business incentive program. The assumptions are detailed later, but here are the results:

- For each dollar invested in this well-designed business incentive program, the present value of per-capita earnings of the original state residents will increase by $3.14. As explained in the previous chapter, this increase in state per-capita earnings is this book's definition of economic development benefits. The "present value" calculation simply restates these future earnings in present dollars, so that they can be compared with dollars invested in business incentives.[1]

- Roughly three-fifths of these economic development benefits occur because of increases in the employment rates of state residents. The other two-fifths occur because of state residents' moving up to better-paying occupations.[2]

- These benefits occur because of the new jobs created by the business incentive program. These additional employment opportunities have persistent effects on the economic fortunes of many local residents. The extra job experience obtained by state residents increases their job skills, self-confidence, and reputation with employers.

- As discussed in Chapter 2, there are probably some social benefits that accrue to local communities from higher local employment rates. Even those who don't obtain new jobs or better jobs value these improvements for fellow community members.

- The business incentive is modeled as if it were a state tax incentive provided to assisted businesses for a 10-year term. The same dollar amount per job is provided upfront and for each of the next nine years. The 10-year term of the incentive is assumed because it corresponds to common state practice. If the incentives come in the form of services to businesses, the implicit assumption made in this baseline simulation is that these services have the same effect on business decisions as tax incentives of the same costs.

- The business incentive program is assumed to have earnings effects that are scalable with program size. For example, devoting twice as many dollars to business incentives yields twice the earnings effects.

- In this well-designed program, earnings benefits are greater than costs from year one. Earnings benefits for state residents in year one of the program are a little less than twice program costs.

- Suppose this program is designed as a permanent program that begins at a certain level of activity in year one. This level then grows over time with the economy. This permanent business incentive program will have earnings benefits that start at a little less than twice the program costs in year one, decline gradually to about 1.5 times the program costs over the next 10 years, then increase gradually to a "permanent" ratio of earnings benefits to costs of about three and a half times the program costs over the next 45 years. Figure 3.1 shows how this ratio evolves over time.[3]

- This is not a typical business incentive program. It is perhaps best described as representing "current best practice." It is designed so that the business incentives have no adverse impact on the quality of public services. The financing and design of the program are arranged so that the program has no net negative effect on local demand for goods and services. The incentive is delivered so that incentives can be "clawed back" if assisted businesses do not deliver the promised increase in jobs. The program is well-targeted at the businesses whose expansion will best help the economy. Specifically, the program is targeted at export-based businesses paying an above-average wage premium and having a healthy local multiplier. Chapter 5 will discuss these and other ways in which policymakers can improve the design of business incentive programs.

Figure 3.1 Ratio of Annual State Economic Development Benefits to Annual Costs, Ongoing Business Incentive Program

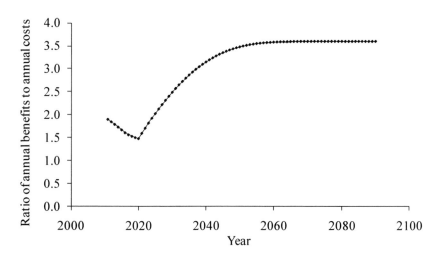

NOTE: The chart shows annual effects on per capita earnings of the original state residents who stay in the state. These earnings effects are this book's definition of state economic development benefits. (As explained in Chapter 2, increases in state earnings that don't increase per capita earnings of the original state residents are not counted—for example, the earnings of in-migrants to the state are not counted.) These effects are stated as a ratio to the annual costs of this business incentive program. This business incentive program is assumed to start in 2011 and remain thereafter on the same scale relative to the state's economy.

- Although these estimates are based on the best available evidence, the results are sensitive to different assumptions. Chapter 6 discusses how policymakers might deal with this uncertainty. Similar issues arise because of uncertainty about the effects of early childhood programs.

These results are generated from a model of how incentives will affect a state economy. There are three main components to this model:

1) Empirical estimates of how business incentives affect business location decisions,

2) Assumptions about how the business incentive program is designed and financed, and

3) Estimates of how the jobs generated will affect the state labor market.

Each of these components will be considered in more detail. First, however, a little more background on what is meant by "business incentives."

TYPES OF BUSINESS INCENTIVES

Many state and local government programs might be said to provide incentives to business. For example, improvements in a state highway system are an incentive for business to expand in that state. In this book, however, I define business incentives more narrowly. I focus on assistance to businesses that is to some significant degree customized to the individual business. Not all businesses will necessarily receive the same assistance. Even similar businesses in similar circumstances may receive different assistance. The actual assistance provided to an individual business is decided with some discretion by an economic development organization.

Most of the dollars in state and local business incentives are provided through tax incentives. The most important single type of incentive is property tax abatements. Property tax abatements allow a new branch plant or a business expansion to pay less than the normal business property tax rate for the new or expanded plant. The business applies for the abatement to some local government agency or board. Property tax abatements are not automatically received by right under state law. State laws differ in whether property tax abatements are permitted, what is the maximum amount and time period of such abatements, what types of industries and businesses are eligible for these abatements, what criteria are to be used in awarding the abatements, and what governmental entities have to approve the award of the abatement.

Other business tax incentives are also important. One increasingly common tax incentive is business rebates for worker income taxes. Under this tax incentive, assisted businesses are provided with tax credits equal to the state income tax payments made by the new workers associated with the business location or expansion decision. The logic is to reward the business for the additional personal income tax revenue generated for the state by the expansion. Businesses apply to a state agency to be granted this incentive. These tax credits are in some cases refundable. That is, the amount of these tax credits may exceed the business's tax liability under the state's corporate income tax. If the tax credit is not refundable, the maximum tax credit cannot exceed the business's tax liability under the corporate income tax. If the tax credit is refundable, then the business may receive a net cash payment from the state. As with property tax abatements, these tax credits are provided over some considerable time period after the location or expansion decision.

Another important tax-related business incentive is tax increment financing (TIF). In a TIF project, the increased property taxes from new development in a particular small geographic area go into a special fund. This special fund can only be used to promote the development of that small geographic area. Often this fund pays off bonds used to make public improvements in the geographic area.

Enterprise zones often provide tax incentives to business. Most enterprise zone programs are authorized by state government laws under a variety of names. (In Michigan, for example, they are known as Renaissance Zones.) The federal government also has had an "Empowerment Zone and Enterprise Community" program since 1994. Under enterprise zones, businesses that locate in or expand in a particular geographic area receive some type of favorable tax treatment. The actual tax break received varies with a state's particular program. Some enterprise zone tax incentives are reduced property taxes, others are credits against state corporate income taxes, and still others are reduced sales taxes on the business's purchase of inputs or on the goods and services it sells. Enterprise zone incentives are typically awarded as a matter of right to any business that meets the program's criteria for being located in the zone. However, there is some government discretion in designating the geographic areas defined as enterprise zones.

Some business incentives are special customized services to business. Customized job training programs provide new or current workers at a company with training customized to the business's needs. Businesses or local economic development agencies apply to state governments to receive customized training grants. The training is actually delivered by local community colleges.

Customized roads are also common. New plant locations, or major expansions, can apply to state agencies to pay for new or expanded roads needed to support the new location or expansion. Such assistance is awarded on a discretionary basis. It differs from general highway improvements in that the road project associated with the new business moves up to the top of the road construction list.

Other customized infrastructure assistance is also provided to new or expanding businesses. Businesses may be provided with access to water and sewer and other utilities at reduced costs. Businesses may also be provided with reduced-price or free land, sometimes in business parks (or industrial parks, or research parks) where the land is already available and includes all the needed infrastructure.

Manufacturing plants are often provided with various types of extension services. These extension services help the business to adopt or better implement new production technologies or other business practices to help improve the business's productivity and profitability. These extension agencies are operated at the state and local level. However, many of these extension agencies receive at least some funding through federal assistance from the National Institute of Standards and Technology.

Small businesses are provided with a variety of information and training to assist in start-up or expansion. These services are often provided through Small Business Development Centers. Some of the funding for such centers comes through the federal Small Business Administration.

Small business assistance includes entrepreneurial training classes. Such training helps potential entrepreneurs determine whether their planned business is viable and develop a business plan for the new business. Small business assistance also includes advice to existing small businesses on how to deal with specific problems with marketing, financing, or production. Some new or small businesses are also assisted through small business incubators. Such incubators typically combine relatively cheap rents with some shared services (e.g., a receptionist or answering service), and in some cases some on-site business consulting advice.

Another type of business incentive is assistance in raising capital. States in some cases directly provide grants, loans, and investments to support various types of business research and business expansion. In other cases, states will guarantee or encourage private financial institutions or capital financing institutions to provide loans or other capital to businesses.

Finally, state and local agencies provide various types of information and ombudsman assistance to new or existing businesses. New businesses are helped to find a suitable site. The new business might also be helped to get the appropriate environmental and other permits for that site. Existing businesses might be provided with some help in overcoming problems with state or local agencies that could inhibit the business's expansion.

Table 3.1 provides a typical list of business incentive programs. This list is for the state of Michigan. As the chart shows, overall, Michigan devotes almost $1 billion a year to business incentives. Of that amount, about two-thirds is in the form of tax incentives, about half of which are property tax abatements. Over 90 percent of the funding for these business incentives comes from state and local governments in Michigan.

Among the prominent tax incentives in Michigan are property tax abatements, the Renaissance Zone program, tax increment financing zones, and the MEGA program. As mentioned above, Renaissance Zones are Michigan's version of enterprise zones. The MEGA program is a refundable tax credit tied to the income taxes paid by the additional workers that are claimed to be induced by the program, either in a new or expanding plant or a retained plant.

The prominent services in Michigan include several funds that give grants to high-tech businesses or invest capital in these businesses. The state also pays to develop infrastructure for business development in nonmetro areas in Michigan, using federal Community Development Block Grant money.

Finally, considerable sums are spent by state and local economic development organizations in Michigan on business recruitment and on working with existing businesses. State and local staff frequently meet with existing businesses to discuss any problems that might be impeding their expansion or continued operations in business. Staff help resolve these problems. State and local staff also seek to market the state to businesses that are planning to open new facilities. They try to assist such businesses in finding suitable sites in Michigan, and in promptly obtaining the proper permits for building on these sites.

Table 3.1 Michigan's Current Economic Development Budget

Program	Level of government	Tax break or expenditure	Annual dollars (in millions)
Location subsidies			
Property tax abatements	Local, with implicit partial state reimbursement	Tax break	330
Renaissance Zone tax exemptions	5/6 local, 1/6 state, although implicit partial state reimbursement for local share	Tax break	121
Tax increment financing (1/3 of total for TIFs assumed to go to economic development)	Local, with implicit partial state reimbursement	Tax break	100
MEGA tax credits	State	Tax break	62
Brownfield tax credits	State	Tax break	29
Renewal/enterprise community tax credits for parts of Detroit/Flint/Clare County	Federal	Tax break	17
General business retention and recruitment			
State activities (MEDC)	State	Expenditure	27
Local activities (local agencies)	Local	Expenditure	15
Specific economic development services			
Customized job training grants	State	Expenditure	10
Michigan Manufacturing Technology Center: extension services to small and medium-sized manufacturers	36% federal, 31% state, 33% fees	Expenditure	7
Small Business & Technology Development Center network	37% federal, 16% state, 47% local	Expenditure	7

Infrastructure			
Community development block grants for nonurban communities for infrastructure to support economic development	Federal	Expenditure	45
Capital market and applied research grants/loans			
21st Century Jobs Fund: commercialization competition	State	Expenditure, loan, or investment	100
21st Century Jobs Fund: investment fund	95% state, 5% private	Investment	120
Capital Access Program loans to small businesses	State, with banks	Loan	4
SBA guaranteed loans	Federal, with banks	Loan	—
Total			994

NOTE: These figures are annual spending or tax revenue forgone as of 2007 for all economic development programs operating in the state of Michigan, whether financed by the state, local areas, or the federal government. All local tax credits (property tax abatements for new manufacturing plants and expansions, Renaissance Zone tax exemptions, and TIFs) are implicitly partially reimbursed by the state, because the state essentially augments local property tax collections for schools up to the foundation grant amount per student. TIFs in some cases go to downtown development and neighborhood development activities that might be argued to be "community development" rather than "economic development." That is, the TIF might be redistributing economic activity within the metropolitan area more than increasing overall metro economic activity. I conservatively estimate that only one-third of TIF resources go to "economic development," with the other two-thirds assumed to go to "community development." MEGA stands for the Michigan Economic Growth Authority; these credits are refundable tax credits to the business based on the income tax revenue generated by the workers associated with the business expansion, location, or retention decision. Brownfield tax credits provide special tax credits for businesses locating on land with environmental problems that has been designated by the state as a brownfield. The dash for SBA guaranteed loans means that I do not try to calculate an implicit value of these guarantees.

Each state in the United States has a somewhat different array of economic development programs. Emphases on particular types of programs differ across states. However, Michigan's set of programs is not unusual.

As this discussion shows, businesses have access to a wide variety of incentives. However, these incentives are similar in that they all provide assistance to individual businesses associated with some location or expansion decision. Some assistance, such as tax incentives or capital market assistance, has a cash value. Other incentives provide businesses with services that presumably have some cash-equivalent value to the business.

My definition of business incentives excludes assistance that is uniformly provided by law to all eligible businesses. I refer to such business assistance as "entitlement business assistance." For example, consider investment tax credits under the state's corporate income tax. Any firm that makes an investment has a legal right to receive the tax credit. I do not include entitlement business assistance in the category of business incentives because the magnitude of entitlement business assistance is difficult to define. Any change in state tax law that reduces tax revenues from business could be defined as entitlement business assistance. However, entitlement business assistance may have effects that are similar to those of business incentives. One issue considered in this book is whether policymakers should replace business incentives with entitlement business assistance.

The distinction between discretionary business incentives and entitlement business assistance may not be obvious to businesses or policymakers. This distinction may not make a dramatic difference in what tax breaks or services are actually provided. There is an old adage in economic development called the "reverse potato chip rule," in reference to an old TV commercial: with economic development incentives, you can't give out just one. There is political pressure to offer other businesses a similar tax break or service to what you offered one particular business. Therefore, the discretion in nominally discretionary programs is, in practice, less than it appears. This suggests that we should either convert many business incentives to entitlement business assistance, or restore true discretion to how business incentives are awarded.

BUSINESS INCENTIVE EFFECTS

What should we assume about the job-creation effects of state business incentives? My assumptions about business incentive effects can be stated in several ways.[4] One useful approach is to examine the likely effects of typical state and local business incentive programs. (In doing these calculations, I consider the "present value" of the costs of different business incentives. This present value takes the incentives provided in future years and discounts them back to their equivalent in today's dollars using some discount rate.) The average state and local business incentive program has the same present value to assisted businesses as providing a tax incentive, each year for 10 years, of $1,149 per job.[5] (All dollar figures given in this book, unless otherwise noted, are in 2007 dollars.) I express the incentive program as a 10-year promise of tax incentives because most economic development incentives have terms of some medium length. The model used in my research assumes that an incentive of this magnitude will successfully induce a business location or expansion decision 3.6 percent of the time. Suppose 1,000 businesses locating a new branch plant or making a business expansion were provided a 10-year incentive of $1,149 per job in the new plant or expansion. In 36 of these 1,000 cases, the branch plant location or expansion decision would not have occurred but for the incentive. In the other 964 cases, the incentive had no effect. That is, the plant location or expansion decision would have occurred anyway.

These effects are for a program that provides tax incentives or other cash assistance. Programs that provide services to assisted businesses would have an effect equal to their cash equivalent to the businesses. For the model simulation, I assume that if the business incentive was a service, its cash value to the business was just equal to the cost of providing this service. In Chapter 5, I discuss the possibility of providing more productive economic development services. Such services would provide more than a dollar's worth of services to businesses per dollar of cost.

Another way to express the effects of incentives is the ratio of the present value of the incentives to the jobs created.[6] The model used in my research assumes that the ratio of the present value of incentives to the number of jobs created is about $200,000 (to be precise, $199,220).

What this means is that if a program offers incentives that businesses judge to have a present value per job of $10,000, we would expect the incentive to be decisive about 5 percent of the time. (This should not be extrapolated to mean that if a program was crazy enough to offer $200,000 per job, that it certainly could take credit for completely determining the location decision. I have yet to see an incentive offer whose present value was even close to $200,000 per job. Newspaper stories that imply larger figures sometimes simply sum incentive offers over 20 years or value loans as if they were cash grants. The evidence suggests that the largest incentives have a present value of about $31,000 per job.[7] These very large incentives might be responsible for tipping the location decisions of about one-sixth of the businesses they assist.)[8]

These assumptions about the effectiveness of business incentives are based on the economics literature on the effects of overall state and local business taxes on business location. The overall business tax literature can be used to infer the effects of business incentives if we assume that business location decisions depend on business costs. Whether costs are lowered through lower overall state and local business taxes, or through business incentives, the effects of a given cost reduction should be similar.

Why use the research on the business location effects of overall business taxes? Why not use research on the business location effects of specific incentives? The research literature is far more extensive on overall business taxes than on incentives. Furthermore, measures of overall business taxes are usually more accurate than measures of incentives.

I base my assumptions about the effects of state and local business taxes on a literature review by Michael Wasylenko (1997). He concludes that the "suggested estimate" of the elasticity of business activity with respect to state and local business taxes is −0.2. This elasticity of −0.2 means that if overall state and local business taxes are lowered by 10 percent, holding all other factors constant, local business activity in the long run will increase by 2 percent.[9] This elasticity is within the range suggested by my prior research review of −0.1 to −0.6. An elasticity of −0.2 can be used to derive this book's estimated ratios of incentive costs to jobs created.[10]

The cost-effectiveness of business incentives is quite sensitive to variations in elasticity estimates. The incentive cost per job created is proportional to 1 over this elasticity. Thus, if the elasticity is −0.1 rather than −0.2, the ratio of costs to jobs created will double. If the elasticity is −0.6 rather than −0.2, the ratio of costs to jobs created will be one-third of its previous value.

This uncertainty has implications for public policy. The estimated ratios of earnings effects to costs in this chapter could be off by a factor of 2 to 3. Chapter 6 discusses the implications of this uncertainty for public policy.

FINANCING AND DESIGN OF INCENTIVES

The business incentive program modeled here is assumed to be a well-designed program. It corresponds to current best practice.

I will argue in Chapter 5 that current best practice could be improved upon in various ways. Chapter 5 also will include quantitative evidence on how the effectiveness of business incentives will vary with the financing and design of business incentives. In the current section of this chapter, I describe the design of best-practice business incentives.

Best-practice business incentives are *not* financed by cutting public services. Cuts to public services have two types of adverse effects on local economic development. First, cutting public spending will cut demand for local goods and services. For example, cutting public spending will lead to lower employment and wages of public employees such as teachers, police, etc. Lower earnings of these public employees reduce demand for other local workers. Cutting public spending also reduces demand for local suppliers to the government.

Second, cutting public spending may cut the quality of public services that are valued by business. We know that business location decisions are sensitive to the quality of public services such as education and highways. Several studies have found that cuts in business taxes, when financed by cutting public services, may actually discourage business location (Bartik 1991a, p. 48).

The current best-practice business incentive program also needs to avoid adverse demand effects, which may occur if the program is financed by increases in household taxes. Increased household taxes reduce household demand for local goods and services.

How can business incentive programs be financed without adverse effects on local demand or public service quality? The business incentive program could be part of a budget-neutral reform of business taxation. This budget-neutral program would reduce the tax burden on business expansions by business incentives. The tax burden on businesses that do not invest or expand would be raised by broadening the business tax base or increasing average business tax rates for businesses. This base-broadening and these increased average business tax rates would be offset for new or expanding business by business incentives.[11]

Most business incentives fall short of current best practice. For example, business incentives are typically not part of a budget-neutral business tax reform. In many cases, business incentives are an ad hoc add-on to the current business tax system. Typically, business incentives are not subject to a budget constraint. Business incentives frequently expand over time because of political pressures. For example, a property tax abatement initially intended for manufacturers may be expanded to wholesale businesses or big box retailers. Rebates to businesses for worker income taxes may initially only provide rebates for income taxes associated with new employees. But political pressures may lead to rebates for income taxes associated with retained jobs.

When business incentive programs expand in an ad hoc fashion, adverse effects from their financing are more likely to occur. The loss of revenue may reduce public spending and public services, and increase household taxes.

I assume that the business incentives are equal in effectiveness to simply giving businesses cash via tax incentives. Chapter 5 discusses how some customized services to business may have greater effectiveness than cash incentives.

The business incentives are assumed to be provided to assisted businesses over a 10-year period. This reflects current best practice. Delaying incentive payments makes it easier to base incentives on the business's performance in providing more local jobs. If the business does not perform, the incentives yet to be paid can be recovered. On the other hand, providing incentives over 10 years is less effective in altering business location decisions than providing incentives up front. Businesses tend to have large discount rates on future cash flows.

The business incentives are assumed to be provided only to export-based businesses. Export-based businesses are those that either 1) export goods and services outside the local economy (a metropolitan area or state) or 2) substitute for imports of goods and services from outside the local economy. Incentives to non-export-based businesses may increase the activity of the assisted businesses. However, much of the increased activity of the assisted businesses will reduce activity in other local businesses that serve the same local market. This displacement of other local business activity reduces the effectiveness of business incentives to non-export-based businesses. For example, helping one local retailer may reduce sales at other local retailers.

This assumption means that the estimates provided here would not be applicable to business incentives provided to sports teams and sports stadiums. The estimates provided here would also not be applicable to incentives provided to so-called destination retailers such as Cabela's and Bass Pro Shops. Although sports activities and destination retailers have an export-based component, a considerable portion of their sales reduces the sales of other local businesses.

The assisted businesses are assumed to have a healthy multiplier of 1.8.[12] This multiplier means that for every 10 jobs created in assisted businesses, eight jobs are created in other local businesses. These multiplier jobs occur in part in local suppliers to the assisted businesses. Multiplier jobs also occur in local retailers that sell goods and services to the workers of the assisted businesses and their local suppliers.

A multiplier as large as 1.8 requires that assisted businesses have a good network of local suppliers and pay good wages. Multipliers of this size are more likely for manufacturing than for nonmanufacturing businesses.

I assume that the assisted businesses and the spinoff businesses together pay an average wage premium. That is, the average wage of the total jobs created, with the multiplier, is about equal to what one would expect, given the skill requirements of those jobs. Because many service industries pay below-average wages compared to their skill requirements, this implies that the businesses that actually receive the incentive pay above-average wages.

If instead the jobs created pay below-average wages, this has adverse effects on local wage standards. As shown by previous studies, reduced wage standards in the local economy will reduce local earnings (Bartik 1993b). This reduction in earnings will occur in part because of lower wages in the newly created jobs. In addition, these lower wage standards will reduce wages and labor force participation rates throughout the local economy.

I assume that nothing special is done to match local workers to newly created jobs. Matching workers to newly created jobs might increase the share of jobs that go to local workers who would otherwise not be employed, as opposed to in-migrants to the local economy.

EFFECTS OF LOCAL JOB GROWTH ON LOCAL WORKERS

For unemployment rate effects of local job growth, I assume effects that start out at 30 percent of the growth shock. That is, for every 10 jobs created, three of those jobs reduce the local unemployment rate. These effects on the unemployment rate then steadily decline to zero over the next five years. This pattern of effects is consistent with the evidence presented in Bartik (1991a, 1993a) and in Blanchard and Katz (1992).

Effects on local labor force participation rates are assumed to be more persistent. This is consistent with evidence (Bartik 1993a) that the effects of local job growth on labor force participation rates do not diminish much for at least 17 years. As was discussed in Chapter 2, this empirical evidence can be rationalized by theories of labor market hysteresis. An increase in local job growth provides valuable labor market experience. This experience increases the future employment rates of local residents.

However, we would not expect hysteresis effects to persist indefinitely. Hysteresis effects are due to the long-term effects on local residents of short-term labor market experiences. Such hysteresis effects will be reduced over time as these local residents die or move to other local labor markets.

I assume effects on labor force participation rates that start out at 30 percent of the growth shock. These effects then "depreciate" based on the proportion of the original local residents who will be both still alive and still working in the local labor market. These migration rates are based on information on what proportion of a state's population are still living in their birth state as of different ages.[13] The resulting effects on labor force participation are consistent with Bartik (1991a, 1993a).

Figure 3.2 shows the time pattern of effects on unemployment rates and labor force participation rates.[14] The effects on labor force participation rates do not diminish much over the first 10 to 20 years. However, by 60 years after the local job growth shock, these effects on labor force participation have diminished to close to zero.

Effects on occupational upgrading are assumed to follow the same time pattern as effects on labor force participation. This is based on the empirical evidence that occupational upgrading effects are quite persistent. In addition, this assumption is based on the hypothesis that the persistence of occupational upgrading effects is due to hysteresis effects. Such hysteresis effects would diminish because of mortality and outmigration. Occupational upgrading effects are calibrated so that their average effects on earnings during the 10 years after the job increase match the occupational upgrading effects estimated in Bartik (1991a).[15, 16]

Figure 3.2 Assumed Effects of Increase in State Employment on State Unemployment Rates and Labor Force Participation Rates

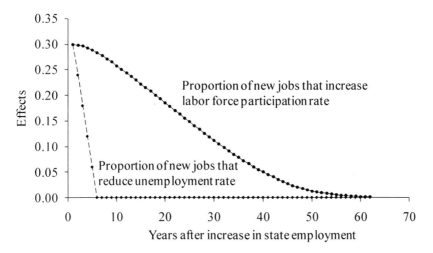

NOTE: Figure shows the assumed effects on state unemployment rates and labor force participation rates of a once-and-for-all increase in state employment. The effects are stated as a proportion of the employment shock. For example, both effects start in year 1 at 0.30. This means that for every 10 jobs created, three reduce local unemployment, three increase local labor force participation rates, and the remaining four increase local population. The derivation of these effects is described in the text.

RESPONSE TO POSSIBLE OBJECTIONS

The argument presented here goes against conventional wisdom. Among many liberals, and some conservatives, the belief is that business incentives are too small a percentage of costs to matter much. As a result, business incentives are too expensive per job created.

As examples of the belief that business taxes are too small a percentage of costs to affect location decisions, consider the following quotations:

> Incentives, for all their cost to state and local governments, are still too small to matter much. Typically, a firm's wage bill will be much greater than its tax bill; for the average manufacturing firm in the U.S., payroll is about 11 times the firm's state and local taxes before incentives . . . Thus fairly small geographic differentials in wages could easily outweigh what appear to be large tax and incentive differentials. —Fisher and Peters (2004, p. 31)

> State and local taxes are not typically a significant cost of doing business. All state and local taxes combined make up but a small share of business costs and reduce profits only to a limited extent. —Lynch (2004, p. vii)

> The fact is that the value to a firm of a state's typical, limited-term incentive package pales when compared to factors such as overall tax burdens; a reasonably priced, skilled labor force; the relative cost of compliance with regulations; efficient transportation facilities; crime rates; utility services and costs; education quality; and the general quality of life. —Reed (1996, p. 37)

It is certainly true that labor accounts for a greater share of business costs than state and local business taxes. But labor costs are harder for state and local governments to change than are state and local business taxes.

Labor costs adjust across the United States in response to other cost differentials. There are wide variations in labor costs across the United States. But much of this variation simply responds to other factors affecting the relative attractiveness of different locations to businesses or households. The more limited variation in state and local business taxes or business incentives is more readily controllable by policymakers than are regional variations in labor costs.

A similar argument can be made for most other business costs that vary across state economies. Business tax costs and business incentives are readily controllable. Cost factors such as the crime rate, the quality of education, and the local quality of life are more difficult for policymakers to control in the short run.

These cost factors can be affected in the long run. Therefore, these cost factors should also be considered as part of economic development policy. This book's main purpose is to argue for considering policies such as pre-K education as economic development policy. But the importance of long-term cost factors does not deny the importance of cost factors that are easier to control in the short term.

The argument that state and local taxes make up a modest proportion of costs tells us nothing about how businesses respond to changes in these tax costs. What is relevant to the effect of business incentives on location decisions is the closeness of relative profitability across different locations. If, after all factors are considered, profits are relatively close in one state versus another state, then a small business incentive may prove decisive, even if business tax costs are modest in size.

Business incentives may lead to changes in labor costs. When business incentives cause increased job growth, that increased job growth will raise local prices and wages. These increased local costs help limit the size of the effect of business incentives upon job growth. But these increased local costs cannot eliminate any effect, because the increased costs ultimately depend upon a greater local population bidding up the price of scarce land.

Suppose local costs do not matter much to business location. Then it is hard to see how state and local policies to improve public services can make an area more attractive for business location. The argument against business incentives can be used to argue for the impotence of almost any state or local economic development policy.

A less extreme view is that business incentives matter, but not enough. Incentives do not affect a sufficient number of business location decisions. Therefore, the forgone revenue per job created is excessive. Consider the following quotations:

> The best case is that incentives work about 10 percent of the time and are simply a waste of money the other 90 percent.
> —Fisher and Peters (2004, p. 32)

> Even with optimistic assumptions, for each private-sector job created by state and local tax cuts, governments may lose between $39,000 and $78,000 or more in tax revenue annually.
> —Lynch (2004, p. viii)

Part of the issue is that my own analysis disagrees somewhat with the figures used by these authors. I get a somewhat smaller percentage of location decisions affected by incentives, and a somewhat smaller cost per job created.[17]

However, the more important issue is that the benefits per job created are quite high. Jobs created by business incentives may have multiplier effects. Even though not all of these jobs go to local residents, many do, and for a long period of time. Furthermore, the job creation also allows for occupational upgrading benefits for state residents that are persistent. As a result, the state economic development benefits per job created by business incentives are estimated in this book to have a present value of almost one-half million dollars per job.

This half-million-dollars-per-job benefit only considers earnings benefits for state residents who get new or better jobs. As discussed in Chapter 2, there also would be social benefits to other state residents who care about their fellow state residents.

Because the benefits of state job creation are so high, policymakers should be willing to pay a great deal to achieve such benefits. Even affecting only a small percentage of business location decisions may be a worthwhile policy.

Of course, the benefits of state job creation could be much lower than is assumed here. A market-clearing model of the labor market could be used to argue that creating jobs has only slight benefits. As was discussed in Chapter 2, in such a model, the market wage only slightly exceeds the "reservation wage" of the newly employed workers.

Such a market-clearing model also implies much smaller benefits from the many possible policy interventions in the labor market. Programs such as job training, education, and public service jobs would also have much smaller benefits. Many of the benefits of such programs come from increasing the employment rates of former participants. Reservation wages' being close to market wages implies that only slight benefits would come from increases in employment rates.

CONCLUSION

The research summarized in this chapter suggests that business incentives can produce sizable benefits for state economies. These incentives can produce state economic development benefits whose present value exceeds the incentive costs by a ratio of three to one.

These ratios of benefits to costs are for an incentive policy that meets standards for best current practice. This requires that the incentives not adversely affect public spending and the quality of public services. Many or even most current business incentive programs would not meet these best practice standards. Chapter 5 will consider issues related to the quality of business incentives.

There also is some uncertainty about the magnitude of business incentive effects. Chapter 6 will consider the implications of this uncertainty for public policy.

Incentives have a high ratio of benefits to costs because of the large benefits of higher local employment rates and occupational attainment. These sizable labor market benefits provide a rationale for business incentive policies that have high costs per job created.

Business incentives are not the only way to increase state employment rates and occupational attainment. The next chapter turns to specific estimates of the state economic development effects of pre-K programs and other early childhood programs.

Notes

1. The present value of all benefits and costs is evaluated using a real social discount rate of 3 percent to further adjust dollar flows that are already expressed in 2007 dollars. The real discount rate adjusts for factors that mean a dollar in real terms in future years may be worth less than a dollar at the present day—for example, because per capita income is increasing over time. Chapter 7 discusses the discount rate issue.
2. The precise percentages are as follows: 57.8 percent of the benefits are due to higher employment rates, and 42.2 percent are due to better occupational attainment.
3. A table in Appendix 3A gives the numbers behind Figure 3.1. Appendix 3A is available on-line from the Upjohn Institute, or via e-mail from the author.
4. Appendix 3B shows the mathematics behind the relationship between these various approaches.

5. This figure is derived from Table 3.7 in Peters and Fisher (2002, pp. 74–75), which gives the average present value of state and local economic development subsidies across 75 cities in 13 leading industrial states, and including enterprise zone incentives, at $5,048 in 1994 dollars, where they calculate present value using a 10 percent discount rate. This present value and discount rate correspond to annual subsidies of $1,149 over 10 years in 2007 dollars. Note that I am not assuming that a 10 percent discount rate is a valid discount rate; in fact, in later calculations, I assume that 3 percent is the appropriate social discount rate, while 12 percent is the discount rate actually used by corporate decision makers. Rather, I use the 10 percent discount rate actually used by Peters and Fisher to translate their present values into corresponding annual flows, as their present values were actually calculated using the 10 percent discount rate for annual flows; I am merely reversing the process. My calculation of annual flows will not depend on the discount rate used by Peters and Fisher, to the extent to which typical economic development subsidies in fact are flat annual subsidies lasting around 10 years.

6. As explained in Appendix 3B, this is the present value as judged by the business being offered the incentive. Businesses probably use relatively high discount rates. According to Poterba and Summers (1995), the discount rate used by businesses in making investment decisions is 12 percent. Therefore, these present values of tax incentives provided over time need to be calculated using a 12 percent discount rate to determine their effectiveness in altering business location decisions. The social costs of these incentives need to be evaluated using the appropriate social discount rate, which I assume in this book to be 3 percent. (See Chapter 7.)

7. This is based on Peters and Fisher's estimate that in 2007 dollars, and evaluated at a 10 percent discount rate, the largest incentives have a present value of $33,515 per job (Peters and Fisher 2002, Table 3.7, pp. 74–75). If we assume these typical incentives have a 10-year term, the annual incentive value would be about $4,959. The present value of such an incentive at a 12 percent discount rate is $31,382.

8. These largest incentives have an annual value of about $5,000 per year for 10 years. That is, they are equivalent to reducing the cost of labor by about $2.50 per hour for 10 years. It does not seem wildly implausible that such an incentive might tip the location decision of one out of six businesses receiving the incentive. This is a substantial reduction in the average cost of labor. In 2007 dollars, average private industry labor costs per hour of labor were $27.69 (BLS 2008). A $2.50 per hour reduction is almost a 10 percent reduction in labor costs, which we would expect to have substantial effects upon decisions.

9. Note that holding other facts constant includes holding the quality of public services constant. Thus, the cut in state and local business taxes must be financed in a way that does not diminish the quality of state and local public services.

10. Appendix 3B provides the details behind this assertion.

11. A second possibility is for the business incentive program to be financed by increased household taxes, but with offsets to boost local demand. For example, if the business incentives were in local services such as customized job training, the increased spending on these services would help boost the local economy.

12. This calculation is based on data on MEGA that were used by the author and col-

leagues in previous work on Michigan's economic development programs (Bartik, Eisinger, and Erickcek 2003). The median multiplier reported by the MEGA program for its subsidized firms is 1.98. This is calculated by the University of Michigan using the well-respected REMI model (Treyz 1993). Therefore, I suspect that the multiplier figures are reasonable. However, the MEGA program is much more selective than the typical economic development program, and is one of the few programs that performs an impact analysis before the incentive is awarded. In addition, Michigan may have higher multipliers for export-based businesses than the average state, as Michigan has particularly dense networks of industrial suppliers. So, I suspect that MEGA multipliers are higher than average for economic development incentives. For the analysis in this book, the assumed multiplier of 1.80 is equal to the fortieth percentile of the multipliers reported for MEGA subsidies.

13. The proportion still in the state and still living is based on an elaborate calculation. I use population numbers from the U.S. Census on the number of persons ages 16 to 79 in the U.S. population. I then use employment rates by ages 16 to 79 to determine how employment is allocated across these different persons. I assume that the employment shock has permanent effects on labor force participation rates that are divided among different ages based on their share of total employment in the state at the time of the employment shock. I then used age-specific mortality rates to determine what proportion of those benefiting from that employment shock would still be alive in different years. I furthermore used data on what proportion of Americans living in their birth state at different years would still be living in that state in later years. (Specifically, the likelihood of whether someone is living in the state at age A1 if they were living there at age A0 is equal to the ratio of the proportion of persons living in the birth state at age A1 versus age A0.) The age-specific mortality rates were taken from life tables published by the National Center for Health Statistics (2005). The estimated out-migration from the state was based on the percentage living in their birth state, which I calculated from the PUMS data from the 2000 U.S. Census.

14. Appendix 3C provides the numbers behind this figure.

15. Specifically, it turns out that if the labor force participation rate effects on earnings are multiplied by 83.3 percent, the average effects of occupational upgrading on earnings will be 0.238 percent during the 10 years after the local job growth shock, which matches the estimates in Bartik (1991a, p. 150).

16. There are a few other assumptions needed to generate the results. First, to calculate the earnings effects of this increase in labor force participation rates and reduction in unemployment rates, I needed to make some assumptions about wages. I assumed that average wage per hour was initially a weighted average of the wage rate calculated from the 2004 Outgoing Rotation Group of the Current Population Survey. (The wage rate was later adjusted to 2007 prices.) The weight used was the percentage of employment in each age group from age 16 to age 79. Because this group, which is affected by the job growth shock, will age, the wage rate of the affected group is also allowed to adjust based on the employment shares of each age group that will be in the affected state, according to assumed age-specific

mortality rates and out-migration rates from each state. In addition, this model—and all models in the book—assume long-run annual growth rates of real wages of 1.2 percent. Therefore, subsequent annual wage rates for this group affected by the growth shock were adjusted upward by 1.2 percent for each year. All of these estimated effects are for a single group affected by a business incentive–induced growth shock in 2011. Similar effects were estimated for a permanent business incentive program by assuming that the 2012 group would have 1.2 percent higher wages every year and be 0.3 percent bigger, and so on for subsequent groups affected by a permanent growth shock. (The default model throughout this book also assumes annual population growth of 0.3 percent.) Real wage growth projections come from Holtz-Eakin (2005); population growth projections come from the board of trustees of the Social Security system (OASDI 2005). Finally, the costs of a permanent business incentive program were assumed to increase by 0.3 percent (to have the same percentage effect on jobs relative to population) plus 1.2 percent (under the assumption that the real cost of inducing a job via business incentives will grow at the same rate as the real wage rate).

17. Appendix 3B provides more details. I also respond further in Appendix 3D to other points made by Robert Lynch. My response explains some of the differences between his estimated costs per job created and my estimated costs per job created.

4
The Economic Development Effects of High-Quality Early Childhood Programs

The previous chapter estimated how a state's economic development is affected by business incentives. This chapter estimates how a state's economic development is affected by early childhood programs. These economic development benefits are effects on the earnings per capita of state residents. Early childhood programs have not usually been thought of as economic development programs. But these programs have effects on state residents' earnings, per dollar of program costs, that are of a similar order of magnitude to business incentives.

This chapter provides estimates of economic development effects for three different early childhood programs: 1) universal prekindergarten (pre-K) education, 2) the Abecedarian program, and 3) the Nurse-Family Partnership program.[1] The universal pre-K program that is examined would provide free pre-K education to all four-year-olds for three hours per day during the school year. The program is modeled after the Chicago Child-Parent Center program and the Perry Preschool program. The Abecedarian program provides disadvantaged families with free, high-quality child care/early education. This child care/education is "high-quality" in that it has low class sizes, high-quality teachers, and a curriculum focused on optimal child development. The child care/education is full-time and full-year for five years, from birth to age five. The Nurse-Family Partnership program provides first-time mothers from disadvantaged backgrounds with 30 nurse visits from prenatal to age two. These nurse home visits are focused on better prenatal care and better child care for the child. These visits also help the mother by providing advice and support for improvements in the mother's education, job, and family life.

The economic development effects are for operating these programs at full scale. For universal pre-K, "full scale" means sufficient for all four-year-olds whose parents choose the program. The other two programs are targeted at disadvantaged families. For them, "full scale" means sufficient slots for all disadvantaged families.

CONTEXT OF THESE THREE EARLY
CHILDHOOD PROGRAMS

Why study these three programs?

There are many early childhood programs. For example, the federal Head Start program serves almost one million children annually. This includes 8 percent of all three-year-olds and 11 percent of all four-year-olds. State-funded pre-K education programs have expanded in recent years. As of 2007–2008, such programs are estimated to enroll more than 1.1 million children. This includes 4 percent of all three-year-olds and 24 percent of all four-year-olds (Barnett et al. 2008). Federal- and state-subsidized child care for current and former welfare recipients probably serves more than 2 million children per year (Besharov, Higney, and Myers 2007). Many programs seek to improve parenting practices through home visits and parenting classes.

These three particular programs—universal pre-K, the Abecedarian program, and the Nurse-Family Partnership program—were chosen for this project for two reasons. First, these three programs had evaluation data that allowed for reasonable calculation of economic development effects. Estimation of the economic development effects of early childhood programs requires estimates of program effects on the adult employment and earnings of former child participants. Out of the many early childhood programs, these three programs have the best long-term follow-up data on former child participants.

Second, these three programs are model early childhood programs. I aim here to estimate the economic development effects of best current practice in early childhood programs. Focusing on best current practice is analogous to the previous chapter's focus on well-designed business incentives.

These best current practices are often only observed in small-scale experimental programs. This raises the issue of whether such results can be duplicated in full-scale implementation. I will explore this issue further in Chapter 5, which considers program design, and in Chapter 6, which considers uncertainty about program impacts.

Even though much of the evidence for these three programs comes from small-scale programs, this evidence is consistent with what we know about larger-scale programs. For universal pre-K education, although the Perry Preschool program was small-scale, the Chicago Child-Parent Center program was run at a large scale. For state-funded pre-K programs, well-designed studies in five states have found evidence of short-term cognitive effects (Gormley et al. 2005; Wong et al. 2008). Based on these studies of large-scale programs, it is plausible that full-scale implementation of these three "best practice" programs could have significant benefits.

On the other hand, not all large-scale early childhood programs are equally effective. Head Start has had mixed evaluation results (Barnett 2007; Besharov and Higney 2007; Currie 2007). The most recent Head Start impact study, using random assignment, finds that most impacts fade out by the end of first grade (Puma et al. 2010). This fading of Head Start impacts reflects the average performance for the Head Start treatment group relative to the control group, who experienced a variety of early childhood programs, including state pre-K programs. Although former Head Start participants continue to learn over time, the control group participants eventually catch up. Chapter 5 will consider what design features of early childhood programs are most likely to lead to long-term benefits.

SUMMARY OF ECONOMIC DEVELOPMENT BENEFITS

The state economic development benefits of early childhood programs can be summarized using various metrics.

This book's definition of state economic development benefits is the increase in earnings per capita of state residents. I consider these early childhood programs' effects on the present value of the future earnings of state residents. I analyze the ratio of these present value effects to the present value of program costs. (Present value calculations take future dollars and restate them in present-day dollars using some discount rate. Chapter 7 will discuss the issue of discounting further.[2]) For these three programs, this ratio is in the range of $2 to $3 per dollar of costs. This is roughly the same order of magnitude as the economic development benefits-to-cost ratio for high-quality business incentive programs. As Chapter 3 showed, such business incentive programs increase the present value of state residents' earnings by $3.14 per dollar of costs.

More specifically, high-quality universal pre-K education increases the present value of state residents' earnings by $2.78 per dollar of costs. An Abecedarian child care program increases the present value of state residents' earnings by $2.25 per dollar of costs. The Nurse-Family Partnership program increases the present value of state residents' earnings by $1.85 per dollar of costs.

Three aspects of these programs cause these increased state earnings per capita (which I define as state economic development benefits). The first type of effect is the stimulation of the state economy from increased state government spending, when that spending is financed by taxes. The second type of effect is due to the increased education or labor supply of parents. The third type of effect is due to the increased adult education, employment, and occupational attainment of former child participants. For both the parental and former-child-participant effects, only a portion of earnings effects occur because of increased educational attainment. Even holding educational attainment constant, these programs appear to have some effects on the labor quality of parents and children that increase employment rates and earnings.

The benefits these programs achieve through more spending are small. I will explore in more detail later why these stimulative effects are small. The short answer is that most of the stimulative effects of spending are offset by increased taxes.

The relative importance of effects on parents, versus former child participants, varies across programs. Programs that provide more child care, or that target the parent for assistance, have larger effects on parents. The Abecedarian program and the Nurse-Family Partnership provide roughly half of their benefits through benefits for parents. (The other half occurs through earnings increases for former child participants.) The Abecedarian program provides five years of full-time and full-year free child care. This explains its relatively large effects on parents. The Nurse-Family Partnership's program model emphasizes improving the "life course" of parents as one important goal. Universal pre-K education provides almost all of its earnings effects through former child participants. The child care is too limited in scope and time (three hours a day for the school year for four-year-olds) to dramatically affect parents' earnings.

Figure 4.1 graphically shows the breakdown of the various "transmission mechanisms" by which these programs provide economic development benefits to a state's residents. These transmission mechanisms are spending, effects on parents, and effects on former child participants.

The economic development benefits of early childhood programs are stronger in the long term than in the short term. Suppose a state

Figure 4.1 State Economic Development Benefits of Early Childhood Programs, Divided among Various Mechanisms for Causing Such Effects

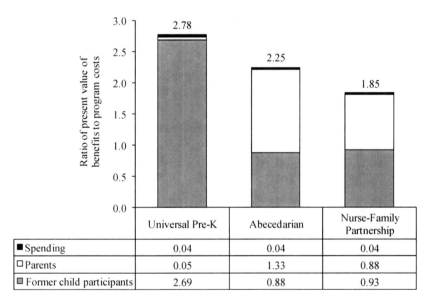

	Universal Pre-K	Abecedarian	Nurse-Family Partnership
■ Spending	0.04	0.04	0.04
□ Parents	0.05	1.33	0.88
▨ Former child participants	2.69	0.88	0.93

NOTE: For each early childhood program, this figure shows the ratio of the present value of effects on state residents' earnings to the present value of costs. These earnings effects are this book's definition of state economic development benefits. The earnings effects are divided among three mechanisms for achieving such effects: 1) effects of spending more money on early childhood programs, 2) effects on parents of participants in these programs, and 3) effects on former child participants in these programs when they grow up and enter the labor force.

in 2011 adopted full-scale versions of these early childhood programs. Suppose that these programs were permanent. Under these assumptions, these programs would have some significant earnings benefits in the short term. But these earnings benefits would be less than costs. For example, these early childhood programs would provide state economic development benefits in the first year (2011 in this simulation) whose ratio to costs ranged from 0.17 to 0.31. As these programs continued, the ratio of annual earnings effects to annual spending would increase. But this ratio would not exceed 1.00 for any of these programs until the 2030s. The ratio of annual earnings effects to costs then continues upward until eventually all these programs have annual ratios of earnings effects to costs of 2.86 or greater.

The delay in receiving economic development benefits from early childhood programs is due to these programs' inherent nature as child development programs. The earnings effects on former child participants do not begin to occur until these former participants reach age 16. Furthermore, the bulk of the earnings effects occur when former child participants begin to reach prime earnings years, at age 30 or 40 or greater. A universal pre-K education program that begins providing services to four-year-olds in 2011 will not increase the earnings of this cohort until they reach age 16 twelve years later, in 2023. The earnings effects on this first cohort will be much greater when they reach higher earnings years at age 30 or 40 (the years 2037 or 2047).

The short-run earnings effects of early childhood programs are due to the stimulative effects of spending or to effects on parents. But spending effects, as previously stated, are small. Although parent effects are important for some programs, the effects on former child participants are important for all early childhood programs, as one might expect.

In contrast, as discussed in Chapter 3, business incentives can provide a greater immediate boost to state earnings. A well-designed business incentive program can increase state residents' earnings in its first year of operation by almost twice the costs. Such a well-designed business incentive program immediately creates a relatively large number of jobs for state residents. Figure 4.2 provides a summary of the ratio of annual earnings effects to costs for these three early childhood programs and for a well-designed business incentive program.

Many state and local political leaders are focused on short-term benefits. Increasing the political attractiveness of early childhood pro-

**Figure 4.2 Ratio of Annual State Economic Development Benefits to
Program Costs, Each Year after Permanent Program Is
Begun, for Three Early Childhood Programs and a Business
Incentive Program**

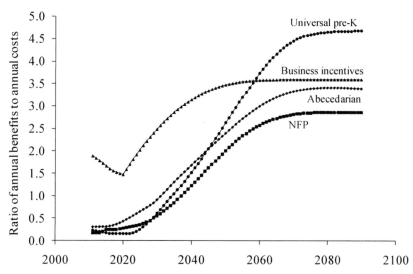

NOTE: This figure assumes that one of these three early childhood programs is begun
in 2011 and continued permanently. The figure reports effects on state residents' earnings due to increases in the earnings of the state's original residents who remain in the
state. These earnings effects are this book's definition of state economic development
benefits. For comparison, the figure also shows effects for a permanent program of
business incentives whose scale remains at the same percentage of the state economy
over time. The calculations show the effects for each program, assuming that it is the
only program being run. Possibilities of synergy effects among these programs are
ignored. Synergy effects are discussed in Bartik (2008). NFP stands for the Nurse-
Family Partnership. Appendix 4A presents the numbers behind this figure. (Book
appendices are available on-line at the Upjohn Institute's Web site.)

grams may depend in part upon redesigning these programs or their
financing to increase the short-term ratio of program benefits to costs.
This topic will be considered in Chapter 7.

　　These three programs differ in their size when operated at full scale.
A universal prekindergarten education program has the largest number of participants. I estimate that if such a program were operational
throughout the United States, it would have slightly less than 3 million

participants. The other two early childhood programs are targeted at disadvantaged families. Therefore, fewer children would participate in a full-scale national implementation: 600,000 children for the Abecedarian program and 400,000 children for the Nurse-Family Partnership program.

The programs also differ in spending per participant. The Abecedarian program is the most expensive. Providing free, high-quality, full-day and full-year child care for five years is quite expensive. The present value of net costs per child for the Abecedarian program is over $60,000.[3] (This figure adjusts for cost savings from reduced spending on other pre-K and child care.) The present value of net costs per child for the other programs is much less: $10,000 for the Nurse-Family Partnership program and $5,000 for universal pre-K. The cost figure for universal pre-K is also a net cost figure, as it saves money on existing publicly funded pre-K programs. (The earnings benefits for these early childhood programs are also calculated as net benefits. Net benefits show the earnings effects of these programs, compared to the earnings effects of the pre-K or child care program participation that they displace.)

Combining these factors, universal pre-K and a full-scale Abecedarian program would be far bigger programs than a full-scale Nurse-Family Partnership program. Full national implementation of the Abecedarian program would cost about $40 billion for an annual cohort of children. Universal pre-K would cost almost $15 billion for an annual cohort of children. The Nurse-Family Partnership costs less than $4 billion per annual cohort. The Abecedarian program costs "real money" because of its high costs per participant. Universal pre-K has moderately high costs because it has many participants. The Nurse-Family Partnership program has modest overall costs because it has both a modest number of participants and a modest cost per participant. Table 4.1 summarizes this information.

As pointed out above, all three of these early childhood programs have healthy ratios of state economic development benefits to costs. But because these three programs are of dramatically different scales, the sizes of their effects on a state's economic development are quite different. A state that adopted a full-scale Abecedarian program would increase the present value of state residents' earnings by 1.7 percent. The effect of a state universal pre-K program is a little less than half as large: universal pre-K would increase the present value of state residents' earnings by 0.75 percent. In contrast, the earnings impact of a full-scale Nurse-Family Partnership program would be far smaller: this program would increase the present value of state residents' earnings by slightly more than 0.1 percent. Table 4.2 summarizes these calculations. (The table also includes net effects after subtracting the present value of program costs, which tells a similar story of relative program effects.)

These results suggest that you get what you pay for. Early childhood programs that are of modest scale in both number of participants and the intensity of intervention per participant are unlikely to have large economic development benefits. If state policymakers want large effects from investing in children, they need to make large investments. Of course, the investments also need to have a high payoff.

Another metric for judging these programs' effects is their long-term percentage effects on a state's employment or earnings. In the long run, a state that implemented a full-scale Abecedarian program would increase its employment and earnings by between 2 and 3 percent. The long-run effects of a state's implementing universal pre-K education would be about half as much, or about 1.2 percent. The Nurse-Family Partnership program would have much smaller long-run effects of 0.2 percent on jobs and earnings.

Full-scale implementation of any one of these three early childhood programs can be compared with business incentives of the same cost. There is no unique scale for a business incentive program. The model assumes that a business incentive program will have its effects scaled with incentive costs. These calculations show that all three early childhood programs have larger long-run effects on state residents' employment than business incentives of the same costs. Table 4.3 presents the detailed numbers.

A different picture is presented by comparing the long-run effects on earnings of early childhood programs versus business incentives. For early childhood programs, long-run percentage effects on earnings are somewhat greater than long-run percentage effects on employment. But for business incentive programs, long-run percentage effects on earnings are much greater than long-run percentage effects on employment. Therefore, the advantage that early childhood programs have over business incentive programs in long-run employment effects is lessened or even reversed when looking at long-run earnings effects. For example,

Table 4.1 Comparison of Scale of Three Early Childhood Programs When Operated at Full Scale, in Number of Child Participants per Cohort, Present Value of Net Costs per Child, and Present Value of Costs per Cohort

	Number of child participants in a single annual cohort (in millions)	Present value of net program costs per participant ($)	Present value of costs per annual cohort ($ billions)
Universal prekindergarten education	2.892	4,933	14.3
Abecedarian program	0.619	64,297	39.8
Nurse-Family Partnership	0.373	10,033	3.7

NOTE: This table shows the number of participants and the present value of total costs per cohort if these three early childhood programs were to be implemented at full scale in all states. The table also shows the present value of net costs per child participant in each program. Net costs adjust, in the case of the Abecedarian program and universal pre-K, for offsets from reduced spending on other pre-K or child care programs. All dollar figures are in 2007 dollars. Present value calculations use a 3 percent real social discount rate.

Table 4.2 Present Value of Earnings Effects on State Residents, Costs, and Net Effects of Three Early Childhood Programs

	Present value of earnings effects on state residents, as a percentage of state residents' earnings	Present value of program costs, as a percentage of state residents' earnings	Present value of net effect (= earnings effects − costs) as a percentage of state residents' earnings
Universal prekindergarten education	0.75	0.27	0.48
Abecedarian program	1.69	0.75	0.94
Nurse-Family Partnership	0.13	0.07	0.06

NOTE: These calculations report the present value of earnings effects of each program for state residents, and the costs of each program, as a percentage of the present value of state residents' earnings. (Thus, 0.75 is three-quarters of 1 percent.) Present value calculations use a 3% real discount rate. Both earnings effects and costs are measured for the program relative to whatever early childhood program participation they displace. That is, if existing pre-K or child care programs have fewer participants as a result of introducing one of these three programs on the scale assumed here, this both saves on costs and reduces earnings effects. The net effect calculation subtracts program costs from "state economic development benefits," which are defined as the earnings effects on state residents.

Table 4.3 Long-Run Percentage Effects on State Residents' Employment and Earnings of Three Early Childhood Programs, Compared to Business Incentives

	Percentage effects on jobs as a percentage of state jobs	Percentage effects on jobs of business incentive program of same cost as this early childhood program	Percentage effects on state residents' earnings as percentage of state earnings	Percentage effects on state residents' earnings of business incentive program of same cost as this early childhood program
Universal prekindergarten education	1.19	0.54	1.24	1.02
Abecedarian program	2.34	1.51	2.62	2.85
Nurse-Family Partnership	0.19	0.14	0.21	0.27

NOTE: Effects are percentage increases in state residents' employment and earnings in the long run—here operationalized as 2090, 79 years after program initiation—due to permanent full-scale adoption of each of these three early childhood programs. These effects for each early childhood program are compared with a permanent business incentive program of the same cost as that particular early childhood program.

universal pre-K still has greater long-run effects on earnings than business incentives of the same cost. But pre-K's advantage over business incentives in long-run earnings effects is not as great as it is for long-run employment effects. For the Abecedarian program, and for the Nurse-Family Partnership program, long-run effects on earnings are slightly less than those of business incentives of the same cost.

Therefore, compared to business incentives, early childhood programs have greater relative effects on employment than on earnings. This pattern occurs because of which socioeconomic groups are served by early childhood programs, compared to business incentives. Early childhood programs provide their greatest assistance to disadvantaged individuals. The resulting increase in employment occurs at below-average wages. Business incentive programs create jobs at closer to average wages. Business incentive programs do help some nonemployed individuals get jobs, but they also increase the occupational attainment of the overall workforce.

One implication of this analysis is that early childhood programs, compared to business incentives, probably have more progressive effects on the income distribution. These distributional effects are explored in Chapter 8.

WHY YOU SHOULD CARE ABOUT 1 PERCENT EFFECTS ON EARNINGS

Some readers may be underwhelmed by these estimated effects. The effects of both early childhood programs and business incentive programs may seem small. The effects are around 1 percent or 2 percent of earnings. Why should we care?

We should care for several reasons.

First, 1 or 2 percent of earnings is a large number. The estimated long-run effects on the total U.S. economy would amount to hundreds of billions of dollars per year. For example, the implied long-run effect on national annual earnings of universal pre-K education is about $300 billion (Bartik 2006).

Second, these earnings effects, for both early childhood programs and business incentives, are two to three times their costs. A wise society should follow the rule of making such investments. If such a rule is consistently followed, then society will repeatedly benefit from adopting innovations that raise net incomes. Over time, the cumulative effect of numerous such decisions will be far more than 1 or 2 percent.

Third, the estimates used here are deliberately based on a conservative model of benefits. The model is conservative because it is "static." What do I mean by a static model? I examine the direct effects of programs on earnings. However, I do not examine potential dynamic effects on savings and investment.

For example, it could be argued that a portion of the higher earnings from early childhood programs or business incentives will be saved. Such savings may stimulate private business investment. One could also argue that a portion of the higher earnings will be taxed. Some taxes may be invested in other educational programs that will enhance economic development.

Increased savings and private investment, or increased taxes and public investment, can increase long-run economic growth. The sequence of events is as follows: Increased earnings stimulate private and public investment. Increased investment further increases the size of the economy. This further stimulates private and public investment. Depending on the model of how private and public capital affect the economy, it is possible to get permanent effects on growth rates.

Recent Brookings Institution studies on universal pre-K and the Abecedarian program incorporate such dynamic effects (Dickens and Baschnagel 2008; Dickens, Sawhill, and Tebbs 2006). A wide variety of long-run dynamic effects can be obtained, depending on what economic growth model is used. In some of these models, the percentage effect on the economy keeps on growing indefinitely over time.

Why am I not comfortable in adopting such dynamic models? First, there is not widespread agreement among economists about what is the "right" economic growth model. Therefore, there is a large range of dynamic estimates of these programs' effects on long-run earnings.

In addition, these dynamic effects are contingent on assuming that increased earnings will be invested in private and public capital. It seems more conservative to simply estimate the direct effects on earnings and note the possibility that further effects may occur if these earnings are used for investments. If households and governments choose to consume all of the increased earnings, then these dynamic effects will not occur.

Finally, one could get huge and unbounded long-run economic effects from *any* program that raises economic activity. This same type of argument could be used for any tax cut or government program that raises overall economic activity. It seems strange to argue that any program that raises economic activity will have unbounded effects over time. This confuses the effects of the program with the normal process by which increased economic activity may contribute to higher long-run growth.

However, readers should be aware of these possible dynamic effects. These dynamic effects are real potential effects of programs that raise earnings by 1 or 2 percent. Increasing the size of the economic pie always has the potential of leading to a virtuous cycle of investment and growth. The crucial issue in initiating such a growth process is whether the program's direct economic benefits exceed its costs. If so, then the program may permanently increase economic growth. Long-run effects could far exceed the programs' direct effects of 1 or 2 percent.

PROGRAM DESCRIPTION

To better understand the above estimates, the following sections provide an expanded description of each of the three programs.

I include some description of how previous studies' results were used to generate this book's estimates.[4] Most estimated effects that I use from previous studies are statistically significant or close to statistically significant. However, I use the best estimate even when it is not statistically significantly different from zero. This issue is discussed further in Chapter 6, which deals with uncertainty about program effects. A short rationale is that the rule of using the best estimate is most likely to yield the best decision about whether to adopt a program.

Universally Accessible Prekindergarten (pre-K) Education Program

The universal pre-K program used in this book is based on a program design of Lynn Karoly and James Bigelow of the RAND Corporation. They developed this program design in 2005 to estimate the effects of universal pre-K in California (Karoly and Bigelow 2005).

I picked Karoly and Bigelow's program design for two reasons. First, as shown below, Karoly and Bigelow's assumptions about the effects of pre-K are moderate. They do not assume some perfect pre-K program that is unlikely to be implemented on a large scale. Karoly and Bigelow's assumed effects are considerably below those of previous small-scale pre-K programs. Second, I wanted to avoid using my own program design, to alleviate possible concerns that I might have manipulated my program design to get the desired results.

Karoly and Bigelow's universal pre-K program is based on the Chicago Child-Parent Center program. However, it differs in some crucial features. The program is assumed to be universally available to all four-year-olds. ("Universal" does not mean mandatory.) Seventy percent of all four-year-olds actually participate in this voluntary program. The program operates for three hours per day during the school year for one year for all participants. It has a class size of 20 children. A certified teacher is the lead teacher, and the teacher's aide is a paraprofessional.

Following Karoly and Bigelow's lead, I assume that the effects of universal pre-K on child participants are 23 percent of the effects per participant of the Chicago Child-Parent Center (CPC) program. This 23 percent is based on Karoly and Bigelow's assumptions about how much program effects per participant might be reduced from the CPC program. Two factors might reduce the Karoly/Bigelow program's effects relative to CPC effects. First, a universal pre-K program would include many middle-class and upper-class families, whereas the CPC program was targeted for low-income families. Second, the estimated effects of the CPC are relative to those for other families who are not in any pre-K program, whereas some of the children in universal pre-K would have otherwise been in some other pre-K program. The 23 percent assumption also acknowledges the somewhat larger class size and shorter duration for universal pre-K compared to the CPC program. The modeled universal pre-K program has student-to-staff ratios of 20-to-2, whereas the CPC program averaged 17-to-2. Some researchers of pre-K education believe such a class size differential will not alter a program's effectiveness (Schweinhart et al. 2005, p. 202). However, I maintain that it might lower effectiveness somewhat.

I assume that the net cost of this program, per child participant, is $4,933. This net cost is arrived at after allowing for cost savings on other public pre-K programs and child care programs. The gross cost of the program per participant is $6,823. These net cost and gross cost assumptions are derived from Karoly and Bigelow.[5] From the available evidence, this amount seems sufficient to fund a high-quality program.[6]

The modeled universal pre-K program is provided only for four-year-olds, whereas the CPC program was offered at ages three and four. However, only about half of the CPC program participants actually participated in the program for two years. Estimated program effects did not differ by large amounts between one-year participants and two-year participants (Reynolds et al. 2002, p. 285).

The CPC program was a pre-K program started in 1967 in various Chicago schools. The program is still continuing today. Estimates of its effects are based on nonexperimental evaluations. However, the comparison group appears to be quite similar to program participants. Estimated effects on former child participants are based on all 989 CPC participants who were born in 1980 and who participated at 24 different CPC sites at 24 Chicago public schools. The outcomes for these former child participants are compared with outcomes for 550 children born in 1980 who attended five Chicago public schools that did not have the CPC program but were otherwise similar in socioeconomic status to the participating schools. (The description of the CPC program and of research results from the CPC program are based on various publications by Arthur Reynolds of the University of Minnesota and his colleagues, and particularly on Reynolds et al. [2002] and Temple and Reynolds [2007]. These descriptions are also based in part on Galinsky [2006].)

As of ages 20 and 21, the CPC program has reduced the percentage of high school dropouts by 11 percentage points (Reynolds et al. 2002). I assumed a universal program would reduce the dropout percentage by 23 percent as much. I used data on how employment rates and wages vary with educational attainment to estimate effects of universal pre-K on the jobs and earnings of former child participants.

I wanted to estimate longer-term effects of universal pre-K on subsequent educational attainment and employment, beyond ages 20 and 21. To do so, I relied on estimates from the Perry Preschool program, but modified to be appropriate for the CPC program. The Perry program was conducted from 1962 to 1967 in Ypsilanti, Michigan. The 58 randomly assigned experimental child participants and 65 randomly assigned control group children have been followed to measure program effects. (The descriptions of the Perry program and its associated studies are based in part on Schweinhart et al. [2005] and on Galinsky [2006].)

The Perry program was similar to CPC but somewhat more intensive. Perry averaged 13 students to two teachers, as opposed to the CPC class-size ratio of 17 students to two teachers. In addition, all of the Perry teachers were certified teachers, whereas only the lead CPC teacher was required to be certified. Both the Perry program and the CPC program were half-day programs that only operated during the school year. Both were offered for two years, for ages three and four. However, 80 percent of the Perry children participated for two years, versus only half of the CPC children. Finally, the Perry program, but not the CPC program, included a one-and-a-half-hour weekly home visit.

One estimated effect of the Perry program on former participants at age 19 was to reduce the high school dropout rate by 22 percent (Schweinhart et al. 2005). This is a little less than twice the CPC program's effect on high school dropouts at age 20 (Reynolds et al. 2002). Based on this, I assume that the long-run effects of the CPC program on educational attainment or employment rates will be about one-half of the Perry effects. In turn, the effects for universal pre-K are assumed to be 23 percent of the imputed CPC effects.

The Perry program's effects on long-run employment rates are far greater than could be predicted based on educational attainment. For example, the Perry program is estimated to increase the employment rate by 14 percent at age 40, but the program's effects on educational attainment predict that the employment rate will only increase by 2 percent (Bartik 2006, Table 11; Schweinhart et al. 2005). Presumably these "extra employment rate" effects are due to better and more-job-relevant skills that are not reflected in higher educational attainment. These "extra employment rate" effects of Perry are used in my model. I infer long-run employment rate and earnings effects for universal pre-K beyond those predicted by educational attainment.

The effects of universal pre-K on parents are based on research on how child care costs affect mothers' labor force participation rates. (See Anderson and Levine [2000], Blau [2001], and Blau and Hagy [1998]. Also see discussion of the implications of this research in Bartik [2006], p. 41.) Based on this research, the increase in mothers' labor force participation rates is estimated to be about one-fifth of the percentage reduction in child care costs. (For example, a 100 percent reduction in child care costs—that is, making child care free—would be assumed to increase mothers' employment rates by 20 points. If the base employment rate was 30 percent, free child care would increase the employment rate to 50 percent). However, free half-day school-year child care for one four-year-old child does not reduce child care costs by 100 percent. I made a number of adjustments to determine the effective reduction in child care costs. Half-day school-year child care is about one-fourth of yearly work time. About 47 percent of the participants in Karoly et al.'s model of universal pre-K would have already received free child care from another pre-K program. Thirty-nine percent of parents of four-year-olds also have a younger child.[7] I ended up concluding that for the average family in universal pre-K, child care costs are only reduced by 8 percent (Bartik 2006).

Abecedarian Program

The Abecedarian program was operated as a random-assignment experiment from 1972 to 1977 in Chapel Hill, North Carolina. It provided disadvantaged families with five years of free full-time and full-year child care and pre-K education (from 7:30 a.m. to 5:30 p.m., five days a week, 50 weeks a year). Services began when the child was six weeks of age and continued until the child entered kindergarten. The program also included home visits every other week. The child care incorporated educational goals from the very beginning, but with a highly individualized curriculum. Group-size-to-staff ratios changed from 6 infants to 2 teachers for the first year, to 8 toddlers to 2 teachers for the second year, to 10 preschoolers to 2 teachers for the third year, and to 14 preschoolers to 2 teachers for the fourth and fifth years. Teachers were high school graduates for children from birth to age two.

Teachers were college graduates for children from ages three to five. Salaries were competitive with public school salaries. (The description of the Abecedarian program is based on various papers from this project, but particularly Ramey and Campbell [1991]. I also used information from descriptions of the Abecedarian program by Galinsky [2006] and Ludwig and Sawhill [2007].)

The Abecedarian program had high costs. The present value of gross program costs per child is almost $80,000. These high costs are due to the intensive nature of the program. Class sizes were small. The program devoted substantial time to each child. Children potentially received over 12,000 hours of services from this program (5 years × 50 weeks per year × 5 days per week × 10 hours per day, minus the first 6 weeks at 5 days per week and 10 hours per day = 12,200 hours).

The program's gross costs of $78,411 per child are reduced to net program costs of $64,297 per child. This reduction occurs because of reduced use of other publicly subsidized pre-K programs and child care. The assumed magnitude of this reduction was derived from Ludwig and Sawhill (2007).

The Chapel Hill environment of this experiment probably resulted in good follow-up services for the Abecedarian students and families. The public school system in Chapel Hill was considered to be one of the two best public school systems in the state (Galinksy 2006, p. 14). Chapel Hill schools had a relatively small percentage of disadvantaged children. The school district also had a large number of different support services for children who were behind. In addition, among both the treatment and the control group, half of the children were randomly assigned to additional school-age interventions. In these school-age interventions, home/school resource teachers helped provide supplemental materials for parents to work on with their children. Therefore, the estimated effects of the Abecedarian intervention represent the effects of early childhood intervention when subsequently these children are frequently eligible for a variety of services. If early childhood services have positive synergistic effects with school-age services, this may increase the effects of the Abecedarian program.[8]

The Abecedarian program was targeted at families who scored high on a risk index. This index was based on a number of factors: low educational level of the mother or father, low family income, whether the family was a single-parent family, family receipt of welfare, and low-

IQ mother or father. It is difficult to determine exactly what percentage of the U.S. population would meet the Abecedarian criteria. Ludwig and Sawhill (2007) suggest that a full-scale Abecedarian program could achieve similar results by targeting families below the poverty line. I adopt their assumption, which results in about 15 percent of all children participating in a full-scale Abecedarian program.[9]

The estimated effects of the Abecedarian program rely on random assignment. Random assignment allows us to be confident that the differences between the treatment group and the control group are not due to differences other than program assignment. This experiment included 57 children in the program group and 54 children in the control group.

The free child care provided by the program would be expected to increase the labor supply of parents during the five years of the program. As discussed above for universal pre-K, we have good estimates from previous research of how child care prices affect mothers' labor supply. The extra employment of mothers during the program's five years should increase their subsequent labor supply and wages. Program data provide direct evidence that mothers' employment and earnings increase by sizable amounts after program completion. In addition, the Abecedarian program results suggest that the program increases postsecondary education of mothers. The model simulates short-run effects on mothers' employment and earnings due to the free child care. The model then simulates long-run effects on mothers' employment and earnings due to the greater short-run employment experience and greater educational attainment.

The Abecedarian experiment estimated an increase in attendance in college BA programs for former child participants as of age 21. I use the program's estimated effects on education activity and enrollment at age 21 to project final educational attainment of Abecedarian program participants. These effects on educational attainment imply effects on employment rates and wage rates. In addition, it appears that former child participants are more likely to be employed at age 21 than one would expect, given their educational attainment. As discussed above, results from the Perry Preschool program suggest that early childhood interventions may have employment rate effects beyond their effects on educational attainment. I use estimated results from Perry to predict how the Abecedarian results for former child participants at age 21 might change at older ages.

Nurse-Family Partnership Program

The Nurse-Family Partnership (NFP) program has been subject to three experimental studies: Elmira, New York, starting in 1977; Memphis in 1987; and Denver in 1994. The program now operates in 32 states and serves over 21,000 families (Nurse-Family Partnership 2010; Olds 2005). The NFP's target group for assistance is disadvantaged first-time mothers. Each mother is provided with two and a half years of regular nurse visits, 75–90 minutes long, from prenatal to age two. On average, about 7 visits occur prior to the child's birth, and 23 after. (These descriptions of NFP are based on Kitzman et al. [2000]; Olds [2002]; Olds et al. [1997, 1998]; Olds, Kitzman, et al. [2004]; and Olds, Robinson, et al. [2004].)

The "curriculum" presented in the nurse visits has three goals: 1) healthier prenatal care, 2) more sensitive child care, and 3) a better maternal life course. A better maternal life course includes better spacing and planning of subsequent pregnancies, help for the mother in completing her education and finding work, and more constructive involvement of the father in the family (Olds 2002). The goals of the NFP focus at least as much on the mother as on the child. First-time mothers are targeted on the theory that they will be more open to the program's influence. Nurses are used as home visitors because of their credibility with mothers and their health care knowledge. The Denver experiment suggests that nurse home visitors are more effective than paraprofessional home visitors (Olds, Robinson, et al. 2004).

In the initial NFP experiment, in Elmira, the program targeted modestly disadvantaged first-time mothers. However, research suggested that the program had greater effects for more disadvantaged women (Karoly et al. 1998; Olds et al. 1997). Therefore, subsequent tests of the program have been targeted more greatly at disadvantaged women. Isaacs (2007) estimates that a full-scale NFP program might qualify 9 percent of all children as eligible. I adopt Isaacs's assumption.

The NFP has far fewer hours of intervention per family than the Abecedarian program or universal pre-K education. The NFP only interacts with its target group for perhaps 45 hours over two and a half years (30 visits × 90 minutes per visit). The Abecedarian program interacts with children for up to 12,000 hours. Of course, the theory behind the NFP is that interventions at a crucial period with the mother will have large effects later on. There is evidence from the experiments of such effects on the mother's behavior. The Elmira and Memphis experiments indicate that the program reduced subsequent pregnancies. The Denver experiment indicates effects in delaying the time until a second birth (Olds et al. 1997; Olds, Kitzman, et al. 2004; Olds, Robinson, et al. 2004). Fewer subsequent pregnancies, or delayed second births, are likely to improve the quantity and quality of the mother's interaction with the first child.

The lower intensity in hours of service of the NFP program is not fully matched by lower costs. Costs of the NFP program per child are about one-eighth of the costs per child of the Abecedarian program (about $10,000 per child versus $78,000 per child). The hours of service per child of the NFP program are less than 0.5 percent of the hours of service per child of the Abecedarian program (45 hours versus 12,000 hours). The lower differential in costs than in service hours probably reflects several factors. The NFP relies more on one-on-one service: nurses meet individually with the mothers, whereas there are multiple Abecedarian children per teacher. More NFP resources are devoted to nondirect service hours. Finally, salaries may be higher for NFP nurses than for the average Abecedarian employee.

The three NFP experiments have larger sample sizes than the Abecedarian program. Larger samples allow program effects to be estimated with greater statistical precision. Sample sizes for the treatment group and the control group at each site are in the hundreds.

The NFP's effects on increasing the employment of mothers and reducing welfare usage are greater in the Elmira experiment than in the Memphis and Denver experiments. The lower effects in the later experiments may reflect changes in welfare policy that increase pressure on welfare mothers to be employed. (Olds, Robinson, et al. [2004] note no effects on mothers' use of welfare in the Denver trial. This result differs from the effects estimated in Memphis and Elmira. They speculate that this may be due to welfare reform.) After welfare reform, reductions or delays in subsequent pregnancies are less likely to affect mothers' employment. Because of welfare reform, I use a more conservative estimate by relying on the Memphis and Denver experiments to estimate the NFP's effects on mothers' employment and earnings.

The Memphis and Denver results suggest modest effects of the experiment on increasing mothers' high school graduation rates (Olds,

Kitzman, et al. 2004; Olds, Robinson, et al. 2004). They also suggest some short-run increases in mothers' employment, during the period from the child's second to fourth birthdays, beyond what is predicted based on educational attainment (Kitzman et al. 2000; Olds, Robinson, et al. 2004). However, these short-run extra employment effects then fade away (Olds, Kitzman, et al. 2004).

None of the three experiments has direct evidence on former child participants' employment or earnings, or their educational attainment. Therefore, earlier indicators of effects on former child participants must be used to predict effects on their employment and earnings as adults. Estimates from Memphis suggest small effects of the NFP on age six reading and math scores (Olds, Kitzman, et al. 2004). These reading and math score test results can be used to predict adult employment rates and earnings. The Elmira results also report large effects of the program on reducing the former child participants' arrests through age 15 (Olds et al. 1998). These juvenile arrests can be used to predict reductions in adult criminal activity. Predicted reductions in adult criminal activity can then be used to predict changes in adult employment rates.

MODELING ECONOMIC DEVELOPMENT EFFECTS, PART 1: SPENDING

These estimates of program size and program effects were then used to simulate effects on the employment and earnings of state residents. These simulations were based on a model of how a state economy responds to labor demand and labor supply increases.

The first type of economic development effect is due to increased public spending. The additional spending on early childhood programs will increase demand for goods and services produced within the state. The increased program spending will create jobs for the staff of the early childhood program. The increased spending will also create some jobs in state-based suppliers to the early childhood program (e.g., suppliers of paper, furniture, books, toys, etc.). The workers in the early childhood program and its suppliers will spend some of their salaries on locally produced goods and services. This multiplier effect on demand for locally produced goods and services will increase jobs and earnings at these local producers. In turn, there will be further effects as a portion of these increased jobs and earnings in other local producers is respent locally.

However, we also have to take into account the effects of increased state taxes on demand for goods and services produced within the state. I assume that the increased state spending on early childhood programs is 100 percent financed by increased state taxes. These increased state taxes will reduce the disposable income of state residents. Lower disposable income will reduce state residents' demand for goods and services, including goods and services produced within the state. This lower demand for goods and services produced within the state will reduce jobs and earnings from these employers.

Intuition might suggest that the stimulus from increased program spending will be completely offset by higher taxes. The increased state spending and taxes are the same dollar amount; therefore, they might be assumed to have equally sized but opposite effects on demand.

This intuition is wrong. It overlooks an asymmetry in the first-round effects of increased spending versus increased taxes. The increased spending in the first instance directly creates jobs and earnings in the early childhood programs. In this first round, 100 percent of the increased state spending affects demand for locally produced goods and services. This increased spending then goes on to have indirect effects, as a portion of the state spending is respent by early childhood workers.

In contrast, higher state taxes have no direct effect in reducing jobs and earnings in the state. The increased taxes reduce after-tax disposable income. Only a portion of the reduction in disposable income is reflected in reduced demand for locally produced goods and services. The rest of the reduction in disposable income is reflected in reduced demand for goods and services produced outside the state, or reduced savings.

Consider this example. Suppose a state increases taxes by $50,000 to pay for the salary and benefits of one lead pre-K teacher. All of this $50,000 in increased spending goes to increasing jobs and earnings in the state. However, of the $50,000 in increased taxes, some of that $50,000 would have been spent on mail orders from L.L. Bean or trips to other states. Some of the $50,000 might have been saved. And even for the portion of the $50,000 that is spent locally, not all of that spending boosts jobs and earnings in the state. For example, reduced spending on clothing at local stores, if the clothing is produced outside the state, would be in large part reflected in reduced production outside the state. (Of course, there would be some reduction in demand for the retail services provided by local clothing retailers. Some local jobs would be lost by clothing salespeople.)

This stimulative effect of an equal-sized increase in government taxes and spending is well known in economics. It is referred to as the balanced budget multiplier. The relevance of the balanced budget multiplier to state government budget decisions has been emphasized by many economists, including Nobel Prize winner Joseph Stiglitz and President Obama's first director of the Office of Management and Budget, Peter Orszag (Orszag and Stiglitz 2001).

To estimate the net effects on a state economy of an equal increase in early childhood program spending and state taxes, I use a well-known regional econometrics model, the REMI model (Regional Economic Models Inc). These estimated effects are then scaled up or down depending upon the size of the particular early childhood program.

But this book measures "state economic development" as the increase in the employment and earnings of the original state residents. The estimated effects on the demand for labor from the REMI model need to be translated into effects on the employment and earnings of the original state residents.

To measure these effects on the employment and earnings of state residents, I use the same methodology that was used to measure the effects of business incentives. Both business incentives and increases in early childhood spending can create jobs in a state economy. I use the same assumptions as were used in Chapter 3 about what proportion of those jobs in the short run and the long run will be reflected in higher labor force participation rates and lower unemployment rates. I use the same assumptions about how job creation in a state will allow some state residents to move up to better-paying jobs. And I use the same assumptions about how these effects change over time because of mortality, or because of state residents moving to other states.

However, spending more money on early childhood programs turns out to have small "demand effects." As mentioned earlier in this chapter, the demand effects of increased state spending on early childhood programs only increase the earnings of state residents by four cents per dollar of state spending.

In contrast, a dollar devoted to business incentives is estimated to increase the earnings of state residents by $3.14. Why this discrepancy in demand effects?

This discrepancy occurs for two reasons. First, state spending on early childhood programs must spend 100 percent of a job's earnings to directly create that job. In contrast, inducing a job's creation through business incentives costs only a portion of the job's earnings.

Second, the jobs created by state spending on early childhood programs will only continue if state spending is kept at that higher level. If the spending goes away, so do these jobs. In contrast, the model of business incentives assumes that once a job is attracted by business incentives, that job (although not necessarily that business) will remain in the local economy. The market demand in the national and world economy for that business will remain even after the incentive is gone. Maintaining a job through continuous spending is obviously more costly than permanently inducing a job through a one-time package of tax incentives.[10]

MODELING ECONOMIC DEVELOPMENT EFFECTS, PART 2: STATE LABOR MARKET EFFECTS OF INCREASED LABOR SUPPLY OF PARENTS OR FORMER CHILD PARTICIPANTS

As discussed in Chapter 2, this book's definition of state economic development only includes the increased employment and earnings of state residents who stay in the state. To measure the state economic development effects for each early childhood program, I adjust for parents and former child participants who would be expected to die at various ages. I also adjust for what proportion of parents and former child participants will remain in the state.[11] I note, in Chapter 2, the finding that more people stay in the same state than one might think.

The proportion that stays may vary with features of the local economy, e.g., its size. This issue is explored further in Chapter 9. Local economic development effects of early childhood programs may vary in metropolitan areas versus states, and with the size and growth rate of the metropolitan area.

From a national perspective, we would include the increased employment and earnings for parents or former child participants in early childhood programs who move to other states. Chapter 10 will consider the national perspective.

We also allow for the possibility that increased labor supply may cause displacement effects. The increased quantity or quality of labor supply of parents or former child participants does not directly create jobs in a state's economy. The net effect on state residents' employment and earnings depends upon how employers respond to this increase in state labor supply.

As discussed in Chapter 2, I assume one-third displacement effects of early childhood programs. For every three jobs that parents or former child participants who remain in the state will hold due to their higher employment rates, I assume that net jobs in the state go up by two jobs. The other job displaces some other state resident from employment and is not counted in my simulations. Similar displacement effects are assumed for increased earnings due to parents or former child participants getting better jobs. Allowing for displacement effects scales back the economic development effects of early childhood programs by one-third. I believe that this one-third displacement assumption is reasonably supported by empirical evidence.[12] I also note that these assumptions—i.e., scaling back the economic development benefits of early childhood programs by one-third—are conservative.

DOES THIS ANALYSIS TREAT EARLY CHILDHOOD PROGRAMS FAIRLY COMPARED TO BUSINESS INCENTIVES?

> Some economic developers don't believe that multipliers for child care count. They think multipliers are relevant in other fields—like manufacturing or construction—but not for a service industry like child care . . . Some will say that multipliers count for some services such as banking or education, but not for child care. We believe that multipliers count for both and that is the approach we've taken in this report [on the economic impact of child care].
>
> —Mildred Warner (2005)

The educational impact on children has been a primary focus for many researchers [on the impact of early childhood programs] and the significance of this long-term benefit is clearly responsible for the growing interest in universal Pre-Kindergarten. However, the short-term economic returns that accrue from increased and stable parental employment . . . as well as the child care industry as a whole . . . should not be underestimated. Policy makers who face budget cuts for early care and education or propose new spending on early childhood services appreciate the research establishing the short-term returns on the investment. Clearly, early childhood education generates short- and long-term benefits for children, parents and society and all economic aspects of the field should be explored to justify the level of investments needed.

—Dana Friedman (2004, p. 3)

This book is not the only attempt to analyze the economic effects of early childhood programs; many research studies and consulting reports analyze the economic impact of the child care industry. How do these estimates compare? Do these alternative studies suggest any issues with this book's estimates?

Many of these economic studies of child care have involved two groups of researchers. One group is associated with the Linking Economic Development and Child Care project at Cornell University, whose principal investigator is Professor Mildred Warner. A second group is associated with the Insight Center for Community Economic Development, formerly the National Economic Development and Law Center. The Web site of the Insight Center lists 12 studies done by the Insight Center from 2001 to 2008 on the economic impact of child care. These include the states of California, Hawaii, Illinois, Massachusetts, Minnesota, Montana, North Carolina, and Ohio, and the cities of Los Angeles and Washington, DC. The Web site of the Cornell project lists 74 studies done from 1997 to 2008 on the economic impact of child care. These studies are written by a variety of researchers, including some of those from the Cornell project as well as the Insight Center. (Thus, there is some overlap between the two lists.) These include studies for the states of South Carolina, Alaska, West Virginia, Indiana, Missouri, Oregon, Iowa, Louisiana, Virginia, Colorado, South Dakota, Washington, North Dakota, Connecticut, Arizona, Oklahoma, Mississippi, Texas, Florida, New York, Maine, Rhode Island, and Vermont, as well as for the cities of Buffalo, San Francisco, New York, and Memphis.

Many studies come up with much larger estimates of the spending impacts and parental labor supply impacts of early childhood programs than I do in this book. For example, one study estimates that spending on the child care industry increases employment by 2.0 percent. In addition, the employment and earnings associated with parents who are freed up by child care to work amounts to 11 percent of total employment and 12 percent of total earnings (M Cubed Consulting Group 2002). These are immediate impacts, not long-run impacts. In contrast, my estimates of spending and parental labor supply effects are much lower. Consider my estimates of the spending and parental labor supply effects of the Abecedarian program, which is a full-time and full-year child care program. The immediate spending impact of a full-scale implementation of the Abecedarian program is to provide job creation and earnings benefits equivalent to 0.02 percent of a state's employment or earnings. This spending impact increases over a four-year period to a maximum of 0.07 percent of employment and 0.10 percent of earnings, before declining toward zero. The immediate parental labor supply impact of a full-scale implementation of the Abecedarian program is to provide job creation benefits and earnings creation benefits of 0.05 percent of state employment and 0.02 percent of state earnings. Eventually these parental labor supply effects become much larger. These parental labor supply benefits increase steadily over time to their long-run values of 1.1 percent of state employment and 1.4 percent of state earnings. (Figures are calculations by the author, from this book's simulation model.)

These different impact estimates are obviously important to evaluating the social benefits from early childhood programs. In particular, the size of the immediate benefits may be extremely important to political support for early childhood programs. As Dana Friedman points out in the second quotation given above, "Policymakers . . . appreciate the research establishing the short-term returns . . . "

Therefore, an important question is, which estimate of short-term effects is right? Have I missed something in evaluating the economic development benefits of early childhood programs? Is my methodology somehow biased against early childhood programs? Mildred Warner in the first quotation above criticizes researchers who count multipliers for business incentives but not for early childhood programs. Is that the problem here?

The short answer is no. I use a consistent methodology for counting the economic development benefits of business incentives and early childhood programs. I do count multipliers for the spending effects of early childhood programs, just as I do for those of business incentives.

Why, then, are the impact estimates in this book, versus this large body of studies, so much smaller? I believe there are three reasons for these differences in estimates. First, there are different definitions of "economic impacts." Second, there are differences in the size of the "program" being studied. Third, there are differences in the "counterfactual" used to define impacts.

On the first point, I use a more narrow definition of economic development benefits than is used by these child care studies. I use this definition consistently for estimating both business incentive effects and early childhood program effects. However, this measure does yield smaller numbers.

Specifically, as discussed in Chapter 2, this book focuses on increases in the employment rate and earnings per person of state residents who remain in the state. I do not include increases in state employment and earnings that are associated with in-migration. As explained in Chapter 2, this measure does focus consistently on measuring the benefits from economic development that accrue to specific individuals. Growth in a state or local economy is not a benefit in and of itself. It is only a benefit to the extent that such growth enhances the well-being of specific individuals.

In contrast, the economic impact studies of child care include all increases in jobs and earnings of state residents. This definition of economic impact includes job growth and earnings growth that do not provide benefits to any individual. For example, this definition includes benefits that accrue to in-migrants who could have found similar jobs and earnings elsewhere.

In my opinion, the child care studies' definition of economic impact is inferior to my definition. However, the child care studies' definition is similar to the definitions of economic impact used by some state and local economic developers. As discussed in Chapter 2, some state and local economic developers often focus on overall local growth. Who is actually benefiting from that growth is not a focus.

On the second point, the early childhood programs I am considering are smaller than the overall child care industry. Smaller programs will have smaller impacts. For example, the most expensive program I consider, the Abecedarian program, is at full scale assumed to have the participation of 15 percent of U.S. children under the age of five. For the child care industry, about 35 percent of U.S. children under the age of five are in child care delivered by some "nonrelative" (Johnson 2005, Table 1).

On the third point, my estimates of economic development effects are compared to a different counterfactual world than these child care studies. Any impact statement implicitly compares two hypothetical worlds. I believe my comparisons are more relevant to real world policy alternatives. However, the child care studies might be more politically useful for dramatizing the importance of child care.

In my estimates, I am comparing a world with a particular early childhood program to a counterfactual world without the early childhood program. This includes the effects due to financing the program. Thus, I include all the multiplier effects of the spending on the early childhood program. But I also include all the multiplier effects of the increased taxes.[13]

In addition, in this book the parental labor supply effects are calculated based on the effects of free child care, compared to the labor supply in some counterfactual world where child care prices are unchanged. Also, the parental labor supply effects add in other effects of the program on parental labor supply due to mentoring effects or educational attainment effects. Again, these effects are measured by comparing what happens in a world with the program compared to a world without the program. These effects on parental labor supply will provide extra labor market experience, which will over time increase employment rates and earnings.

What is the counterfactual in these child care studies? This counterfactual is usually not explicitly stated. However, we can imagine some counterfactuals that would yield impact estimates similar to the numbers produced by these studies.

For example, consider spending impact estimates based on the size of the child care sector, plus its multiplier effects on suppliers and local retailers. These impact estimates would be relevant if all current child care was externally financed by someone outside the state or local economy, for example the federal government. The impact estimates answer the question, "What would a state's economy be like in a world in which all child care was financed by the federal government, compared to a world in which there is no government financing for child care?" Neither world is the world in which we live or are likely to live. Therefore, these gross comparisons of child care spending impacts, with multipliers, do not seem relevant to any real world policy change.

However, comparisons of worlds in which there is a little more or a little less federal government financing for child care may encompass worlds we might live in. They answer the policy-relevant question, "What are the economic benefits to a state of getting a little more federal financing of child care?"

Even so, these spending comparisons do not answer the question of how the world would differ if we expanded child care using increased state taxes. Therefore, the spending impact estimates of the child care sector do not tell us much about how a state or local government on its own can positively affect its economy through spending more on child care.[14]

On parental labor supply, some of the child care impact studies estimate the economic impact of eliminating all parental earnings associated with child care. Some studies only include eliminating one parent's earnings per household (under the implicit assumption that child care frees up only one parent to work). Other studies include earnings of both parents in households that use child care. Some studies then go on to calculate multiplier effects, as these lower parental earnings reduce demand for other local industries (e.g., M Cubed Consulting Group 2002).

Such parental labor supply impact estimates could be interpreted as a comparison of the world we live in to a world in which all nonparental child care is made illegal. If somehow this occurred, one parent might drop out of the labor force. The disappearance of this parent's earnings would then have multiplier effects on the local economy.

This comparison is perhaps useful as a thought experiment for dramatizing the crucial nature of the "child care industry." A sizable chunk of the economy does depend upon our permitting nonrelative care of children.

However, I do not think that this comparison is relevant to any policies that might be feasibly considered. Outlawing paid child care, let alone nonparental child care, has no political feasibility. Furthermore, even if such a law were somehow passed, it would be difficult to enforce.

Therefore, I would argue that my spending impact estimates and parental labor supply estimates are more relevant to real world policy. My estimates do correspond to the economic development benefits for a state of implementing at full scale some early childhood programs. These benefits for individuals who live in and stay in the state can be compared with the costs of the state's paying for these programs.

The modest short-run benefits from early childhood programs may make these programs less politically attractive to policymakers interested in short-run returns. Chapter 7 will consider how to deal with this problem.

CONCLUSION

The best estimates suggest that high-quality early childhood programs can provide a state's residents with substantial economic development benefits. These economic development benefits are of similar magnitude to the benefits of high-quality business incentive programs. Early childhood programs have particularly strong benefits in the long run.

I now turn in the next chapter to exploring what designs work best for early childhood programs and business incentive programs. Subsequent chapters explore the implications of uncertainty about these estimated effects, as well as other issues related to these estimates.

Notes

1. The reports on which this book is based also included estimates for the Parent-Child Home Program, a home visitation program. However, these estimates were largely derived from one study. I have been persuaded by an anonymous reviewer of this book that this evidence base is too scanty to put much weight on the results for PCHP.
2. Present value is calculated using a real discount rate of 3 percent. Chapter 7 considers alternative discount rates.
3. In present value, expressed in 2007 dollars. As mentioned in a previous chapter, all dollar figures in this book, unless otherwise noted, are in 2007 dollars. Present value calculations use a 3 percent social discount rate.
4. Appendix 4B provides more detail. This detail includes a description of the statis-

tical significance of the various point estimates used. As mentioned previously, all appendices are available on-line from the Upjohn Institute.

5. I update their cost estimates to 2007 dollars, and I also allow for costs to increase by 1.2 percent per year from 2004 until the original start year of 2009. This 1.2 percent allows for real wage increases over time. These same start-year costs were retained when the start year was changed to 2011. I also modified their adjustment for offsets by assuming that all universal pre-K participants who previously participated in other public pre-K programs had the same average costs; Karoly and Bigelow implicitly assumed that some had zero costs.

6. Gault et al. (2008) suggest that lower costs are needed for a high-quality program. According to them, a similar three-hour-per-day school year program and a lead teacher paid public school wages costs $4,071 per year per child at a class size of 20-to-2, $4,506 per year per child at a class size of 17-to-2, and $4,893 per year per child at a class size of 15-to-2. These figures are current figures and might increase somewhat by the assumed start-up date of this universal pre-K program of 2011. In any event, it seems that the gross costs assumed in this book are easily more than enough to pay for a high-quality program. Even if program offsets from other programs are not as forthcoming as are assumed in this analysis, the net costs assumed in this book should be able to pay for a high-quality program.

7. These are the author's calculations using data from the Current Population Survey for March of 2004.

8. In this case, positive synergistic effects mean that the school-year services differentially increase the success of participants in the Abecedarian preschool program versus nonparticipants. This may take place if the Abecedarian services help children become better able to benefit from the school services. On the other hand, the school services may be differentially targeted at children who are behind, which may differentially help children who do not participate in Abecedarian preschool services. This would be a negative synergistic effect. Finally, it is possible that the school services equally help both participants and nonparticipants in Abecedarian preschool services.

9. Their calculations also assume about a 75 percent take-up rate for the program among families with eligible children.

10. This assumption is backed up by evidence that shocks to levels of local employment have very persistent effects. For evidence, see models estimated by Blanchard and Katz (1992) or Bartik (1991b). In other words, local employment can be thought of as following a random walk. One way to think about this is to note that the business that has been incentivized will eventually decline or leave. But in the meantime, the agglomeration economies associated with that business will have attracted other export-based jobs, beyond those predicted by multiplier effects on local suppliers and retailers. The negative effects of the gradual disappearance of the jobs in incentivized businesses are offset by the positive effects of the agglomeration economies that occur before those jobs disappear.

11. The details on these predictions are in Appendix 4B.

12. Appendix 2B provides the evidence to back up that claim.

13. Such effects are also implicitly included in the calculations for the business incen-

tive program. In Chapter 3, I am implicitly assuming no net demand effects, positive or negative, from the business incentive program. This requires that the business incentive program either be financed by increased average business tax rates, or that the business incentive program be composed of some mix of tax incentives with customized business services. Alternatives to these assumptions are considered in Chapter 5. In any event, the net demand effects of business incentive programs in the baseline of Chapter 3 are assumed to be zero. The balanced budget multiplier demand effects of more spending on early childhood programs are assumed to be positive.

14. This is true also of child care spending impact estimates that use Type I multipliers, which exclude household respending effects, rather than Type II multipliers, which include such respending effects. (Warner and Liu [2006] present some estimates that distinguish between these two impact estimation approaches.) There is no reason for the elimination of household respending effects to necessarily have the same effect as the negative impact of households financing the program through increased taxes.

5
Design Matters

What Features of Business Incentive Programs and Early Childhood Programs Affect Their Economic Development Benefits?

The preceding chapters have argued that business incentive programs and early childhood programs can provide large economic development benefits, *if* these programs are high-quality programs. But what constitutes quality in these programs? What program designs are most effective?

This chapter discusses in turn some key features of, first, business incentive programs and, second, early childhood programs that affect their economic development benefits. Program design's effects on economic development benefits turn out to be large.

BUSINESS INCENTIVES

Chapter 3 estimates that each dollar invested in business incentives increases the present value of the earnings of state residents by $3.14. In this book's terminology, that means that, per dollar of costs, the "economic development benefits" for state residents are $3.14. This return on business incentives depends upon particular assumptions about the features of a business incentive program. These economic development benefits might be altered up or down by changes in these features. The economic development benefits of business incentives are principally altered by three features: 1) how the incentives are financed, 2) which businesses the incentives target, and 3) how the incentives are designed.

Incentive Financing

> I conclude with a two pronged warning about why we can't keep giving money away in wasteful corporate subsidies. We have far more urgent needs to spend our money on to really create good jobs. Instead of steering so much money into private deals that are unaccountable and ineffective, we need to get back to basics and invest in public goods, especially our skilled labor base and our infrastructure.
>
> —Greg LeRoy (2005, p. 197)

> The fact that public spending can stimulate the economy more than tax cuts should come as no surprise. After all, when taxes are cut, part of the forgone tax revenue will not be spent locally—some of it will be saved, some will be spent out of state, and some will be taxed by other jurisdictions. But when taxes are raised in order to increase public services, the additional spending is typically done locally.
>
> —Robert Lynch (2004, p. 46)

In Chapter 3, I estimated the economic development benefits of business incentives, under certain assumptions. One assumption was that the incentives were financed without negative effects on demand for goods and services in the regional economy. I also assumed that the incentives were financed without negative effects on the quality of public services. Reduced quality of public services might negatively affect business location and expansion. As Greg LeRoy argues in the above quotation, local job creation depends upon the quality of an area's labor force and infrastructure.

Suppose instead that business incentives are financed by increases in household taxes. This will negatively affect local demand for goods and services because it reduces the after-tax income of local households. The incentives transfer resources from local households to the owners of firms. Because many of these owners live out of state, the increased income of owners will have little impact on local demand.

I estimate that household tax financing of business incentives will reduce the present value of the earnings increase for state residents, per dollar of resources devoted to business incentives, from $3.14 to $3.07. This estimate is based on simulations using a well-respected regional econometric model, the REMI model.[1]

Suppose instead that the business incentives are financed by cuts in public services. Suppose initially that the public services cuts are *not* valued by businesses, and hence play no role in altering business location decisions. But this public spending cut will still reduce demand for local goods and services. Based on the REMI model, this cut in public spending will reduce the state economic development benefits of business incentives, per dollar of resources devoted to business incentives, from $3.14 to $3.03.[2]

The negative demand effect of lowering public spending is greater in magnitude than the negative demand effect of increasing household taxes. Why is this so? The public spending cut has a direct effect on reducing the demand for local goods and services and reducing local jobs. The tax increase on households only has indirect effects on reducing demand for local goods and services. A portion of the reduction in after-tax household income will be reflected in lower spending on local goods and services. But some portion of the reduced after-tax income will lead to household adjustments that do not lower spending on local goods and services. For example, as Robert Lynch points out in the above quotation, households may reduce savings, or purchases from on-line retailers, or out-of-state travel and tourism. In addition, only a portion of the lower spending on local goods and services affects local jobs, as only a portion of the value of local goods and services is produced locally using local workers. Because public spending cuts have a 100 percent effect on local jobs in the first instance, and tax increases only have a partial effect, financing a business incentive program through public spending cuts has larger effects on reducing the net benefits of the business incentive program.

These negative demand effects of incentive financing are modest. Why are demand effects small relative to incentives' other effects? A permanent business incentive program creates new jobs each year. This annual job creation will tend to be of similar magnitude over time. As a result, the state's job level will continually change. But demand effects of incentive financing have mostly a once-and-for-all effect on reducing the level of jobs in the state economy.[3]

The modest negative demand effects of incentive financing are not generalizable to across-the-board business tax cuts. Across-the-board business tax cuts lose much more revenue in the short run than business incentives. Business incentives are cheaper to finance because they target business tax breaks (or customized business services) at businesses making new business investment decisions. According to a study I did with my colleagues George Erickcek, Wei-Jang Huang, and Brad Watts (2006), negative demand effects are much more important in analyzing across-the-board business tax cuts. In the case we examined, financing a general business tax cut through increased household taxes reduced the tax cut's effects by about one-fourth over a 10-year period. Financing a general business tax cut through cuts in public spending reduced the tax cut's effects by almost one-half over a 10-year period. These larger negative demand effects occur because of the larger revenue loss due to general business tax cuts.

Cuts in public services could have an additional negative effect on economic development if these public services are valued by business. For public services valued by business, a cut in the quality of these public services may negatively affect business location and expansion decisions.

Some studies suggest that cuts in business taxes, if financed by cuts in some public services, may actually have a net negative effect on a state's economic development. Helms (1985) estimates that a tax cut, if financed by cuts in any type of public spending except welfare spending, would negatively affect a state's personal income. Munnell (1990) estimates that tax cuts that cut public capital spending would negatively affect the growth of state private employment. And in Bartik (1989), I estimate that business tax cuts, if financed by cuts in local school spending or fire protection spending, would negatively affect a state's rate of small business starts. I also estimate that cuts in property taxes, if financed by cuts in spending on higher education or health care, would negatively affect a state's manufacturing output (Bartik 1999). Bania and Stone (2007) estimate that a cut in taxes, financed by cuts in what they call "productive services and infrastructure" (e.g., education, roads, and public safety), will reduce per capita income growth in all but the four highest-tax states.[4]

How can a business incentive program avoid negative effects on public services? One way to avoid hurting public services is to impose a budget constraint on the annual dollar volume of business incentives. The amount of resources to be devoted to business incentives can then be part of an overall plan that avoids some of these negative financing effects. Without a plan for financing business incentives within a budget constraint, it is easy for business incentive programs to expand over time and thus threaten the state and local tax base that supports public services.

One possible plan would impose an overall revenue goal for net business tax revenue, after accounting for business incentives. This plan would require that an increase in business incentives be financed by offsetting increases in business tax revenue. These offsetting increases in business taxes would be designed to avoid negative effects on business location decisions. For example, special tax breaks for non-export-based businesses may be eliminated without adverse consequences for overall business activity. As another example, increases in average corporate tax rates and investment tax credits may raise offsetting revenue while having a neutral effect on business location decisions.

For such plans to be workable, it must be possible to impose a meaningful budget constraint on the annual dollar volume of business incentives. This can be readily done for business incentives that are customized public services to business.

It is more difficult to impose an annual budget constraint on business incentives that are special tax breaks. It is politically difficult for policymakers to deny business tax incentives to any business that meets the eligibility criteria. Therefore, in practice, nominally "discretionary" business tax incentives become "entitlement" tax breaks, which will go to any business that meets the eligibility criteria. "Discretionary" business tax incentives end up being quite similar to tax breaks that are written into the law and are legal entitlements to eligible businesses.

If discretionary business tax incentives in practice are equivalent to entitlement tax breaks, is there any reason not to incorporate such "discretionary" incentives into the tax code? Incorporating discretionary incentives into the tax code avoids any illusion that such incentives will be withheld from eligible businesses. The legislative authorization of business tax breaks as part of the tax code may be more likely to raise issues of the appropriate balance of business taxes versus household taxes, or of lower taxes versus higher public spending.

However, business tax breaks to promote economic development will yield greater economic development benefits if targeted at particular categories of eligible businesses. As will be discussed below, we would want to target such business tax breaks at investment and employment expansion decisions by businesses that are "export-based" and pay a higher wage premium. This targeting can readily be done with discretionary business incentives. It can also be done as part of the business tax code. However, such targeting as part of the business tax code requires that the legislative process be willing to prioritize economic development benefits. Political pressures from other businesses for "fairness" may discourage such targeting.

Even if business tax incentives for economic development are incorporated into the tax code, business incentives that are public services cannot be made entitlements. For example, the customized job training program that meets the needs of one business will not meet the needs of some other business. Such services must be customized and to a large extent discretionary.

In accounting for business incentive costs, it is important to be moderate in estimating any possible revenue offsets to such incentives. Economic developers sometimes talk as if tax incentives have no costs. Their argument is that if the tax incentive is decisive in tipping the business location decision, then there is no forgone revenue from the incentive, as otherwise the business would not be there. But this ignores the estimate, discussed in Chapter 3, that incentives are decisive in only 4 percent of the cases in which they are awarded. Therefore, business incentives have net costs, because of the many cases in which they reward businesses that would have located in the local economy without the incentive. Plausible estimates indicate that typical business incentives are unlikely to have more than 20 percent of their net costs offset by fiscal benefits (Bartik 2005).[5]

Business tax incentives are one type of "tax expenditure." Tax expenditures are provisions in the laws that reduce revenue compared to some "normal" tax code. These tax expenditures are usually undertaken for some particular purpose; for example, business tax incentives are intended to promote economic development. For a business incentive program to be financed with minimum negative effects on public services, business incentives' costs must be budgeted for realistically and must be discussed in the context of the overall state and local budget. This requires that this type of tax expenditure, along with other tax expenditures, be regularly reviewed. If the costs are excessive relative to the benefits, business incentives and other tax expenditures should be curtailed.

States are increasingly taking account of tax expenditures. For example, 33 states now have some reasonably complete reports on tax expenditures (Corporation for Enterprise Development 2007). However, these tax expenditures are in many cases not subject to the same intensity of legislative and executive review as are spending programs.

Incentive Targeting

Business incentives will also be more effective if targeted at businesses that will yield greater economic development benefits for state residents. Three factors are particularly important in determining the economic development benefits from a particular business: 1) the wage premium of the growth generated, 2) the multiplier effect of the created jobs, and 3) whether the business is an export-based business.

As discussed in Chapter 2, different industries and businesses do not always pay the same wage for the same quality of labor. Some businesses choose to pay relatively high wages compared to the educational and other credentials of the workers hired. Paying higher wages reduces the time and money costs of hiring good workers, reduces worker turnover, and encourages high worker productivity. Other businesses choose to pay relatively low wages compared to worker credentials. This saves on wage costs, but may increase hiring and turnover costs and decrease productivity. These positive and negative wage premiums relative to worker credentials vary systematically across industries. Some industries pay higher wages than others for the same worker credentials. Within industries, different firms may follow different wage strategies (Groshen 1991).

The calculations of Chapter 3 assumed that, on average, the jobs attracted by business incentives pay no positive or negative wage premium relative to the local economy's regular wage standards. The jobs attracted by business incentives include the jobs directly induced by the business incentives. It also includes the job growth due to the multiplier effect. The estimate that a dollar of business incentives increases the present value of state earnings by $3.14 assumes that the growth will increase state employment rates and allow some state residents to move up to better paying jobs. But it does not assume further effects due to increasing or reducing state wage standards.

Estimates indicate that if local employment growth has a positive or negative wage premium relative to the area's wage standards, this will have some positive or negative effects on local earnings. Some of these positive or negative effects are direct effects of the newly created jobs paying more or less. But the wages paid by new jobs may have spillover effects on wage standards for existing jobs. In addition, higher or lower wages may encourage or discourage additional labor supply of local workers. The estimates suggest that for each extra dollar in wages due to new jobs paying higher wage premiums, total earnings in the local area go up about $2.84 (Bartik 1993b).[6]

Based on these estimates, the economic development benefits of business incentives vary greatly depending on the wage premiums in the newly created jobs. If the new jobs pay a 10 percent wage premium compared to prevailing wages in the state economy, the effect on the present value of state residents' earnings, per dollar invested in business incentives, increases from 3.14 to 4.03, an increase of almost one-third. Of course, this effect also goes in reverse. If the new jobs pay 10 percent less, controlling for worker credentials, compared to what jobs customarily pay in the state economy, then the economic development benefits per dollar spent decrease from 3.14 to 2.25.[7]

I emphasize that these calculations are based on the wage premiums for all the jobs created. This includes jobs created through the multiplier effect. If most of these jobs are in service industries rather than supplier industries, these jobs may tend to pay relatively low wages. Therefore, the average wage premium in the jobs *directly* attracted by the business incentives may not represent the average wage premium for all jobs created as a result of the business incentives.

Calculating the wage premium in all newly created jobs requires a regional econometric model or input-output model that can determine the likely industry composition of the newly created jobs. In addition, the wage practices of the firms that are attracted may differ from industry standards. These firm-specific wage premiums should also be taken into account.[8]

The economic development benefits from business incentives also will be affected by the magnitude of multiplier effects. The calculations of Chapter 3 assume a healthy multiplier of 1.8. Lower or higher multipliers, all other factors being equal, will proportionately raise or lower these economic development benefits. For example, if the multiplier effect is only 1.4, which would not be unusually low, then the present value of earnings effects, per dollar devoted to business incentives, would decline from 3.14 to 2.44.[9]

Multiplier effects will vary with the types of jobs created and the nature of the local economy. Multiplier effects depend in part on the likely density of local supplier links. If an attracted business uses more local suppliers, multiplier effects will be greater. Multiplier effects also depend on demand effects on local retailers. Demand effects on local retailers will tend to be greater if the direct jobs and supplier jobs pay more wages, either because of greater worker skills or because of greater wage premiums. Estimating the magnitude of these multiplier effects also requires a good regional econometric model or input-output model.

The economic development benefits from business incentives will be affected by whether the direct jobs attracted are export-based jobs. The calculations of Chapter 3 assumed that 100 percent of the businesses targeted by business incentives are export-based businesses. If some percentage of the targeted businesses are *not* export-based businesses, then even if any such businesses are induced to locate or expand by the incentives, their location or expansion will reduce jobs in competing businesses. For example, consider the provision of business incentives to restaurants. Even if a business incentive successfully induces a new restaurant to open or an existing restaurant to expand, these "induced" new restaurant jobs will reduce jobs in other local restaurants. There is no reason to think that business incentives will magically increase local demand for restaurants. Therefore, the increased sales at the restaurants associated with the business incentives will reduce sales at other local restaurants.

For this reason, the expected economic development benefits from business incentives should be reduced proportionately by the percentage of targeted businesses that are not export-based businesses. For example, if 50 percent of targeted businesses are not export-based businesses, the present value of expected earnings benefits, per dollar of resources devoted to business incentives, will be reduced from 3.14 to 1.57. Benefits are halved.[10]

Focusing on export-based businesses with reasonably large multipliers and reasonable wage premiums is conventional wisdom in the economic development profession. However, this focus is not always successfully practiced. Two major types of business incentives are subsidies for sports teams and subsidies for retail businesses. In most cases, such subsidies violate these principles for what types of businesses should be targeted by business incentive programs.

One significant type of business incentive is a subsidy for sports teams and sports stadiums. The average subsidy from a host city to a typical major league sports team now exceeds $10 million per year (Noll and Zimbalist 1997, p. 494). In the case of sports stadiums, only a portion of the revenue gained will generate new jobs for state residents, for several reasons. First, many of the fans attending the games are local residents who would have otherwise spent their money on some other in-state activity. Second, much of the revenue from professional sports goes to athletes, who largely spend their money outside the state. On the other hand, the sports stadiums may attract outside visitors who otherwise would not have visited, and who spend money in the state on activities other than the sports themselves. However, this additional spending does not make up for the displacement of other local spending and the flow of revenue to nonstate residents (Blair and Swindell 1997).

In addition, most sports-related visitor spending supports relatively low-wage employees working concessions or working in local hotels. The resulting multiplier effects are likely to be modest. In addition, the low wages will tend to lower local wage standards.

Another significant type of economic development subsidy is subsidizing retail businesses. For example, subsidies are frequently awarded to such "destination retailers" as the outdoors outfitter Cabela's. Such subsidies are more common in the 31 states in which local governments are to some extent financed by local sales taxes (Cline and Neubig 1999). Local governments in these states often engage in incentive wars to attract retailers, in order to raise their local sales tax base. For example, I know from personal conversations with economic developers and local news media that such incentive wars over retail businesses are common in Alabama and Arizona.

Even in the case of "big box" retailers or specialty retailers that offer some unique product or pricing, most of the new sales for such subsidized retailers will come from state residents who would otherwise have spent money at some other retailer in the state. Therefore, a sizable portion of the new jobs at the subsidized retailers are offset by displacement of jobs at other state retailers who lose sales. Furthermore, the new jobs at retailers frequently pay low wages. This reduces the size of the multiplier effect of any new retail jobs that are directly created from attracting out-of-state spending, as the new employees' increased expenditures on state consumer goods are necessarily modest. The low wages may also lower local wage standards.

Poor targeting can dramatically alter the effectiveness of business incentives. Consider the following targeting: Only 30 percent of the assisted business's activity is assumed to be export-based. In addition, I assume a lower multiplier of 1.5. Finally, I assume that the newly created jobs pay 10 percent less relative to worker credentials than is typical for that state's economy. All of these assumptions seem quite plausible for many sports stadium projects or big box retailers.

Under these assumptions, business incentives provided to retailers or sports teams will only generate $0.57 in present value earnings for state residents per dollar of costs. Under the baseline assumptions, business incentives provided to high-paying export-based firms generated $3.14 in present value earnings for state residents per dollar of costs. The 30 percent export-based assumption means that even if the new business activity is induced by the subsidy, only 30 percent of this new activity is truly net new activity to the state. As a result, the effectiveness of the subsidy is decreased by 70 percent. The lower multiplier of 1.5 versus 1.8 further decreases the effectiveness of the subsidy in creating jobs by another 17 percent. Finally, the 10 percent below normal wage premium further reduces the benefits by another 28 percent.[11]

Incentive Delivery Approaches

> In this era of heightened capital mobility, investments in skills and infrastructure are especially wise because, unlike a call center or a widget plant, they don't up and run away. If a business fails or moves, at least the taxpayers in the area retain the value of their past investments: the dislocated workers will take their skills to new jobs, and the infrastructure will still be there, helping other businesses.
>
> —Greg LeRoy (2005, p. 198)

The economic development benefits of business incentive programs will also depend on how the program's assistance is delivered. Three aspects of program delivery are particularly important: 1) the timing of assistance, 2) whether the program's assistance is cash or in-kind services, and 3) whether and how the program seeks to shape the hiring practices of assisted businesses.

To summarize the importance of the timing of incentives: business incentive programs may yield greater benefits if the assistance is provided up-front. However, up-front assistance must try to recover the public's investment from assisted businesses that do not fulfill their job creation commitments. The details of why up-front assistance makes sense and how to design such up-front assistance follow.

The estimated effectiveness of the business incentives in the baseline simulation in Chapter 3 relies on the assumption that the incentives are paid out over a 10-year period. This reflects customary practice. Business incentives are paid out over a number of years in part because this allows some costs to be postponed, which is politically preferable. In addition, this allows incentives to be credited against tax payments rather than paid out explicitly in cash. Finally, postponing some payments lessens potential problems caused by a business's receiving incentives but then leaving after a few years. If a business leaves, state and local economic developers would like if possible to "claw back" all or part of the incentive given to induce the location decision. This is often done through legal clawback agreements (Weber 2002, 2007). Most local governments report that they always require such clawback agreements (Bartik 2004a). However, such agreements can sometimes be difficult to enforce. But if part of the incentive has only been agreed to and not yet paid, then there is no problem in not paying the remaining part of the incentive if the business leaves town.

However, we know that businesses apply relatively high real discount rates to future flows of profits in making corporate decisions. Pressures from the stock market for short-run profits lead to an exaggerated focus on the short run. Studies suggest that the real discount rate used by corporate executives in making decisions averages about 12 percent per year (Poterba and Summers 1995). A 12 percent real discount rate implies, for example, that even without inflation, a dollar of profits 10 years from now is equivalent to only 32 cents today. In contrast, the suggested real discount rate for government investment decisions (the social discount rate) is 3 percent per year. (Chapter 7 will discuss the social discount rate issue in more detail.) At a 3 percent real discount rate, a dollar of inflation-adjusted profits 10 years from now is equivalent to 74 cents today. The discrepancy between corporate and social discount rates means that the government can affect corporate location decisions more, at the same present value from the public's perspective, by paying a higher proportion of business incentives up-front. For example, rather than providing one dollar of incentives 10 years from now, providing incentives between 32 cents and 74 cents immediately will affect corporate location decisions more, at lower present value costs to the taxpayer.

Paying more of the incentives up-front has a downside. Up-front incentives make more acute the issue of whether the incentives can be recovered if the business leaves the area. One way to make up-front incentives more recoverable is to pay more of them in the form of worker training, or infrastructure such as access road improvements and utility provision (e.g., this was suggested in Bartik [2005], as well as in the quotation given above from LeRoy [2005], p. 198). This assistance is valuable to firms but is largely recoverable if the business leaves. If the business leaves, the access roads and utility infrastructure will remain, and most of the trained workers will probably stay. This physical capital and human capital will help the area attract a replacement business. In addition, providing incentives through services spending also provides an immediate boost to the local economy. The stimulating effects on local labor demand of hiring workers to provide the training or build the infrastructure will exceed the depressing effects of the added taxes to pay for the training and infrastructure.

Resimulating the model with these up-front, in-kind incentives results in greater economic development benefits. Up-front economic development services increase the present value of state residents' earnings, per dollar of present value costs, by $4.47. This compares to $3.14 under the baseline assumptions. Of that $4.47, $4.36 occurs because these up-front incentives are more cost-effective in creating jobs. The other $0.11 is due to the economic stimulus of spending government money on job training and infrastructure.

Suppose that the timing of business incentives is held constant. Cash assistance such as tax incentives, and in-kind services such as customized job training, can both be delivered up-front. But the in-kind services may still be more productive than tax incentives if the services reduce business costs by more than $1 per dollar of government spending.

Many studies suggest that economic development services can be effective.[12] However, only two studies allow a comparison of their job-creating effects versus tax incentives.

My colleague Kevin Hollenbeck studied a customized job training program for incumbent workers in Massachusetts (Hollenbeck 2008). This program provided competitive grants to Massachusetts for incumbent worker training. The typical training grant had a government cost of about $1,300 per worker, with a matching contribution by the business. Training on average lasted 18 months. Two-thirds of assisted businesses were in manufacturing. One-third of assisted businesses had fewer than 50 employees, and seven-eighths had fewer than 500 employees.

Hollenbeck analyzed survey data that asked the businesses about the training's impact. Economists are wary of self-reported impacts. However, it is unclear why businesses would have a strong incentive to lie about these impacts. In many cases, businesses seemed quite willing to report that these training grants had no impact on job creation.

About 30 percent of the businesses reported that they hired new workers as a result of the training grants. Among the 30 percent of firms affected, an average of 12 workers were hired as a result of the training grant. About 20 percent of businesses reported that the training prevented layoffs. Among the 20 percent of firms affected, the average number of layoffs reported to have been prevented was 12.

To analyze job creation effects per training dollar, Hollenbeck counted only the reported new hires or prevented layoffs in export-based businesses. The created jobs were assumed to have a multiplier effect of 2 on jobs in Massachusetts. Based on these calculations, this customized job training grant program cost about $9,000 per job created. This is only 6 percent, or one-sixteenth, of the cost of creating jobs through tax incentives.

Taken at face value, these estimates imply that a dollar invested in the Massachusetts customized job training grant program would increase the present value of state residents' earnings by over $50. This estimate could be scaled back in various ways. We could only count jobs added, not averted job layoffs. We could assume a lower multiplier. We could assume that businesses may exaggerate the impact of the training grants. However, even with these adjustments, it still seems plausible that customized job training is more cost-effective in creating jobs than tax incentives.

Hoyt, Jepsen, and Troske (2008) compare the effects of customized training incentives versus tax incentives in Kentucky counties. This study relies on statistical analysis of the correlation of these incentives with county employment growth. They find that customized training incentives have roughly 10 times the job-creating impact of tax incentives. This is consistent with Hollenbeck's results.

Other economic development services also seem to be effective in altering business behavior:

- A random assignment experiment analyzed the effects of entre-preneurial training for unemployed workers who expressed an interest in starting their own businesses. Forty-nine percent of the group receiving entrepreneurial training successfully started their own businesses, compared to 28 percent of the control group (Benus, Wood, and Grover 1994).[13] It is not easy to know how to translate these results into labor market effects. However, this study suggests the potential for help to entrepreneurs to be cost-effective.

- Several studies of manufacturing extension services suggest these programs can increase business productivity (Jarmin 1999). For example, the Industrial Resource Center program in Pennsylvania is estimated to increase annual productivity growth in assisted firms by 3.6–5.0 percent, compared to growth in similar but un-assisted firms (Oldsman and Russell 1999). Other estimates suggest that these programs lower business costs by $3 per dollar of program costs (Michigan Manufacturing Technology Center 2008).[14]

Determining the jobs impact of manufacturing extension is complicated. On the one hand, helping firms to improve productivity may cost jobs, holding output constant. On the other hand, helping firms to be more competitive may expand output and jobs. A careful analysis is done in a study by Ehlen (2001). This study suggests that manu-facturing extension, compared to business tax incentives, is about nine times more cost-effective in creating jobs. This implies that per dollar invested, manufacturing extension produces state economic develop-ment benefits of over $28.[15]

The economic development benefits of business incentives can also be increased by increasing the proportion of new jobs that go to state residents rather than in-migrants.[16] In the baseline simulations, I assume, based on previous studies, that in the short run 6 out of 10 jobs go to state residents and the other 4 to in-migrants. Of the six jobs going to state residents, three go to the unemployed and three go to persons out of the labor force. The effects of job creation on state residents' unemployment are assumed to quickly fade. The effects on state labor force participation are assumed to slowly fade with out-migration and mortality of the original state residents. In addition, the greater the number of jobs that go to in-migrants, the fewer the possibilities for state residents to get promotions to better-paying occupations.

Increasing the proportion of jobs that go to state residents can have considerable effects on the jobs and earnings generated for state residents. Suppose we increased the proportion of new jobs going to state residents from 6 out of 10 to 8 out of 10. I assume that this is evenly divided between more jobs for the unemployed and more jobs for state residents who are out of the labor force. The pattern of fading of effects over time is assumed to be similar. But because the initial effect is that more state residents get job experience, these state residents will develop increased job skills, a stronger self-confidence, and an improved reputation with employers. As a result, these state residents' future employment and wage rates will be higher. In addition, I assume that effects on occupational upgrading are blown up proportionately with the effects on labor force participation. With fewer in-migrants being hired, more job vacancies will go to already-employed state residents as well as to nonemployed state residents. This provides more opportunities for occupational upgrading.

Under these alternative assumptions, the present value of real earnings generated for state residents, per $1 of business incentives, is $4.19. This is one-third higher than under the baseline assumptions.

The share of jobs that goes to in-migrants depends on the availability of state residents with suitable skills for the job opportunities created by economic development programs. The in-migrant share may also depend on the ease with which employers and local job seekers can get information about suitable job matches. Programs that provide carrots or sticks to encourage firms to hire local residents for the jobs created by economic development programs may be helpful. For example, some local areas, such as Berkeley, California, and Portland, Oregon, have used "First Source" programs to encourage more local hiring. Under First Source programs, businesses receiving incentives are required to consider local job seekers who are screened and referred through the local job training and placement system. Businesses are not required to hire those who are referred. The effectiveness of these programs in altering businesses' hiring practices depends upon whether the programs provide effective training and screening services. If these training and screening programs are effective, then businesses may get better quality hires at less cost by using these First Source programs.[17]

In addition, greater availability of suitably skilled state residents may increase the share of jobs that go to state residents. For example, any program that improves the employability and job skills of state residents may increase the proportion of the jobs created by economic development that will go to state residents. Among such programs are early childhood programs. Early childhood programs are therefore potentially complementary to business incentives. High-quality early childhood programs may increase the effectiveness of business incentives in providing state residents with higher earnings.

EARLY CHILDHOOD PROGRAMS

> Supporters of a stronger government role [in early childhood care and education] . . . argue that high-quality [early childhood] programs have bigger positive impacts and that the ingredients of a high-quality program can be specified with some precision . . . Opponents of a stronger government role . . . question whether high-quality programs can be identified with any degree of accuracy.
>
> —William Gormley (2007a, pp. 634–635)

> There are . . . a few "overarching principles" that these three interventions [the Perry Preschool program, the Chicago Child-Parent Center program, and the Abecedarian program] had in common . . . They began early . . . They had well-educated, well-trained and well-compensated teachers—with resulting low staff turnover . . . They maintained small class sizes and high teacher-child ratios . . .

> They were intensive programs . . . Intensity can be described in several ways, including the contact hours with the child in the program, work with parents and extension into the school-age years . . . They focused on children's learning—not just their achievement.
>
> —Ellen Galinsky (2006, pp. 19–20)

I have identified three early childhood programs that produce large economic development benefits: universal high-quality pre-K education (modeled after the Chicago Child-Parent Center program and the Perry Preschool program), the Abecedarian program, and the Nurse-Family Partnership program. But why were these programs successful? Can we identify program features that were crucial to these programs' success? Do we know enough to be able to replicate these programs' success on a larger scale? As pointed out by Gormley (2007a) in the above quotation, opponents of a stronger government role in early childhood care and education often argue that we don't really understand how to create high-quality early childhood programs. This section of the chapter will explore these issues.

Imitating Successful Programs

One strategy for making early childhood programs successful on a large scale is to imitate successful small-scale programs. This strategy might focus on imitating those features of these successful programs that could plausibly alter program effectiveness. As noted by Galinsky in the above quotation, the pre-K and child care programs with the most rigorous research evidence of success share some common features that might plausibly affect child participants. These pre-K and child care programs tend to have educated and trained staff and small class sizes. They also are intensive in the hours devoted to each child. Finally, these programs are administered locally rather than being subject to federal rules.

On the other hand, we don't know for sure whether these are the crucial program details. The devil is in the details. For example, if staff quality is important, how is that best ensured? Are education credentials the most important determinant of staff quality? Or does staff quality depend more on some combination of staff aptitude for work with young children, good training, and low turnover?

From the analysis in Chapter 4, we do know that intensity affects the total benefits of early childhood programs. A program that is small in both number of participants and program hours per participant may have high benefits per dollar spent. But it will be difficult for such a program to have large total benefits because of its limited size and scope. As discussed in Chapter 4, the Nurse-Family Partnership program has large economic development benefits for state residents per dollar spent, but not large total economic development benefits. This program is targeted at disadvantaged groups and also has a moderate level of services per participant. These factors limit total benefits. In contrast, universal pre-K education and the Abecedarian program are designed to be larger, more intense programs. As shown in Chapter 4, the potential total benefits of implementing such programs on a larger scale are therefore larger.

The Head Start Issue: Avoiding the Limitations of Programs with More Modest Effects

Another strategy for making early childhood programs higher quality is to avoid imitating early childhood programs that seem to be less successful. We might focus on avoiding features of these less successful programs that intuitively seem plausible reasons for these programs' being less successful.

Any discussion today of quality in early childhood programs has to address recent research findings on Head Start. The Head Start program was started in 1965 and currently serves almost 1 million children. The program provides a mix of early education and other services (e.g., health services) to three- and four-year-olds. The impact of Head Start has long been controversial. (For some recent reviews of the debate from different perspectives, see Barnett [2007], Besharov and Higney [2007], and Currie [2007].)

But the most recent entry into the Head Start debate is the January 2010 final report of the Head Start Impact Study (Puma et al. 2010). This study is particularly noteworthy because the study was rigorous: it evaluated Head Start using random assignment. Applicants to Head Start at age three, and at age four, were randomly assigned to either a treatment group that was allowed to enroll in a local Head Start center or a control group that was not allowed to enroll at that center.

The findings of the final report were disappointing to Head Start advocates. Interim reports had shown some positive effects on children's cognitive outcomes as of the end of Head Start. But the final report indicated that almost all these cognitive effects faded out by the end of kindergarten and first grade. By "faded out," what is meant is that although former Head Start participants continued to make progress in learning, the control group of children caught up.

A variety of arguments can be made about these findings. (Barnett [2008] provides a useful discussion.) There certainly is some possibility of effects of Head Start on unobserved noncognitive skills that may increase future success of Head Start participants. The Head Start Impact Study is comparing Head Start not with parental care but with a wide variety of other pre-K programs and child care programs. The control group actually spent more hours per week in nonparental care than was true for the Head Start treatment group. If some of these pre-K programs and child care programs used by the control group are of high quality, then this reduces Head Start's relative impact. But this need not imply that quality pre-K programs are unimportant.

Head Start may be a program that needs to improve to catch up with recent improvements in other pre-K and child care programs. Some rigorous studies suggest that Head Start has positively affected participants in the long run (Currie and Thomas 1999; Garces, Thomas, and Currie 2002; Ludwig and Miller 2007).[18] These long-range positive results can be reconciled with the recent Head Start Impact Study in two ways. First, it could be that these long-range results reflect noncognitive benefits of Head Start that were not measured in the Head Start Impact Study.[19] Second, these long-range studies inevitably are studying the effects of Head Start on participants from many years ago. It is possible that Head Start was much better than alternative child care and pre-K programs many years ago, but that these alternatives have improved in quality in recent years.

However, another reaction to these recent research findings is that high-quality early childhood programs should avoid imitating some of the features of Head Start. For example, traditionally Head Start has not required that its teachers have high academic credentials. Furthermore, perhaps Head Start's attempt to deliver multiple services in addition to early education distracts program staff from sufficiently focusing on educational goals for the child participants.[20] Finally, Head Start is a federal program, which arguably restricts its flexibility to respond to local needs. (Some of these possible issues with Head Start are being addressed by recent Head Start reforms. For example, legislation passed in 2007 requires that 50 percent of all Head Start lead teachers must have a bachelor's degree by 2013. In addition, the federal government is implementing a variety of accountability standards for local Head Start centers [see Administration for Children and Families 2010].)

However, again the point can be raised that we don't know which features of Head Start may be impeding its success. For example, will requiring that more Head Start teachers have bachelor's degrees provide benefits sufficient to justify this requirement's costs?

It should also be noted that some Head Start programs are considerably more effective than the average Head Start program. For example, the Tulsa, Oklahoma, Head Start program seems to produce greater cognitive gains at kindergarten entry than is true in the Head Start Impact Study (Gormley et al. 2009). (The cognitive gains are not, however, as large as those for Oklahoma's pre-K program.) More research is needed on how the features of Head Start programs alter their effectiveness in improving children's life chances. Gormley et al. (2009) suggest that Tulsa's Head Start program differs from other Head Start programs in spending more time on instructional activities. This raises a broader issue, to which we now turn: what can we tell from research on all pre-K programs about which program features promote program effectiveness?

Disentangling the Effects of Different Features of Early Childhood Programs

It would be useful to find good research that identifies how different factors alter the effectiveness of early childhood programs. I focus attention on pre-K and child care programs because there is more research evidence for such programs than there is for the Nurse-Family Partnership. I also bring in evidence from the research literature on what determines school quality. It seems plausible that program attributes that affect school quality for kindergartners and first-graders might also be relevant for pre-K education programs.

The economic development benefits of early childhood programs may be affected by six features of these programs:

1) The structural features of these programs, such as class size and staff qualifications;

2) The process quality of these programs, such as what goes on in the interactions between the child and program staff;

3) The time intensity of these programs—for example, the number of hours per day, the number of days per year, and the number of years of program services per child participant;

4) Whom the program serves—for example, whether the program is targeted at children from disadvantaged families or has a wider clientele;

5) Whether the program is delivered by the public sector or the private sector; and

6) Whether the program's design and administration are dominated by federal control or involve more state or local flexibility.

It could be argued that ultimately all of these six features only affect program effectiveness by affecting process quality. The interaction between the child and program staff is the ultimate factor that determines program outcomes. Other program features such as class size, staff qualifications, the amount and structure of program time, whom the program serves, and who administers the program, may be important because they affect how staff interacts with children.

However, in practice, those shaping policy interventions can choose to work separately on these six features. There is a difference between policy interventions that directly seek to target process quality and policy interventions that indirectly seek to improve process quality by targeting other program features, such as class size and teacher qualifications.

In the following analysis, I try to quantify the effects of changing some of these features of early childhood programs. Specifically, I estimate the economic development benefit within the state. This benefit is the increase in the present value of state residents' earnings. This estimate can be compared with estimates of the present value of the costs of the quality change.

In doing this analysis, I rely on estimates of the effects of features of early childhood programs on early elementary test scores. These effects on early childhood test scores can then be used to predict later earnings. This prediction relies on studies that link childhood test scores with later earnings.[21]

This methodology for estimating the benefits from design improvements in early childhood programs is conservative. It is conservative because the resulting estimates are likely to provide a lower bound, compared to the true benefits from design improvements. The estimated effects of pre-K programs on adult earnings significantly exceed what one would expect based on eventual educational attainment, or on earlier test scores. This greater effect may be explained by effects of early childhood programs on noncognitive skills that are less significantly correlated with higher test scores and educational attainment. This greater effect may also be due to early childhood programs' impacts on reducing former participants' prison or jail time and criminal records. These effects on noncognitive skills or crime are unlikely to be fully captured by relying on effects on test scores.

As will become clear in the below discussion, in discussing the effects of program features on the effectiveness of early childhood programs, I am walking into a minefield. These are controversial issues. In part, the problem is that there is little rigorous experimental evidence on how variation in program features affects outcomes. The evidence used in the below discussion is usually from natural variation in program features. Researchers try to control for the influence of different program features, but many program features may be unobserved. This creates some uncertainty about all of the below results. I try to reflect this uncertainty in considering different scenarios for how different program features affect program quality. Chapter 6 will discuss implications of uncertainty for program design.

Structural Quality

Class size

Lower class size in a pre-K program or child care center probably significantly improves program effects. The overall research literature is mixed.[22] However, the best studies do seem to find significant effects from lower class size.[23]

The Tennessee Class Size Study uses experimental methods to show that lower class size in kindergarten through third grade significantly improves test scores in the short run and long run (Krueger 2003; Schanzenbach 2007). This strongly suggests that lower class size should make a difference in pre-K.

The National Day Care Study combined experimental and non-experimental methods to look at what variables affected child care quality for three- and four-year-olds (Travers and Goodson 1980). Average group size proved to be one of the most significant variables affecting test score gains by a center's children. These results for average group size are from nonexperimental analyses of the study's data.

The implied "effect sizes" in the National Day Care Study are perhaps twice as large as those in the Tennessee Class Size Study. The Tennessee Class Size Study implies that lowering kindergarten class sizes from 22 to 15 students will raise test scores by about 0.2 "standard deviation units"—that is, by about one-fifth of the standard deviation of test scores across students in the sample (Krueger 2003; Schanzenbach 2007). The National Day Care Study implies that a similar decrease in class size will raise test scores among students ages three and four by about 0.4 standard deviation units.[24] This is consistent with the notion that group size may be more important for younger children. On the other hand, the Tennessee Class Size Study's estimates of the effects of class size are based on random assignment experimentation, whereas the National Day Care Study's results for class size are based on analysis of natural variation in class size. Therefore, it could be argued that the Tennessee Class Size Study's results will be more reliable.

Based on such studies, we can roughly quantify the effects of lowering pre-K class size. The baseline estimates in Chapter 4 assumed a pre-K group size of 20 students per class, which is slightly above the class size of the Chicago Child-Parent Center program. Perry Preschool averaged a class size of 12 or 13 students. I consider the possible effects of reducing pre-K class size from 20 students to 15 students, which will move us close to the Perry Preschool model. This is a class size reduction for which we have good estimates of the increase in per-student costs (Gault et al. 2008).

Suppose I take the conservative approach of relying on the class-size effects from the Tennessee Class Size Study. This is a conservative approach because there is some reason to think that these rigorous Tennessee results for kindergarten will understate the effects of lower class size for pre-K. To calculate the change in economic development benefits from lower pre-K class size, I must estimate how the lower class size will affect adult earnings. I do so by relying on prior research on how early test scores affect adult earnings (Currie and Thomas 1999; Krueger 2003).

Based on these calculations, lower pre-K class size has state economic development benefits that significantly exceed costs. As discussed in Chapter 4, at the baseline class size of 20, the ratio of state economic development benefits to costs for universal pre-K was 2.78. That is, the present value of the increase in state residents' earnings was 2.78 times the program's costs. Lowering class size to 15 is estimated to increase state economic development benefits by 83 percent of the original costs per participant. That is, the present value of the earnings effects for state residents goes up from the original value of 2.78 times the original program costs; it rises to 3.61 times the original program costs. As a percentage of the original program costs, this is an increase of 83 percent (= [3.61 − 2.78] ÷ 1.00). As a percentage of the original earnings effects, it is an increase of 30 percent (= 0.83 ÷ 2.78). Program costs are estimated to increase by 28 percent of the original costs per child participant. Therefore, there are net benefits per child participant equal to 55 percent of the original program costs (55 percent = 83 percent − 28 percent).[25]

These estimates use only the increase in test scores from lower class size to infer the long-run economic development effects of lowering class size. Yet we know that the economic development effects of pre-K go well beyond the effects that would be predicted based on pre-K's effects on educational attainment. Apparently, pre-K education has some effects on "noncognitive" skills that are important in explaining earnings, but are not as important in determining educational attainment or test scores. Therefore, these estimates may be a lower bound to the true economic development benefits of lowering class size.

Both the Tennessee Class Size Study and the National Day Care Study suggest that class size is the key driver of quality, not the ratio of students to adults. Obviously lower class size will tend to be associated with a lower ratio of students to adults. But once we control for class size, lowering the student-to-adult ratio (by, for example, adding a classroom aide) does not seem to increase student progress in kindergarten classrooms or in child care centers for three- and four-year-olds (Schanzenbach 2007; Travers and Goodson 1980).

What explains these results for class size? According to observational evidence in the National Day Care Study,

> when the total number of children in the classroom was small, lead teachers tended to spend time in various forms of social interactions with small clusters of children; when the total number of children was large, lead teachers tended to spend time in passive observation for the group as a whole. Children in small groups showed more creative, verbal/intellectual, and cooperative behavior than their peers in larger groups. They were less likely to be non-participants in classroom activities, and they had higher gains on standardized tests from fall to spring. (Travers and Goodson 1980, p. 239)

Adding an aide does not help that much, if at all, because

> high [staff/child] ratios often imply a kind of dilution of adult responsibility, as well as requiring that the lead teacher divert some of her energies to managing other adults . . . The number of children present with one or more caregivers, measured by a total head count, effectively determines the size of the "subgroups" toward which lead caregivers typically direct their attention. As the number of children assigned to a classroom increases, the size of these subgroups increases, regardless of the prevailing staff/child ratio. That is, classes are rarely divided into smaller groups of roughly equal size, even when enough adults are present to permit such division. Rather, lead caregivers appear to supervise most or all of the children in the class at once, although aides may occasionally take one or a few children aside for special activities. (Travers and Goodson 1980, pp. 241, 235–236)

Therefore, class size matters because it affects the process of what goes on in the classroom. Process can also be affected more directly, as I will discuss below.

Staff educational credentials

Research on early childhood programs has reached mixed results for the effects on children of increases in the *general* educational credentials of staff. Some studies of pre-K or child care find no significant positive effects of the lead teacher's having a BA degree (Currie and Neidell 2007; Early et al. 2007; Mashburn et al. 2008; Travers and Goodson 1980). Other studies of pre-K and child care find positive effects on children of teacher educational credentials (Barnett 2004; Bueno, Darling-Hammond, and Gonzales 2010; Gormley 2007a; Kelley and Camilli 2007). The lack of easy-to-detect effects of general educational credentials is analogous to research on K–12 student achievement and teacher credentials. A master's degree for a K–12 teacher is not associated with greater achievement gains for his or her students.

The effects of teachers' educational credentials on early childhood program quality may depend greatly on context. For example, requiring a BA degree might help improve early childhood program quality if there is sufficient funding that highly qualified teachers can be recruited and retained, but not otherwise. If there is insufficient funding to pay salaries competitive with K–12 teachers' salaries, requiring a BA degree for pre-K teachers might lower quality by restricting the hiring pool or increasing turnover. On the other hand, if a BA credential requirement is accompanied by commensurately higher salaries, this may reduce teacher turnover. Lower teacher turnover should increase program effectiveness; we know from research on K–12 education that first-year teachers tend to be less effective (Gordon, Kane, and Staiger 2006). The effect on program quality of a BA credential versus an AA (associate's degree) credential may depend upon the relative quality of these colleges, which varies across states. The value of different educational credentials may also depend upon the specific majors of the individuals with those credentials: a BA or an AA degree with a major in early childhood education may matter more than a BA or an AA degree without those specialized classes.

Specialized staff training and education in early childhood development often has positive effects on child outcomes. For example, the National Day Care Study found that "lead caregivers with specialized education or training played a more active role with children than those without such preparation, and children under their supervision made relatively rapid gains on standardized tests" (Travers and Goodson 1980, pp. 241–242). Some of David Blau's research also is consistent with this conclusion that specific staff training matters (Blau 1997, 2000).[26]

Given the uncertainty in the effects of requiring different educational credentials for early childhood teachers, I consider instead a hypothetical question: how big would these effects have to be for increased educational credentials to have state economic development benefits that exceed costs? I consider variations in the credentials of lead teachers in pre-K programs. Chapter 4's baseline calculations assumed that the lead pre-K teacher had a BA degree and was paid wages competitive with public schools. Suppose the credential requirement was lowered, so that the lead pre-K teacher only was required to have a child development associate (CDA) credential. This credential "requires a high school diploma (or GED), at least 120 hours of formal education across eight areas of early childhood education/child development/ professional practice, and at least 480 hours of direct experience working with preschool children" (Gault et al. 2008, p. 4, footnote g). Based on research by Gault et al., lowering the lead teacher credential from a BA to a CDA might at most save 29 percent of costs.[27]

Based on research on the relationship between early elementary test scores and adult earnings, requiring a higher credential for lead pre-K teachers would pass a benefit-cost test even if such a credential requirement only increases student test scores slightly. Average test scores need only increase by an "effect size" of 0.045 for a BA requirement (rather than a CDA) to have benefits exceeding the extra salary costs.[28] This required effect is quite small: the effect size is probably equivalent to increasing what the average student learns during the pre-K year by about 5 percent.[29] In other words, requiring the lead teacher to have a BA rather than a CDA will pay off if average learning rates increase by more than 5 percent. The required effect size is so small because of the large state economic development benefits of increasing student achievement. Even a tiny increase in former participants' earnings, added over many years, adds up to a considerable sum.[30]

Composition of student body in pre-K education: economic integration versus economic segregation

One structural quality issue that has not been adequately explored by research is whether overall child benefits from pre-K education would be improved by greater integration of students from different economic backgrounds in pre-K classes. This topic is highly relevant to the debate over universal pre-K education versus programs that target the disadvantaged, such as Head Start.

There is some evidence that pre-K peer effects are important. Henry and Rickman (2007) found statistically significant and substantively large peer effects in Georgia pre-K classrooms. Their results suggest that the abilities of a child's peers in his or her classroom, as measured at the beginning of the pre-K school year, had large effects on the test score gains of pre-K students. A one standard deviation increase in peers' measured prior abilities was associated with effects of more than three-tenths of a standard deviation on several post pre-K tests.[31]

This suggests that children from disadvantaged backgrounds will benefit from being placed in pre-K classrooms with children from more advantaged backgrounds who have higher test scores. But what about effects on the children from advantaged backgrounds? These children might have their pre-K gains lowered by being placed in classes with children whose prior abilities were lower. If peer effects are of similar magnitude for children from all income groups, then the overall benefits from "income mixing" of pre-K classrooms will be nil.

As far as I know, there is no good research evidence on how peer effects vary for children from different economic backgrounds.[32] If peer effects are greater for low-income children than for upper-income children, then economic integration will raise overall pre-K effectiveness. At the extreme, if peer effects are important for low-income children, but not important for upper-income students, we can validly claim that economic integration will help low-income children at little cost to upper-income children. On the other hand, if peer effects are important, but of similar magnitude for different income groups, then the policy choices are more difficult. Economic integration would then have little effect on overall pre-K effectiveness. However, economic integration would promote greater achievement among lower-income students at the expense of reduced achievement among upper-income students. Even if a policy wonk might favor such redistribution, it is unlikely to have much political popularity.

More research is clearly needed on peer effects and how they vary across income groups. As of right now, we don't know whether economic integration will raise the overall effectiveness of pre-K education, nor how it will redistribute the effectiveness of pre-K education across income groups. We need better information to give more reliable advice.

Process Quality

The overall message of this section is that there is little convincing evidence that structural child care inputs affect child outcomes, while there is more evidence that "process quality" has a positive effect on child development. These findings are rather similar to those in the school quality literature, in which many studies find that structural inputs such as class size, teacher education and experience, and teacher pay have little impact on student outcomes, while more intangible teacher characteristics (captured by teacher fixed effects) are strongly associated with student outcomes . . .

—Blau and Currie (2006, p. 1195)

Even the minority of researchers who are unconvinced that class size and teacher credentials affect child outcomes (such as Blau and Currie in the above quotation) agree that child outcomes are affected by "process quality."[33] "Process quality" is jargon for the quality of the interaction between the teacher and the child. It is intuitively plausible that the effectiveness per hour of early childhood programs mainly depends on the quality of the interaction between the teacher and the child. Structural features of the early childhood program, such as group size and the teacher's training, may be important because of their effects on the interaction between teacher and child.[34]

Two studies provide good measures of how the quality of teacher-student interactions affects children's learning gains in pre-K. The first study is the National Day Care Study (Travers and Goodson 1980). This study included a measure of the "social interaction" between the lead teacher and children in the centers. This measure is based on the proportion of time that the teacher engages in particular types of activities. Specifically, the measure is equal to the proportion of time that the teacher engages with children by questioning children, responding to children's questions, comforting children, and praising children, minus the proportion of time that the teacher is simply passively observing. (Other uses of teacher's time, which include giving commands to children, correcting children, and instructing children, as well as interacting with adults, are ignored. This implicitly treats these other activities as neutral activities.) The study measures across 53 centers how this "social interaction" variable affects student learning gains from the fall to the spring. These estimates control for the influence of average group size in the center. Smaller average group size is positively correlated with a higher level of this social interaction variable. Because group size is controlled for, there is some reason to believe that these empirical estimates reflect the influence of better "social interaction" between teachers and students, and do not just proxy for the benefits of smaller group size.

A more recent study looks at more than 2,400 children in 671 pre-K classrooms in 11 states with well-established programs (Mashburn et al. 2008). This study included a measure of the instructional quality of teacher-child interactions. Trained outside observers assessed whether teacher-child interactions encouraged children to further develop concepts and thinking skills, and whether teachers provided children with high-quality feedback. The empirical work examined how instructional quality predicted test score gains, controlling for child characteristics but not other program characteristics. Therefore, estimated effects of instructional quality could proxy for other program characteristics. The empirical work suggests that instructional quality is greater when group size is smaller.

The two studies yield similar results: pre-K classes in which teachers interact with children more frequently to develop concepts and thinking skills, and provide higher-quality feedback, have modestly greater test score gains. Such test score gains predict modestly greater economic development benefits. I consider the effects of an increase in instructional quality of one standard deviation of its variation across the 53 centers (the National Day Care Study) or 672 classrooms (the state pre-K study). (This is a large but not unusual change. If instructional quality were distributed normally across centers or classrooms, a one standard deviation improvement would move a center or classroom at the median level of instructional quality to the eighty-fourth percentile.) Such an increase would yield increases in test scores of 0.074 (NDCS) or 0.045 (state pre-K study) in "effect size" units—that is, as a proportion of the standard deviation in test scores across individual students.[35]

This increase in test scores would be expected to increase the state economic development benefits, in increased present value of state residents' earnings per dollar of costs, by an amount equal to 0.47 (NDCS) or 0.29 (state pre-K study). Therefore, these process improvements would pass a benefit-cost test unless they increased pre-K program costs by more than 47 percent or 29 percent. Obtaining such process quality improvements might require some improvements in management quality. But it seems unlikely that such improvements in management would inevitably necessitate increases in costs of 29 or 47 percent.

Better "process quality" in pre-K is positively associated with smaller class size (Mashburn et al. 2008; Travers and Goodson 1980). It is also positively associated with more staff training in early childhood development (Travers and Goodson 1980). Therefore, it is plausible that these structural changes achieve their effects through improving the "process" of what goes on in the classroom.

Can process quality also be improved through better pre-K curricula? The evidence is mixed but suggestive. In a recent randomized experimental test of 14 different pre-K curricula, 12 out of the 14 did not have consistently positive effects on student achievement compared to the "normal" curriculum used in the control classes. However, 2 out of the 14 curricula did have consistently significant positive effects on student learning in either reading or mathematics. In another recent randomized program study, two out of the three curricula that were studied had significant positive effects on student learning.[36] In addition, in most cases the control classrooms also used pre-K curricula that have their advocates. A random assignment study of the "Tools of the Mind" curriculum suggests that this curriculum, compared to a control curriculum, helped pre-K students to significantly improve their ability to stay self-disciplined and focused (Diamond et al. 2007).[37] Finally, in another study, which used rigorous but not experimental methods, the researchers found that "scientifically based" reading instruction in pre-K seems to have statistically significant effects on some literacy indicators but not all (Jackson et al. 2007). I conclude that there is potential for systematic experimentation with pre-K curricula to improve the effectiveness of pre-K education in improving student outcomes.

Time Intensity of Services

The baseline pre-K program in Chapter 4 assumed a half-day pre-K program, operating only during the school year, for four-year-olds only. What about the effects of a longer pre-K school day, or more pre-K days per year, or adding a three-year-old program to the four-year-old program?

The available research suggests that having children spend more hours in pre-K increases economic development benefits. However, it may not always increase economic development benefits by more than the increased costs. This is particularly true for spending more hours per day in pre-K education.

The only rigorous study of the effects of the pre-K day length is a study by Robin, Frede, and Barnett (2006). They look at an experiment in New Jersey that used a random assignment lottery to admit applicants to a special program that increased the pre-K day to eight hours. The pre-K day in control classrooms was two-and-a-half to three hours. (The experiment also increased the length of the pre-K year by four weeks, from 41 weeks to 45 weeks.) Increasing the length of the pre-K day does have cognitive benefits for test scores. These test score effects average 0.205 of a standard deviation. Based on these test score gains, I estimate that a pre-K program with a longer school day has a 56 percent greater effect on state residents' earnings. On an original cost basis, benefits per dollar increase by 155 percent of the original costs, from 2.78 times the original costs to 4.33 times the original costs (1.55 = 4.33 − 2.78; 56 percent = 1.55 ÷ 2.78).[38]

These estimates not only reflect benefits from greater cognitive attainment for former pre-K students when they grow up, they also reflect greater child care benefits from a longer pre-K day. In addition, because this expanded pre-K involves greater government spending, there are also balanced-budget multiplier benefits from a longer pre-K day.

However, costs also go up significantly. Using cost estimates from a study by Gault et al. (2008), I estimate that costs would almost quadruple, swelling to 3.62 times the original cost base. The new full-day pre-K program would have economic development benefits exceeding costs (4.33 is greater than 3.62). So the full-day pre-K program would be better than not having a program. But the increase in the present value of benefits, as a proportion of the original costs, of 1.55 (4.33 − 2.78) is less than the increase in the present value of costs of 2.62 (3.62 − 1.00). The added state economic development benefits are less than the added program costs. From a state economic development perspective, the move from a half day to a full day does not have a net payoff.

Of course, there may be other benefits of a longer pre-K day that are not captured by test-score gains and state economic development benefits. For example, perhaps there are noncognitive benefits of a longer pre-K day. However, they would have to be very large to justify the extra expense. Furthermore, a longer pre-K day might in some cases have harmful effects on behavior.

However, a full-day program may allow more families to have access to a high-quality pre-K program. A half-day pre-K program may not be accessible to some families unless they can find affordable child care for the rest of the parents' or guardians' workday. This may require that half-day programs be accompanied by some type of subsidized child care program. This would add to the costs of a half-day program.

In addition, perhaps the child care benefits of a longer pre-K day could be better exploited with some program add-ons. The pre-K program could be combined with programs that would target the adults in the pre-K participant's family for training and work. This issue will be considered further in Chapter 7.

For the Chicago Child-Parent Center program, Arthur Reynolds has done some analysis of the effects of adding a second year of pre-K education (Reynolds 1995). By adding a second year, we generally mean having the child enrolled in pre-K programs at age three and age four rather than just at age four. The second year improved test scores by about 0.253 of a standard deviation.[39] These higher test scores translate into predictions of higher earnings for former participants. In addition, a second year of pre-K adds child care benefits for parents. Adding a second year increases costs by a little more than double. (It costs more than double because there is a lower proportion of three-year-olds currently enrolled in public pre-K programs, and therefore less saved costs on existing programs.) Doubling costs also increases the balanced budget multiplier effects of pre-K. Summing up all the benefits, adding a second year of pre-K education increases the effects on state residents' earnings by 47 percent.[40] As a ratio to the original cost basis, benefits increase from their original value of 2.78 to 4.09, an increase of 1.31. This is slightly more than the increase in costs of 1.25 (from 1.00 to 2.25 with the second year added).[41]

The state economic development benefits of adding a second year of pre-K education are only slightly greater than the added costs. However, these calculations are only based on the cognitive test score gains caused by pre-K. If the second year of pre-K has even modest noncognitive benefits, then the second year's net benefits will increase significantly.

Why does adding more hours per day have lesser net benefits than adding more days? Perhaps there are limits to how much pre-K students can learn during a day. Adding learning time may be more productive when adding days rather than adding hours per day.

There are no rigorous studies of the effects of a longer pre-K year. However, it seems likely that adding days to the year may have similar effects to adding a second pre-K year.

Targeted versus Universal Programs

The effects estimated in Chapter 4 of high-quality universal pre-K programs assume that the benefits of universal pre-K are greater for children from low-income families than for children from upper-income families. The greater effectiveness of pre-K for lower-income families is plausible based on what we know about child development. There is significant evidence that middle- and upper-income families are more frequently successful in encouraging vocabulary development and higher-order thinking skills (Hart and Risley 2003). Therefore, pre-K education has a smaller deficit to fill for middle- and upper-income families. This suggests that pre-K's effects will be smaller for these families.

If this pattern of effects occurs, then there is a possible argument for targeting pre-K programs to children from lower-income families. The economic development benefits per dollar spent will be greater.

The issue of targeted versus universal pre-K programs will be more fully considered in Chapter 8. I note here the bottom-line conclusions of Chapter 8: Although targeting may increase benefits per dollar spent, universal pre-K programs have both economic and political advantages. It seems likely that pre-K's benefits for the middle class are extensive enough that broadening pre-K services beyond a lower-income target group has net economic development benefits. Furthermore, universal pre-K services seem more likely to develop stronger political support precisely because of those same middle-class benefits. These overall political and economic benefits of universal pre-K are more important than benefits per dollar spent. The purpose of public policy is to increase overall social benefits, not to maximize ratios of benefits to costs. Therefore, universal pre-K is probably preferable to targeted pre-

K, although changing political circumstances or research evidence may alter that conclusion.

Institutions Delivering Pre-K Education

What institutions deliver pre-K education does not seem crucial to quality—or at least, there is no strong evidence that institutions matter to quality. Oklahoma's near-universal pre-K system is mostly delivered through its public schools. Georgia's extensive pre-K system is largely delivered through payments to private pre-K providers. Both systems have significant evidence of success in improving educational outcomes.[42] Either public or private provision of pre-K education seems potentially compatible with high quality.

The Federal versus State/Local Role in Early Childhood Programs

Federal involvement in early childhood education may affect quality. The pros and cons of federal involvement will be considered further in later chapters, particularly Chapters 10 and 13.

CONCLUSION

As this chapter shows, program design makes a huge difference to the economic development benefits of both business incentive programs and early childhood programs. The devil is in the details of these programs' designs.

The estimates of economic development benefits in this chapter, and in Chapters 3 and 4, rely heavily on results from empirical research. There is always considerable uncertainty in social science research. Are the estimates valid? Can they be generalized to a larger-scale program? The next chapter considers how policymakers should respond to this uncertainty.

Notes

1. Specifically, this is based upon previous simulations that I have done with George Erickcek examining the short-run demand-side effects of spending cuts and tax increases on Michigan's budget (Bartik and Erickcek 2003). Based on this analysis, an increase of $x in taxes in Michigan will have an immediate demand-side impact of about 1.8 times the impact of reducing spending and taxes by $x. (Compare $554.4 million with $308.8 million in personal income impacts in the table in Bartik and Erickcek [2003] labeled "Economic Impact of $925 Million in Adjustments to the Michigan State Budget FY 2004.") We know from the analysis of pre-K that the balanced budget multiplier effects have a present value of $0.04 compared to the present value of costs. Therefore, for the same present value of costs, cutting public spending will have impacts of 1.8 times 0.04, or 0.07.

2. This calculation is based upon Bartik and Erickcek (2003). Cutting public spending by $x is estimated to have immediate demand-side effects that are about 2.8 times the effects of cutting both public spending and taxes by $x. (Compare $863.2 million and $308.8 million in the table in Bartik and Erickcek [2003] labeled "Economic Impact of $925 Million in Adjustments to the Michigan State Budget FY 2004.") The calculated present value of balanced budget multiplier earnings effects per dollar of program costs is 0.04. Multiplying 0.04 by 2.8 yields a demand-side impact of the public spending reduction of 0.11. Of course, as the text points out, the supply-side impact of cutting public services could be orders of magnitude higher, and indeed could wipe out the beneficial supply-side effects of business tax incentives.

3. This argument is the same as the rationale given in Chapter 4 for why balanced budget multiplier effects of early childhood programs are modest.

4. Bania, Gray, and Stone (2007) provide some additional theory and evidence for this model.

5. Even the most effective business tax incentives are unlikely to be free. Bartik and Erickcek (2010) consider the most recent data on Michigan's MEGA tax incentive program. Because of its focus on auto-related manufacturing in a state with strong supplier links and high wages, MEGA's most recent data shows an extremely high estimated multiplier effect in the long run, at 3.88. We estimate that MEGA may have two-thirds of its gross costs offset by fiscal benefits. But there still are net budgetary costs of MEGA.

6. This estimate weights the gains to whites versus gains to blacks that are reported in Bartik (1993b) at 84.4 percent versus 15.6 percent. This is based on my calculations, using CPS data, of non-Hispanic white and black percentages in the United States.

7. These calculations are based on taking the earnings generated under the original estimates and multiplying these by the percentage wage premium times 2.843. The assumption is that the wage premium effect on local residents depends upon those local residents whose employment rates or wage rates are directly altered by

the new job opportunities, with proper allowance made for the spillover effects of higher or lower wage premiums.

8. The notion that business incentive programs should take into account wages of assisted businesses is broadly consistent with the philosophy behind living wage campaigns (Pollin and Luce 2000). It also is broadly consistent with the philosophy behind the so-called high road approach to economic development that is associated with Joel Rogers and the Center on Wisconsin Strategy (e.g., Luria and Rogers 1999). However, the details of exactly how higher-wage businesses should be targeted pose some complex issues. Targeting businesses that pay high average wage premiums relative to the skills they require is not exactly the same as conditioning business incentive availability on the lowest wage paid by an assisted business. However, under some circumstances, it may be a useful simplifying political approach to the issue. I discuss some of the complexities in Bartik (2004b).

9. This revised number of 2.44 is based on multiplying 3.14 times the ratio of a 1.4 multiplier to a 1.8 multiplier.

10. For business tax incentives awarded to all eligible businesses (as opposed to incentives targeted at some eligible businesses), the analysis of economic development impact is more complicated. If tax incentives are awarded to all retail businesses, or all service businesses, it seems likely that the incentive will be to some extent shifted forward in the form of lower prices. Lower prices for retailers or service businesses for consumers will tend to increase real wages. This will attract in-migrants, which may lead to some downward pressure on nominal wages. This increased availability of labor may attract some increased business activity. It seems likely that the resulting job creation effect per dollar of incentive will be lower than the job creation effect per dollar for incentives to export-based businesses. But the job creation effect will not be zero. In the case of incentives to businesses providing services to other local businesses, these incentives may result in lower prices for local business inputs. This will also result in some job creation effects because of lower business input costs. Although these job creation effects are not zero, they are likely to be lower than for incentives to export-based businesses.

11. $0.57 = 3.14 \times 0.3 \times (1.5 / 1.8) \times 0.72$.

12. For example, there are a variety of studies of job training programs that are quite similar in structure to customized job training programs. These include studies of sectoral job training programs (Pindus et al. 2004), such as the Wisconsin Regional Training Partnership (Dresser and Rogers 1997).

13. The Corporation for Enterprise Development provides a wide variety of ideas for programs to promote regional economic development through entrepreneurship. See the organization's Web site at http://www.cfed.org.

14. Luria and Rogers (2008) provide a broader perspective of the possible role of manufacturing extension services in improving regional economic development.

15. Ehlen (2001) estimates a cost-per-job figure that is only 1/9.06 times as great as the cost-per-job figure for business tax incentives. Therefore, the earnings effects per dollar invested will be at least 9.06 times as great. Multiplying the 3.14 ratio for business tax incentives times 9.06 yields a figure of 28.45. In addition, the up-

front spending stimulus will provide a net positive effect of 0.11 of the cost of the program. Therefore, per dollar invested, the Ehlen study implies economic development benefits with a present value of $28.56. These calculations were originally developed in Bartik (2009d).

16. An extensive exploration of the issue of "who gets the jobs" is undertaken in Persky, Felsenstein, and Carlson (2004).

17. For more information on Portland's programs, see Bartik (2001), pp. 256–258, and for more information on Berkeley's programs, see Bartik (2004a), p. 363. For more information on both, see Molina (1998).

18. Although these studies don't use random assignment, they are rigorous in that the differences between Head Start participants and nonparticipants are arguably exogenous and result from a reasonable "natural" experiment. Currie and her colleagues' studies rely on comparing Head Start participants with their siblings who did not attend Head Start. This controls for many of the unobserved family characteristics that may affect children's later success. Ludwig and Miller's research relies on comparing counties whose poverty rates were high enough to trigger special assistance from the Office of Economic Opportunity in the mid-1960s in doing their Head Start applications, to counties that were slightly above the poverty rate threshold that triggered such OEO assistance.

19. For example, as shown in Gormley et al. (2009), Head Start may produce greater gains in child health than is true of programs that are more focused on cognitive gains. It is certainly possible that even if there are no long-run cognitive effects of Head Start, health gains from Head Start could contribute to greater long-run success in life.

20. Of course, it could also be true that some of Head Start's noncognitive goals could contribute to long-run life success.

21. I rely on Krueger's (2003) estimate that a one standard deviation increase in these early test scores increases long-run earnings by 16 percent. This estimate is based on a study by Currie and Thomas (1999), using British data. These estimated effects are then adjusted in my simulation model for out-migration and displacement effects. Krueger's estimated effects of early test scores on earnings are quite similar to a more recent study by Chetty et al. (2010). This more recent study finds that one standard deviation–higher test scores in kindergarten increase future earnings, as of age 27, by 14.8 percent.

22. However, Gormley (2007a) summarizes the literature by saying that "in general, researchers have concluded that lower child-to-staff ratios are better, especially for infants."

23. I should mention that Blau (1997) seems to find no effects from structural features of preschool and child care when he looks at the effects of variations in these features within centers. I owe this point to Gormley (2007a). My own take on this issue is that variations within centers will in many cases be endogenous in ways that may obscure effects. For example, more parents may ask for a better teacher, or a better teacher may be asked to take on more students by a center director. In addition, students with special needs may be put in smaller classes. Therefore I rely more on studies that look at effects that are either exogenous (Tennessee Class

Size Study, a pure random assignment experiment) or that appear to plausibly vary exogenously across centers (the National Day Care Study).

24. From Table 5.1 on p. 192 of Travers and Goodson (1980), I infer that the standard deviation of PSI scores among students within centers is 3.56. I use the coefficient in Table 5.2 on the logarithm of observed group size of −3.89 to infer that the effect of a reduction in group size from 22 students will increase test scores by 0.42 standard deviation units. I note that according to the study, most of these child care centers had group sizes of between 12 and 24 students (pp. 31–32), which is within the range considered here.

25. The calculations begin with the estimates of Chapter 12 that a 0.1 "effect size" increase in early elementary test scores for one student provides an increase in the present value of earnings in the state—i.e., state economic development benefits—of $8,312. This estimate is derived from studies of how early elementary test scores are associated with later earnings (Currie and Thomas 1999; Krueger 2003). I then calculate what this means for the effects of changes in test scores at the end of the pre-K program. Test score effects of a pre-K program would be expected to decay over time. Based on the meta-analysis by Camilli et al. (2010), the decay rate between the end of the pre-K program and early elementary school is assumed to be such that a program's effects on elementary test scores will be 38 percent of its test score effects at the end of the pre-K program. (This is based on their estimate of mean effect sizes of 0.50 at the end of the early childhood program versus 0.19 between ages 5 and 10.) Camilli et al.'s results seem consistent with evidence on the Tennessee Class Size Study from Schanzenbach (2007). As a result, a one standard deviation or one "effect size" increase in test scores at the end of the pre-K program is estimated to provide state economic development benefits of $31,586 (= $8,312 × 10 to get a one standard deviation change × 0.38 to convert from the end of the pre-K program to early elementary school). This estimated effect indicates that a one standard deviation improvement in test scores at the end of a pre-K program will provide state economic development benefits of 6.40 times the net cost per student of the pre-K program considered in Chapter 4, which had a net cost of $4,933 per student (6.40 = $31,586 ÷ $4,933). Based on Schanzenbach's analysis of the Tennessee Class Size Study, a reduction in class size in kindergarten from an average of 22.4 students per class to 15.1 students per class increases test scores at the end of kindergarten by an effect size of 0.187 (Schanzenbach 2007, Tables 2 and 4). This analysis is considering a reduction in pre-K class size from 20 to 15 students. This reduction of five students is slightly smaller than the Tennessee class size reduction of 7.3 students. I assume the effect size for a pre-K class size reduction of five students is 0.128 (= 0.187 × 5 ÷ 7.3). Based on this effect size at the end of the pre-K program, the resulting economic development benefits for former child participants' earnings will increase, as a proportion of the original net cost of the pre-K program, by 0.82 (= 0.128 × 6.40). I assume that child care and social spillover effects of pre-K programs do not vary with class size. Balanced budget multiplier effects will go up with higher costs and spending, which I turn to next. Gault et al. (2008) provide estimates that suggest that reducing class size from 20 to 15 students will increase per-student

costs by 20.2 percent. I assume this increase applies to the gross pre-K costs per student that were assumed in Chapter 4 of $6,823. Net costs are lower at $4,933 because of reduced costs of other programs. An increase in gross costs per student of 20.2 percent is equivalent to an increase in net costs of 27.9 percent (= 20.2% × $6,823 ÷ $4,933). This program cost increase of 27.9 percent also increases balanced budget multiplier effects by 27.9 percent, from their original ratio to the original program cost basis of 0.04 to a new value of 0.05, an increase of 1 percent of the original cost basis. Combining the effects on child participants' earnings with balanced budget multiplier effects, total state economic development benefits increase by 83 percent of the original program costs. This exceeds the increase in program costs of 28 percent of original program costs.

26. The importance of program staff credentials has also been studied for the Nurse-Family Partnership programs. Although these findings are important in designing parenting programs similar to NFP, the NFP findings are not necessarily generalizable to pre-K education or other early childhood programs. The Nurse-Family Partnership did a random assignment experiment that compared a control group with two treatments that differed in whether the "home visitor" was a nurse or a paraprofessional. The paraprofessional was required to have a high school degree but was specifically required to not have a bachelor's degree or any college education in "helping professions." However, preference was given to hiring paraprofessionals with some background in working in human services. Furthermore, referrals were sought for the best-quality paraprofessional home visitors from existing home visiting programs. All nurses and paraprofessionals in the experiment received one month of extensive training prior to providing services. From evaluation evidence gathered when the children were 21 months old, the nurse home visitors, compared to paraprofessionals, had twice as much effect in improving mother and child outcomes. However, by age four, the effects of nurse home visitors and paraprofessionals were more similar. The nurse home visitors had greater effects on child outcomes, whereas the paraprofessional home visitors had greater effects on the mothers (Olds et al. 2002; Olds, Robinson, et al. 2004).

27. Gault et al. (2008) estimate that lowering the requirement from a BA-I credential (BA paid public school wages) to a CDA credential saves 21.2 percent at a class size of 20 (Gault et al. 2008, Table 2). This reduction is applied to Chapter 4's gross costs per student of $6,823. As a percentage of net pre-K program costs, this reduction in costs is 29.3 percent (= 21.2% × $6,823 ÷ $4,933).

28. The cost savings is 0.29 on the original cost basis. A one standard deviation reduction in test scores at the end of pre-K reduces state economic development benefits by 6.40 times the original cost basis, from a previous endnote. This downgrading in educational credentials is a bad idea if it only reduces test scores at the end of pre-K by 0.045 of a standard deviation (0.045 = 0.29 ÷ 6.40).

29. For example, in the study by Lamy et al. (2005), typical learning during the preschool year on many tests is about equal to an effect size of 1.

30. Gault et al. (2008) calculate cost effects of various credentials for different types of pre-K programs. I consider their case of a BA-I credential (a BA degree paid at public school wages) versus an associate's degree and a CDA, for a school year

program of three hours per day and a class size of 20, which is the pre-K program modeled in this book (Gault et al. 2008, p. 10, Table 2). The percentage differentials calculated by Gault et al., as a percentage of the BA-I credential, are a reduction of 17 percent for going from a BA-I to an associate's degree and a reduction of 21 percent in going from a BA-I credential to a CDA credential. These percentage reductions are applied to the gross per-child cost of this book's modeled pre-K program of $6,823 (see Chapter 4), but are then recalculated as a percentage of this book's net per-student costs of $4,933 as 24 percent and 29 percent, respectively. The dollar savings per student of going from a BA to an AA are $1,190, and the dollar savings in going from a BA to a CDA are $1,436. In Chapter 12, I calculate that the present value of the future earnings effects of increasing one student's test scores in early elementary school by an effect size of 0.1 is $8,312. Therefore, upgrading the credential from an AA to a BA, which costs $1,190, will generate an increased present value of earnings equal to or greater than $1,190 if the increase in elementary test scores is greater than or equal to: $0.014 = 0.1 \times \$1,190 \div \$8,312$. Similar calculations can be done for moving from a CDA to an associate's degree, or from a CDA to a bachelor's degree.

31. Qualitatively similar results were found in a smaller study by Schechter and Bye (2007).

32. Henry and Rickman (2007) recognize this issue and identify it as a future research priority. They say that "future studies should include estimates of the effects of peer abilities on children with both high and low initial levels of skills. We were unable to obtain reliable estimates, because of the limited number of children within the classes on whom the peer skills were estimated. It is very important to have estimates of the effects on children at both ends of the skills continuum to inform policy deliberations related to mixing of students at . . . [a] time when publicly subsidized pre-Kindergartens and preschools are rapidly developing across the U.S." (p. 111).

33. As pointed out in endnote 23, Blau's finding that structural quality does not matter to child outcomes in child care centers is based on considering variation within centers (Blau 1997). As argued by Gormley (2007a), the variation within centers may be endogenous, which may make it difficult to find causal effects of structural quality. As for the K–12 research literature, also referred to by Blau and Currie (2006), there is a long-standing debate over the strength of the evidence on whether class size and other resources affect student test score gains. Krueger (2002, 2003) represents one side of the debate, arguing that lower class size does significantly improve student achievement. Hanushek (2002) represents the other side of the debate, arguing that there is no convincing evidence that lower class size or more resources per student affect student achievement, at least once resources per student are beyond some minimum threshold. As is obvious from the text, my own views agree with Krueger that the Tennessee Class Size Study, with its use of random assignment, tips the balance of the research evidence in favor of the proposition that more resources per student can improve student achievement.

34. Goffin (2010), in a recent research brief, argues that structural quality is important for how it affects process quality. Goffin, however, adds the point that providing

better structural quality, such as lower class size, in addition to improving process quality, such as the quality of teacher interactions with children, may also augment the effects of higher-quality teacher interactions with children. Thus, structural quality may have an effect independent of process quality. This may be true with respect to measured teacher-student interaction quality. However, it would be difficult to refute the proposition that lower class size may affect various aspects of unmeasured teacher-student interaction quality. Thus, even if structural quality features have effects independent of measured process quality, it may be that these occur through affecting unmeasured process quality.

35. This calculation was done as follows. First, I consider the calculation for the NDCS study. The process variable whose effects I examined from this study was its "social activity" variable. "Social activity" is defined as a linear combination of the proportion of time spent in various activities in Table 6.1, p. 224 (Travers and Goodson 1980). This linear combination is the sum of the time that the lead teacher spends directly questioning, responding to, comforting, and praising students, minus the time that the lead teacher spends observing students. The study's Table 3.3 (p. 79) and Table 3.4 (p. 82) provide standard deviations and correlations of the time the lead teacher spends in each of these activities. (Statistically insignificant correlations are omitted. I treat these as zero.) From these standard deviations and correlations, I generated an estimated variance of the social activity linear combination.

However, this variance is for the individual observation for a lead teacher. The actual measure used in the regressions is aggregated to the center level. The report mentions that the "generalizability" of this social activity measure is 0.2 (p. 226). This means that the proportion of the variance in the individual observations that can be explained by the center is 0.2 (p. 63). Therefore, I assume that the center mean of this social activity variable has a variance of 0.2 times the variance of the individual lead teacher–measured variable. The resulting calculation yields an estimated standard deviation in this social activity center mean variable of 0.06877.

The estimated effect of social activity on the Peabody Picture Vocabulary Test (PPVT) is 8.63 (p. 234). The estimated standard deviation in the PPVT test, based on unadjusted PPVT test scores, is 8.03 (derived from Table 5.1, p. 192). Therefore, a change of one standard deviation in the social activity variable is estimated to increase the PPVT test score by 0.074 standard deviation units.

For the state pre-K study (Mashburn et al. 2008), the process variable I focus on is the Classroom Assessment Scoring System "Instructional Support" (CLASS IS) variable. This CLASS IS measure is derived from a factor analysis. CLASS IS reflects whether teachers promote thinking skills and creativity and provide high-quality feedback to students.

I focus on the effects of the CLASS IS variable on the three tests for which standard deviations were reported. These three tests are the Peabody Picture Vocabulary Test (PPVT), the Oral Expression Scale from the Oral and Written Language Scale (OWLS), and the Woodcock-Johnson III Test of Achievement, in the area of applied problems. Each of these tests has a standard deviation of 15.

I focus on the average effects of the CLASS "Instructional Support" (IS) measure on these three tests. The average reported effect of a one-unit change in CLASS IS on these three tests is 0.807. But because the standard deviation of each of these tests is 15, the effect in "standard deviation units" is 0.054 = 0.807 ÷ 15. The reported standard deviation of the CLASS IS variable is 0.83 across the classrooms included in the study. Therefore, a one standard deviation increase in the CLASS IS variable will increase test scores by an effect size of 0.045 (= 0.83 × 0.054).

For comparison, the standard deviation of group size in the National Day Care Study was 5.6, which is a little bit greater than the five-student reduction in group size considered earlier.

36. In the 14-curricula study, by "consistently" statistically significant, I mean that the effects were significant both at the end of pre-K and at the end of kindergarten. The two curricula that had significant consistent effects were 1) DLM Early Childhood Express supplemented with Open Court Reading Pre-K and 2) Pre-K Mathematics supplemented with DLM Early Childhood Express math software (Preschool Curriculum Evaluation Research Consortium [PCERS] 2008). In the "Project Upgrade" study (Layzer et al. 2007), the two successful curricula are RSL and BTL. It is interesting that RSL did not have statistically significant effects in the PCERS study even though it was included. This may reflect differences in the quality of the curriculum used in the control classrooms. The Project Upgrade report suggests that the baseline standards for literacy in their sample pre-K classrooms were weak.

37. The Tools of the Mind curriculum appears to increase what is known in educational research jargon as "executive functions" or "cognitive control."

38. This calculation is done similarly to calculations reported in other endnotes in this chapter. A 0.205 effect size due to a longer pre-K day is estimated to increase adult earnings of former pre-K participants by a proportion that is 1.31 of the original costs (1.31 = 0.205 × 6.40 effect of a one standard deviation increase in pre-K test scores).

This is an increase in adult earnings effects of 49.5 percent of the original earnings effects of 2.65 for former child participants only, from Chapter 4. I assume that social spillover effects are blown up by a similar amount, going from 0.04 to 0.06 on an original cost basis, an increase of 0.02.

Child care hours increase by a factor of 3.24 (= 8 hours ÷ 3 hours per day × 45 weeks ÷ 37 weeks). Accordingly, I assume that child care benefits, which originally had a present value of 0.05 as a proportion of the original cost base, will expand by 0.11, becoming 0.16 of the original cost base.

I assume that the expanded-time pre-K program will cost 3.62 times as much as the original pre-K program. This is derived from figures from Gault et al. (2008). They calculate that a three-hour-per-day program will cost $4,071 per school year, and that a nine-hour-per-day program will cost $10,884 (Gault et al. 2008, p. 10). I extrapolate this to the relative cost of an eight-hour-per-day program by multiplying by eight-ninths, and to the relative cost of a 45-week program by multiplying by 45/37. The resulting cost increases are used to blow up the Chapter 4 baseline program's gross costs of $6,823, and then are reexpressed as a proportion of the Chapter 4 net costs per student of $4,933.

This expanded time increases the original cost basis to a new cost basis that is 3.62 times its original value. In addition, it expands balanced budget multiplier effects: they increase from 0.04 on an original cost basis to 0.15 on an original cost basis, an increase of 0.11.

The total effect is to increase benefits, on an original cost basis, to 4.33 (= 2.78 + 1.31 + 0.02 + 0.11 + 0.11). However, the cost basis has increased to 3.62. The new ratio of benefits to costs still exceeds 1 (4.33 ÷ 3.62 = 1.20), but the increased benefits of 1.55 (= 4.33 − 2.78) are less than the increased costs of 2.62 (= 3.62 − 1.00).

39. This simply averages Reynolds's results across the three test score measures for kindergarten, reported in his Table 3 on p. 15.

40. Readers may note that the percentage effect on earnings is smaller for the second year of pre-K than for the move from a half-day pre-K program to a full-day program, even though the effect on test scores is greater for adding a second year of pre-K. The reason, as detailed in other endnotes, is that the benefits and costs of adding an extra year of pre-K are scaled back based on some displacement of usage of other pre-K programs. For the move from a half-day to a full-day pre-K program, I do not adjust benefits or costs for any reduced usage of other pre-K programs.

41. The 0.253 effect size for the second year of pre-K suggests an earnings effect for former child participants of 1.62 on the original cost basis. However, this should be cut back somewhat to allow for the displacement of other public pre-K programs by universal pre-K, and to allow for possible lower benefits for middle- and upper-income children. According to Barnett et al. (2008), public pre-K enrollment of four-year-olds is 35 percent and of three-year-olds is 12 percent. The calculations in Chapter 4 scaled back pre-K benefits for four-year-olds by 77 percent because of other public enrollment and lower benefits for other groups. I assume this scale-back factor is proportional to enrollment in public pre-K, and thus I scale back gross three-year-old benefits by a factor of 26 percent (= 77% × 12% ÷ 35%). This reduces the earnings benefits for former child participants from the added year at three years of age to 1.19 on the original cost basis (= 1.62 × [1 − 0.26]). This is an increase of 45 percent compared to the original earnings benefits of former child participants (45% = 1.19 ÷ 2.65).

Social spillover benefits on labor productivity are also assumed to expand by 45 percent, from 0.04 to 0.06.

Child care benefits will double, from 0.05 to 0.10. Balanced-budget multiplier benefits will increase by the increase in costs, which I calculate next.

Gross costs increase by the assumed gross costs per pre-K participant of $6,823. But these gross costs will be reduced by some offset from saved costs on existing programs. The Chapter 4 calculations assume that net costs will be lowered from $6,823 to $4,933, a scaling back of 28 percent (28 % = [6,823 − 4,933] ÷ 6,823). I assume that this scaling back is reduced proportionately with the lower existing public enrollment of three-year-olds (12%) vs. four-year-olds (35%).

Therefore the scale-back factor from gross costs for three-year-olds is 10 percent (10% = 28% × 12% ÷ 35%). The increased costs on the original net cost basis will then be 1.25 (= [1 − 0.10] × $6,823 ÷ $4,933). Balanced-budget multiplier effects will then be 2.25 of their original value, increasing from 0.04 to 0.09, an increase of 0.05.

Total benefits on the original cost basis will be 4.09 (= 2.78 + 1.19 + 0.02 + 0.05 + 0.05). This is an increase of 1.31 on the original cost basis (1.31 = 4.09 − 2.78). Of course, the original cost basis increases from 1.00 to a new cost basis of 2.25. The state economic development benefits of 1.31 are slightly greater than the increase in costs of 1.25.

42. For Oklahoma, see the various papers by William Gormley, such as Gormley et al. (2005). For Georgia, see the review by Levin and Schwartz (2007).

6
Dealing with the Known Unknowns

How Policymakers Should Deal with
Dueling Estimates from Researchers

Thus far, this book's analysis of business incentives and early child-hood education has ignored that these benefits are uncertain. Business incentive programs are estimated to increase the present value of state residents' earnings per dollar spent by $3.14. Early childhood programs are estimated to increase the present value of state residents' earnings per dollar spent by $2–$3, with specific dollars-and-cents figures given for each program. But these figures are best estimates. These best esti-mates are surrounded by considerable uncertainty. How much might uncertainty affect benefits? What are the sources of this uncertainty? How should this uncertainty affect our decisions about adopting these programs? How should uncertainty affect program design? This chapter addresses these questions. I conclude that despite uncertainty, we can move forward with needed program expansions, while designing pro-grams to increase our understanding of what works.

SOURCES OF UNCERTAINTY

> I read the research literature to say that preschool programs can probably make a marked improvement in the lives of disadvan-taged children, but that we have only a partial idea of how they should be organized and managed, that is, brought to scale.

—Douglas Besharov (2007, p. 3)

> My conclusion based on [my experience with studies focused on state fiscal policy] is that we are uncertain about the effects of eco-nomic development policies, including broad state fiscal policy, on economic growth.

—Therese McGuire (1992, p. 458)

> We examine the results of some of the programs considered to be early education models—including Perry Preschool, Chicago Child-Parent Studies, Abecedarian, and Head Start—and find the research to be flawed and therefore of questionable value.
>
> —Darcy Olsen and Lisa Snell (2006)

> The upshot of all of this is that on the most basic question of all—whether incentives induce significant new investment or jobs—we simply do not know the answer. Since these programs probably cost state and local governments about $40–$50 billion a year, one would expect some clear and undisputed evidence of their success. This is not the case.
>
> —Peter Fisher and Alan Peters (2004, p. 32)

As with most social science research, the research findings on early childhood programs and business incentives are viewed as "uncertain," "disputed," or "questionable" by some observers. The above quotations give some examples of such views. There is indeed some uncertainty in the research on early childhood programs and business incentives. This uncertainty is sometimes used by critics to argue that the research is "flawed." For example, the above quotation by Olsen and Snell comes from a report by the libertarian Reason Foundation, in which they give many reasons why there might be uncertainty about the success of early childhood programs in different research studies. Although there is uncertainty in research results, its magnitude is sometimes exaggerated, and such uncertainty is inevitable in any social science research.

The uncertainty in estimated economic development benefits of early childhood and business incentives programs has multiple sources. These sources include the following:

- Small sample size in some studies
- Methodological differences across studies
- Problems in identifying causation
- Difficulty in observing long-term effects
- The use of local labor market models to infer labor market effects
- The complexity of defining "quality"
- Challenges in generalizing from studies and analyses to new and often broader programs

The small sample sizes of some studies of these programs makes their estimates more uncertain. This small sample size is particularly a problem for some (not all) studies of early childhood programs. Two of the best random assignment studies, of Perry Preschool and the Abecedarian program, have low sample sizes. The Perry Preschool program had 58 treatment-group children and 65 control-group children. The Abecedarian program had 57 treatment-group children and 54 control-group children. These small sample sizes make it surprising that these studies found any statistically significant effects. Statistically significant effects only occurred because some effects were large. The small sample sizes make these studies vulnerable to attack by critics. Critics such as Olsen and Snell can push hard on whether these studies "prove" that early childhood programs work. As another example, the Cato Institute has argued that many of Perry's effects "disappeared when the scientific standard [of statistical significance] was used" (Schaeffer 2008). (Although some of Perry's results are not statistically significant, many of its most important economic development effects are statistically significant. For example, effects on educational attainment and employment rates are usually statistically significant at least at the 90 percent level, and sometimes at the 95 percent level.)[1] Some econometricians argue that the Perry program's multiple tests of outcomes may have led to some overstatement of the statistical significance of program results (Anderson 2008).

A larger source of uncertainty is differences across studies. For example, the business incentive estimates in this book are derived from studies of how state and local business taxes affect business location or state and local economic growth. The estimates used here are average effects across studies. However, effects differ widely across various studies. In my 1991 book, I concluded that plausible estimates of how business taxes affect state and local economic development could be one-half to three times the figures used here (Bartik 1991a).[2]

Moreover, a plausible alternative methodology is to infer the effects of business incentives from the effects of overall business costs. Using business taxes to infer the effects of business tax incentives already assumes that "a dollar is a dollar": the effect on business location decisions of a dollar of business incentive is the same as that of a dollar's reduction in business taxes. But why infer the effects of business incentives from the effects of business taxes? Instead, we can infer the effects of business incentives from the effects of a more comprehensive measure of business costs. Estimates suggest that state and local economic development is less than half as responsive to overall business costs as to business tax costs. For some unknown reason, state and local economic development is much less sensitive to labor costs, which dominate total business costs, than to business tax costs. Which estimates are more accurate measures of how businesses will respond to business incentives? As pointed out in Bartik (1991a), there are arguments on both sides. I argue in Bartik (1991a) that it is more likely that the estimated labor cost effect is biased toward zero. However, the discrepancy raises doubts about the estimated business tax effect.

The estimated business responsiveness to incentives has a large effect on these programs' ratios of economic development benefits to program costs. For example, the well-known REMI regional econometric model estimates a sensitivity of local business activity to business costs that can be used to estimate the cost per job created of business incentives. This estimated cost per job created is 2.55 times the cost per job created of business incentives that is assumed in this book (Bartik et al. 2006). The baseline ratio of economic development benefits per dollar of business incentives is 3.14. Using the REMI estimates, this ratio would be reduced to 1.23 (= 3.14 ÷ 2.55). Other estimates could reduce this ratio below 1.[3]

For early childhood programs, there are also wide variations across studies. For example, results for home visitation programs vary widely. The Nurse-Family Partnership program gets consistently favorable reviews. Many other home visitation programs do not seem to have large positive effects. For example, according to Steve Barnett and Ellen Frede, codirectors of the National Institute for Early Education Research, "Home visitation programs for children under age three are popular, but most fall short of their goals for improving children's learning and development" (Barnett and Frede 2009, p. 5). According to re-searcher Deanna Gomby, "For every outcome, as many as half of the studies and programs [involving home visiting] demonstrate extremely small or no benefits at all" (Gomby 2005, p. 44). These disparate findings suggest that home visitation programs may need especially good designs or program contexts to be successful. High-quality pre-K education programs tend to have more consistent positive effects. (Even Head Start on average has short-term positive results, although more modest than many high-quality pre-K programs or exemplary Head Start centers.) This may reflect the greater number of contact hours with the child in high-quality pre-K programs than in home visitation programs.

Another source of uncertainty is that it sometimes is difficult to be sure that we have identified causal effects of the programs. For example, the Chicago Child-Parent Center program was not evaluated using random assignment. Instead, outcomes for former participants in CPC programs were compared with outcomes for students in similar neighborhoods without CPC programs. This procedure is reasonable. But it means there could have been other differences between the two groups of students than access to the CPC program. In contrast, the evaluations of many other early childhood programs are based on random assignment. This includes Perry Preschool, the Abecedarian program, and the Nurse-Family Partnership program. Random assignment implies that estimated effects should be unbiased estimates of causal effects of the program. Absent random assignment, estimates could be biased by other systematic differences between program participants and the control group.

In business incentive studies, state and local business tax rates may be endogenous, which biases estimates. Business tax rates are sometimes measured by dividing business tax revenue by some measure of economic output or income. Using such measures, business tax rates will be affected by state economic growth. Better measures of business tax rates would hold the economy constant. For example, rates could be measured by business taxes as a percentage of business profits or value added for a hypothetical firm whose characteristics are held constant. Even with this better measurement, business tax rates are obviously chosen by state and local government. State legislators and other political leaders may base these choices on the economy.

The endogeneity of business taxes may bias estimates. The estimated "effect" of state and local business taxes on the state economy may instead represent effects of the economy on taxes. Studies try to control for this endogeneity. For example, if lagged tax rates are used, the measured tax rate will not be directly affected by today's economic growth. But there are no perfect solutions. Lagged economic growth and today's economic growth may be positively correlated. The estimated correlation of lagged tax rates with today's economy may in part reflect the influence of the past economy.

Another source of uncertainty is that studies usually only observe the effects of programs in the short term. But the economic development benefits of these policies depend greatly on their long-term effects. Such long-term effects may be inferred but are usually not directly observed. For example, the estimated effects of business taxes are typically based on studies that look at new location decisions, or at business growth over some short-term time period. To get long-run effects of business taxes, we must make assumptions about how local economies behave. For example, I assume that business activity only adjusts gradually to some change in business tax rates (see Bartik 1991a, p. 237). I also assume that a local economy's output and employment follow a random walk. Under this hypothesis, an induced increase in business activity that is due to business incentives will permanently persist at the same level, rather than gradually depreciating or appreciating. (This issue was previously addressed in an endnote to Chapter 4.) The random walk behavior is consistent with data on how local economies behave (for example, in the well-known article by Blanchard and Katz [1992]).[4] However, this assumption is a plausible model, not a proven objective fact.

For early childhood programs, observed effects on former child participants never encompass their entire lifetime work history. How could they, unless the studies extended for 70 years? The Perry Preschool program has effects estimated through age 40. This gives a fairly good idea of total career effects. For the other early childhood programs I consider (Abecedarian, NFP), the estimated effects are largely inferred from effects observed at age 20 or earlier. I look at effects as of age 20 on educational attainment, employment rates, earnings, and criminal activity. Effects on these indicators can be used to project lifetime earnings effects. These estimates are plausible, but they are extrapolations.

A related problem is that even long-term impact studies may not tell us the impact of programs today. As Ludwig and Phillips (2007, p. 3) point out, "[There] is a generic challenge to understanding the long-term impacts of contemporaneous government programs—we can only estimate long-term impacts for people who participated in the program a long time ago." Programs implemented a long time ago were implemented in a different social context. There will always be some uncertainty as to whether the same program implemented today will have similar long-term impacts.

For example, the best long-term evidence for the impacts of early childhood programs is from the Perry Preschool program. This program has now followed former childhood participants up to age 40. But the Perry Preschool study is based on a program in which enrollment began in 1962. The United States was quite a different country in 1962 than it is today. One crucial difference is that back in 1962, there were relatively few pre-K programs available for low-income families. This is no longer true today. As a result, any new pre-K program may not have as much "value added" as the baseline programs that are already available.

Another source of uncertainty is that estimated economic development benefits rest on plausible but not totally proven models of how local labor markets respond to supply or demand shocks. Consider the estimated effects of early childhood programs on state residents' earnings. These effects reflect plausible estimates of how many former child participants in early childhood programs will stay in their home state. The estimated effects also use labor market models that suggest that labor supply shocks will have displacement effects of one-third.

Consider the estimated effects of business incentives. These effects assume a particular time path of how state employment growth will affect state population, unemployment rates, and labor force participation rates. As discussed in Chapters 2 and 3, these estimates are based on good empirical evidence. However, these estimates are contested by some prominent researchers, such as Blanchard and Katz (1992).

Another uncertainty is the complexity in defining quality in these programs. This is discussed in Chapter 5 and need not be detailed here. We do have a basis for informed opinions about what makes a good-quality business incentive program or early childhood program. But there is some inevitable remaining uncertainty about what program designs work best.

A challenging issue is whether the estimates derived from particular studies can be generalized to new programs. For example, most of the early childhood programs focused on in this book (Perry Preschool, Abecedarian, and NFP) included extensive involvement of researchers with program design. Furthermore, the Perry and Abecedarian programs are quite small-scale. Will these small, researcher-tended, hothouse programs do as well when transplanted to a different setting, expanded to a large scale, and overseen by a state or local government of average competence? According to psychologist Mark Lipsey, large-scale programs tend to have about half the effects of their small-scale, researcher-run counterparts (Lipsey 2009). It is reassuring that the Child-Parent Center program, which was run on a large scale by the Chicago Public Schools, does appear to have been successful.

This book's estimates also assume that estimated effects of overall business taxes can be generalized to business tax incentives. In addition, this book's discussion of business incentives that are services to business assumes some generalization from small-scale to large-scale programs. I assume that programs providing customized job training, manufacturing extension services, entrepreneurship training, or small-business development help, will be equally effective per dollar spent if they are scaled up.

THE BEST RESPONSE TO UNCERTAINTY

> We need . . . large-scale state demonstrations with careful evaluations. Then—and only then—will we be justified in having a true national movement and spending serious money—the $20 billion, $30 billion, $40 billion per year it will cost to make sure that all of our at-risk kids get a high-quality preschool program.
>
> —Ron Haskins, codirector, Brookings Institution Center on Children and Families (Haskins and Rolnick 2006, p. 7)[5]

> My message to policymakers is that the effects of state and local tax policy are so uncertain that concern over this issue should not be a driving force in general fiscal policy decisions.
>
> —Therese McGuire (1992, p. 458)

> The more fundamental question . . . is whether we should wait until we have developed the perfect program before we move to extend Head Start to all eligible children. Obviously the answer is "no." Research and expanded funding for Head Start can be compatible. We can make funds available for grantees that are willing and able to evaluate the effectiveness of various aspects of their programming while expanding enrollments.
>
> —Janet Currie (2007)

How should our decision-making about policy respond to these many sources of uncertainty? There are at least three types of responses. (However, a strategy might combine these three types.) The possible responses include the following:

1) Wait for better evidence. (Haskins and McGuire in the above quotations seem to take this perspective.)

2) Go ahead with large-scale program implementation, based on the best empirical estimates, of what we currently know to be the best-quality design of the program.

3) Go ahead on a large scale with the best design of these programs, but design the program structure so as to maximize our learning from the programs' experience. (Currie in the above quotation seems to take this perspective.)

Waiting has its attractions. We can imagine many fine social experiments that would enormously increase our knowledge about what works in business incentives and early childhood education. If such experiments were not too costly, in both money and time, then it clearly would be better to wait. If waiting could provide better proof of what strategy makes the most sense, at low costs, who could object?

But of course experiments are costly. The main cost is not the money cost. The most important cost is a time cost or opportunity cost. Waiting means that in the interim we forgo the economic development benefits of earlier, large-scale implementation of these programs. It is a cliché to say that children only grow up once. If they miss having a good pre-K experience now, our later learning about a possibly better program will not make up for what past cohorts of children have missed. A similar argument could be made for business incentives: If we wait for more studies, some jobs will not be created in this state today. Some state residents will not be employed who otherwise would be employed. This lack of employment experience has long-lasting effects on these state residents' wages, employability, and self-confidence.

An attractive option is to move ahead with large-scale implementation of our best current estimate of the optimal business incentive programs and early childhood programs. Suppose a policymaker is faced with many decisions about what public policies to implement. Suppose there is considerable uncertainty about each decision. With many uncertain decisions, the best course of action is to be guided by the expected net benefits of each decision. This course of action maximizes the total net benefits from all the decisions, judged collectively. If the uncertainty in each individual policy decision is uncorrelated with the uncertainty in the other policy decisions, the positive and negative surprises will tend to balance out.[6]

However, an even better option is to have our cake and eat it too. We can implement at a large scale our current best guess about an optimal business incentive or early childhood program. But we can also design these programs so their quality can be continuously improved. How can such learning capabilities best be designed into a large-scale program?

First, learning will be advanced if the program tests a variety of planned variations in program design. We should test variations that plausibly might improve performance, but for which we don't know enough about effectiveness. For example, some business incentive programs should test variations in the length of customized training programs, whether these customized training programs focus on new or incumbent workers, and the size and industry of businesses participating in the programs. As another example, pre-K programs should be tested that systematically differ in class size, weekly hours, days per year, and one versus two years of pre-K education. We should also explore planned variation in pre-K curricula, and in teacher credentials and training.

Second, data should be systematically collected on program outcomes, program structure and costs, and program processes. For example, early childhood programs should all collect data on the same measures for child achievement, child behavior, child mental health, and family behavior. Data should also be collected on key structural features of each program, such as class size and teacher qualifications. Data should be regularly collected on what is actually going on in each program's interactions with children and/or parents. Programs might also choose to collect data on other measures, but some measures should be collected by all programs.

For business incentive programs, core data should be collected in all programs on selected measures of businesses' assessment of the programs' quality, and on the programs' impact on jobs, productivity, and wages. Data should also be collected from state data files—available in all states from the unemployment insurance program—on the employment and earnings of individual businesses. In addition, data should be collected on the costs and design features of the program. For example, data should be collected from customized training programs on the dollar costs per trainee, the class size of customized training, and who delivers the training. For manufacturing extension services, data should be collected on the number of hours of advice per business, and the technical expertise of the person providing the advice. Furthermore, data should be collected on qualitative features of the program. These qualitative features might include what types of skills are taught in customized training, or what specific types of information are provided in manufacturing extension services. Collection of data on core measures allows programs to be compared.

Third, program learning will also be facilitated if there is room for creative new program designs by local program operators. This means that ideas for additional variations in program design should not just be generated from the top down, but also from the bottom up.

Several researchers have highlighted the greater measured effects on early childhood educational development of state-run prekindergarten programs relative to Head Start. Even prior to the recent final report of the Head Start Impact Study, Steve Barnett, codirector of the National Institute for Early Education Research, summarized the research literature as concluding that "Head Start's effects on learning may be smaller than those of many state and local pre-K programs . . ." (Barnett 2008, p. 18). The smaller effects of Head Start are surprising because Head Start is more expensive per child. Of course, Head Start has broader goals than educational development, such as family health. But some researchers have argued that Head Start may also suffer from some rigidity because of its centralized federal control. For example, economist Art Rolnick of the Minneapolis Fed has argued that "Head Start . . . [has] performed well below expectations because [it] approach[es] the problem of early childhood development from the top down" (Haskins and Rolnick 2006). Ron Haskins of the Brookings Institution has argued that "we're not going to figure this [early childhood education] out at the federal level . . . The states are really the key to this" (Jacobson 2007, p. 16).

For business incentives, no one would argue that federal agencies have led the way in creating new program approaches. The U.S. Economic Development Administration is not the source of most new ideas in economic development. It is state and local agencies that have provided the creativity in coming up with new program approaches. The federal role has mostly been to provide supportive funding.

We don't have to assume that state and local governments are inherently more creative than federal agencies to see some merit in multiple approaches. More new ideas are likely to be generated if there are more groups that have the freedom to try new ideas. Providing some considerable autonomy to state and local initiatives is one way to do so.

Fourth, the results of these programs should be measured by comparing program results for program participants to results for similar nonparticipants. This requires that data on the core program success measures be collected for these similar nonparticipants. Adding in nonparticipants adds considerably to the costs of data collection: more data must be collected, and collection of data from nonparticipants may be more difficult.

This comparison of program participants with nonparticipants requires identifying similar nonparticipants. In some cases, it may be possible to do random assignment. However, random assignment is frequently politically and ethically difficult. How do you refuse to admit a child to a universal pre-K program? How do you refuse to provide extension services to a manufacturer struggling with difficult competitive issues? Therefore, it is necessary to develop approaches that will plausibly identify similar nonparticipants without random assignment.

Without random assignment, high-quality program evaluation can still be pursued. Program design may often cause program participation to vary because of factors that do not dramatically alter program participants' success. If such factors affecting program participation can be modeled, then the evaluation can come up with reasonable estimates of the causal effects of the program. For example, child participation in a universal pre-K program that charges income-based fees may vary with whether the family's income is below or above the cutoff for charging fees.[7] Child participation in a universal pre-K program may also vary with where pre-K facilities are located relative to the family's location.[8] For a business incentive program, a business's participation may also vary with the business's location relative to the location of the program's service provider. Business incentive programs may also do selective or random marketing of the program to different businesses. This difference in marketing to individual businesses may result in variation in business program participation that is independent of likely business success. Such variation in program participation may generate evidence on the true effects of the program on various business success measures.[9]

For these measures and evaluations to be credible, they need to be conducted independently of program providers. However, program providers will need to cooperate in helping collect the needed data on program design and from program participants. For the evaluations to be comparable, they need to be coordinated according to uniform standards.

To implement all these creative program features, such programs should allow for considerable state and local discretion. However, the federal government is the only plausible source of uniformity in standards. We need uniform national standards for data collection, for the program variations that will be prioritized for testing, and for the methodology of program evaluations. These standards should be accompanied by the federal funding needed to support this large-scale data collection and evaluation. Therefore, some combination of state and local program management, with federal funding and standards for systematic program learning, seems the most sensible division of government responsibility. These general principles leave room for arguing about the exact division of responsibility between the federal government versus state and local governments.[10] (Chapters 10 and 13 include further discussion of appropriate federal versus state and local roles in business incentive programs and early childhood programs.)

CONCLUSION

Uncertainty need not paralyze action. Despite uncertainty, we have reasonable estimates of the economic development benefits of business incentives and early childhood programs. We also have reasonable estimates of what program designs will maximize those economic development benefits.

We can both realize the expected benefits from expanding these programs and also learn more about what works. To do so, program expansions must allow for testing a wide variety of creative program approaches. These tests should include requirements to collect good data on key program success measures and key program operation details. A combination of state and local creativity, with good federal standards for data collection and evaluation, seems the best way to move forward.

It is a cliché to say that state and local governments are laboratories of democracy. State and local governments, left to their own devices, will clearly experiment with different designs for business incentives and early childhood education. But without federal support and requirements for data collection and evaluation, these laboratories of democracy will not be good laboratories. Strong federal incentives must be provided so that these laboratories will produce knowledge about what works that is useful to the nation.

Notes

1. The Perry effects used in Chapter 4 are reviewed in Appendix 4B of this book, available on-line from the Upjohn Institute. This appendix includes a discussion of whether various effects are statistically significant. The educational attainment and employment rate effects are statistically significant at some ages at the 95 percent level, and at other ages at the 90 percent level. In all cases, however, these effects are substantively large. Most of the statistical evidence reviewed in Appendix 4B comes from Schweinhart et al. (2005).
2. This book uses Wasylenko's summary estimate that the elasticity of state and local economic activity with respect to state and local business taxes is −0.2. The range of plausible estimates in my book is from −0.1 to −0.6. Studies that control for fixed effects or public services tend to find larger elasticities (in absolute value). One can easily find studies outside that range, including some very good studies. For example, Hines's (1996) estimates find an elasticity of −0.65. His estimates use an unusually good methodology. He compares the location decisions among U.S. states of foreign corporations from countries that only allow a deduction for U.S. taxes versus countries that allow a full credit for U.S. taxes. This different treatment of state and local business taxes seems a plausible exogenous shift in the tax price of different U.S. states.
3. For example, the estimated long-run elasticity of business activity with respect to wages is −0.67 (Bartik 1991a, p. 51). Labor costs are about 14 times state and local business tax costs (p. 49). Therefore, based on the wage elasticity, we would expect the long-run elasticity with respect to state and local business taxes to be about −0.05 (= −0.67 ÷ 14). The elasticity used in the current book is −0.20. Using an elasticity of −0.05 would quadruple the costs per job created of business incentives. The ratio of economic development benefits to program costs would decline from 3.14 to 0.79 (= 3.14 ÷ 4).
4. This random walk behavior is also consistent with theories of why city size distributions look the way they do. A regularity in city size distributions is that the

product of a city's population and the city's population rank among cities in the country is a constant for a given country and time period. This regularity can be derived if city growth shocks are random draws from a distribution, which is random walk behavior. See Gabaix (2008).

5. This quote from Ron Haskins comes from Haskins and Rolnick (2006), which is a transcript of a discussion between Ron Haskins and Art Rolnick.

6. Ludwig and Phillips recently commented on this issue in the context of Head Start: "Some observers have focused on the fact that many of the estimated impacts in the recent randomized experiment evaluation of Head Start are not statistically significant, and so follow the usual scientific convention of assuming that any estimates that cannot be statistically distinguished from zero are zero . . . But . . . the expected value of a program's benefits and costs may be a more relevant framework for making policy decisions than statistical significance, and the expected net value of Head Start is positive" (Ludwig and Phillips 2007, p. 4).

These comments came before the recent release of the final report of the Head Start Impact Study. I do not know whether Ludwig and Phillips still believe that the findings of the Head Start Impact Study support the notion that the expected net benefits of Head Start are positive. However, the point they make remains valid in concept, although perhaps not in this specific application.

7. This is sometimes called a regression discontinuity approach. Outcomes are assumed to vary smoothly with family income. Yet participation in the program varies discretely as the income cutoff is crossed.

8. An approach such as this was used by David Card to estimate the causal effects of college education on earnings (Card 1995).

9. If the marketing is selective, we have a regression discontinuity model. Business success without the program would vary smoothly with whatever cutoff is used to select businesses for marketing. Yet participation will vary discretely around the cutoff. Alternatively, random marketing will yield experimental estimates. The marketing will cause random variation in the percentage participating in two different groups. The difference in success measures in the two groups can be divided by the difference in the percentage participating to yield a plausible estimate of program effects. This is similar to the approach used in any regular experiment for converting "intent to treat" estimated effects to actual program effects.

10. For example, one hot political issue is the future of Head Start. Some more conservative analysts, such as Ron Haskins, have advocated converting Head Start to a block grant to state and local governments. Other more liberal analysts, such as Jens Ludwig and Deborah Phillips, have worried about the risk in allowing this radical change in Head Start program design.

7
Bringing the Future into the Present

How Policymakers Should Deal with the
Delayed Benefits of Early Childhood Programs

As discussed in Chapter 4, early childhood programs and business incentives differ in their benefits' timing. Business incentives deliver sizable economic development benefits almost immediately. Jobs are attracted, and this immediately increases employment rates and upgrades many state residents to better jobs. In contrast, most benefits of early childhood programs are long delayed. Early childhood programs have some economic development benefits in the short term. Free child care and other services to parents increase parental labor supply. Spending more money stimulates the state economy. But these short-term economic development benefits are modest. During the years right after these programs are begun, earnings of state residents go up by only 20 to 30 percent of program costs. Annual earnings effects of these programs do not exceed annual costs until at least 20 years later. (Figure 7.1, which reproduces Figure 4.2, shows the time pattern of effects.) These delays in benefits occur because so many of the benefits are due to the improved adult labor supply of former child participants. Better child development's benefits are only achieved in the long run.

The delayed nature of benefits from early childhood programs raises two issues. First, how should policymakers weight future benefits versus current costs? I will argue that policymakers should not discount future benefits too much. At any reasonable discount rate, benefits exceed costs for high-quality early childhood programs. However, policymakers often do drastically discount or disregard social benefits that are in the future. This leads to the second issue. Given that policymakers discount the future too much, what can be done to encourage policymakers to adopt early childhood programs? How can we get policymakers to adopt programs that are socially beneficial but politically unattractive because their benefits are delayed? Various approaches will be discussed to making such programs more attractive. We can work on

**Figure 7.1 Ratio of Annual Economic Development Benefits for State
Residents to Program Costs, Each Year after Permanent
Program Is Begun, for Three Early Childhood Programs and
a Business Incentive Program**

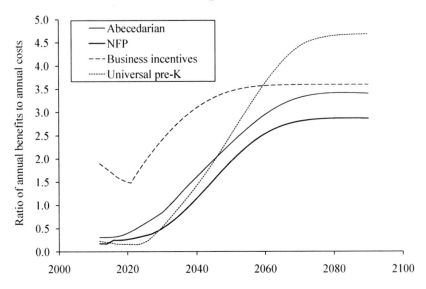

NOTE: As defined in this book, annual economic development benefits for state residents are just effects on state residents' earnings per capita. This figure assumes that
one of three early childhood programs is begun in 2011 and continues permanently.
The figure reports effects on state residents' earnings due to increases in the earnings
of the state's original residents who remain in the state. For comparison, the figure also
shows effects for a permanent program of business incentives whose scale remains at
the same percentage of the state economy over time. This figure is identical to Figure
4.2.

costs. Short-run costs can be postponed or reduced. Alternatively, we
can work on benefits. Long-run benefits can be shifted toward the present. Short-run benefits can be increased.

Improving the short-run benefits versus costs of early childhood
programs would put these programs on a more level playing field with
business incentive programs. As will be discussed below, business
incentive programs use various techniques to increase short-run benefits relative to costs. The magnitude of short-run benefits versus costs is
not an immutable attribute of a program, but can be affected by policy.

DISCOUNTING

What social discount rate should be used for evaluating public policies? This question has been extensively debated in the economics literature. Recently, the debate over discount rates has been reignited in discussing environmental issues. Environmental issues such as global warming often involve trade-offs between short-run costs and long-run environmental benefits. The discount rate used to compare future benefits with current costs makes a big difference in whether specific policies pass a benefit-cost test. Low social discount rates support stringent environmental policies. High social discount rates support lax environmental policies.

For this book, I assume we are determining a discount rate for comparing consumption over time. What is the value of a dollar of consumption a year from now, or 10 or 30 years from now, compared to a dollar of consumption today?[1]

The relative value of future consumption versus current consumption should depend on several factors. First, the value of future versus current consumption should depend on how fast one assumes the social value of extra consumption declines with higher per capita consumption. Most economic models assume some growth of per capita consumption over time. If one assumes that the value of an extra dollar of consumption dramatically declines as per capita consumption declines, then future changes in consumption should be down-weighted more heavily. Second, the value of future versus current consumption should depend on how fast one expects per capita consumption to increase. If per capita consumption will increase more rapidly over time, then people in the future will have higher per capita consumption. Other things being equal, this reduces the social value of an extra dollar of consumption in the future versus a dollar today. Third, it is possible that there is some inherent bias toward current consumption over future consumption. Even if per capita consumption did not increase over time, it is possible that many people would value a dollar of consumption today more than a dollar of consumption in the future.[2]

The discount rates used in this book should be compatible with the growth rate of per capita consumption that I assume. For this book, I assumed a rate of growth of real wages (and hence per capita consumption) of 1.2 percent per year. We could assume different rates of per capita consumption growth. But then we would need to adjust future earnings flows as well. For this discussion, I hold real wage growth and per capita consumption growth constant at 1.2 percent per year.

However, there are many possible assumptions about how rapidly the social value of consumption declines as per capita consumption increases. There are also different assumptions about how much the present should be inherently preferred to the future, even if per capita consumption were the same.

The debate over global warming has involved different assumptions about these determinants of discount rates. Sir Nicholas Stern, the lead author of the well-known *Stern Review on the Economics of Climate Change*, which was prepared for the British government, adopted assumptions that led to a relatively low discount rate (Stern 2007). Some of the American critics of the *Stern Review*, such as economists William Nordhaus and Martin Weitzman, adopted assumptions that led to somewhat higher discount rates.

In addition, the leading American academic journal on public policy, the *Journal of Policy Analysis and Management*, recently published an article that made other assumptions about discount rates. The article was titled "Just Give Me a Number! Practical Values for the Social Discount Rate" (Moore et al. 2004). The article tries to provide assumptions that would lead to some consensus on the social discount rate.

For the current book, I explored how it makes a difference to follow all these varying assumptions about discount rates. However, I adjusted all these discount rates to this book's assumption of a 1.2 percent annual growth rate in real wages. Under that wage growth scenario, the *Stern Review*'s assumptions imply a social discount rate of less than 2 percent. Nordhaus's and Weitzman's assumptions imply social discount rates of 3.9 percent and 4.4 percent, respectively (Nordhaus 2007; Weitzman 2007). The Moore et al. assumptions imply a social discount rate of 2.2 percent. Finally, this book's baseline estimates assume a social discount rate of 3 percent.

How do these discount rates affect the benefits and costs of business incentives and early childhood programs? Table 7.1 shows ratios of economic development benefits for state residents to costs for these programs under various discount rates. Notice two points about these results: First, as one would expect, the higher discount rates of Nordhaus or Weitzman make the early childhood programs look somewhat

Table 7.1 Effects of Alternative Discount Rate Assumptions on Ratio of Present Value of State Economic Development Benefits to Program Costs, for Business Incentives and for Three Early Childhood Programs

			Discount rate assumption of:			
		Moore				
	Stern	et al.	This book	Nordhaus	Weitzman	
Implied discount rate on aggregate future earnings (%)	1.6	2.2	3.0	3.9	4.4	
Ratio of present value of earnings effects to costs for:						
Business incentives	3.56	3.36	3.14	2.92	2.82	
Universal pre-K	4.46	3.62	2.78	2.10	1.82	
Abecedarian	1.59	2.54	2.25	1.88	1.71	
Nurse-Family Partnership	1.88	2.23	1.85	1.49	1.33	

NOTE: State economic development benefits are defined in this book as increased earnings per capita of state residents. See Appendix 7A for methodology and references.

worse relative to business incentives. Higher discount rates mean that the future adult earnings of former child participants are not weighted as highly. Second, under all these discount rates, the present value of increased earnings for state residents exceeds the cost of the program. Therefore, even under assumptions that yield relatively high discount rates, these early childhood programs still make sense from a state economic development perspective. Benefits for former child participants are so large that even high discount rates do not make these benefits unimportant.

Another possible way to analyze these different policies is in terms of their rate of return. The "rate of return" of a proposed public policy is the maximum discount rate at which the project is still worth pursuing. This maximum rate of return helps reveal whether the project would be worth doing under more extreme assumptions about appropriate discount rates. As is well known in benefit-cost analysis, this rate of return should not be used to rank projects. The present value, calculated using the correct discount rate, should be used to rank projects. The discount rate's purpose is to allow a comparison of the relative value of consumption at different points of time.

Table 7.2 shows these rate-of-return calculations. Business incentives yield benefits exceeding costs immediately. Therefore, business incentives will have a positive return at any discount rate. Early childhood programs are all worth doing unless real social discount rates exceed 5.7 percent. Such high discount rates are implausible.

This discussion focuses on what policymakers should do. Research on the social discount rate suggests that policymakers should discount the future, but not too much. Therefore, policymakers should be willing to implement early childhood programs, even though many of their benefits are far in the future.

Unfortunately, this is probably not the way many state, local, and federal policymakers actually view the world. These early childhood programs do not have benefits exceeding costs for the remaining political career of most policymakers. In the short run, while the policymakers considering these programs are in office, these early childhood programs have benefits that fall short of costs.

Many policymakers may have implicit discount rates that exceed 10 percent. Research suggests that corporate executives evaluate investment projects at discount rates that average 12 percent (Poterba and

**Table 7.2 Annual Rate of Return to Business Incentives and Three
Early Childhood Programs, from a State Economic
Development Perspective**

Program	Annual rate of return, state perspective
Business incentives	Infinite or undefined
Universal pre-K	6.7
Abecedarian	7.7
Nurse-Family Partnership	5.7

NOTE: This table shows the highest real interest rate at which the present value of
effects of the program on state residents' per capita earnings exceeds the present value
of program costs. Business incentives' benefits exceed costs regardless of how high
the real interest rate is, as estimated program benefits in the first year exceed costs.
Therefore, the "rate of return" to business incentives can be seen as infinite or undefined. Note that all these "rates of return" only include "economic development benefits" for the state. Thus, these rates of return do not count, for example, the benefits of
reduced crime, or spillover effects on earnings of residents of other states.

Summers 1995). Government policymakers might be at least as short-
sighted. If policymakers' discount rates are 10 percent or greater, the
value of the earnings benefits from early childhood programs will fall
short of these programs' costs.

Can anything be done to change the net benefits of early childhood
programs, as perceived by policymakers? We could simply argue for
adopting a long-term perspective. However, changing such underly-
ing attitudes is difficult. Political pressures encourage policymakers to
worry about reelection.

A more politically feasible alternative is to adjust the benefits and
costs of early childhood programs to increase their short-term payoff.
Short-term costs can be postponed or otherwise reduced. Long-term
benefits can be shifted toward the short term, or short-term benefits can
be otherwise increased. The rest of this chapter considers the options
for increasing the short-term economic development payoff of early
childhood programs.

REDUCING SHORT-RUN COSTS: POSTPONING COSTS THROUGH BORROWING

One way to reduce short-run costs of early childhood programs is to finance the programs through borrowing. Borrowing delays program costs, allowing the timing of costs to better match the timing of economic development benefits.

Borrowing is generally accepted as a way for the government to pay for "physical capital"—roads, public buildings, prisons. The rationale for this borrowing is that it allows the costs of building or rehabilitating physical capital to be better matched to the stream of benefits from such capital. For example, building a new highway has large up-front costs. Yet its benefits will be received for many years to come.

Allowing borrowing for early childhood programs would put these programs on a more level playing field with business incentives. Business incentive programs can postpone many of their costs by promising future incentives to business. Because these programs can postpone costs, they become more attractive to policymakers.

However, most state constitutions severely restrict public borrowing, except for the building or redevelopment of tangible physical capital. In most states, it would be illegal for the government to sell a 30-year bond to pay for early childhood programs.

State and local governments have come up with creative ways of borrowing to get around these constitutional restrictions. States have sometimes securitized streams of revenues they will receive from dedicated sources. For example, states have sold off future revenues that they will receive from the settlement with tobacco companies, and have used the proceeds to finance public programs (Scheppach 2003; Sindelar and Falba 2004). Some states have sold off the rights to collect tolls on a public highway (Burwell and Puentes 2009).

In economic development policy, one common program is tax increment financing (TIF) (Dye and Merriman 2006). In a TIF program, the increase in property tax revenue in a particular geographic area is dedicated to a special TIF fund. For example, this geographic area might be a downtown area. This dedicated revenue can only be used for purposes determined by the authority overseeing the TIF district. It is common to use TIF revenues as backing for bonds that are sold to finance various public improvements in the TIF district. For example, in a downtown area, the TIF revenues might be used to finance parking ramps, or for marketing the downtown.

TIFs are being used in more creative ways. Of particular relevance here is that TIFs are starting to be used for educational programs. Michigan recently passed a "Promise Zone" law, which was inspired by the Kalamazoo Promise. Under the Kalamazoo Promise, private donors guaranteed that they would pay up to four years of tuition at Michigan public universities and community colleges for all graduates of Kalamazoo Public Schools. The Michigan Promise Zone law allows for TIF zones to help finance similar programs in other areas of Michigan. A school district or some other local government can develop a plan to provide free college tuition to all students within the district or government jurisdiction. If this plan is approved by the state of Michigan, the plan can in part be funded by TIFs. The plan would receive the state education property tax revenue from the increase in property values in the designated area.[3]

Similar TIFs could be created to finance early childhood programs. Some portion of the increment in a tax's revenue could be dedicated to a fund to support early childhood programs. The incremental tax revenue would not have to necessarily be property tax revenue. Early childhood TIFs could be financed with incremental revenue from the sales tax or income tax. The dedicated revenue in that fund could be used to support bond issues to pay the up-front costs of early childhood programs.

What objections might be raised to borrowing for early childhood programs? One is that borrowing only makes sense if the early childhood program does produce sizable future benefits. If the early childhood program does not produce sizable long-run benefits, then it would be a mistake to borrow to pay its costs.

A second objection is that allowing borrowing for the operating costs of public programs, even highly desirable programs, might lead to abuses. There are good historical reasons why state constitutions often restrict public borrowing. In the early nineteenth century, American states were extraordinarily active in borrowing. This borrowing was often used to support corporations that promoted state economic development, such as investments in canals, railroads, and banks. However, this large-scale borrowing led to eight states defaulting on their debts during the economic downturn of the 1840s. Subsequent state constitutional amendments put significant limitations on state debt issuance and investment in corporations (Wallis 2000).

A third objection is that the current period does not seem the most favorable time to expand debt. The recession that began in December 2007 is widely attributed to excessive promotion of overly risky debt by many different financial institutions and government agencies. The financial system might not be ready for new forms of government financing. The political winds might not support such government borrowing.

It is somewhat disconcerting that a few years ago, Citigroup was promoting the financing of early childhood education with debt financing. In October 2006, the managing director of the Student Loan Group of Citigroup made a presentation to a group of early childhood advocates on this topic (Sheldon 2006). According to the meeting summary, the Citigroup director pointed out that "because early care education [ECE] spending is a capital formation expenditure . . . , an optimal way for society to pay for ECE costs would be to match the repaying of cash to the time when benefits are received . . . He proposed this might be accomplished via a financing mechanism similar to the federal government's student loan program . . . Under such an arrangement, the same entities (parents, federal and state governments) that currently pay for early education would be responsible to pay under [this new financing] proposal" (Invest in Kids/PAES 2006). These are all cogent points. However, now does not seem the best time for new creative financing schemes.

REDUCING SHORT-RUN COSTS: POSSIBLE OFFSETS FROM REDUCED SPECIAL EDUCATION COSTS

One significant short-run cost offset to early childhood programs is reduced special education costs. High-quality early childhood programs have been shown to significantly reduce the percentage of students in K–12 special education. For example, the Perry Preschool project reduced special education assignments for mental impairment from 35 percent in the control group to 15 percent in the treatment group (Schweinhart et al. 2005). Reductions of about half as much in special education assignments were found in the Chicago Child-Parent Center program: from 25 percent down to 14 percent (Reynolds et al. 2002). The more intensive and more expensive Abecedarian program had somewhat larger effects on special education assignments: it reduced them from 48 percent to 25 percent (Masse and Barnett 2002).[4]

Reducing special education assignments even modestly can yield significant cost savings. Special education is expensive. It is estimated that special education assignment costs an average of more than $10,000 a year per special education student. This is an extra $10,000 cost above regular education costs (Parrish et al. 2004, Part II; updated to 2007 dollars using the CPI). These special education costs can extend over many years, from kindergarten through high school (and even beyond in some cases). Because special education costs such a great amount per year and extends for many years, the cost savings from reducing special education assignments can be large.

Early childhood programs might also cause other savings for the education system, the social welfare system, and the criminal justice system. However, in the present context, we are focusing on cost savings that are short-term. Reducing grade retention saves costs only in the long run. The costs that are saved from reduced criminal activity also take many years to be realized. Savings in child welfare costs from reduced abuse and neglect cases may be more immediate. However, the evidence suggests that such savings for the child welfare system are small relative to special-education cost savings. For example, for the Chicago Child-Parent Center program, cost savings for the child welfare system are only 11 percent of estimated cost savings from reduced special education costs (Reynolds et al. 2002). Estimates for the Nurse-Family Partnership also suggest modest fiscal savings from reduced child-welfare system costs (Aos et al. 2004, Technical Appendix, p. 96).

I added reduced special education costs into my simulation model of universal pre-K and a full-scale Abecedarian program. I used this revised simulation model to recalculate the flows of benefits versus costs of these programs over time. This revised simulation model calculates "net costs" of these early childhood programs for each time period. These net costs subtract out the reduced special education costs.[5]

Figures 7.2 and 7.3 show the results.[6] As the figures show, the ratio of economic development benefits to net costs increases significantly.

**Figure 7.2 Ratio of Annual State Economic Development Benefits to
Net Program Costs, Before and After Adjusting for Reduced
Special Education Costs, for Universal Pre-K Education**

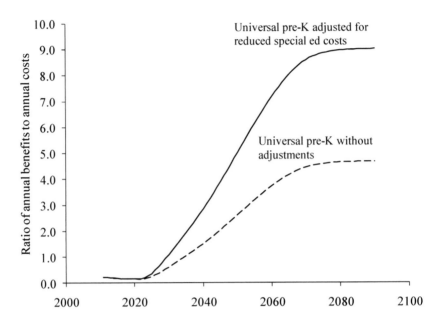

NOTE: Program is assumed to start full scale in 2011 and continue indefinitely. Ratio
shown is earnings benefits for state residents in each year, divided by program costs
in that year. Assumptions used are described in text and text endnotes. Appendix 7B
shows the numbers behind this figure.

Calculations suggest that the ratio of benefits to net fiscal costs increases
from 2.78 to 4.90 for universal pre-K education. For the Abecedarian
program, this ratio increases from 2.25 to 3.21.

However, the short-term perspective on these programs only modestly improves. For example, under these revised calculations, which
consider reduced special education costs, it takes 19 years after universal pre-K is implemented for annual economic development benefits
to exceed annual net costs. (In terms of the figure, this happens when
the ratio of annual economic development benefits to net costs exceeds
1.) This is an improvement over the baseline calculations. In the baseline calculations, it took 24 years for economic development benefits to

Figure 7.3 Ratio of Annual State Economic Development Benefits to Net Program Costs, Before and After Adjusting for Reduced Special Education Costs, for Abecedarian Program

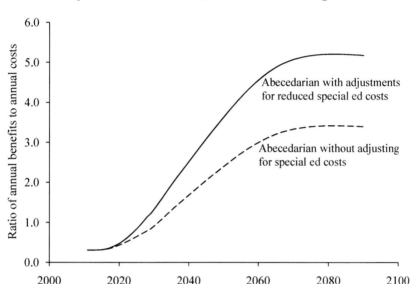

NOTE: Program is assumed to start full scale in 2011 and continue indefinitely. Ratio reported is ratio of earnings benefits for state residents for that year, divided by net program costs for that year. Assumptions used are described in text and text endnotes. Appendix 7B shows the numbers behind this figure.

exceed costs. However, 20 years is still a long time to wait for economic development benefits to dominate costs.

In addition, during the first 10 years or so, the ratio of benefits to net costs only modestly improves if one considers special education cost savings. For example, 10 years after the universal pre-K program is begun, annual benefits are 17 percent of net costs, up from 16 percent in the original simulation.

For the Abecedarian program, under these revised calculations, it takes 16 years for annual economic development benefits to exceed annual net costs. In the baseline calculations, it took 21 years. Sixteen years is a long time to wait for annual economic development benefits to exceed costs.

In addition, 10 years after a full-scale Abecedarian program is begun, annual economic development benefits are 54 percent of net costs. This is only up modestly from the 47 percent figure calculated before, which did not consider special education cost savings.

In sum, even when special education cost savings are considered, early childhood programs are only attractive to policymakers who possess the patience needed to take a long-term perspective.

REDUCING SHORT-RUN GOVERNMENT COSTS: FINANCING PRE-K OUT OF THE K–12 SCHOOL BUDGET

Universal pre-K education or other early childhood programs could be financed without increasing taxes or borrowing. Some other spending category could be reduced. This budget reallocation would promote state economic development if this other spending category has lower economic development benefits than the early childhood program.

Politically, the most likely spending cut to finance universal pre-K would be to cut K–12 spending. Local school districts are likely sponsors of pre-K education. If they choose to finance universal pre-K education, and voters are not inclined to increase taxes, then universal pre-K's costs are implicitly being financed by reduced K–12 spending. At the state level, state governments frequently have special funds for support of public education spending. In addition, public education spending proposals are often considered together as part of a particular appropriations bill. Moreover, public education spending proposals often are considered together by the same committee. In this political process, achieving increased funding for high-quality pre-K education may involve some reduction in K–12 spending. This reduction may be explicit or it may be implicit. Because of expanded pre-K spending, K–12 spending may not increase as fast as it otherwise would. However, it would be politically naïve to deny the possibility of a political trade-off between pre-K funding and K–12 funding.

This political trade-off does not reflect any necessary logical consequence of increased pre-K spending. Increased pre-K education spending can logically be financed by cutting any spending category, not just K–12 spending. We can increase pre-K spending without increasing taxes or government borrowing by cutting such budget categories as prisons, Medicaid, state employee benefits, and others. However, these logical possibilities are less politically likely than financing universal pre-K through reduced K–12 spending.

Suppose we did finance 100 percent of the costs of universal pre-K through reduced K–12 spending. Then this budget reallocation would have no net government spending cost. The short-term tax costs of increasing pre-K spending are eliminated. State policymakers need not worry about proposing tax increases to pay for universal pre-K.

But what would be the consequences of this budget reallocation for state economic development? Universal pre-K education increases state economic development largely by increasing the earnings of former child participants. K–12 education has similar types of effects on state economic development. The quality of K–12 education affects the earnings of former students. The quantity and quality of the labor supply of former K–12 students who stay in the state will affect the state's economic development. A cut in K–12 spending may damage the quality of K–12 education, which will adversely affect state economic development. If universal pre-K is funded, but K–12 spending is cut, which of these policy changes will dominate the state's future economic development? Will state residents' earnings increase or decrease?

To address these questions, I used this book's simulation model to estimate the economic development benefits derived from reallocating K–12 spending to universal pre-K education. To do so, I needed an estimate of how reductions in K–12 spending will affect the earnings of former students.

For this simulation, I used a maximum plausible estimate of how large the effects of cutting K–12 spending could be. I used estimates derived from economist Alan Krueger's estimates of how spending on reduced class size in grades K–2 affected future earnings (Krueger 2003).

Krueger's estimates are derived from the Tennessee Class Size Study. This study was a random assignment study in which students were randomly assigned to either "normal" K–2 classes that averaged 22 students or "experimental" lower class sizes that averaged 15 students. The study estimated effects of this lower class size on early elementary test scores. Krueger used these test score effects to estimate effects on future earnings. For his benefit-cost analysis, he also estimated what percentage increase in K–2 spending was needed to achieve these results. Under reasonable assumptions, lower K–2 class sizes clearly passed a benefit-cost test. For example, under discount rate and wage growth assumptions similar to this book's assumptions, the present value of future earnings benefits is about three times the extra K–12 spending costs.[7]

Suppose we use Krueger's estimates to estimate the earnings effects of all changes in K–12 spending. Krueger's estimates imply that a 1 percent decrease (increase) in K–12 spending that occurs for one year of a student's K–12 career will decrease (increase) that student's future earnings by 0.03 percent. This is derived by assuming that the earnings effects of any change in K–12 spending will be the same as the earnings effects of changes in spending on smaller class sizes in grades K–2.[8]

I regard this as a maximum plausible estimate of the effects of lower K–12 spending for several reasons. First, not everyone accepts Krueger's estimates. For example, there is an ongoing dispute between Krueger and other education researchers such as Eric Hanushek about whether K–12 class size and spending have effects as large as those estimated by Krueger (Hanushek 2002; Krueger 2002). Second, even if we accept Krueger's estimates, it is unlikely that most changes in K–12 spending have as large an effect on student learning and future earnings as K–2 class size. Therefore, there are less damaging ways to cut the K–12 budget than increasing K–2 class size. As a result, we would expect the future earnings effects of an optimal cut in the K–12 budget to be less than the effects estimated by Krueger for K–2 class size.

Financing universal pre-K education is estimated to cost 2.8 percent of the K–12 budget.[9] Therefore, the simulations consider the economic development effects of implementing universal pre-K by cutting the K–12 budget by 2.8 percent.

Many effects of reduced K–12 spending are long delayed. In the first year, the spending cut only reduces the quality of education of students leaving K–12 for one year. Based on the Krueger estimates, a cut of 2.8 percent in K–12 spending experienced for only one year will reduce future earnings by only 0.08 percent ($= 2.8 \times 0.0296$). After two years, this impact doubles. It keeps going up for each successive cohort of students for the next 13 years. After 13 years, we have students who have experienced 2.8 percent lower school funding from kindergarten through twelfth grade. Using the Krueger estimates, the 13 years of lower school funding is estimated to reduce earnings by 1.08 percent. After 13 years, each successive cohort of students leaving public schools is estimated to have its members' lifetime earnings reduced by 1.08 percent.[10]

These effects on students' earnings are entered into this book's simulation model. As was done with early childhood programs, I make assumptions, based on reasonable estimates, on how many former K–12 students will survive to various ages and how many will stay in their home state. I also make similar assumptions that one-third of this change in the state's labor supply is offset by displacement effects. Due to the funding cuts, students leaving the K–12 system have lower labor force participation and job skills. This increases job opportunities for other state residents. These increased job opportunities offset one-third of the direct negative effects on state earnings due to students who remain in the state.[11]

The reduced K–12 education spending also has some immediate economic development effects. Reduced education spending reduces demand for labor in the K–12 sector and also reduces the need for taxes to finance the expanded preschool. The reduced K–12 spending offsets 1-for-1 the balanced budget multiplier effects of the extra universal pre-K spending.

Figure 7.4 shows the estimated economic development effects of financing universal pre-K through reduced K–12 spending. The chart shows the annual effects of pre-K education by itself on the earnings of state residents, as a percentage of total state earnings. The chart also shows the negative effects on state residents' earnings of reducing K–12 spending. Finally, the chart shows the net effects of both changes combined.

As the figure shows, at first this budget reallocation has little or no net effect on state residents' earnings. However, after about 16 years, this budget reallocation begins to have positive effects on state economic development. These positive effects steadily increase until they max out, as a percentage of the state economy, at about a 0.75 percent boost to the economy, after about 60 years.

The negative effects of reduced K–12 spending are estimated to offset about two-fifths of the positive effects of universal pre-K education.[12] Why are there gains from this budget reallocation? These gains occur because the estimated effects of universal pre-K on child develop-

**Figure 7.4 Effects on State Economic Development of Financing
Universal Pre-K Education by Reducing K–12 Spending**

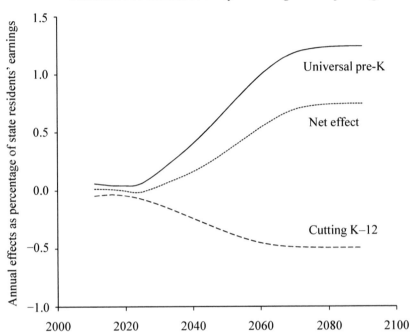

NOTE: Effects for universal pre-K are as previously described in Chapter 4, and in
Bartik (2006). Effects of cutting K–12 are modeled as described in chapter text, and
follow estimates of Krueger (2003). The net effect is simply the difference between
the two. Appendix 7C provides the detailed numbers behind this figure.

ment and adult success are significantly greater than the effects of later
intervention. One can explain this as being due to the inherent advantages of earlier intervention. One could also hypothesize that increasing
the time that children spend in school may be somewhat more productive per dollar than increasing the quality of that time.

None of this means that this budget reallocation is the best alternative. All the estimates say is that if we assume that the total K–12 plus
pre-K budget is fixed, reallocating funds from K–12 to pre-K seems to
have net positive effects on state economic development. But increasing total spending on pre-K and K–12 may also pay off. Recall that
Krueger's estimates show a positive benefit-cost ratio for increasing

K–12 spending. In the present scenario, earnings benefits are scaled back, as I only count earnings effects due to former students who stay in the state, and I assume that extra quality of labor supply has some displacement effects. But I still conclude that reducing K–12 spending has negative economic development effects that are 22 percent greater than the resulting budget savings.[13] In this simulation, cutting K–12 spending is a bad idea from a state economic development perspective.

Therefore, the best alternative would be to increase spending for universal pre-K, and finance this in some way other than cutting K–12 spending. Cutting K–12 spending is definitely a "second-best" way of financing universal pre-K education.

What are this simulation's limitations? One obvious limitation is that the simulation does not allow for any interaction between universal pre-K education and reduced K–12 spending. The simulation assumes the effects of universal pre-K education and reduced K–12 spending are additive. But what if the effects of universal pre-K depend on the level of K–12 spending? Then the effect of the budget reallocation will differ from simply adding the two effects.

It has sometimes been argued that early childhood interventions will have stronger long-term effects if these interventions are coupled with a quality K–12 school system. For example, some believe that the effects of the Abecedarian program were enhanced by the relatively high quality of the Chapel Hill school system. According to Galinsky, the public school system in Chapel Hill at the time of the experiment was considered one of the two best public school systems in the state. The Chapel Hill public schools had a relatively small percentage of disadvantaged children, and a large number of different support services for children who were behind. Perhaps this excellent school system helped the Abecedarian treatment group more than the control group.

Therefore, it is possible that the estimated impacts of universal pre-K will be reduced if the quality of subsequent K–12 education is reduced, beyond the prediction from adding up the separate effects of these two interventions. In that case, Figure 7.4 may overstate the net benefits of this budget reallocation.

On the other hand, perhaps universal pre-K has greater impacts on children when K–12 school quality is lower. In that case, the combined impact of the budget reallocation will be more positive than shown in Figure 7.4.

Another issue is whether reducing K–12 spending will have the earnings effects estimated by Krueger. As mentioned above, it seems plausible that there are better ways to cut the K–12 school budget than by increasing K–2 class size. For example, in 2006, Mark Tucker and his colleagues at the National Center on Education and the Economy advocated that we consider getting rid of at least the senior year in high school for most students, as the senior year often seems unproductive. This is just one of many possible K–12 changes that could cut spending at lower costs to student achievement and earnings than by raising early elementary class sizes.

Finally, although funding universal pre-K through cutting K–12 spending avoids short-run tax increases, it does not produce short-run economic development benefits. As the figure shows, under this scenario, there are few economic development benefits for 25 years. This budget reallocation is only attractive to a policymaker with great patience.

INCREASING SHORT-RUN BENEFITS THROUGH CAPITALIZATION

Benefits of early childhood programs would be realized earlier if some of these benefits were "capitalized" into higher property values. A state or local government that implements at full-scale a high-quality early childhood program is providing a service that is valuable to families. The increased future earnings of former child participants should be valued by parents. Parents should be willing to pay more to obtain access for these future benefits. This willingness to pay could be reflected in a willingness to pay more to buy a house or rent an apartment in the state or local area that offers these services. This willingness to pay more for housing should increase property values. This increase in property values may occur as soon as buyers and sellers of property fully understand the future benefits provided by early childhood programs. These increased property values do not have to wait for these future benefits to occur if sufficient numbers of buyers and sellers of property believe that these benefits will occur. Therefore, capitalization of future earnings benefits into property values could increase the up-front benefits of early childhood programs.[14]

The value of property should also reflect the property's taxes. However, the economic development argument for early childhood programs is that these future earnings benefits significantly exceed the costs of financing these programs. Furthermore, as other authors have pointed out, early childhood programs provide many medium-run and long-run fiscal benefits. These fiscal benefits include the lower special education costs mentioned above. They also include other reductions in spending, such as lower criminal justice system costs and lower costs for welfare and Medicaid. Fiscal benefits also include increases in taxes due to the increased earnings in the state economy. Some simulations suggest that fiscal benefits greatly outweigh the costs of these programs (Bartik 2006; Dickens and Baschnagel 2008; Lynch 2007). The medium-run and long-run fiscal benefits are great enough that at modest discount rates such as 3 percent, the adoption of these programs has a positive net present fiscal value, not a cost.

How buyers and sellers of property value these short-run fiscal costs versus long-run fiscal benefits is uncertain. This may depend in part on how short-run fiscal costs are paid for. If all short-run fiscal costs are reflected in higher property taxes, costs may loom larger in property owners' minds. If short-run fiscal costs are financed in ways that are less visible, less tied to property purchases, or less a burden on the general taxpayer, then these short-run costs may have less influence on how typical buyers and sellers value property. For example, if these short-run costs are financed through higher sales taxes, they may be less visible to many households and therefore not affect property bids much. If short-run costs are financed through an increase in the top rate on a graduated state income tax, then these costs may not affect property bids that much.[15]

Will buyers and sellers of property perceive the benefits of early childhood programs as benefits that should increase their valuation of property? This seems much more likely for programs such as universal pre-K education that provide widespread benefits to many households. On the other hand, it seems less likely that property values will go up if early childhood programs only provide benefits to relatively few households. Some early childhood programs help relatively few households because they are targeted at disadvantaged households. This includes programs such as the Abecedarian program. It also includes many home-visiting programs, such as the Nurse-Family Partnership.

Whether universal pre-K education will affect property valuation depends in part on whether it provides benefits that are visible to prospective property owners in the state or local area. Some benefits of universal pre-K education do manifest themselves in the short run in a way that we know is visible enough to affect property valuation. Specifically, high-quality universal pre-K will affect elementary school test scores. We know from previous research that elementary school test scores are visible enough and tied enough to property ownership to affect property values.

Studies suggest that universal pre-K will increase average test scores in third, fourth, and fifth grades by about 0.08 in "effect size" units. This "effect size" jargon of educational researchers means that average test scores will increase by eight-hundredths of the typical standard deviation across students in test scores.[16] Based on previous studies of the housing market, an increase in average test scores in third, fourth, and fifth grades of one standard deviation probably increases property values by 5 to 10 percent.[17] Therefore, because of its effects on average elementary school test scores, universal pre-K should increase a state or local area's residential property values by 0.4 to 0.8 percent. This calculation assumes that property buyers and sellers value the increase in test scores but ignore the possible fiscal consequences of universal pre-K. As outlined above, fiscal consequences might be ignored because these fiscal consequences are on net positive in the long run, or because the short-run fiscal costs are not salient to homeowners' property valuation decision.

Based on typical U.S. property values, if universal pre-K raises residential property values by 0.4 to 0.8 percent, the capital gain from universal pre-K will be 6.4 to 12.7 times the annual gross budgetary costs of universal preschool.[18] If property valuations are unaffected until test scores actually improve, then this property value gain will begin to occur when the original participants in pre-K reach third grade, four years after the universal pre-K program is adopted. At average U.S. property tax rates, such an increased valuation of property would raise property tax revenues of 8 to 17 percent of the annual gross costs of the universal pre-K program.[19]

Universal pre-K would have much larger effects on property values if buyers and sellers of property fully valued its effects on future earnings. This book's simulations allow a calculation of universal pre-K's effects on state residents' earnings. I can also calculate the effects on the earnings of former preschoolers who leave the state. These effects should also be relevant to parents' property valuation decisions. Combining these calculations, we can calculate the net present value of the increase in earnings that can be accessed by buying property in this state.[20]

This net present value obviously depends upon the discount rate typically used by buyers and sellers of property. What discount rate might actually be used by prospective buyers and sellers of property to value earnings effects that occur for their children? The honest answer is, we don't know. However, we can come up with some plausible alternatives. I consider four alternatives. First, prospective home buyers might use the same discount rate as the ideal policymaker. For this alternative, I use a discount rate of 3 percent, which this book has consistently assumed is optimal for the ideal policymaker. A second alternative is to rely on evidence of how parents behave in making investments in children. A study of parental investments in children's health estimated a parental discount rate of 4.70 percent (Agee and Crocker 1996). A third alternative is to estimate what discount rate is compatible with the finding that a one standard deviation increase in test scores raises property values by 5 to 10 percent. I calculated what discount rate would make this property value effect reasonable. I estimated discount rates of 7.48 percent (5 percent property value effect) and 6.06 percent (10 percent property value effect). Finally, as argued by Barrow and Rouse (2004), we might use the average 30-year real interest rate on mortgages. They calculate this to be 7.33 percent. This mortgage rate is quite close to the estimated discount rate associated with a 5 percent property value effect. I combine these two possible discount rates in the analysis.

Table 7.3 uses these plausible discount rates to calculate effects of universal pre-K on property values and property taxes. I consider two scenarios. Under one scenario, I only consider the property value effects of the gross economic development benefits provided by universal pre-K. This scenario ignores the fiscal effects of universal pre-K education. It implicitly assumes that the short-run taxes to support universal pre-K aren't relevant to property buyers and sellers. Perhaps the taxes are not paid by the decisive property buyer or seller. Or perhaps these short-run taxes are perceived as being outweighed by the long-run fiscal benefits of pre-K education in lowering special education costs, criminal justice system costs, and welfare system costs. Under the second scenario, I

Table 7.3 Possible Capitalization Effects of Universal Pre-K Education

Discount rate used	3.00%	4.70%	6.06%	7.33%	Elementary test score effect for comparison
Source of discount rate or estimates	Optimal social discount rate.	Parental discount rate for investment in children, inferred from investment choices regarding children's health.	Discount rate compatible with estimate that a one-standard-deviation increase in test scores increases property values by 10%.	Average 30-year real mortgage rate from Barrow and Rouse. (Also compatible with a one-standard-deviation test score effect of about 5%.)	Due to effects of elementary test scores on property values, and effects of universal pre-K on elementary test scores.
Gross capitalization of economic development benefits					
% effect on property values	18.3	5.1	2.5	1.4	0.4 to 0.8
Ratio of property value effect to annual costs of universal pre-K	292.1	81.2	39.4	22.7	6.4 to 12.7
Property taxes raised as proportion of annual costs of universal pre-K	3.88	1.08	0.52	0.30	0.08 to 0.17
Net capitalization of economic development benefits					
% effect on property values	14.0	3.0	1.0	0.3	
Ratio of property value effect to annual costs of universal pre-K	178.4	38.7	12.9	3.4	
Property taxes raised as proportion of annual costs of universal pre-K	2.37	0.51	0.17	0.05	

NOTE: The figures in the last column come from the previous section of the text, which analyzed capitalization effects on elementary test scores. The remaining columns calculate capitalization under various assumptions about discount rates and whether all of the program costs are deemed relevant to property valuation. The first three rows of numbers simply consider capitalization under the assumption that only gross economic development benefits of universal pre-K are capitalized. Fiscal effects are ignored under the assumption that these are not relevant, either because of the many fiscal benefits (e.g., reduced special ed costs, criminal justice system costs, welfare costs, and child welfare costs) as well as costs of universal pre-K, or because the marginal home buyer may not pay many of those costs (e.g., fiscal costs may not be deemed relevant to property bids if financed by the sales tax, or a progressive income tax, or a business tax). The final three rows of numbers consider the opposite extreme example: all of the program costs of universal pre-K are capitalized, ignoring any fiscal benefits of universal pre-K. Capitalization effects on property values calculate the discounted present value of economic development benefits (or economic development benefits minus program costs) under various discount rates and get the percentage effect by dividing by the estimated total residential property values, which are estimated based on Federal Reserve Board Flow of Funds data (Federal Reserve Board 2009). Property tax collections assume a real property tax rate of 1.33%, based on average national data from Yilmaz et al. (2006) of the Tax Policy Center. The discount rate assumptions are based on different plausible discount rates. 3% is the optimal social discount rate used in this book. 4.7% is an estimate of the average discount rate used by parents for making decisions about investments in their children's health. 6.06% is an estimate of the discount rate that would be needed to explain how elementary test scores affect housing prices, assuming that a one-standard-deviation increase in test scores increases housing prices by 10%. 7.33% is an estimate from Barrow and Rouse of the average real 30-year mortgage rate. 7.33% is also close to the discount rate needed to explain how elementary test scores affect housing prices, under the assumption that a one-standard-deviation increase in test scores increases housing prices by 5%. (The actual discount rate for a 5% effect is 7.48%.)

consider the property value effects of universal pre-K after subtracting out 100 percent of the program costs for universal pre-K. No fiscal benefits from universal pre-K are considered. In the real world, it seems likely that the truth is between these two scenarios.

These property value effects vary widely. However, these results do support several conclusions. First, property value effects of universal pre-K are potentially about three times as great as predicted by effects on elementary test scores. This estimate is derived by comparing the elementary test score effects with the effects of gross economic development benefits using the comparable discount rate. This reflects that universal pre-K has considerably greater effects on the future earnings of former child participants than would be predicted from its effects on elementary test scores.

Second, effects of universal pre-K on property values are often large under plausible discount rates. Effects are many multiples of annual program costs.[21] The property taxes raised from these higher property values are often significant fractions of annual program costs. Under some plausible scenarios, these property tax increases are sufficient to fund universal pre-K.

Third, whether such capitalization effects will actually occur obviously depends greatly on how property buyers and sellers value universal pre-K. This depends in part on whether property buyers and sellers have accurate information about the quality of universal pre-K. It also depends on whether property buyers and sellers understand fully the potential long-run benefits of high-quality universal pre-K. Finally, this valuation depends on how heavily these buyers and sellers discount these benefits to children.

At present, I doubt whether most property buyers and sellers directly include pre-K quality in their property valuation decisions. I doubt this because information on pre-K quality is often weak. Furthermore, many property buyers and sellers may not sufficiently understand the effects of pre-K quality on future earnings of former child participants. Therefore, to the extent that universal pre-K currently has a property value effect, it is probably mostly indirect, through effects on elementary test scores. Elementary test scores are more widely known by prospective home buyers. Parents do believe that such test scores are related to future life prospects for their children.

However, these valuations of universal pre-K by property buyers and sellers may potentially be affected by pre-K advocates. Pre-K advocates might consider disseminating better information for prospective homeowners on the quality, availability, and cost of pre-K in different states and metropolitan areas. Some beginning attempts to provide such information include the *State of Preschool Yearbook* by the National Institute for Early Education Research.

Pre-K advocates might also consider further measures to inform the public about the future earnings effects of universal pre-K education. A fuller understanding of these effects might boost household valuations of these earnings effects.

Finally, public relations efforts that stress how children are affected by early childhood programs might alter parental discounting of these effects. Stressing the effects on children in public discourse may reduce parental discounting of such effects.

The rationale for increasing parental valuations of pre-K's effects is in part to improve parental choice options by providing better information. But public relations efforts to increase parental valuations will also change the incentives facing state policymakers. If pre-K quality, availability, and cost become more salient to prospective home buyers, the effects of these factors on property values and property tax revenues will increase. This will increase the attractiveness of high-quality universal pre-K to state and local policymakers who wish to boost their state or local area in the short run. Short-run boosts in property values and property tax revenues may be more of an incentive to policymakers than long-run boosts to earnings. As I will discuss in Chapter 13, property value effects have been used as an argument by past grassroots American movements to expand education.

One trade-off with increased capitalization is that it transfers some of the benefits of universal pre-K education to property owners. This will be further discussed in the chapter on distributional effects (Chapter 8).

Capitalization effects are relevant when universal pre-K is analyzed from a state perspective. These capitalization effects reflect the relative attractiveness of a given state, versus other states, due to the state's offering high-quality universal pre-K. At the national level, we would not expect universal pre-K to lead to capitalization effects. Chapter 10 further considers the national perspective.

INCREASING SHORT-TERM BENEFITS: INCORPORATING PARENTAL EMPLOYMENT PROGRAMS INTO EARLY CHILDHOOD PROGRAMS

The short-run benefits of early childhood programs may also be increased by program modifications. What program components might be added to significantly increase short-run benefits?

It seems reasonable to focus on program add-ons that might have some synergy with the early childhood programs. Otherwise, short-run benefits could be increased by adding any arbitrary program X that has a high ratio of short-run benefits to costs. But if program X's social returns do not depend on the existence of the early childhood programs, and vice versa, then it is unclear why we would consider the early childhood programs plus program X as a package. For example, perhaps some antipollution regulation would have large short-run benefits relative to costs. But it would seem strange to claim that we have "solved" the problem of delayed benefits to early childhood programs by adding an antipollution regulation to the policy package.

One program add-on that might have some synergy with early childhood programs is an employment and training program for the parents of the child participants. It seems possible that early childhood programs that provide some free child care, such as universal pre-K and the Abecedarian program, might make employment and training services for the parents more effective.

Employment and training services for parents may provide more short-run economic development benefits than are provided by early childhood programs. Increases in parental employment and wages will occur immediately, while improvements for former child participants have to wait until the children grow up.

What are plausible returns to high-quality employment and training programs for the parents of the child participants in universal pre-K or the Abecedarian program? How might adding on parental employment and training programs affect the short-run benefits from an early childhood program package?

We don't know the answer. There has not been much experimentation to explore the social returns to adding parental employment programs to early childhood programs.

I wanted to gauge the potential for adding on parental programs. To do so, I considered what would happen if the add-on parental employment program had a rate of return that matched the highest rates of return that have been reliably estimated for employment and training programs. I consider two scenarios. First, I consider an add-on parental job-training program that matched the highest rates of return that have been estimated for federally run job training programs. Second, I consider an add-on program that matched the highest rates of return that have been estimated for state or locally run job training programs.

For the first scenario, I assumed the parental employment and training program had returns as high as the estimated effects of Job Training Partnership Act (JTPA) programs on disadvantaged adults. JTPA was the main federally funded job training program from 1982 to 1998. It was evaluated by a random assignment experiment in the late 1980s and early 1990s.

The random assignment experiment indicated that JTPA had extremely high rates of return for adults. The experiment indicated modest effects per trainee on average earnings. Annual earnings for trainees increased by over $1,200 (Friedlander, Greenberg, and Robins [1997], updated to 2007 dollars). The evidence suggests that these earnings increases persisted without much change for at least five years after training (GAO 1996).[22] These increased earnings were achieved at a cost per adult trainee of about $2,000 for women and $1,400 for men. The real rate of return to society from JTPA training for adults exceeds 70 percent per year under any reasonable assumptions (Friedlander, Greenberg, and Robins 1997).

Although these rates of return to JTPA are high, the annual earnings effects are modest, at only $1,200. Why not consider a training program that had more dramatic effects on annual earnings than $1,200? For federally funded job training programs, research does not find any training programs that have persistent annual earnings effects for broad groups that exceed the $1,000 to $2,000 range (Bartik 2001, Chap. 4). Furthermore, until recently, most of the job training research literature has not found job training programs with annual earnings effects that exceed the $1,000 to $2,000 range. This research literature finds that the annual earnings effects for training programs, once they exceed some minimum threshold for services per trainee, do not significantly increase with program spending per trainee (Greenberg, Michalopoulos, and Robins 2003).

Recently, however, there have been some estimates suggesting that job training programs may have annual earnings effects that are greater, at least for some job training programs that are state or locally directed, and are somewhat higher-cost. Hollenbeck and Huang (2006, 2008) have estimated annual earnings effects of some state and locally directed job training programs that exceed $4,000 annually. These large annual earnings effects are sometimes persistent.

These recent estimates are less rigorously estimated in that they are not derived from random assignment experiments. Instead, the estimates are derived by estimating the postprogram earnings experiences of participants in job training programs with nonparticipants who are matched on their preprogram characteristics and earnings. Although this matching eliminates observed preprogram characteristics and earnings as an explanation of the postprogram earnings differences, there could also be unobserved preprogram differences between program participants and nonparticipants that might explain the differences. However, it is noteworthy that Hollenbeck and Huang's estimates for federally funded job training programs are similar to previous estimates for federally funded job training programs that use experimental methods. Hollenbeck's estimates for annual earnings effects for programs under the Workforce Investment Act (WIA), the successor program to JTPA, seem roughly consistent with the experimental estimates for JTPA. This similarity adds some credibility that such nonexperimental methods may be reliable in this context.

One possible explanation for these higher earnings effects in Hollenbeck and Huang's research is that training programs may be better directed by state and local governments than by the federal government. Prior research suggests that job training programs may be more effective if they work closely with local employers (Bartik 2001, Chap. 4). Local employers can help identify higher-wage jobs that have strong local growth and a shortage of available workers with suitable skills. Local employers can also help identify what job skills are best addressed by training. Perhaps greater state and local discretion will allow for sufficient flexibility to facilitate better partnerships with local employers. Federally funded job training programs, such as JTPA and WIA, allow for state and local administration. However, federal rules may inhibit the flexibility that is needed to work with local employers to meet local needs.

For the second scenario, I assumed that the add-on parental job training program had annual earnings effects similar to those estimated by Hollenbeck and Huang for community college job prep programs in the state of Washington. These community college programs provide training for individuals that leads directly to jobs, rather than to transfer to a four-year college or university. Hollenbeck and Huang estimate annual earnings effects of $4,758 as of three quarters after exiting training, and $3,962 as of three years after exiting training.[23]

These large annual earnings effects come at considerable program cost. The estimated additional community college tuition costs, plus state subsidized costs that are not part of tuition, amount to $11,231 per trainee (Hollenbeck and Huang [2006, p. 179], updated to 2007 dollars). The costs of this type of training are over $9,000 greater than the average costs per trainee of most federally funded job training, such as the JTPA program. However, this $9,000 in extra costs pays off, because it increases annual earnings effects by over $2,500 (e.g., $3,962 − $1,200 for JPTA = $2,762). These extra earnings effects appear to be persistent, so these estimates suggest that the more expensive training investment is worth it.

Costs of this community college training program are so much greater because the program is more intense. The program modeled is assumed to last 1.9 years on average. During those 1.9 years, the program requires full-time attendance at the community college. In contrast, average costs for JTPA, WIA, and other federally run job "training programs" reflect that for many "trainees," the training provided is mostly job placement assistance and very short-term training.

I resimulated the economic development benefits and costs of universal pre-K and the Abecedarian program with these two types of add-on training programs for parents. In one simulation, I assumed that the program had costs per trainee and earnings effects per trainee that were similar to the JTPA program's effects for adult women.[24] In the second scenario, I assumed that the add-on program had costs and earnings effects per trainee that were similar to the state of Washington's community college job prep programs.[25] I assumed that 75 percent of the families involved with the Abecedarian program would enroll in training, as the Abecedarian program targets disadvantaged families. I assumed that 75 percent of the "high-risk" families enrolled in universal pre-K would enroll in training, along with 25 percent of "medium-risk" families. This assumption means that 26.3 percent of all families in universal pre-K would enroll in training. In calculating increased earnings of state residents, I make my usual adjustments to include only survivors who stay in the state, and to adjust for labor market displacement.

Figures 7.5 and 7.6 show the annual ratio of economic development benefits to costs for universal pre-K education and the Abecedarian program with these two types of adult training add-ons. For comparison, the figures also show the annual ratios without the adult training add-ons.[26]

As shown in Figure 7.5, adding training to universal pre-K has the potential for significantly improving the short-term and medium-term economic development benefits of pre-K. The original program has annual economic development benefits that hover at about 15–23 percent of costs for the first 13 years or so after the program is initiated. With the add-on adult training, economic development benefits steadily increase during those first 13 years. This package of pre-K and adult job training yields much bigger benefits sooner. For example, five years after the original program is initiated (the year 2016), annual economic development benefits are only 16 percent of annual costs. With the add-on of JTPA-style training, by five years after program initiation, annual economic development benefits are 35 percent of annual costs, or twice as great. With the add-on community college job preparation training, by five years after program initiation, annual economic development benefits are 47 percent of annual costs. Annual economic development benefits of the original program did not exceed annual costs until 24 years after the program's start. With the JTPA-style training add-on, annual economic development benefits exceed costs after 18 years— six years earlier. With the community college job preparation training, annual economic development benefits exceed costs after 15 years.[27]

The potential for greater short-term ratios of benefits to costs is limited in a universal program because of the assumption that training benefits will be restricted to disadvantaged families. A more targeted pre-K program would have its short-term benefits-to-cost ratio boosted more by adult training add-ons. Alternatively, a training program that had high returns to more advantaged workers could increase the short-term benefits-to-cost ratio.

**Figure 7.5 Ratio of Annual State Economic Development Benefits to
Program Costs, Universal Pre-K Education, with Two Types
of Adult Training Components, Compared to Similar Ratio
without a Training Component**

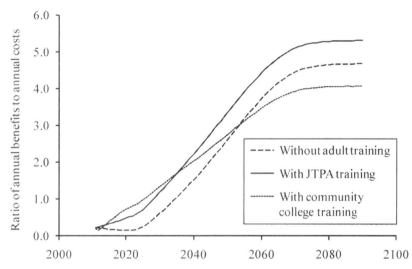

NOTE: Methodology is explained in chapter text and Appendix 7D. Economic development benefits are increases in earnings of state residents. The figure shows how
the ratio of these annual economic development benefits to costs, for universal pre-
K education, changes when either of two types of adult job training is added to the
pre-K program. All these calculations are for a permanent universal pre-K program,
with any adult job training add-ons also being permanent, that starts in 2011. As is
discussed in the text, what is particularly important is how these add-on training programs affect short-run ratios of benefits to costs.

As Figure 7.6 shows, adding adult training to the Abecedarian program does not much affect the time pattern of the ratio of benefits to
costs.[28] The lack of effect reflects the large costs of the Abecedarian
program. The modest earnings benefits provided by adult training do
not loom large compared to the large costs per child participant in the
Abecedarian program.[29] In addition, the Abecedarian program already
has considerable short-term benefits for parents, even without adult
training add-ons.

These potential effects of short-term training are hypothetical. It
would seem important to do some demonstration projects and experi-

Figure 7.6 Ratio of Annual State Economic Development Benefits to Program Costs, Abecedarian Program, with Two Alternative Adult Training Components, Compared to Similar Ratio without a Training Component

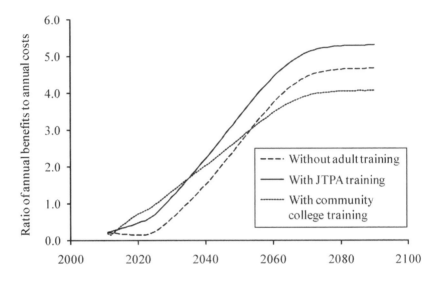

NOTE: Methodology is explained in chapter text and Appendix 7D. Economic development benefits are increases in earnings of state residents. The figure shows how the ratio of these annual economic development benefits to costs, for the Abecedarian program, changes when either of two types of adult job training is added to the program. All these calculations are for a permanent Abecedarian program, with any adult job training add-ons also being permanent, that starts in 2011. As is discussed in the text, what is particularly important is how these add-on training programs affect short-run ratios of benefits to costs.

mentation with adding training and employment services for adults to early childhood programs.

It is particularly important to do such experimentation because there may be synergies between early childhood programs and adult training and employment programs. High-quality early childhood services may increase the return to adult training and employment programs by providing free child care and peace of mind to parents. Improved parental employment and earnings may increase the rate of return to early childhood programs. Higher family income may reduce stresses of poverty that harm child development and adult outcomes for those children. For example, research by Duncan, Kalil, and Ziol-Guest (2008) suggests that among families with less than $25,000 in annual income, increasing a family's income by $1,000 per year increases the future earnings of children in that family by 6 percent.[30] The calculations so far do not reflect these potential synergies, which may be important.

To gauge the potential importance of such synergies, I reestimated the economic development benefits from the adult training add-ons to the Abecedarian program, but this time including possible effects of adult training programs on the earnings of their children. I used Duncan, Kalil, and Ziol-Guest's estimates to do this reestimation. Including effects on the children of trainees increased the net present value of benefits of the JTPA-style training program by 22 percent. Including children's effects increased the benefits of the community college training program by 30 percent.[31] The benefit-cost analysis of adult job training programs is significantly altered by considering effects on children.[32]

It should be an important research priority to investigate the potential for programs that integrate services to children with services to their parents.

CONCLUSION

The economic development benefits from high-quality early childhood programs are mostly long-term. This is a problem for policymakers with short time horizons. What can be done about this problem?

Based on this chapter, a variety of solutions seem possible:

- Do calculations that demonstrate the likely savings in special education costs from early childhood programs.

- Establish systems of regularly rating the scope, quality, and costs of state and local pre-K education programs in a comparable way. Promote these quality rating systems to potential property owners. Also, promote the importance of pre-K education to potential property owners. Such rating systems and promotion efforts would improve family awareness of the importance and quality of preschool. As a result, high-quality universal pre-K programs would be more likely to increase property values in the short run.

- Do demonstration projects and experiments that add adult employment and training programs to early childhood programs. See what works and what doesn't work, and what potential synergies there are in combining such efforts.

- If policymakers are reluctant to raise taxes to improve early childhood programs, urge policymakers to finance such programs with reductions in other government spending that has lower rates of return.

- Once the current U.S. financial crisis has passed, explore options such as tax increment financing to fund expansion of high-quality early childhood programs.

Of all these options, I believe there are two options that offer the most promise: 1) promoting capitalization benefits and 2) experimenting with combining early childhood programs with programs for parents. We can increase capitalization by increasing information on pre-K education programs. This option directly addresses the central problem: policymakers undervalue the most important benefits of universal pre-K, the future benefits for former child participants. If parents have sufficient information that these benefits for children are reflected in property valuations, then these future benefits become visible to policymakers in the short run. Furthermore, greater parent knowledge and valuation of pre-K education is also likely to affect how parents vote. Such a change in voting behavior would certainly affect state policymakers. Finally, a sustained effort to promote better information on pre-K across states is relatively cheap compared to its potential benefits.

Comprehensive programs that include assistance to parents directly increase short-term benefits. We may find that such comprehensive programs offer higher returns. Early childhood programs may increase the rate of return of adult job training programs, and adult job training programs may increase the rate of return of early childhood programs. Experimentation should explore such possibilities. But even if these synergies are modest, a comprehensive program will have greater short-term benefits relative to costs.

This chapter has focused on the distribution of the benefits of early childhood programs over time. The next chapter focuses on the distribution of the benefits of early childhood programs and business incentive programs across different income groups.

Notes

1. Savings and investment issues may complicate the discussion. Suppose the policy affects savings and investment flows. Suppose further that the social value of a dollar of savings or investment exceeds the social value of a dollar of consumption. Under these assumptions, we need to determine some shadow prices of savings and investment to adjust the different dollar flows to consumption equivalents.

   The financing of the policy's costs may affect savings and investment in several ways. The financing may affect incomes, which will affect savings. Borrowing may affect interest rates. Extra taxes may affect the returns on savings and investment.

   But the benefits of the project may also affect savings and investment in several ways. Project benefits may also affect incomes. The project may also create a fiscal surplus. This may reduce borrowing's burden on interest rates, or affect the need for taxes that distort the returns on savings and investment.

   The shadow price of savings and investment may exceed 1 because of tax wedges between the private before-tax return on investment and the private after-tax return on savings. In addition, the shadow price of savings and investment may exceed 1 because of the social return on investment's exceeding the private before-tax return on investment. For example, if there are agglomeration economies, then investment may have external benefits for the economy.

   As mentioned in Chapter 4, I avoid in this book taking account of these long-run dynamic effects of changes in savings and investment. I avoid these dynamic investment effects because I think there is no consensus among economists on the magnitude of such effects. Dynamic investment effects can lead to unbounded effects of policies under certain assumptions, but not under other also plausible assumptions. Dickens and his coauthors have models of early childhood programs that incorporate dynamic investment effects (Dickens and Baschnagel 2008; Dickens, Sawhill, and Tebbs 2006).

2. Appendix 7A provides a more technical discussion. This includes an equation for the discount rate. It also includes discussing plausible values in that equation. Like all the appendices, Appendix 7A is available from the Upjohn Institute Web site.

3. Under Michigan's school finance law, this diversion would not significantly reduce revenue for the local schools or other governmental units in the area that approved the Promise Zone. The state education property tax is paid into the state School Aid Fund. Other state revenues are also paid into the state School Aid Fund. These School Aid Fund revenues are used to provide sufficient aid to each school district to make up the difference between capped local property taxes for schools and a largely state-determined foundation grant per student. This foundation grant per student constitutes essentially all local school district general operating revenue. A Promise Zone would reduce overall revenue going into the state School Aid Fund. This would tend to reduce overall foundation grants per student, unless state policy offsets this loss of revenue. However, the consequence of one Promise Zone for the foundation grant per student would be quite small. Therefore, each

Promise Zone has very little impact on the operating revenue per student of its own school district. But if many Promise Zones are designated, the program as a whole might significantly reduce K–12 school funding in Michigan.

4. This ratio compares the Abecedarian control group to the entire Abecedarian treatment group. Ramey et al. (2000) point out that the Abecedarian group that only received services prior to kindergarten, without extra K–12 support services, only had a special education services receipt rate of 12 percent. They argue that the extra K–12 services may have increased the recognition of special education service needs. However, the group that received only services prior to kindergarten has a sample size of 23. Therefore, to be conservative, I decided to use the comparison between the overall Abecedarian treatment group and the control group to calculate the special education cost savings for the Abecedarian program.

5. The simulation was done in the following way: I assumed that the reduced special education percentage due to universal pre-K education would be 2.3 percent of all participants. This is 23 percent of the approximately 10 percent effect found in the Chicago Child-Parent Center (CPC) program. This same 23 percent factor was used to scale back the CPC effects for all earnings effects of the program, and reflects the assumption that a universal program will have somewhat smaller effects on more-middle-class children and on children who would have attended pre-K even without the universal program.

For the Abecedarian program, I assumed that special education assignments would be reduced by 23 percent of all participants. This 23 percent has nothing to do with the CPC scale-back factor. The Abecedarian 23 percent is based on experimental evaluations of the Abecedarian program that show a reduction in special education assignments from 48 percent in the control group to 25 percent in the treatment group.

Increased special education costs were initially assumed to be $10,054 in 2007 dollars. This is based on Parrish et al. (2004, Part II) figures on special education costs for 1999–2000 of $8,080 (p. 22). These special ed costs are updated to 2007 dollars using the CPI-U. I assume that only 10 percent of special education costs are paid by the federal government and 90 percent by state and local governments. This seems consistent with the figures in Parrish et al. I only count as cost savings the state and local cost savings, as in this book I am focusing on the state perspective.

It is assumed that the cost savings from reduced special education assignments accrue for all 13 years from kindergarten through twelfth grade. This implies that special education cost savings for a given cohort of early childhood participants begin accruing one year after the universal pre-K program begins, and five years after the Abecedarian program begins. For each cohort, it is assumed that special education costs after 2011 increase in real terms by 1.2 percent a year, which is this simulation model's assumption about average real-wage increases. As in the regular simulation models, each subsequent cohort is assumed to be 0.3 percent bigger, as this is the population growth assumption of these models. In addition, each subsequent cohort is assumed to have 1.2 percent higher special education costs per student, to reflect wage growth. These assumptions about increasing real special education cost trends are modest, given that data from Parrish et al. suggest that special education costs have increased in real terms by an average of 1.6 percent a year from 1977–1978 to 1999–2000.

The simulations also allowed for reduced balanced-budget multiplier effects from the reduced special education spending. This reduces economic development benefits. However, this reduction in benefits is less than the reduction in net costs. Reduced balanced-budget multiplier effects were calculated the same way balanced-budget multiplier effects were calculated for the original simulations.

6. Appendix 7B presents the numbers behind these figures.

7. This comes from the scenario in Krueger where the social discount rate is 3 percent and the annual productivity growth rate is 1 percent. I use the same social discount rate and a wage growth rate of 1.2 percent. Under Krueger's assumptions, the present value cost of this intervention per student is $7,660 in 1998 dollars, and the present value of future earnings benefits is $21,667 (Krueger 2003, Table 5, p. F56). The resulting ratio of the present value of benefits to the present value of costs is 2.83.

8. Krueger estimates that earnings will go up by 3.2 percent because of smaller class sizes. These smaller class sizes require a 47 percent increase (e.g., 22 over 15 = 1.47) in funding. This estimate assumes that when class sizes are lower, all elements of per-pupil spending must increase proportionately, not just the ratio of teachers to students. The average experimental student in the Tennessee Class Size Study experienced these smaller class sizes for 2.3 years. If we divide 3.2 percent by the product of 47 percent and 2.3 years, we get an earnings effect of 0.0296 percent for a 1 percent change in spending for one year of a student's K–12 experience.

9. This is based on the estimates given in Chapter 4 for the costs of implementing universal pre-K. In 2007 dollars, this is estimated to have a net cost nationally of $14.3 billion. This figure is assumed to apply to the 2009–2010 school year. According to the Digest of Education Statistics, total public K–12 operating spending in the 2004–2005 school year was $424.6 billion. Updating to year 2007 prices yields a cost of $459.2 billion. According to projections from the Institute of Education Statistics, real education spending for public elementary and secondary schools is expected to increase by 32 percent from 2004–2005 to 2017–2018, which is an increase of 2.16 percent per year. Applying this annual rate of increase, we get projected K–12 spending for the 2009–2010 school year of $510.9 billion. Pre-K spending of $14.3 billion divided by $510.9 billion is 2.8 percent.

10. The actual simulation calculation is slightly more complicated. Because I am focusing on state residents and state earnings, I adjust these impacts down slightly to account for in- or out-migration during the K–12 school years. Therefore, of students leaving the K–12 school system at age 18, not everyone will have experienced their entire K–12 education in the state that is reducing its K–12 spending by 2.8 percent. This consideration lowers the average effect on earnings after 13 years from 1.08 percent to 0.96 percent.

11. I also have to make assumptions about how many public school students will annually exit the public school system through graduating or dropping out. For

graduates, I start with the figures on public school graduates for 2005–2006 from the Digest of Education Statistics. For dropouts, I use Heckman's figure that the true four-year graduation rate is 77 percent (Heckman and LaFontaine 2007). (Reported high school dropout rates are probably too low.) I calculate from this figure an annual dropout rate. I apply this dropout rate to total public high school enrollment in the fall of 2005 to get the number of dropouts exiting the high schools at that time. These 2005–2006 figures for annual numbers of both graduates and dropouts are adjusted to 2009 by using projections that public school graduates will grow at 0.59 percent per year (*Projections of Education Statistics to 2017* report by Hussar and Bailey [2008]). These 2009 figures are compatible with the 2009 starting date for the original pre-K projections. For 2011 starting numbers, I assume that all effects are the same percentage of total earnings.

12. The long-run positive effects of universal pre-K are a 1.241 percent boost to earnings. The long-run negative effects of reduced K–12 spending in this scenario are −0.495 percent. The ratio of this negative effect to the positive effect is 0.40.

13. This is my calculation using this simulation. I assumed a cutback in K–12 spending of 2.8 percent, and calculated the present value of state earnings losses versus the savings in K–12 program costs. The resulting ratio of the present value of state earnings losses to the present value of savings in K–12 program costs is −1.218.

14. In the model of this developed by Roback (1982) and used by many subsequent researchers, increased household amenities at the interstate or intermetropolitan level could also in theory be reflected in lower wages. However, as was pointed out in Bartik and Smith (1987), for an increase in an amenity that is just valued by households and not businesses, the percentage increase in property values should be much greater than the percentage reduction in wages. Labor is a much larger share of business costs than land, and therefore only very small reductions in wages are compatible with keeping profits the same after an increase in land prices. Furthermore, it could be argued that business will also place some direct value on the "amenity" of better early childhood programs. Any direct benefit to businesses from this amenity will further drive up both property values and wages.

15. These remarks are somewhat speculative. We really don't know the true incidence of many tax and spending programs at the state and local level. Economists seem to believe that higher property taxes will be capitalized into lower property values. There is less agreement about what will happen because of other changes in state and local taxes and spending. The text passage suggests that the incidence may depend in part on how many households mentally classify a particular tax or service as being tied to property ownership. Property taxes are clearly tied to property ownership. By longstanding tradition, the quality of public education is also tied to where a household lives, and so is mentally considered to be part of the property purchase. The question is whether households think of early childhood programs as being tied to property ownership. The issue that this section of the chapter explores is whether such a connection either naturally is made (through effects of early childhood programs on school test scores) or can be made through the right marketing of pre-K's benefits.

16. This is based upon estimates from the Chicago Child-Parent Center program that

the program increased participant average test scores in third, fourth, and fifth grades by an average effect size of 0.22 (Reynolds 1995). I assume, as was done in the simulation, that the effects of a universal pre-K program will be only 23 percent of the effects of a program (such as CPC) that is targeted. On the other hand, peer effects will multiply effects by 1.54 times the raw effects. Therefore, the effects on average test scores are $0.08 = 0.22 \times 0.23 \times 1.54$.

17. This statement principally relies on studies by Black (1999); Bayer, Ferreira, and McMillan (2007); and Kane, Riegg, and Staiger (2006). Black found that an increase of one standard deviation in across-school average test scores increased property values by 2.2 percent. Based on studies of test score variation by Bloom (2006) and Kane, Riegg, and Staiger, a one-standard-deviation difference in cross-student test scores is probably between two and five times the standard deviation in cross-school test scores. So Black's numbers imply that a change in average test scores of one standard deviation will increase property values by 4 to 11 percent. Bayer, Ferreira, and McMillan find that an increase in average school test scores of one standard deviation increased property values by 1.8 percent. Multiplying by two to five yields an effect of an increase in average test scores of one standard deviation of 4 to 9 percent. However, Bayer, Ferreira, and McMillan also find effects that are perhaps twice as great if one allows for test scores changing demographic composition of school neighborhoods. It could be argued that the long-run effect of school test-score changes should include such adjustments, which would raise the test score effects on property values to 8 to 18 percent. Finally, Kane, Riegg, and Staiger concluded that an increase in average school test scores of one standard deviation across students increased property values by about 10 percent. Therefore, an effect with a range of 5 to 10 percent seems reasonable.

18. This is based on figures from the Federal Reserve Board's (2009) Flow of Funds report indicating that residential property values in the United States as of the fourth quarter of 2008 totaled 23.1 trillion dollars. (This sums the residential real estate values of the household sector and the noncorporate sector.) Multiplying this by the percentage effects on property values, converting to 2007 dollars, and comparing this figure to the estimated national cost of universal pre-K in 2007 dollars of $14.3 billion, I get the ratio cited in the text.

19. This uses a figure from the Tax Policy Center that typical property tax rates in the United States are 1.33 percent of property value (Yilmaz et al. 2006).

20. I take the total flow of earnings in the state due to universal pre-K, including effects on parents, children, and spending effects. These effects are calculated including displacement effects. I then add in the flow of earnings for former child participants who leave the state. For these leavers, I do not adjust for displacement. The assumption is that prospective property buyers in the state will consider the net effect on their earnings if they stay in the state, which will include displacement effects, and also consider the net effect on their earnings if they leave the state, which will not include displacement effects because the state is assumed to be small relative to the nation.

21. Why are property value effects so much higher relative to annual program costs than the ratio of the present value of benefits to costs? This largely occurs because

216 Bartik

property value effects take into account the entire present value of future benefits, and annual program costs represent just one year's costs. As a result, property value effects can plausibly be tens or hundreds of times the annual program costs of universal pre-K.

22. This is not how GAO spun the results. GAO emphasized that results became statistically insignificant some years after training. However, the results also indicated that results did not statistically significantly change over time. In any job training experiment, one would expect training effect estimates to become more imprecise with time. With more time since training, there are more random shocks to earnings that increase imprecision.

23. These figures take the difference-in-difference, regression-adjusted estimates from Hollenbeck and Huang (2006, Table 6.5, p. 68), adjust these quarterly figures to annual figures, and then use the CPI to adjust these earnings effects to 2007 dollars rather than first quarter 2005 dollars.

24. This add-on JTPA-style program, by itself, had a ratio of the present value of benefits to the present value of costs of 8.78. These benefits are mostly earnings benefits but also include some balanced budget multiplier effects (0.04 out of the 8.78). These benefits only count state economic development benefits, so they adjust downward for out-migration and displacement. These adjustments are similar to those made in Chapter 4 for early childhood programs.

25. This community college program by itself had a ratio of the present value of benefits to costs of 2.63. These benefits are mostly earnings benefits but also include some balanced budget multiplier effects (0.04 out of the 2.63). These benefits only count state economic development benefits, so they adjust downward for out-migration and displacement. These adjustments are similar to those made in Chapter 4 for early childhood programs.

26. The numbers behind the figures are in Appendix 7C.

27. The ratio of the present value of benefits to costs improves from 2.78 to 3.35 with the add-on of a JTPA-style training program. The ratio of the present value of benefits to costs decreases somewhat from 2.78 to 2.72 with the add-on of a community college job preparation program. The annual costs of the add-on JTPA training program are initially about $1.5 billion. The annual costs of the add-on community college job prep training program are initially about $8.6 billion.

28. The ratio of the present value of economic development benefits to the present value of program costs increases from 2.25 to 2.37 with the add-on of a JTPA-style adult training program, and increases from 2.25 to 2.28 with the add-on of a community college job preparation program. The annual costs of the add-on programs are somewhat lower than for universal pre-K because the number of assumed Abecedarian participants is lower than for universal pre-K, owing to the more targeted nature of the Abecedarian program. The annual costs of the add-on JTPA program are initially about $0.7 billion. The annual costs of the add-on community college job prep training program are initially about $4.1 billion.

29. The present value of costs for the add-on JTPA program are about 2 percent of Abecedarian's high costs, but are about 10 percent of costs for the cheaper universal pre-K program. The much more expensive add-on community college job prep

program has costs that are about 10 percent of Abecedarian's costs but 59 percent of costs of the universal pre-K program. Therefore, these add-on programs can sway the short-term and long-term rates of return of universal pre-K much more readily than they can sway the returns to the Abecedarian program.

30. This calculation uses the regression coefficients from Appendix Table 3 in Duncan, Kalil, and Ziol-Guest (2008). I use the coefficient of 0.584 in predicting ln(earnings) using income measured in $10,000 units, and then translate this effect on ln(earnings) into an actual percentage effect.

31. To do these calculations, I relied on Duncan, Kalil, and Ziol-Guest's analysis that a $4,326 increase in average family earnings for low-income families, while children are ages 0–5, will increase adult earnings at ages 25–37 by an annual average of $4,919. I adjusted this effect so that it applied to age 31, and I assumed that the dollar effect varied by age from ages 20 to 79 in the same way as did control-group female earnings in the database used to estimate the adult earnings effects of the Abecedarian program. As discussed in appendices to Chapter 4, these data are ultimately derived from CPS data on black females. Adult earning effects were only calculated from ages 20 to 79. I calculated effects on average earnings when the child is ages 0–5 by using figures for the JTPA and community college program's effects from the time the training starts until five years later. These figures are adjusted downward because of out-migration and displacement. Effects on children when they grow up are also adjusted downward for migration out of the state, death rates, and displacement. Thus, these calculations reflect state economic development benefits, not national economic benefits. Total earnings effects for the child, adjusted for displacement, from ages 20 to 79, are then discounted using a 3 percent discount rate back to age equals zero, when the training is supposed to start. The resulting discounted present value of earnings effects on the children of adult trainees, for the JTPA-style training program, is 2.60 times the program's costs. The discounted present value of earnings effects on the children of adult trainees, for the community college training program, is 1.14 times the program's costs. Thus, either of these programs passes a benefit-cost test based solely on its indirect effects on the earnings of the children of trainees.

32. The overall benefit-cost picture for the Abecedarian program is improved, but not by much, because of the high costs of the program. The ratio of benefits to costs for the Abecedarian program was originally 2.25. With the benefits of add-on adult training for both adults and their children, the ratio of benefits to costs with a JTPA-style add-on increases to 2.41. With a community college job prep add-on, the ratio of benefits to costs increases to 2.39.

I should also point out that although the Abecedarian program also directly increases the earnings of the parents of the child participants, the effects of this parental earnings increase on the Abecedarian child participants, when they enter the labor market, are already captured by the baseline estimates.

Similar calculations do not make as much sense for universal pre-K. An intervention with parents when their children are age four will not substantially affect average earnings from birth to age five. In the Duncan, Kalil, and Ziol-Guest estimates, family earnings when the child is age six and over do not have much effect upon the child's future adult earnings.

8
Who Benefits?

Distributional Effects of Early Childhood Programs and Business Incentives, and Their Implications for Policy

How do early childhood programs affect the poor, the middle class, and the rich? The answer to this question is important for several reasons.

First, effects on different income groups may change these programs' social benefits. In this discussion, I assume that programs that tilt benefits toward the poor are more socially desirable. Policymakers, policy analysts, and voters may favor such a tilt because of special concern for the poor. Alternatively, policymakers, policy analysts, and voters may be concerned with making the income distribution more equal. A more equal income distribution may increase the number of people who can meet social standards for being a respectable member of society. Concern over the income distribution may be greater at present because over the last 30 years the U.S. income distribution has become more unequal. To address concerns about the poor, we need information on whether early childhood programs significantly affect the incomes of the poor. To address concerns about the income distribution, we need information about how the effects on the poor compare with effects on other income groups.[1]

Second, how early childhood programs affect various income groups may influence who will provide these programs with political support. An income group's support for a program may depend on what the program implies in taxes and benefits for that group. Assessing patterns of political support requires comparing the program's benefits with taxes for different income groups. Adopting and sustaining a program requires political support that is sufficiently powerful.

Third, how a program affects different income groups may influence program design. For early childhood programs, one important design issue is whether these programs should be targeted at children in lower

219

income groups, or whether services should be universally available to all children. This is most prominently an issue for pre-K education programs. The targeting versus universal service debate is advanced by looking at specific numbers for how programs benefit different income groups under different designs.

To frame this chapter's discussion, I begin with arguments for targeting pre-K education at the poor versus universalizing pre-K education. I then consider the effects on different income groups of business incentives. The effects of business incentives provide a baseline for considering the income distribution effects of early childhood programs. I then go on to provide estimates of the income distribution effects of pre-K programs under various assumptions about program design and program effects. Finally, I consider the income distribution effects of other early childhood programs.

In this chapter, I show that under a variety of distributional assumptions, early childhood programs have net overall benefits that are progressively distributed. Business incentives are more likely to benefit all income groups, but they provide much less net benefit for the poor. Among early childhood programs, universal pre-K, which combines large benefits for the poor with broad benefits for all income groups, has economic and political advantages.

TARGETED PRE-K VERSUS UNIVERSAL PRE-K

Advocates for targeting pre-K education argue that policymakers should invest where returns are greatest. Targeting advocates perceive returns as being greatest for children from lower income families. Nobel Prize–winning economist James Heckman (2005) makes the following argument: "I think the evidence is very strong that family background is a major predictor of future behavior of children. So a disproportionate number of problem kids come from disadvantaged families. The simple economics of intervention therefore suggests that society should focus its investment where it's likely to have very high returns. Right now, that is the disadvantaged population . . . Functioning middle-class homes are producing healthy, productive kids . . . It is foolish to try to substitute for what the middle-class and upper-class parents are already doing" (p. 24).

Advocates for universal services make two arguments. The first is that even if pre-K's benefits are greater for the poor, pre-K may still have benefits for middle-class children that exceed its costs. Steven Barnett, codirector of the National Institute for Early Education Research (NIEER), argues that "if the development of children in higher-income families is taken as an indicator of what is optimal, then it is clear that not only children in poverty, but children at the median income are entering school far less prepared to succeed than they should be. Children at the median income are as far behind their peers from families in the top income quintile as children in poverty are behind their peers from middle-income families" (Barnett 2006).

Barnett (2006) admits that "the weight of the evidence seems to indicate that effects [of pre-K education] are somewhat smaller for children who are not economically disadvantaged. However, these effects are not trivial and are proportionately large enough that long-term economic benefits [of pre-K] for middle-income children could easily exceed costs."

The second argument is that universal programs are more politically feasible and sustainable than programs targeted at the poor. This argument has been made with great force by Harvard sociologist Theda Skocpol (1991):

> Rarely . . . do advocates of targeted benefits or specially tailored public support services face up to the problem of finding sustained political support for them . . . When U.S. antipoverty efforts have featured policies targeted on the poor alone, they have not been politically sustainable, and they have stigmatized and demeaned the poor . . . It seems highly unlikely that further redistributive benefits or intensive services targeted on the poor alone can succeed politically. We still live amidst the backlash against the War on Poverty and the Great Society . . . Instead of policies for the disadvantaged alone, targeting within universalism is the prescription for effective and politically sustainable policies to fight poverty in the United States. (pp. 414, 420, 434)

By "targeting within universalism," Skocpol means policies that provide disadvantaged groups with extra services within a program that has universal accessibility.

Targeted programs may lack the political support needed to be enacted or sustained. Even if the programs can be sustained, lack of political support may mean there is inadequate funding or political attention to maintain program quality. Steven Barnett restates the often-used phrase, "The truth is that programs for the poor are too often poor programs." Barnett (2006) argues that pre-K programs targeted at the poor too often do not follow the best program designs:

> The targeted programs provided to low-income children have never been closely modeled on those that produced the largest benefits. Preschool teachers in many targeted programs are required to have only a high school diploma. Even Head Start requires only half of its teachers to have a two-year college degree. Many state-funded preschool programs do not require college degrees. Looking at subsidized child care policy at both federal and state levels, there is little evidence of a commitment to anything more than warehousing young children. Preschool teachers are paid about half what public school teachers earn, and child care staff are even more poorly paid.

The counterargument is that universal programs are much more expensive. Providing expensive services to the affluent may be politically controversial. Heckman (2005) outlines the following argument which might be made against universal pre-K education:

> Unfortunately, in discussions of early childhood interventions, people often bundle political issues with economic issues. Part of the appeal of universal early childhood intervention is that it provides universal day care, so some groups favor universal early childhood education because it effectively subsidizes women's working. But bundling in this way also creates an opposition group saying, "Why should we subsidize affluent working women?" (p. 24)

Robert Greenstein, executive director of the Center on Budget and Policy Priorities, argues that the right kind of targeted programs for the poor can get political support. In contrast, universal programs may run into problems because of large costs. According to Greenstein (1991),

> the evidence . . . indicates that factors other than whether a program is universal or targeted have a significant bearing on the political prospects of social programs. Targeted programs, for example, are more likely to be strong politically when they serve low-income and moderate-income working families as well as the

very poor. They are also more likely to succeed when they are regarded as providing an earned benefit or are otherwise linked to work, when they are entitlement programs with federally prescribed and funded benefits, when they seem effective, and when they are not provided in the form of cash welfare assistance for young, able-bodied people who do not work.

Skocpol's principal conclusion, that those seeking to develop new anti-poverty policies should rely almost exclusively on universal approaches, seems weak on another account as well: it conflicts with current fiscal constraints. Advocates of new universal programs need to acknowledge the political difficulties posed by the large costs of such programs, just as advocates of targeted programs need to acknowledge the political problems inherent in spending tax dollars on a narrow segment of the population. (p. 438)

Whether targeted or universal programs are the better way to deal with poverty is a fascinating philosophical debate. However, numbers can provide greater content to the argument. I now provide some actual numbers for the income distribution effects of different programs. I begin with business incentives before going on to various designs of universal pre-K and other early childhood programs.

BUSINESS INCENTIVES: WHO BENEFITS

I begin by analyzing the income distribution effects of business incentives. This analysis serves as a baseline for analyzing the income distribution effects of early childhood programs. The analysis also introduces the concepts that will be used to analyze income distribution effects.

Unlike the early childhood programs, business incentive programs as I have defined them have no natural scale. My models assume that business incentive programs have similar ratios of earnings effects to costs at different scales. In the following simulations, I scale this permanent business incentive so that its cost, in present value terms, is the same as that of the modeled universal pre-K program. As it happens, such a scale is a lower-bound estimate of what state and local governments typically spend on discretionary tax incentives for businesses (as opposed to specialized business services).[2] Therefore, the effects reported can be interpreted as a lower-bound estimate of the likely effects of a typical state's tax incentives for business. An upper-bound estimate might be one-and-a-half times the effects I report here.

To analyze distributional effects, I consider the effects on different quintiles of the household income distribution (Table 8.1). Quintiles are defined by ranking all households in the United States by household income, then dividing the ranking into five parts.

The quintiles differ widely in their share of overall household income (row 1 of Table 8.1).[3] If each household in the United States had the same income, then each quintile would have 20 percent of total U.S. income. Instead, the lowest income quintile has only 3.4 percent of total household income, which implies that the average household income of this quintile is about one-sixth of the average household income for all U.S. households. In contrast, the highest income quintile has 49.7 percent of total household income. This implies that the average household income of this quintile is about two-and-a-half times the average household income for all U.S. households.

The simulations in this chapter report the effects of a particular program on the present value of household earnings or the present value of taxes. These figures are sometimes calculated as a percentage of the total present value of income for each household income quintile. This analysis thereby includes both immediate and long-term effects of each program on household income. All effects are included by discounting all future earnings, tax, and income flows at a 3 percent real discount rate.[4]

For each quintile, I calculated the estimated dollar effects of business incentives on the present value of household earnings, relative to the average dollar effects for the lowest income quintile. These figures are derived from estimates of how metropolitan income distributions are affected by increases in employment growth (Bartik 1994b).[5]

The dollar effect of business incentives on earnings tends to be lower for lower income quintiles, and higher for higher income quintiles (row 2 of Table 8.1). For example, the dollar effects of business incentives on the present value of earnings for the middle income quintile are a little more than twice the dollar effect on the lowest income quintile. The dollar effect on the highest income quintile is about three times the dollar effect on the lowest income quintile. Why is this the case? Busi-

Table 8.1 Distributional Effects of Business Incentives

Row		Income quintile					
		Lowest		Middle		Highest	Overall
		1	2	3	4	5	
1	Quintile % share of total household income	3.4	8.7	14.8	23.4	49.7	100
	Business incentive effects on:						
2	Relative dollar effects on earnings, disadvantaged group = 1	1.00	1.39	2.25	3.64	3.10	2.38
3	Earnings benefits as % of income	1.532	0.835	0.791	0.811	0.325	0.620
4	Tax costs as % of income	0.249	0.227	0.216	0.206	0.179	0.197
5	Net benefits as % of income	1.283	0.607	0.575	0.606	0.146	0.422
6	Ratio of earnings benefits to tax costs	6.15	3.67	3.66	3.95	1.82	3.14

NOTE: Dollar benefits per participant for each quintile are indexed to lowest income quintile equals 1. All figures for percentages of income report the present value of that item as percentages of the present value of income for the relevant group. Ratios report ratios of the present value of earnings benefits or net income benefit to the present value of tax costs for the relevant group. All present value calculations use 3 percent real discount rate. Overall earnings effects and tax costs come from the simulation model for business incentives of this book. Earnings are translated into income percentages using the labor share figures of Gordon (2009). Earnings effects are allocated across quintiles based on how income effects of labor demand increases are allocated across quintiles in Bartik (1994b). Tax costs are allocated across quintiles based on average quintile incidence of state and local taxes reported in McIntyre et al. (2003). More details are in text and endnotes to text.

ness incentives increase earnings by increasing demand for labor. How much a given income group can respond to this labor demand increase is influenced by its involvement with the labor market and its skill level. Lower income groups have a lower percentage of their income in earnings. Furthermore, they earn lower hourly wages, so a given increase in hours of work has smaller dollar effects. Therefore, an increase in labor demand increases earnings by less, in dollar terms, for lower income groups.

However, as a percentage of income, the effect of business incentives on earnings is much greater for lower income quintiles (row 3 of Table 8.1). For example, the percentage effect of incentives on earnings for the lowest income quintile is about twice the effect for the middle income quintile. The percentage effect on earnings for the lowest income quintile is almost five times the effect on earnings for the highest income quintile. Dollar effects of business incentives decline in lower income quintiles, but not as fast as income, so percentage effects increase in lower income quintiles. Because lower income quintiles have more hours per year of unemployment and nonparticipation in the labor force, there is more room for greater percentage effects on their incomes.

The earnings effects of this business incentive program must be compared to the program's effects the on taxes of each income group. From the previous analysis in Chapter 3, we have estimates of the costs of a business incentive program relative to its effects on earnings. We need to determine how to allocate these costs across different income quintiles. I use estimates from the Institute on Taxation and Economic Policy on the relative percentage burden of state and local taxes across income quintiles (McIntyre et al. 2003; Table 8.1, row 4).[6]

These estimates are consistent with the consensus among public finance economists that state and local tax burdens are distributed in a modestly regressive fashion. That is, state and local tax burdens tend to be a somewhat higher percentage of income for lower income quintiles.

From these estimates of percentage earnings benefits by quintile and percentage tax costs by quintile, I construct two statistics for each quintile to describe income distribution effects. These same two statistics will be constructed for early childhood programs as well. First, for each quintile I calculate the simple difference of earnings benefits minus tax costs (each as a percentage of income). This is the net percentage effect on the present value of income of each income quintile due to the program. Second, for each quintile I calculate the ratio of the present value of earnings effects of the program to the present value of its tax costs. This is the ratio for each quintile of what it pays for the program to what it gets—a type of benefit-cost ratio.

Both these statistics might play a role in whether a given income quintile would support a program. The first statistic gives a "bottom line" for each program in terms of net effects on income. The second statistic reveals whether the program returns much in effects compared to what each income quintile invests in the program.

Both of these statistics are only calculated for effects on state residents' earnings and income. The focus of this book is on economic effects for states. Therefore, these statistics are calculated to reflect the effects of business incentives (and later, of early childhood programs) on the income distribution of a state.

For business incentives, the net percentage effects on each income quintile are positive (Table 8.1, row 5). Furthermore, the ratio of net earnings benefits to net costs is considerably greater than 1 for each quintile (Table 8.1, row 6). Overall, each income quintile has good economic reasons to favor a high-quality business incentive program.

Why do business incentives benefit all income quintiles? First, as discussed in detail in Chapters 3 and 5, this high-quality business incentive program has overall benefits that substantially exceed costs, by a factor of more than three to one. Second, as outlined above, the benefits of stronger local economic growth tend to be spread quite broadly. Higher income quintiles actually gain more in dollar terms from local economic growth, even though they gain less in percentage terms. At the same time, the regressivity of the tax burden from these programs is insufficient to offset the progressive effect that local economic growth has in increasing the incomes of lower income quintiles by a greater percentage.

The income distribution effects of business incentive programs are modestly progressive.[7] Net percentage effects of the program on the lowest income quintile are slightly more than double those on the middle income quintile. Net percentage effects on the middle income quintile are about four times those on the highest income quintile. In terms of ratios, the ratio of earnings effects to costs is about 70 percent greater for the lowest income quintile than for the middle income quintile. The ratio of earnings benefits to costs is about twice as great for the middle income quintile compared to the highest income quintile.

However, the bottom line is that the net percentage effects of business incentives on the lowest income quintile are quite modest. The estimates suggest that a typical state's financial business incentives only raise the income of the lowest income quintile by about 1.3 percent. These programs are not going to dramatically raise the well-being of the poor.

Effects on the poor are modest because the lowest income groups have many labor market problems. Expanding overall labor demand only addresses one of the problems that low income groups have in the labor markets. Given the more limited involvement of lower income groups in the labor market, and given their lower wages, there are limits to how much expanded overall labor demand can do to help the poor.

More progressive distributional effects might be achieved by business incentives that target more labor demand at lower income groups. For example, business incentive programs might encourage assisted businesses to hire more of the local unemployed. As discussed in Chapter 5, greater hiring of the local unemployed can be encouraged through First Source programs coupled with customized job training. Business incentives may also be provided for hiring the local unemployed, such as in Minnesota's MEED (Minnesota Employment and Economic Development) program.

Business incentives could be made more progressive. However, the progressivity of boosts to labor demand is limited by how much such programs can change the job skills of the disadvantaged. Customized job training programs can increase job skills. Getting more job experience through greater labor demand can increase job skills. However, larger changes in skills may require human capital programs that directly focus on skills development. Adding on human capital components to business incentives may have more limited effects on job skills.

Greater help for the labor market problems of the poor requires greater changes in their skills. This is probably most appropriately addressed through human capital programs. Early childhood programs are human capital programs that try to intervene early, when skills are thought to be the most malleable.

PREKINDERGARTEN (PRE-K) EDUCATION: SPECULATION ABOUT POSSIBLE DISTRIBUTIONAL BENEFITS

The challenge in assessing the distributional effects of pre-K education is that there is no direct evidence. The best studies, such as those of Perry Preschool and the Chicago Child-Parent Centers, focus on the long-run effects on children from disadvantaged families. No studies rigorously examine the long-run effects of high-quality pre-K on children from middle-class and upper-class families. For example, although Heckman believes the returns from pre-K are lower for middle-class families than for the poor, he admits that this belief is not proven by empirical evidence: "Now you say, Do I have really hard evidence on this? The answer is no" (Heckman 2005, p. 24).

We can speculate about possible patterns of pre-K effects across different income groups. On the one hand, children in more disadvantaged groups are further from "optimal patterns" of child development. This might make it easier to improve the development path for these children. On the other hand, as Barnett argues, middle-class children also lag behind children from upper-class families. He maintains that there might be considerable benefits for middle-class children.

With respect to later outcomes, children from disadvantaged families will have greater baseline high school dropout rates. Therefore, it might be easier to improve high school graduation rates for disadvantaged groups. On the other hand, children from more advantaged groups might be closer to attaining a college degree. It might be easier for pre-K to positively affect college graduation rates for advantaged groups.

In this context, it is relevant that the dollar return from attaining a college degree is greater than the dollar return from attaining a high school degree. The annual earnings boost from attaining a four-year college degree, versus having only a high school degree, is $19,400 (2005 dollars), increasing average annual earnings from $31,500 to $50,900. The annual earnings boost from attaining a high school degree but no higher degree, versus being a high school dropout, is $8,100, increasing earnings from $23,400 to $31,500 (Baum and Ma 2007). Thus, fewer additional college graduates are needed to raise the population's total earnings by x dollars than would be required using additional high school graduates.

Another way to describe the contending influences is as follows. Disadvantaged groups have lower baseline wages and employment rates than more advantaged groups. On the one hand, this provides more potential for increasing earnings through boosting wages and employment rates. On the other hand, a given boost in employment rates or wage rates will increase earnings by more in dollar terms for groups with higher baseline rates.

The best direct evidence on the distributional effects of universal pre-K education is from studies of Oklahoma's universal pre-K program (Gormley et al. 2005).[8] This evidence is only for short-run effects, as of the beginning of kindergarten. The Gormley et al. study uses an evaluation methodology, "regression discontinuity" analysis, which is regarded as giving rigorous results.[9] Gormley and his colleagues find evidence that pre-K has short-run positive effects on test scores for children from all income groups. As is common in educational research, the only information on income status of children is whether they are eligible for a free lunch under federal rules (family income of less than 130 percent of the poverty line) or a reduced-price lunch (family income between 130 percent and 185 percent of the poverty line), or whether they must pay full price for lunch (family income above 185 percent of the poverty line). Test score effects for the highest income group are quite similar to test score effects for the lowest income group. Test score effects for the middle income group are somewhat higher than test score effects for either the higher income or lower income groups.[10]

Gormley et al.'s results weaken the case that pre-K education will have smaller effects on more advantaged children. Pre-K is about as effective in increasing the test scores of higher income groups as it is for lower income groups.[11]

BASELINE RESULTS FOR DISTRIBUTIONAL EFFECTS OF UNIVERSAL PRE-K

For the baseline results, I use distributional assumptions from Karoly and Bigelow (2005). Their results assume that lower income children are more likely to enroll in universal pre-K than upper income children. In addition, lower income children are assumed to be less likely than upper income children to be enrolled in high-quality pre-K in the absence of a high-quality universal program. Finally, for any particular change in pre-K enrollment brought about by universal pre-K, the dollar benefits are assumed to be more for lower income children than upper income children. For example, consider children who without universal pre-K would not have been in any pre-K program. Karoly and Bigelow assume that in this group of children, benefits for upper income children are one-fourth the benefits for lower income children.[12]

I simulate the distributional effects of universal pre-K under these assumptions (Table 8.2). One part of the simulation calculates the dollar effect of pre-K on the average participant in each income quintile relative to the lowest income quintile (row 2, Table 8.2). These dollar effects are based on Karoly and Bigelow's assumptions. These distributional effects across quintiles assume a quite rapid fall-off in dollar effects from the lowest income quintiles to middle and higher income quintiles. For example, the dollar effects on the middle income quintile are less than a third of the dollar effects on the lowest income quintile. Dollar effects on the two highest income quintiles are less than one-tenth of the dollar effects on the lowest income quintile.[13]

This fall-off of dollar effects with family income is qualitatively consistent with the opinions of other pre-K experts. For example, NIEER codirector Steve Barnett assumed that effects for children in the middle three quintiles would be one-half those of children in the lowest income quintile, while effects for the top quintile would be zero (Barnett 2004). He regards these as "realistic assumptions about program participation and extrapolated benefits" (p. 10). Heckman has not made specific assumptions about how pre-K's returns decline for higher-income children. However, his remarks imply that returns are smaller for middle- and upper-income children, not nonexistent.

Under these distributional assumptions, universal pre-K's benefits are distributed highly progressively. The return per dollar of tax cost is about 25 to 1 for the lowest income quintile (row 6, Table 8.2). This is almost nine times the return per dollar of tax cost for the middle income quintile. Furthermore, the return per dollar of tax cost is about nine times as great for the middle income quintile as it is for the highest income quintile.[14]

Pre-K provides large benefits for the lowest income quintile. The net present value of earnings benefits, even allowing for the regressive

Table 8.2 Distributional Effects of Universal Pre-K Education, Baseline Distributional Assumptions (with comparisons to business incentives)

Row		Income quintile					
		Lowest		Middle		Highest	Overall
		1	2	3	4	5	
1	Quintile % share of total household income	3.4	8.7	14.8	23.4	49.7	100
	Pre-K effects on:						
2	Relative dollar effects on earnings, disadvantaged group = 1	1.00	0.81	0.31	0.08	0.08	0.38
3	Earnings benefits as % of income	6.252	2.133	0.630	0.122	0.057	0.549
4	Tax costs as % of income	0.249	0.227	0.216	0.206	0.179	0.197
5	Net benefits as % of income	6.003	1.906	0.414	-0.083	-0.122	0.351
6	Ratio of earnings benefits to tax costs	25.08	9.38	2.91	0.59	0.32	2.78
	Comparison with business incentive effects on:						
7	Net benefits as % of income	1.283	0.607	0.575	0.606	0.146	0.422
8	Ratio of earnings benefits to tax costs	6.15	3.67	3.66	3.95	1.82	3.14

NOTE: Rows 2 through 6 of table show effects of universal pre-K under the baseline distributional assumptions. Rows 7 and 8 show distributional effects of business incentives and are taken from Table 8.1. Dollar benefits per participant for each quintile are indexed to lowest income quintile equals 1.00. All figures for percentages of income report the present value of that item as percentages of the present value of income for the relevant group. Ratios report ratios of the present value of earnings benefits or net income benefits to the present value of tax costs for the relevant group. All present value calculations use a 3 percent real discount rate. Overall earnings effects and tax costs come from the simulation model for universal pre-K used in this book and described in Chapter 4. Earnings are translated into income percentages using the labor share figures of Gordon (2009). Earnings effects for former child participants and parents are allocated across quintiles based on the Karoly and Bigelow (2005) distributional assumptions, which are applied to quintiles as explained in Appendix 8A. Balanced-budget multiplier spending effects on earnings are allocated across quintiles based on how labor demand increases are allocated across quintiles in Bartik (1994b). Tax costs are allocated across quintiles based on average quintile incidence of state and local taxes reported in McIntyre et al. (2003). More details are in text and endnotes to text.

nature of state and local taxes, is more than 6 percent of income for the lowest income quintile.[15] This large effect is not surprising. The estimates for the lowest income quintile are based on studies of the Chicago Child-Parent Center program. This program gained fame because it was so effective.[16]

On the other hand, under these distributional assumptions, pre-K's benefits are distributed quite broadly. There are net positive benefits for the bottom three income quintiles, and thus net positive benefits for over half the population. The net benefits for the middle income quintile are a little more than 0.4 percent of income. Even the two upper income quintiles get some nonnegligible benefits. The highest income quintile gets 32 cents in benefits for every dollar that this quintile pays in taxes to support pre-K. The next-highest income quintile gets 59 cents in benefits for every dollar of taxes paid for pre-K. These benefits occur partly due to the broad labor demand benefits of simply spending more money. But they also occur because pre-K's benefits are so large for the disadvantaged that even benefits for upper income quintiles that are drastically scaled back have some importance.

But universal pre-K's benefits are more progressive, and hence less broad, compared to business incentives. For example, consider a universal pre-K program and a business incentive program of the same cost. For the lowest income quintile, the net benefits of the pre-K program are almost five times the net benefits of the business incentive program (Table 8.2, row 5 versus row 7). Yet the business incentive program overall has higher net benefits and returns. The upper three quintiles clearly gain much more from business incentives than from universal pre-K.

Universal pre-K's benefits are more progressive than those of business incentives because of how dollar benefits vary across income quintiles. As discussed above, the research literature suggests that increases in labor demand yield considerably higher dollar benefits for higher income quintiles. On the other hand, everyone seems to agree that dollar benefits of universal pre-K are highest in the lowest income quintile.

ADDING IN POSSIBLE CAPITALIZATION EFFECTS

As was discussed in Chapter 7, universal pre-K programs may lead to some property value increases. Property buyers and sellers may recognize the benefits of universal pre-K in increasing the earnings of former child participants and their parents. If they do so, property value increases will "capitalize" some of the benefits of universal pre-K. Benefits will be transferred from workers to property owners. This capitalization is likely to make the returns to pre-K more regressive.

The extent of capitalization depends upon whether property buyers and sellers recognize the future earnings benefits of pre-K. Capitalization also depends upon what discount rates are used by property buyers and sellers to value these future earnings benefits. I will assume here the maximum possible capitalization that has some empirical support, as discussed in Chapter 7. Specifically, I will assume that property buyers and sellers take full account of future earnings effects. I assume the taxes associated with these programs are ignored by property buyers and sellers. I assume property buyers and sellers use a real discount rate of 4.7 percent in considering how the earnings benefits from universal pre-K should affect property valuations. These assumptions yield a relatively large amount of capitalization. Other plausible assumptions about how property buyers and sellers behave would yield lower degrees of capitalization. Based on these assumptions, I calculate that universal pre-K will increase property values by 5.1 percent. How this particular property value increase is derived is discussed in Chapter 7.

I simulate the distributional effects of universal pre-K education under this capitalization assumption (Table 8.3). A considerable percentage of the total earnings benefits of pre-K are capitalized into higher values. I estimate that pre-K leads to property value increases that are about two-fifths of the present value of earnings benefits.[17]

Furthermore, the costs and benefits of this capitalization are distributed in a manner that makes distributional effects less progressive. For example, the lowest income quintile has a much higher percentage loss (about four times as great) from higher consumer housing prices than is true for the highest income quintile (0.681 percent versus 0.177 percent; row 3 of Table 8.3). But the highest income quintile has a somewhat higher percentage gain from higher property values than the lowest income quintile (0.261 percent versus 0.216 percent, more than one-fifth greater; row 4 of Table 8.3).

Higher consumer housing prices have larger costs for lower income quintiles because housing expenditures are a greater percentage of income for lower income quintiles. Higher property values provide greater benefits for the highest income quintile because the highest income quintile owns more property relative to its income.

Therefore, on net, capitalization makes the distribution of the benefits from universal pre-K less progressive. The lower income quintiles gain less, and the highest income quintile gains more.

However, the earnings benefits from universal pre-K are so great for the lower income quintiles that their net benefits from universal pre-K are still quite high. For example, for the lowest income quintile, capitalization only lowers the ratio of net after-tax benefits to costs from about 25 to about 23. (Compare rows 8 and 10 in Table 8.3.) This is still a very progressive program.

Capitalization does significantly increase the payoff from universal pre-K to the highest income quintile. The highest income quintile now receives 79 cents in benefits for every tax dollar invested. This is more than double the 32 cents that accrues without capitalization (rows 8 and 10, Table 8.3).[18]

ALTERNATIVE DISTRIBUTIONAL ASSUMPTIONS

The baseline distributional assumptions for universal pre-K seem reasonable. As Karoly and Bigelow say, these distributional assumptions "can arguably be viewed as quite conservative." Given current evidence, the most reasonable assumption is that pre-K benefits significantly decline as we go from disadvantaged families to middle income families, but not to zero.

However, because of the lack of evidence on long-term distributional effects of universal pre-K, it seems prudent to consider alternative distributional assumptions. I consider two sets of alternative assumptions. One set is that the dollar benefits for the children of all income groups are the same as the dollar benefits for the children of the disadvantaged. This set of assumptions broadens benefits. Given

Table 8.3 Distributional Effects with Capitalization Effects of Universal Pre-K Education

Row		Income quintile					
		Lowest		Middle		Highest	Overall
		1	2	3	4	5	
1	Quintile % share of total household income	3.4	8.7	14.8	23.4	49.7	100
	Pre-K effects with capitalization						
2	Earnings benefits as % of income	6.252	2.133	0.630	0.122	0.057	0.549
3	Costs of increased housing prices to consumers	0.681	0.360	0.267	0.223	0.177	0.234
4	Benefits of increased housing prices to property owners	0.216	0.210	0.207	0.210	0.261	0.234
5	Net benefits before taxes and after capitalization (row 2 − row 3 + row 4)	5.787	1.983	0.570	0.109	0.141	0.549
6	Tax costs as % of income	0.249	0.227	0.216	0.206	0.179	0.197
7	Net benefits as % of income	5.538	1.755	0.353	−0.097	−0.038	0.351
8	Ratio of before-tax benefits to tax costs	23.21	8.72	2.63	0.53	0.79	2.78
	Comparison to pre-K effects without capitalization						
9	Net benefits as % of income	6.003	1.906	0.414	−0.083	−0.122	0.351
10	Ratio of before-tax benefits to tax costs	25.08	9.38	2.91	0.59	0.32	2.78

NOTE: Rows 2 through 8 of table show effects of universal pre-K when housing prices increase. Rows 9 and 10 show effects without such capitalization effects and are taken from Table 8.2. Earnings effects and tax costs for capitalization cases are also taken from Table 8.2. Overall capitalization effects are based on the assumption that property buyers and sellers have full knowledge of the overall earnings effects of universal pre-K, and on using a 4.7 percent discount rate to value such effects. This leads to a 5.1 percent increase in property values, as explained in Chapter 7 (Table 7.3 and surrounding text). This property value increase is recalculated as a percentage of the present value of overall income, using figures on earnings and a labor share of income of 73.5 percent (Gordon 2009). The effects of this housing price increase are allocated across consumers based on each income quintile's share of total shelter expenditures in the

Consumer Expenditure Survey for 2007 (see the Bureau of Labor Statistics' Web page http://www.bls.gov/cex/2007/Standard/quintile .pdf). The effects of this housing price increase are allocated across property owners based on figures used in Bartik (1994b) on how home ownership, ownership of rental property, and ownership of business real estate are divided across income quintiles. How these calculations are done is detailed in Bartik (1994b), but the allocation is largely based on CPS information on each income quintile's share of rental and dividend income, and of self-employment income, and on each income quintile's home ownership, combined with American Housing Survey data on home values by income quintile.

that everyone seems to agree that dollar benefits actually decline with increasing family income, this set of assumptions captures one bound that contains the possible assumptions. The other set of assumptions assumes that benefits are zero for the children of nondisadvantaged income groups. Given that there should be some benefits of pre-K for middle-class children, this second set of assumptions captures another bound that contains the possible assumptions.

I did simulations that compared the distributional effects of universal pre-K under three sets of assumptions: the baseline assumptions and these two sets of extreme-bound assumptions (Table 8.4). I focused on comparing three types of effects for each income quintile: 1) the dollar benefits of pre-K relative to the lowest income group, 2) the present value of the net after-tax benefits of universal pre-K as a percentage of income, and 3) the ratio of the present value of earnings benefits to the present value of tax costs.

Despite the extremity of the assumptions, the results have some elements in common. First, under all these assumptions, overall net benefits are positive. Second, under all these assumptions, the distribution of the benefits of universal pre-K is highly progressive.

Overall net benefits are positive in all three cases because the benefits of universal pre-K for the disadvantaged group alone are greater than the overall costs of universal pre-K. Extra benefits for nondisadvantaged groups are icing on the cake. Furthermore, benefits are always distributed progressively because the most regressive assumption is that different income groups have the same dollar benefit from pre-K. Even with this extreme assumption of equal dollar benefits, the percentage benefits from pre-K will be much greater for lower income quintiles.

Of course, there also are some large differences in results. As one would expect, universal pre-K's overall benefits are much greater when we assume that pre-K's large dollar benefits for the disadvantaged broadly extend to all income groups. Overall net benefits more than triple. (Overall net benefits increase from 0.351 percent of income under the baseline assumptions to 1.216 percent under the equal dollar benefits for all group assumptions. See rows 3 and 6, Table 8.4.) This broadening of benefits means that all income groups have net benefits from universal pre-K education, not just the first three quintiles (rows 3 and 6). In contrast, universal pre-K's benefits are much lower when benefits are restricted to the disadvantaged. Overall net benefits

Table 8.4 Distributional Effects of Universal Pre-K Education under Alternative Distributional Assumptions

Row		Income quintile					
		Lowest		Middle		Highest	Overall
		1	2	3	4	5	
1	Quintile % share of total household income	3.4	8.7	14.8	23.4	49.7	100
	Pre-K effects under:						
	Baseline distributional assumptions						
2	Relative dollar effect on earnings, disadvantaged group = 1	1.00	0.81	0.31	0.08	0.08	0.38
3	Net benefits as % of income	6.003	1.906	0.414	−0.083	−0.122	0.351
4	Ratio of earnings benefits to tax costs	25.08	9.38	2.91	0.59	0.32	2.78
	"Equal dollar" distributional assumptions						
5	Relative dollar effect on earnings, disadvantaged group = 1	1.00	1.00	1.00	1.00	1.00	1.00
6	Net benefits as % of income	6.003	2.408	1.738	1.253	0.507	1.216
7	Ratio of earnings benefits to tax costs	25.08	11.59	9.03	7.09	3.83	7.16
	"Only disadvantaged benefit" distributional assumptions						
8	Relative dollar effect on earnings, disadvantaged group = 1	1.00	0.67	0.00	0.00	0.00	0.26
9	Net benefits as % of income	6.003	1.557	−0.194	−0.192	−0.173	0.180
10	Ratio of earnings benefits to tax costs	25.08	7.85	0.10	0.06	0.03	1.91

NOTE: Top rows of table show effects of universal pre-K under the baseline distributional assumptions. These figures are taken from Table 8.2. The next two sets of results resimulate these effects under alternative distributional assumptions. These alternative distributional assumptions assume the same dollar effects per participant for children in the lowest income quintile. What changes is what these dollar effects per participant are for other income quintiles. The "equal dollar" assumptions assume that the dollar effect per participant is the same for all quintiles. The "only disadvantaged benefit" distributional assumption assumes that the dollar effects per participant only occur for the disadvantaged group in Karoly and Bigelow (2005), which is in the bottom 35 percent of the household income distribution. Tax costs are not reported in this table, but are the same as in Table 8.2. All percentage effects are for the present value of the relevant variable as a percentage of the present value of income.

of universal pre-K are cut in half when only the disadvantaged benefit. (Overall net benefits decrease from 0.351 percent under the baseline assumptions to 0.180 percent. See rows 3 and 9, Table 8.4.) The program redistributes income from the upper three quintiles to the bottom two quintiles. If only the disadvantaged get earnings benefits from the program, the upper three quintiles all lose about 0.2 percent in income from the increased taxes they have to pay for the universal pre-K program (row 9, Table 8.4).

TARGETED VERSUS UNIVERSAL PRE-K

Given the distributional possibilities, should pre-K be targeted at the disadvantaged rather than be universally accessible?

I consider the implications of targeting pre-K on Karoly and Bigelow's disadvantaged group (Table 8.5). That group is the lower 35 percent of the household income distribution. Targeting considerably lowers pre-K costs. Because of lower enrollment, the total costs of this targeted pre-K program are only 26 percent of the costs of a universal pre-K program. Karoly and Bigelow's assumptions imply that only 26 percent of enrollment in a universal pre-K program will be in this disadvantaged group.[19]

These lower program costs reduce the tax cost of pre-K for all income groups. To calculate these costs, I scale back the costs of universal pre-K for each income group by 74 percent.

Targeting also means that benefits will be the same under all three sets of distributional assumptions. As discussed above, the different sets of distributional assumptions differ in the dollar benefits for nondisadvantaged groups relative to disadvantaged groups. If services are only targeted at children from the disadvantaged group, then these distributional assumptions are irrelevant in determining gross or net benefits.

I calculated net benefits, and the ratio of benefits to tax costs, for each income group from a targeted pre-K program. This targeted program has a very high overall ratio of benefits to costs—more than seven (row 5 of Table 8.5). Targeting services to a disadvantaged group that is estimated, based on several good studies, to have high returns to pre-K obviously will result in a program that has high overall returns.

The returns to the bottom two quintiles are particularly high. These two quintiles receive much the same benefits from services as under a universal program. Benefits go down a little bit because of lower economic development benefits from pre-K spending. But this lowering of benefits is slight. However, the targeting lowers tax costs by 74 percent. The ratio of earnings benefits to tax costs for the two bottom quintiles more than triples (Table 8.5, row 5 versus row 7). However, this corresponds to only increasing the net benefit to the lowest income quintile by 0.1 percent of income (row 4 versus row 6, Table 8.5). Net benefits to the second lowest income quintile actually go down, because some households in this quintile are excluded from pre-K services with targeting.

On the other hand, the targeting means there is no possibility of substantial economic development benefits for the upper three quintiles. (There are no child benefits at all in these groups; there are some assumed benefits from the spending.) However, the targeting does hold down the tax burden from pre-K. Under a pre-K program that is strictly limited to households in the lower third of the household income distribution, the top three quintiles all suffer net losses from paying taxes to support the targeted program.

It should again be noted that this analysis focuses on economic development benefits. An analysis that also considers the benefits of reduced crime would probably come up with larger benefits overall, and some additional benefits for the upper three quintiles.

Given these data, then, which is better, targeted or universal pre-K? I will consider two perspectives. The first is that of some objective policymaker or policy analyst. This policy wonk is trying to choose the policy that maximizes some weighted sum of overall efficiency benefits plus benefits from making the income distribution more progressive. The other perspective is that of a political operative. Which program will be easier to get enacted, and to sustain and grow over time at a high-quality level?

From the first perspective, the targeted versus universal pre-K issue depends upon which world we live in. Do we live in a world in which pre-K only benefits the disadvantaged? Or do we live in a world in which pre-K has at least some significant benefits for the nondisadvantaged?

Table 8.5 Distributional Effects of Targeted Pre-K Program vs. Universal Pre-K Program, under Alternative Distributional Assumptions

Row	Targeted or universal program?	Distributional assumptions	Variable calculated to right for each quintile	Lowest 1	2	Middle 3	4	Highest 5	Overall
1			Quintile % share of total household income	3.4	8.7	14.8	23.4	49.7	100.0
2	Targeted	Consistent with all 3 sets	Tax costs of targeted as % of income	0.064	0.058	0.056	0.053	0.046	0.051
3	Universal		Tax costs of universal as % of income	0.249	0.227	0.216	0.206	0.179	0.197
4	Targeted	Consistent with all 3 sets	Net benefits as % of income	6.099	1.691	−0.053	−0.050	−0.045	0.313
5			Ratio of earnings benefits to tax costs	96.15	29.91	0.05	0.05	0.03	7.16
6	Universal	Baseline	Net benefits as % of income	6.003	1.906	0.414	−0.083	−0.122	0.351
7			Ratio of earnings benefits to tax costs	25.08	9.38	2.91	0.59	0.32	2.78
8	Universal with capitalization	Baseline	Net benefits as % of income	5.538	1.755	0.353	−0.097	−0.038	0.351
9			Ratio of earnings and housing price effects to tax costs	23.21	8.72	2.63	0.53	0.79	2.78
10	Universal	"Equal dollar"	Net benefits as % of income	6.003	2.408	1.738	1.253	0.507	1.216
11			Ratio of earnings benefits to tax costs	25.08	11.59	9.03	7.09	3.83	7.16
12	Universal	"Only disadvantaged benefit"	Net benefits as % of income	6.003	1.557	−0.194	−0.192	−0.173	0.180
13			Ratio of earnings benefits to tax costs	25.08	7.85	0.10	0.06	0.03	1.91

NOTE: After the top row showing quintile income shares, each of the next pairs of rows considers results from the simulation of one scenario, with one row showing net benefits as a percentage of income, and the other row showing the ratio of benefits to tax costs. The columns "Targeted or universal program?" and "Distributional assumptions" show the assumptions made under that scenario for that pair of rows. (For example, rows 6 and 7 both show results when program is universal and the distributional assumptions are the baseline assumptions.) The top 2 rows of results consider tax costs of a targeted versus a universal program. The next pair of rows considers the effects of a targeted program on net income and the ratio of earnings effects to tax costs. For comparison, the following rows compare these effects to effects of a universal pre-K program under various distributional assumptions. The baseline distributional assumption results for universal pre-K are taken from Table 8.2. The results with capitalization are taken from Table 8.3. The results for the "equal dollar" and "only disadvantaged benefit" distributional assumptions are taken from Table 8.4. The targeted program only includes pre-K for the disadvantaged group, which is in the bottom 35 percent of the household income distribution and makes up 26 percent of the enrollment in a universal program. Therefore, the tax costs in the top row are simply 26 percent of the universal program's costs. The net benefits and benefit-to-cost ratios for the targeted program are simulated by assuming the same effects for disadvantaged children and parents as under the universal program, but setting such effects for all other groups to zero because they will not be enrolled. The balanced budget multiplier effects of spending are also reduced to 26 percent of the original spending effects for all groups. As in all the tables in this chapter, effects as a percentage of income are the present value of relevant variable effects as a percentage of the present value of income. Ratios are ratios of present values of relevant variables. Present value calculations use a 3 percent discount rate.

If we live in a world in which pre-K only benefits the disadvantaged, then a targeted pre-K program is the better policy. In that world, the net overall benefits from a targeted program are more than 70 percent greater than those of a universal program (0.313 percent versus 0.180 percent, from row 4 versus row 12, Table 8.5). All income groups will be better off with a targeted pre-K program than with a universal program (row 4 versus row 12).

At the other extreme, if we live in a world in which pre-K's dollar benefits do not decline with family income, then a universal program is the better policy. In that world, the universal program's overall net benefits are almost four times as great as those of the targeted program (row 10 versus row 4, Table 8.5). Both the targeted and the universal program have the exact same "bang for the buck," delivering more than $7 in benefits for every dollar of costs (row 5 versus row 11). But the universal program operates at an almost a four times greater scale. Four out of the five income groups gain more from the universal program than from the targeted program, and the benefits for the lowest income group are the same in either program (row 10 versus row 4).

But these are the extreme cases. More interesting is the set of baseline distributional assumptions. What if we live in a world, as we probably do, in which pre-K's benefits do decline significantly with income, but there are still considerable benefits for middle-income families? In that case, I think the objective policymaker would probably favor universal pre-K over targeted pre-K. Targeted pre-K does have a higher bang for the buck than universal pre-K: targeted pre-K has overall benefits of more than $7 for every dollar of cost. These benefits are more than twice as great per dollar of cost as those of universal pre-K, which has benefits of less than $3 per dollar of cost (row 5 versus row 7). However, net overall benefits of universal pre-K are about 12 percent greater (0.351 percent of overall income versus 0.313 percent, from the last column of row 6 versus row 4). And under universal pre-K, the second-lowest and the middle income quintiles do better than under targeted pre-K. The lowest income quintile's net benefits are almost unchanged. And the two highest income quintiles do somewhat worse under universal pre-K (row 6 versus row 4). Therefore, universal pre-K would seem to be preferable on efficiency grounds to targeted pre-K, as net benefits are higher. And universal pre-K would also seem preferable to targeted pre-K on distributional grounds, as it redistributes more income from the highest income quintiles to the low and middle income quintiles.

From a policy wonk's perspective, there are net efficiency and distributional benefits to choosing universal pre-K over targeted pre-K. Returns to pre-K are lower as we extend services to higher income families. However, these returns are high enough that the gains for lower-middle and middle income quintiles outweigh the losses to the highest income quintiles. Cutting off pre-K service to middle-class families doesn't make sense. The benefits of such services to middle-class families outweigh the costs. The benefit-cost ratio is not as high as it is for lower income families, but it still exceeds 1.

But the practical political perspective is just as important. What conditions will make a program easier to enact and sustain? From a political perspective, what is important is what people perceive to be the benefits of universal pre-K. Perceived benefits may differ from actual benefits.

From a political perspective, expanded pre-K is more feasible and sustainable if it is perceived as having broader benefits for the middle class and if the proposal is for a broad program. In that case, the universal program will probably benefit a majority of the population. A targeted program, in contrast, relies for its support on some altruism from a majority of the population.

This political case for universal pre-K over targeted pre-K is strengthened if the public and political actors believe universal pre-K may be capitalized into higher property values. Capitalization creates larger benefits of pre-K for the politically powerful upper income quintile. The ratio of benefits to tax costs for this quintile more than doubles (row 9 versus row 7). Targeted pre-K, with its narrower eligibility, seems less likely to lead to capitalization. With capitalization, the net losses for the upper income quintile from adoption of a pre-K program are slightly lower for a universal program than for a targeted program (row 8 versus row 4).

Three other factors may increase the policy-wonk and political case for universal pre-K over targeted pre-K: 1) administrative costs, 2) stigma costs of targeting, and 3) reduced peer effects due to targeting. My simulations of strict targeting assume that administrative costs are unchanged because of adding income-targeting to a pre-K program. I assume these costs are slight because all the program has to do is accept or reject some participant. However, if these costs prove to be significant, they would lower net benefits of the targeted program, which would hurt the case for targeting. For example, administrative costs of targeting could be significant if there were political demands to recertify eligibility every month or every calendar quarter. Administrative costs of targeting could also be significant if there were political demands to push the error rate in targeting too close to zero, which would require extensive documentation of eligibility. In contrast, a more reasonable targeting system for a single year of pre-K would have more modest documentation demands and would certify eligibility once at the beginning of the pre-K year. "Good enough" targeting is considerably cheaper than "close to perfect" targeting.

Targeting may also impose stigma costs on participation. Targeting means that pre-K is now identified as a program that serves the disadvantaged. Some disadvantaged parents may choose not to participate in a targeted program but would participate in a universal program. If this occurs on a large scale, then the benefits of targeted pre-K may be significantly reduced.

Finally, targeted versus universal programs may affect peer effects. The work of Henry and Rickman (2007) provides evidence of significant peer effects in pre-K education. Targeting, compared to universal programs, means that the publicly funded pre-K will have less middle-class and upper-class participation. This may reduce positive peer effects on disadvantaged students. On the other hand, this greater income integration may have negative peer effects on middle- and upper-class students. It is often assumed in discussions of income integration in K–12 education that peer effects are asymmetric by income group (e.g., Kahlenberg 2001). It is assumed that the positive effects on the lower income students from the presence of middle-class and upper income students will exceed the negative effects on the middle and upper income students from the presence of lower income students. The rationale for this asymmetry is that the academic achievement of lower income students may be more sensitive to school culture. If this asymmetry is true, then reducing income integration will lower the overall effectiveness of early childhood experiences in preparing children for future success. Even if this asymmetry of peer effects is untrue, peer effects mean that the reduction of income integration in a targeted program will hurt the academic achievement of lower income students.

For all of these reasons, if universal pre-K has some significant actual and perceived benefits for middle-class students, then I think a universal program is preferable to targeting pre-K education at the disadvantaged. A program with broader middle-class benefits makes more economic and political sense. If such benefits are at all plausible in public debate, universal pre-K is the way to go.

But what if the vision of broad benefits for pre-K does not win out in the political marketplace of ideas? For example, what if the "research consensus" moves toward finding that these programs only benefit the disadvantaged? In that case, a targeted pre-K program is a reasonable fall-back position. Such a targeted program would deliver significant benefits to low income groups. (For example, the net benefits for the lowest income quintile are more than 6 percent of income.) And the tax costs for the middle and upper income quintiles are modest: the net losses for these three upper income quintiles are only about 0.05 percent of income (row 4). If the public does not believe that universal pre-K has broad benefits, this may be all the public is willing to pay for.

TARGETING WITHIN UNIVERSALISM: UNIVERSAL PRE-K WITH INCOME-GRADUATED FEES

What about a more moderate targeting effort that maintains universal accessibility? Specifically, I did simulations that considered the possible effects of running a universal program with some fees for children from upper income families.

To try to preserve middle-class benefits, these fees are only imposed on families in the upper 40 percent of the income distribution (greater than $62,000 in household income). In the baseline set of assumptions, this upper 40 percent of households was the group with the lowest benefits from pre-K. In contrast, the lower three quintiles all had significant benefits from pre-K. Therefore, restricting fees to the upper 40 percent seems more likely to increase efficiency than a broader fee structure. Imposing fees on the bottom three quintiles might discourage use from those quintiles, which after all have the highest benefits. Furthermore, it seems politically wise to only impose fees on a minority of the population. This is consistent with the political advice, given above, by Robert

Greenstein of the Center for Budget and Policy Priorities that "targeted programs . . . are more likely to be strong politically when they serve low-income and moderate-income working families as well as the very poor."

The fees I considered were half of pre-K costs for upper income families. This ends up being a fee of $4.70 per hour.[20] This seems roughly consistent with what upper income families might be willing to consider paying. Data suggest that families in such income brackets average paying $3.90 per hour for all types of paid child care.[21] Paying a little more for high-quality pre-K seems feasible.

Charging fees to upper income families should reduce their demand for the pre-K program. I used estimates from a previous study by Blau and Hagy (1998) of how overall demand for all types of child care responds to changes in hourly fees. However, we would assume that the change in usage of one type of child care, a public pre-K program, in response to a fee would be larger than the change in usage of all types of child care in response to fees. Other types of child care and private pre-K programs are substitutes for the public pre-K program. The availability of these substitutes will increase the demand response. Households can more readily reduce demand for any good or service if there are adequate substitutes for that good or service. Therefore, I assumed that the change in public pre-K demand due to the fee would be twice the overall child care demand response estimated by Blau and Hagy.

With this assumption about the demand response to fees, usage of pre-K among households with incomes greater than $62,000 (the top 40 percent) is reduced by 26 percent. This demand response seems plausible. Overall usage (and costs) of the pre-K program is reduced by 13 percent. Fee revenue makes up 20 percent of the overall costs of the program. Fees do have significant effects on the size and financing of the program.

A targeted program that charges fees should have some extra administrative costs. The program will have to determine household income and the appropriate fees, and collect those fees. I assumed that these extra administrative costs from fees amount to about 5 percent of program costs.[22] The exact magnitude of administrative costs depends upon being reasonable about how much documentation of income is required and how often such documentation is required.

What are the effects of charging income-based fees in a universal pre-K program? I do simulations using the baseline distributional assumptions (Table 8.6).[23] The simulations suggest that the addition of these fees has almost no effect on the overall net benefits of the program (row 7 versus row 11; a 0.352 percent net benefit versus 0.351 percent). The fees do promote economic efficiency to some extent by cutting back usage from upper income quintiles whose benefits from the program are low. On the other hand, charging fees does add administrative costs to the pre-K program. Furthermore, the new program does reduce economic development benefits somewhat. This occurs for some of the upper income families that now forgo pre-K. It also occurs for all income quintiles because of the reduced spending and size of the program. On net, all of these factors turn out to be a wash.

However, adding fees does have some important redistributive effects. First, charging fees redistributes some income from the two upper income quintiles to the three lower income quintiles. This redistribution is relatively modest. The net losses for the two top income quintiles, and the net gains for the three bottom income quintiles, are all less than 0.1 percent of income (row 7 versus row 11). This redistribution takes place for two reasons: The reduced demand for pre-K from upper income families 1) reduces benefits for pre-K for the upper two income quintiles and 2) reduces costs for pre-K services for the three lower income quintiles. The fees paid by the upper income families also reduce net benefits for the top two income quintiles and reduce the taxes that the three lower income quintiles pay to finance the program.

Second, charging fees redistributes how program cost is financed in the upper two income quintiles. Some program cost is shifted from upper income households that do not use this pre-K program to families that do. For upper income households that do not use pre-K, what is relevant is the change in their tax cost from the program. This tax cost is reduced by a little more than one-quarter for these upper two income quintiles (row 3 versus row 10). Although this is large as a percentage of the tax burden of the program, it is modest in relation to income—again less than 0.1 percent of income. For upper income households that use pre-K, they now are charged a fee for the program. However, they still presumably are better off having the program than having no program, or else they would not have chosen to enroll their children and pay the fee. In addition, I note that the estimates suggest that the earnings ben-

Table 8.6 Distributional Effects of Universal Pre-K with Income-Based Fees

Row	Fees or free?		Lowest 1	2	Middle 3	4	Highest 5	Overall
					Income quintile			
1		Quintile % share of total household income	3.4	8.7	14.8	23.4	49.7	100
	Effects of universal pre-K with fees on:							
2	Fees	Earnings benefits as % of income	6.238	2.128	0.628	0.092	0.042	0.533
3		Tax costs as % of income	0.182	0.166	0.158	0.150	0.130	0.144
4		Net benefits after taxes as % of income	6.057	1.962	0.471	-0.058	-0.088	0.389
5		Ratio of earnings benefits to tax costs	34.37	12.85	3.99	0.61	0.33	3.71
6		Tax-plus-fee costs as % of income	0.182	0.166	0.158	0.229	0.167	0.181
7		Net benefits after taxes and fees as % of income	6.057	1.962	0.471	-0.137	-0.125	0.352
8		Ratio of earnings benefits to tax-plus-fee costs	34.37	12.85	3.99	0.40	0.25	2.95
	Effects of universal pre-K that is free on:							
9	Free (baseline)	Earnings benefits as % of income	6.252	2.133	0.630	0.122	0.057	0.549
10		Tax costs as % of income	0.249	0.227	0.216	0.206	0.179	0.197
11		Net benefits after taxes as % of income	6.003	1.906	0.414	-0.083	-0.122	0.351
12		Ratio of earnings benefits to tax costs	25.08	9.38	2.91	0.59	0.32	2.78

NOTE: The first set of rows, 2 through 8, examines the effects of a universal pre-K program with income-based fees. These rows analyze net benefits, and ratio of benefits to costs, in two ways. One way simply looks at benefits versus tax costs. The other way includes fees as part of costs. The inclusion of fees is proper for an overall social benefits analysis. However, the analysis without fees is more relevant for households that do not use universal pre-K. The second set of rows, 9 through 12, considers the case of universal pre-K without any fees. These estimates are taken from Table 8.2. The fees are set and analyzed as described in the text. The reduced usage induced by fees requires that both tax costs and balanced-budget multiplier effects be recalculated for all groups. In addition, the earnings benefits of pre-K must be recalculated for all groups. I assume that the usage of pre-K that is due to fees is distributed equally across the top two income quintiles. The effects as a percentage of income are the present value of the relevant variable as a percentage of the present value of income. The ratio is formed by the present value of benefits divided by the present value of costs. Present value calculations use a 3 percent discount rate.

efits for upper income families who use the program exceed the fees.[24]

Does charging income-based fees improve universal pre-K? From a policy wonk's perspective, the fee-based program might be slightly preferable. The fee-based program does not affect the overall net benefits of the program. However, the modest redistribution from the upper two quintiles to the bottom three quintiles would be desirable.

From a perspective of political practicality, it is unclear whether charging fees makes universal pre-K easier to enact and sustain. The political attractiveness of fees depends on the political influence of upper-class households who don't use pre-K versus those who do. The upper-class "nonusers" may be more supportive of a universal pre-K program that holds down costs by charging fees. They may be less supportive of a free universal program that can be framed as subsidizing "affluent working women" (Heckman 2005). On the other hand, the upper-class users of pre-K may resent paying these income-based fees while other families receive free services. This may reduce this group's support for universal pre-K. Whether fees make sense from a political perspective depends on how fees and their rationale are perceived by both pre-K users and nonusers in upper-class groups.

An interesting analogy is made by comparing need-based fees for universal pre-K to need-based college scholarships. There is general public support for providing college scholarships based on need. But despite this, it appears that college scholarship programs for the needy are underfunded. Based on the U.S. experience with need-based college scholarships, it is apparently politically feasible to base education assistance on needs, but doing so does not ensure a well-funded program.

THE ABECEDARIAN PROGRAM: DISTRIBUTIONAL EFFECTS OF A LARGE-SCALE TARGETED PROGRAM

As described in Chapter 4 and its references, the Abecedarian program is an intense and costly intervention targeted at children from disadvantaged families. The program provides full-time, full-year, and high-quality child care and pre-K from birth to age 5. The program potentially provides over 12,000 hours of service to each child. Because of the program's intensity, the Abecedarian program is very expensive per child. The present value of gross costs for each child is close to $80,000. Of course, in return for those intense services, the program produces large economic development benefits. As outlined in Chapter 4, of the various early childhood programs considered here, the Abecedarian program yields the largest economic development benefits per child participant. This is partly due to the large effects on the future earnings of former child participants. But it also is due to the much larger effects on parents' labor supply of five years of free child care, compared to the more limited intervention of other early childhood programs, such as one year of part-time, school-year prekindergarten education.

To analyze the income distributional effects of the Abecedarian program, I assume that services would be restricted to the bottom quintile of the population. As outlined in Chapter 4, Ludwig and Sawhill (2007) estimate that a full-scale Abecedarian program could achieve similar results to those of the original model by targeting families below the poverty line. This would involve providing services to families in the lowest 15 percent of the family income distribution.

Why not an Abecedarian program that is universal? First, there is no research basis for estimating the effects of such a program. Second, as will be seen below, the costs of a full-scale Abecedarian program for 15 percent of the population are already extremely high. A universal Abecedarian program would be prohibitively expensive.

Targeting for the Abecedarian program faces some complications because the program lasts five years. If targeting were based strictly on each year's family income, families would cycle in and out of the program. This would reduce the program's effects. If targeting were based solely on family income just prior to admission to the program, when the child was an infant, then a significant number of family participants would greatly exceed income cutoffs sometime in the next five years.

A pragmatic approach to targeting for the Abecedarian program is to require that families at admission score high on some number of risk factors. These risk factors would be family characteristics that are known to be good predictors of a family having persistent poverty. For example, risk factors might include family income, single-parent family, teenage mother, welfare receipt, low education of the parents, etc. To be admitted to the program, families would have to score high on a certain number of these risk factors, as well as having family income below some cutoff. Once admitted to the program, the child and his or her family would stay in the program for the full five years. With these procedures, the overwhelming majority of participating families would be in poverty or close to poverty for most of the five-year period. This risk-factor targeting approach is similar to how the original Abecedarian program participants were selected. It is also similar to how children are selected for some state pre-K programs. For example, Michigan's state-funded pre-K program requires that the child and his or her family have at least two risk factors from a list of 25 (Daniel-Echols and Schweinhart 2007).

The simulations of the distributional effects of the Abecedarian program used similar methods to those used for universal pre-K education. Therefore, the results can be compared (Table 8.7).

As previously shown in Chapter 4, a full-scale Abecedarian program has quite large net benefits. Overall net benefits are almost twice those of universal pre-K education, even though these benefits are confined to the lowest quintile (row 4 versus row 6).

Furthermore, a full-scale Abecedarian program results in extraordinary net benefits for the lowest income quintile. The program boosts net income for this group by over 35 percent. This is nearly six times the effects on the lowest income quintile of universal pre-K education (row 4 versus row 6).

Why are effects on the lowest-income quintile so high for the Abecedarian program compared to pre-K education? The greater effects for Abecedarian compared to pre-K probably occur because of the more intense services provided by the program to both children and their parents. Five years of full-time, high-quality child care and pre-K education is a far more extensive intervention in the lives of children than one year of part-time, school-year pre-K education. Five years of full-time, full-year free child care changes the working opportunities for parents far more than one year of part-time, school-year, free child care.

However, the Abecedarian program is so large and so redistributive that it imposes large net costs on the upper 80 percent of the income distribution. The upper 80 percent of the population gets very little direct economic development benefit from the Abecedarian program. (There are some economic development benefits for these upper income groups from the increased spending, but these benefits are small.) The upper 80 percent of the household income distribution suffers average net losses

Table 8.7 Distributional Effects of the Abecedarian Program

| Row | | Income quintile | | | | | |
| | | Lowest | 2 | Middle | 4 | Highest | Overall |
		1		3		5	
1	Quintile % share of total household income	3.4	8.7	14.8	23.4	49.7	100
	Abecedarian program's effects on:						
2	Earnings as % of income	35.814	0.033	0.031	0.032	0.013	1.240
3	Tax costs as % of income	0.696	0.635	0.604	0.574	0.500	0.551
4	Net benefits as % of income	35.118	−0.602	−0.574	−0.542	−0.487	0.689
5	Ratio of earnings benefits to tax costs	51.45	0.05	0.05	0.06	0.03	2.25
	Comparison to universal pre-K's effects on:						
6	Net benefits as % of income	6.003	1.906	0.414	−0.083	−0.122	0.351
7	Ratio of earnings benefits to tax costs	25.08	9.38	2.91	0.59	0.32	2.78

NOTE: Rows 2 through 5 show distributional effects for a full-scale Abecedarian program. Rows 6 and 7 show distributional effects for a universal pre-K program. These bottom rows are taken from Table 8.2. The overall size, effects, and costs of an Abecedarian program are derived in Chapter 4. The earnings effects due to effects on former child participants and their parents are derived by assuming all of these effects are allocated to the lowest income quintile; see text for the rationale for this assumption. Balanced-budget multiplier effects of spending are allocated across quintiles based on results in Bartik (1994b) for distributional effects of labor demand. Tax costs are allocated across quintiles based on results in McIntyre et al. (2003). These procedures are similar to what was done for universal pre-K in Table 8.2. All effects as a percentage of income are effects on the present value of the relevant variable as a percentage of the present value of income. Ratios are the present value of benefits divided by costs. Present value calculations use a 3 percent discount rate.

in income from a full-scale Abecedarian program of about 0.5 percent of income (row 4). This far exceeds the net losses for any income quintile from universal pre-K. And of course universal pre-K results in net gains for the middle income quintile and below.

The Abecedarian program is so expensive per participant that its tax burden for the population is almost three times as great as universal pre-K, even though universal pre-K is projected to have more than four times as many participants. (See Table 4.2, and compare the overall tax cost in Tables 8.2 and 8.7.) Because of its more limited number of participants, the Abecedarian program has many fewer direct beneficiaries, and these beneficiaries are concentrated in the lowest income quintile.

This analysis, as is true of all the analysis in this book, only looks at economic development benefits. Studies have not found evidence that the Abecedarian program reduces crime, so anticrime benefits for the overall population cannot be counted on. There may be some benefits for other income quintiles in reduced social service costs.

However, overall, a full-scale Abecedarian program appears to be economically promising but politically troubled. The program could deliver large antipoverty benefits. However, achieving such benefits puts great demands on the altruism of the majority of the population, which is ineligible for the program.

THE NURSE-FAMILY PARTNERSHIP: DISTRIBUTIONAL EFFECTS OF A SMALLER-SCALE ANTIPOVERTY PROGRAM

As detailed in Chapter 4, the Nurse-Family Partnership (NFP) provides disadvantaged first-time mothers with nurse home visits from the prenatal period to age two. These visits focus on delivering a curriculum that includes healthier prenatal care, more sensitive child care, and a better maternal life course. Direct hours of interaction during the visits with each mother total perhaps 45 hours over this two-and-a-half-year period. Estimates suggest that a full-scale NFP would perhaps include about 9 percent of all children.

The NFP is much less intense and costly in services per child than the Abecedarian program. The NFP has a present value of $10,000 per child. This compares to almost $80,000 for the Abecedarian program.

The NFP is also highly targeted on the disadvantaged population compared to universal pre-K: the NFP serves less than 10 percent of all children, whereas universal pre-K is estimated to serve about 70 percent of all children. As shown in Chapter 4, the NFP has an economic development benefits-to-cost ratio that exceeds 1, at 1.85. But the highly targeted nature of the NFP, and its relatively modest costs per child, shape the magnitude and distribution of its economic development benefits.

I simulated the distributional impact of a full-scale version of the NFP (Table 8.8). The methodology was identical to that used for universal pre-K and the Abecedarian program, to allow comparisons.

This full-scale NFP program is assumed to deliver all of its benefits to children and mothers in the lowest income quintile. This is because the full-scale program that is modeled is a targeted program. There is no research basis to project what impact the NFP would have if delivered universally. The NFP was designed to address the needs of disadvantaged families. Early experiments with the NFP suggested that its benefits were greater for more-disadvantaged women (Karoly et al. 1998; Olds et al. 1997).

As expected based on Chapter 4, the NFP has net benefits overall. And given how the NFP is targeted, these benefits are delivered in a highly progressive way (row 4).

However, the lesser intensity of the NFP has two consequences. First, the NFP only has moderate percentage effects on the income of the lowest income quintile, even though this quintile receives most of the NFP's benefits. The NFP increases the income of the lowest income quintile by 2.7 percent (row 4). This is less than one-half of the effects on the lowest income quintile of universal pre-K (row 6 versus row 4). These lesser effects occur even though the NFP is a far more targeted program than universal pre-K. But the hours of services per participant are far less for NFP than for universal pre-K. It is therefore not surprising that its benefits are smaller for lower income groups.

Second, the cost of the NFP for the remaining upper 80 percent of the income distribution is quite modest. The NFP costs about one-twentieth of 1 percent of income for these upper income groups (row 4). In contrast, the costs of the Abecedarian program for upper income quintiles are more than 10 times as great (row 8). Compared to the Abecedarian program, the NFP is quite cheap because of the lesser

Table 8.8 Distributional Effects for the Nurse-Family Partnership (NFP)

| | | Income quintile | | | | | |
| | | Lowest | | Middle | | Highest | |
Row		1	2	3	4	5	Overall
1	Quintile % share of total household income	3.4	8.7	14.8	23.4	49.7	100
	NFP's effects on:						
2	Earnings as % of income	2.770	0.003	0.003	0.003	0.001	0.096
3	Tax costs as % of income	0.066	0.060	0.057	0.054	0.047	0.052
4	Net benefits as % of income	2.704	-0.057	-0.054	-0.051	-0.046	0.044
5	Ratio of earnings effects to tax costs	42.14	0.05	0.05	0.05	0.03	1.85
	Comparison: Universal pre-K's effects on:						
6	Net benefits as % of income	6.003	1.906	0.414	-0.083	-0.122	0.351
7	Ratio of earnings effects to tax costs	25.08	9.38	2.91	0.59	0.32	2.78
	Comparison: Abecedarian effects on:						
8	Net benefits as % of income	35.118	-0.602	-0.574	-0.542	-0.487	0.689
9	Ratio of earnings effects to tax costs	51.45	0.05	0.05	0.06	0.03	2.25

NOTE: Rows 2 through 5 show effects for full-scale implementation of the Nurse-Family Partnership (NFP). The next set of rows, 6 and 7, shows effects for universal pre-K. The final set of rows, 8 and 9, shows effects from the Abecedarian program. The universal pre-K effects and Abecedarian effects come from Table 8.2 and Table 8.7, respectively. The NFP effects on overall earnings and taxes are derived from the simulation models outlined in Chapter 4. These effects are expressed as percentages of income by using data from Gordon (2009) on the labor share. NFP effects on former child participants and parents are allocated across quintiles under the assumption that all such effects occur in the lowest income quintile. Balanced-budget multiplier effects of NFP are allocated across quintiles based on estimates in Bartik (1994b) for how labor demand affects the income of different quintiles. Tax costs are allocated across quintiles based on estimates by McIntyre et al. (2003). All effects for percentage of income are the present value of the relevant variable as a percentage of the present value of income. All ratios of earnings to tax costs are the present value of earnings effects to the present value of tax costs. All present value calculations use a 3 percent social discount rate.

costs per participant. Compared to universal pre-K, the NFP is cheap because it is far more targeted.

These findings suggest that politically, a full-scale NFP program may be an easier sell than a full-scale Abecedarian program. The net sacrifice required does not put as much strain on voters' altruism. On the other hand, the antipoverty effects of the NFP are more modest.

CONCLUSION

Previous chapters show that high-quality business incentives and early childhood programs can deliver economic development benefits that exceed costs for state residents overall. This chapter shows that all of these programs increase the progressivity of the income distribution and help the poor.

All of the early childhood programs are far more progressive than business incentives in their effects on the income distribution. This is partly because some of these early childhood programs are designed to target assistance to disadvantaged families. But it also reflects the idea that programs to develop human capital may by their very nature deliver more progressive benefits than programs that boost labor demand. The progressivity of boosts to labor demand is more limited by the current capacities of disadvantaged groups. Early childhood programs are not so limited. As a result, business incentives are unlikely to deliver large boosts to the economic well-being of state residents who are poor.

How politically feasible is it for early childhood programs to be targeted to the poor? For smaller-scale programs, such as the NFP, the program cost is low enough that such targeted efforts are probably politically feasible. However, the trade-off is that the antipoverty benefits are modest. Smaller-scale targeted programs such as the NFP have the potential to play an important role in addressing the problems of lower income groups. However, they clearly do not have sufficiently large effects to be the "solution" to poverty. This should not be interpreted as a criticism of these programs. I doubt whether advocates of the NFP think that this program can "solve" poverty on its own.

For large-scale early childhood programs, such as the Abecedarian program and universal pre-K education, their political feasibility may be improved if the program can be plausibly designed to deliver broad benefits across many income groups. These larger-scale programs have a greater potential to deliver large benefits to lower income groups. Whether this potential is politically enacted and sustained depends on whether some combination of the general population's altruism and self-interest can be mobilized to support these efforts. Universal accessibility, if not necessarily universal free access, may be helpful in making credible the notion of broad benefits, including improvements in property values. But if political perceptions change so that broad benefits are not plausible, either because of changing research findings or changing perceptions of these findings, then a more targeted program may be the only politically sustainable fall-back position. However, targeted programs may be more limited than universal programs in terms of the costs that a majority of the public is willing to pay. This more limited willingness to pay may limit the quality and hence effectiveness of a targeted program. It may also limit how many disadvantaged children are able to access a targeted program. Universal early childhood programs may be more politically effective than targeted programs in delivering assistance to the poor.

Notes

1. For a useful and insightful recent discussion of the consequences of income inequality, and recent trends in income inequality in the United States and other industrial democracies, see Kenworthy (2008).
2. The estimated annual cost of universal pre-K if implemented nationwide is $14.3 billion. As stated in Chapter 2, annual costs of state and local business incentives are probably $20–$30 billion. Most of these business incentive dollars come in the form of tax incentives. Based on Michigan's figures, about two-thirds (more precisely, 68.2 percent, or $678 million in Michigan tax incentives out of $994 million total Michigan resources for business incentives) of annual state and local business incentives are tax incentives. Out of a $20–$30 billion total in state and local business incentives, this would imply $13.6–$20.5 billion in annual state and local business tax incentives. So, $14.3 billion is probably a conservative estimate of the magnitude of business tax incentives.
3. Figures on what percentage of each household is in each quintile are reported on-line by the U.S. Census Bureau from the 2008 Annual Social and Economic Supplement to the CPS. This reports data for calendar year 2007. The relevant figures are in Table 2 and Table A-3 of DeNava-Walt, Proctor, and Smith (2008). The cutoffs for each income quintile are as follows: quintile 1 (lowest income),

less than $20,300; quintile 2, from $20,300 to less than $39,100; quintile 3 (middle income), from $39,100 to less than $62,000; quintile 4, from $62,000 to less than $100,000; quintile 5 (highest income), $100,000 or more. These income cutoffs are provided on-line in Table HINC-05, available at the Census Bureau's Web site at http://www.census.gov/hhes/www/macro/032008/hhinc/new05_000.htm (accessed June 22, 2010). Mean income of each quintile, available in Table A-3 of Denava-Walt et al. (2008), is as follows: quintile 1, $11,551; quintile 2, $29,442; quintile 3, $49,968; quintile 4, $79,111; quintile 5, $167,971. The implied mean income of all households is $67,609, which is increased relative to the middle income quintile mean by the high incomes of the top quintiles.

4. All these calculations use figures for current income, and the present value of such, for the relevant group. I used current income rather than permanent income because it is more straightforward to measure, and because there are better data on the effects of policies and programs relative to current income. Permanent income is a concept that is never directly measured but only inferred. Trying to measure distributional effects relative to permanent income adds complications about how to measure permanent income. Is consumption a valid measure of permanent income? How can we incorporate borrowing constraints into a model of effective permanent income? The distributional calculations relative to current income probably exaggerate the progressivity of all programs relative to the permanent income distribution. However, the relative progressivity of the different programs would probably hold even if measured against permanent income.

5. Specifically, I first used this book's model to calculate the present value of earnings increases due to business incentives, as a percentage of the present value of earnings. This was then multiplied by 0.735. This factor of 0.735 reflects the estimated labor share of income (Gordon 2009). I use Gordon's figures for the average labor share from 1998 to 2008. Looking at Commerce Department figures on personal income and compensation, and allowing for proprietors' income to have a two-thirds labor share, yielded similar labor share figures. The overall percentage effect on income for all households was then allocated across income quintiles based on the results in Bartik (1994b). I used my estimates from this paper of how income percentages varied by quintile to calculate percentage effects in each income quintile. These percentage figures were then translated into dollar impact figures using each quintile's estimated share of total income.

6. These estimates use fairly standard incidence assumptions. However, as noted by Reschovsky (1998), they may yield more regressive impacts of state and local taxes than is consistent with many economists' views of tax incidence. Therefore, these estimates are somewhat tilted toward not finding progressive effects of these various economic development programs. As a result, the finding in this chapter of progressive impacts of all these programs is strengthened. I also considered incidence using Pechman's estimates (Pechman 1985, variant 3b, p. 61). I had used Pechman's estimates in Bartik (1994b). Pechman's estimates are somewhat more regressive at the lower end, and more progressive between the middle and high end. The Institute on Taxation and Economic Policy (ITEP) numbers imply the following relative tax rates by quintile, where the overall tax rate average is

indexed as 1.00: quintile 1 (lowest), 1.26; quintile 2, 1.15; quintile 3, 1.10; quintile 4, 1.04; quintile 5 (highest), 0.91. Pechman's numbers imply the following relative tax rates by quintile: quintile 1, 1.48; quintile 2, 1.11; quintile 3, 0.97; quintile 4, 0.91; quintile 5, 1.00. None of the qualitative and quantitative findings of this chapter are altered significantly by using the Pechman incidence assumptions rather than the ITEP incidence assumptions. The interested reader can use the numbers in this endnote to recalculate the numbers.

The allocation first calculates the present value of taxes paid overall for business incentives, divided by the present value of future earnings. This percentage is then multiplied by 0.735 to reflect the share of labor compensation in total income. The overall percentage share of taxes in income is then used to calculate the percentage share of taxes in income of each quintile using the relative percentage tax rates in McIntyre et al. (2003). The specific ITEP numbers I used were state and local taxes before considering the potential federal income tax offset. This is the row labeled "Total taxes" in the table for "Averages for All States." Therefore, there may be some additional net benefits from all these programs, both business incentives and early childhood programs, from federal tax deductibility, particularly for higher income quintiles.

The ITEP figures for tax burden by income quintile are for nonelderly couples and individuals. Therefore, the procedure I use implicitly assumes that tax burdens by household income quintile follow the pattern for tax burdens by income quintile for nonelderly couples and individuals.

7. These calculations focus on the economic development benefits. They do not include the effects on capital gains that were included in my 1994 paper. But including capital gains would not make much difference. The real earnings effects calculated here already adjust for changes in local prices, including changes in local housing prices. Therefore, capital gains due to increases in property values are a net addition to benefits, above and beyond what has been counted so far. These capital gains have an estimated present value of only about 0.05 percent of the present value of income. The ratios of gross earnings benefits plus capital gains to tax costs, by income quintile, are as follows: quintile 1 (lowest), 6.30; quintile 2, 3.83; quintile 3, 3.83; quintile 4, 4.13; quintile 5, 2.08; overall, 3.35. (The identical numbers for this ratio for quintiles 2 and 3 is not a typo; it is merely an odd coincidence.) These ratios are not much of an increase from what is reported in Table 8.1.

8. Although there are other studies of how pre-K effects differ with economic status, all these other studies are potentially subject to much more serious selection effects. Parents choose to send their children to pre-K. As a result of this choice, pre-K attendees differ from nonattendees in many ways, both observed and (most critically) unobserved. This selection will bias estimates of pre-K effects. There is no reason to think that this selection bias will be of similar magnitude or even sign across different income groups. Gormley et al. (2005) use a regression discontinuity approach, which, as outlined in the text and in Lee and Lemieux (2009), is potentially much less biased by selection effects.

9. The merits and issues with regression discontinuity studies are discussed in Lee and Lemieux (2009). Gormley et al.'s (2005) regression discontinuity analysis

exploits the fact that Oklahoma's pre-K program has an age cutoff. The same tests were administered at both the beginning of Oklahoma's pre-K program and the beginning of kindergarten for students who had participated in the pre-K program the previous year. These two groups, one of beginning kindergartners, the other of beginning pre-K students, will tend to be similar on most observed and unobserved characteristics, because both groups of families chose to participate in the state pre-K program. We can also add statistical controls for any observed differences across these two groups that happen to occur. The one observed characteristic that will significantly differ across the two groups is age, as the beginning kindergartners will be older than the beginning pre-K students. However, the sample of beginning kindergartners includes students who in the previous year barely made the pre-K program's age cutoff. Furthermore, the sample of beginning pre-K students includes students who in the previous year barely missed the pre-K program's age cutoff. We can estimate how test scores vary with age, controlling for other student characteristics. We would expect test scores to smoothly vary with age, except that there may be a sharp jump at the age cutoff. Those students above the age cutoff were able to participate in state-funded pre-K for one year. Those students below the age cutoff instead participated in other activities, including private pre-K programs. Gormley et al. find that although test score results improve with age, there is an abrupt jump in test score results at the age cutoff. This abrupt jump is most likely associated with having attended the state's pre-K program. The jump is inferred as being the effects of participating in the state's pre-K program, compared to alternative activities.

10. Gormley and his colleagues do not report the statistical significance of these differentials across different income groups. My own calculations suggest that in comparisons across any two groups for any of the tests, the results are not statistically significantly different across income groups. This can be computed by calculating the difference of estimates, then calculating the variance assuming the coefficient estimates are uncorrelated. They would appear to be uncorrelated in that each estimate comes from separate regression estimates using a different sample. With the three tests involved and three groups, there are nine possible comparisons of two groups for a given test. Six of these nine comparisons have t-statistics on the differences of less than 1 in absolute value. The largest in absolute value t-statistic is 1.47, which is statistically significant only at the 14 percent level.

In some discussions of these results, Gormley's presentation may lead some readers to infer that pre-K's effects are larger for lower income groups. For example, the presentation of results in Gormley et al. (2004) or Gormley (2007b) show larger percentage effects on the test scores of lower income children. Percentage effects are larger for lower income groups because average test scores of lower income groups are lower. Absolute effects on test scores are similar across income groups. The implication of these greater percentage effects for later-life effects is unclear. Will the same absolute increase in test scores have greater effects on later-life success starting from a small base test score compared to starting from a large base test score? I know of no evidence that addresses this question.

11. One could argue that a given absolute increase in test scores will have greater effects on lower income groups. This could occur because of the lower test score base of lower income groups (see endnote 10). Or, it could occur because lower income groups are at greater risk of dropping out of high school, or of becoming involved in criminal activities or other negative activities that may reduce employment and earnings. On the other hand, as noted in the text, middle and upper income groups may be easier to induce to have large absolute earnings increases. These groups have higher employment rates and wage rates, so any given absolute increase in employment rates or wage rates will cause larger dollar effects on earnings. In addition, middle and upper income groups may be closer to the margin of being induced to attain a college degree, which affects annual earnings much more than high school graduation.

12. Appendix 8A summarizes their distributional assumptions and explains how I use them to generate some distributional results by quintile. Appendix 8A, like all of this book's appendices, is available from the Upjohn Institute.

13. Earnings effects per quintile do not fall off quite so fast per household in each quintile. The Karoly and Bigelow enrollment assumptions imply that although a higher percentage of four-year-olds who are low-income enroll in universal pre-K, this enrollment is a lower percentage of households in the lowest income quintile. This probably reflects that the lowest income quintile includes a considerable number of single-person households. The pattern of dollar benefits per household, relative to the lowest income quintile, is as follows: quintile 1, 1.00; quintile 2, 0.87; quintile 3, 0.43; quintile 4, 0.12; quintile 5, 0.12. See Appendix 8A for more details.

14. Because of the way in which these distributional effects are calculated, the model implicitly assumes that such phenomena as peer effects and displacement effects occur within each quintile. If peer effects or displacement effects occur across quintiles, this will broaden the benefits of pre-K somewhat. However, there is no way to reliably estimate the extent of such broadening. It seems unlikely that such broadening would significantly reduce the highly progressive nature of benefits for pre-K and other early childhood programs.

15. This 6 percent figure does not measure the annual percentage effect of pre-K on participants. The 6 percent is the present value of the effect on state residents as a percentage of the present value of the income of that quintile. This will be below the long-run annual effects on former child participants for several reasons. First, some former child participants move out of state. Second, the model allows for displacement effects. Third, because the effect on former child participants is long-delayed, this reduces the present value percentage effect relative to the long-run annual percentage effect. Calculations of annual percentage effects on participants suggest that they average 17.3 percent from ages 16 to 79. This is an unweighted average. The percentage effects do not vary greatly across years. Percentage effects on earnings for each year range from 13.6 to 23.5 percent.

16. Estimated effects for the lowest income quintile are somewhat reduced relative to CPC because the CPC estimates are only assumed to fully apply to lower income children who otherwise would have attended no pre-K program. Some members

of the lowest income quintile would otherwise have attended some other pre-K program. The estimated benefits for these children are assumed to be lower than the CPC program's estimated effects. Overall, the average benefits per participant for the lowest income quintile are about 61 percent of the estimated benefits per participant of the CPC program.

17. Pre-K's benefits lead to a 0.549 percent boost to the present value of overall earnings, as a percentage of the present value of income (Table 8.3, row 2). The property value increase is equivalent to 0.234 percent of the present value of income (row 3). Therefore, capitalization into higher property values captures about 42 percent of the earnings effects of pre-K (42% = 0.234 ÷ 0.549). Overall property value increases do not capture all of the overall earnings effects of pre-K because we assume different discount rates. From a social perspective, we use 3 percent to discount future earnings, but we assume that property buyers and sellers use a higher discount rate in determining property bids. Individuals may be more myopic in their market behavior than is socially optimal.

18. It is apparent from these calculations that even complete capitalization would not eliminate the overall progressivity of universal pre-K education. Even if the overall benefits of pre-K are fully capitalized into higher property values, this does not mean that these benefits are completely capitalized for each income group. We can think of blowing up capitalization benefits so that they are the same as the overall earnings benefits. Under this assumption, the lowest income quintile still gains so much from the higher earnings benefits that the capitalization effects cannot completely offset these effects. Because all income groups participate in the same housing market, capitalization effects cannot perfectly offset earnings benefits for each income group, even if they do so overall.

Why doesn't capitalization differentiate by income groups to capture differential benefits? Differential capitalization is implausible given that land can be reallocated from one housing type to another. In terms of Table 8.3, if capitalization differentiates by income group, then capitalization implies that housing prices of the lowest income quintile would have to go up by much more in percentage terms than those of the average household, while housing prices of the highest income quintile would go up by much less in percentage terms than for the average household. Presumably these housing price changes are due to differential land price changes, as in the long run the price of structural capital should be related to replacement costs. In any event, it would be very difficult to sustain the large differences in land prices between income groups implied by non-uniform capitalization. Perhaps in theory some perfectly enforced zoning and new housing regulations could do so. In practice, the required land price differentials seem likely to overwhelm any such regulatory barriers.

19. This largely occurs because the lower income household groups seem to have fewer four-year-olds. This probably occurs because lower income households have a greater percentage of single individual households.

20. This fee is based on the pre-K program being three hours a day, 175 days a year, and having net costs in 2007 dollars of $4,933. This cost is what was assumed in my original report in 2006. These cost estimates were derived by Karoly and

Bigelow (2005). These are net cost figures that net out cost savings on existing pre-K programs. Therefore, the fee as a percentage of gross pre-K costs would be higher. However, the net cost figures assumed by Karoly and Bigelow end up being similar to some estimates of the gross costs of high-quality pre-K programs. Consider the estimates of the cost of high-quality pre-K education in Gault et al. (2008). There, a similar three-hour-a-day school-year program and a lead teacher paid public-school wages cost $4,071 per year per child at a class size of 20 to 2, $4,506 per year per child at a class size of 17 to 2, and $4,893 per year per child at a class size of 15 to 2. The calculation of pre-K costs also adds in extra administrative costs of 5 percent above this $4,933 per child to monitor family income and regularly collect the fees. (However, fees are set at half of the net costs before these extra administrative costs.)

21. This figure is taken from PPL Table 6B from the on-line version of Smith (2002). It can be found at http://www.census.gov/population/socdemo/child/ppl-964/tab06.pdf (accessed June 28, 2010).

    Specifically, I looked at the weekly child care expenditures divided by weekly child care hours for children less than five, and for families with annual incomes greater than $69,763 per year in 2007 dollars. (In the table, these are families with an average monthly income of greater than $4,500 in 1997 dollars.) I then updated this hourly figure to 2007 dollars using the CPI.

22. Karoly and Bigelow (2005) assume that charging fees will increase administrative costs by 10 percent. However, this appears to be based on a statement by Barnett (1993) that refers to the overall administrative costs of welfare programs, not the extra administrative costs that result simply from charging fees. Studies of administrative costs as a percentage of benefits in the United States suggest that non-means-tested programs such as Social Security have administrative costs of 2.5 percent of benefits, while welfare and unemployment insurance programs have administrative costs of 12.1 percent and 11.8 percent of benefits (Kesselman [1982], of which I was made aware by Besley and Kanbur [1990]). This might suggest that means testing adds 9–10 percent in administrative costs as a percentage of benefits. However, many of the administrative costs of welfare and unemployment insurance programs are due to complex work search rules, as well as administrative procedures that in part are meant to discourage usage. Therefore, I suspect that the extra administrative costs of charging fees to upper income families in a universal pre-K program would be considerably less than 9–10 percent. An extra 5 percent is a somewhat arbitrary but reasonable assumption.

23. A working-paper version of this chapter considers other distributional assumptions.

24. This can be derived by comparing row 2 to the fees paid, which is given by the difference between row 7 and row 3. For income quintile 4, the earnings benefits from pre-K with fees are 0.092 percent of income, whereas fees are 0.079 percent of income. For income quintile 5, the earnings benefits from pre-K are 0.042 percent of income, whereas fees are 0.037 percent of income.

9
Locality Matters

How Economic Development Benefits
Vary in Diverse Local Economies

In this book, up until now, the analysis has focused on economic development benefits for a typical state. For example, consider my statement that high-quality universal pre-K education produces $2.78 in economic development benefits per dollar of costs. That statement is true for an "average U.S. state." In an average U.S. state, high-quality universal pre-K would increase the present value of state residents' per-capita earnings by $2.78 per dollar of program costs. Consider also my statement that high-quality business incentives produce economic development benefits of $3.14 per dollar of costs. That statement, too, is true in an "average U.S. state": in an average U.S. state, high-quality business incentives will increase the present value of state residents' per-capita earnings by $3.14 per dollar of incentive costs.

But states differ. These differences may affect economic development benefits. I show in this chapter that economic development benefits of pre-K education differ somewhat across U.S. states. However, in all states, pre-K education has economic development benefits that considerably exceed program costs.

Furthermore, economic development benefits for a typical state may differ from economic development benefits for a typical metropolitan area. This is important because public policy toward early childhood programs and business incentives is not solely the prerogative of state governments. Local policymakers also make decisions about investing in early childhood programs, or in business incentives.

I show in this chapter that for a typical metropolitan area, compared to a typical state, the ratio of economic development benefits to program costs of early childhood programs is reduced. However, this reduction is small enough that these programs still make sense from a metropolitan area's perspective. Even if local governments in a metropolitan area pay all the costs of pre-K, this investment can still pay off in producing economic development benefits for the metropolitan-area economy.

Local economic development benefits may also vary because of the size and growth rate of the metropolitan area. I show in this chapter that the economic development benefits of early childhood programs will be smaller in smaller metropolitan areas, or in slower-growing metropolitan areas. However, these effects of metro-area size and growth on the returns to early childhood programs are modest. Even in small and slow-growing metropolitan areas, early childhood programs still have local economic development benefits exceeding costs.

I also show that the local economic development benefits of business incentives may be significantly lower in fast-growing metropolitan areas. In metropolitan areas that already have rapidly growing labor demand, policies to add even more jobs have lower benefits. These benefits may be insufficient to justify incentives' costs.

Therefore, local economic development strategy should vary with the local area's growth trends. Areas with plenty of jobs may not benefit much from business incentives. These high-growth areas should instead focus on early childhood programs and other programs to give local residents the skills needed for available jobs. Low-growth areas may benefit more from business incentives. However, low-growth areas will also benefit from early childhood programs and other skill-building programs.

The purpose, then, of this chapter is to explain how locality matters to economic development benefits. This includes quantifying how much it matters.

WHAT THIS CHAPTER IS AND ISN'T

This chapter focuses on characteristics of state and local areas that affect the benefits of early childhood programs or business incentive programs, holding constant who participates in these programs. As previous chapters have explored, benefits of early childhood programs may vary with the income mix of families participating. Benefits of business incentive programs may vary with the wage rates of businesses receiving incentives.

The types of families participating in early childhood programs may tend to vary with a locality's socioeconomic makeup. The types of businesses receiving incentives may tend to vary with a locality's business mix. But who participates in these programs also depends upon program design and administration. The locality's socioeconomic mix and business mix do not completely determine program participation.

This chapter considers how benefits would vary if we had the same mix of participants but were in a different state or local area. For early childhood programs, even with the same income mix of family participants, how would economic development benefits vary with state and local characteristics? For business incentive programs, even with the same types of businesses receiving incentives, how would economic development benefits vary with state and local characteristics?

THE MECHANISMS BY WHICH LOCALITY MATTERS

What characteristics of a state or metropolitan area affect economic development benefits for early childhood and business incentive programs? How do these characteristics affect economic development benefits?

States

For states, the main characteristic affecting economic development benefits of early childhood programs is the out-mobility of residents from early childhood to adulthood.[1] For this book's calculation of economic development benefits of early childhood programs, I only count earnings gains for those who remain in the state.

For states with lower percentages of children remaining in the state during their careers, we would expect economic development benefits of early childhood programs to be lower. I will quantify this below.

Metropolitan Areas

Compared to the typical state, the typical metropolitan area will be smaller and less diverse in amenities and industrial characteristics. As a result, we would expect that fewer children would remain as adults in the same metro area than in the same state. This will lower the economic development benefits of early childhood programs from a metropolitan perspective compared to a state perspective.

It is unclear what the smaller size and reduced diversity of metro areas, compared to states, imply for the economic development benefits of business incentives. On the one hand, the smaller size and reduced diversity of a metropolitan area as opposed to a state might mean that employment growth at the metro-area level will attract fewer in-migrants than at the state level. This would raise the economic development benefits of employment growth for the original residents of the area. On the other hand, the smaller size and reduced diversity of metro areas, compared to states, might mean that there is less likelihood of a good match among the original residents for any newly created jobs. This would reduce the effects of job creation on local employment rates, which would reduce economic development benefits.

In addition, it is possible that the responsiveness of business employment to incentives could differ at a metropolitan level compared to a state level. Business location decisions are more responsive to incentives if the location has more close substitutes. Because the typical metro area is smaller than the typical state, it might be thought to have more close substitute locations. On the other hand, state boundaries sometimes split metropolitan areas and other local labor markets. Two locations within the same local labor market are more likely to be close substitutes than two locations in different local labor markets.

Metropolitan Area Size

Metro area size might affect economic development benefits for reasons similar to why economic development benefits would differ for metro areas versus states. Smaller metro areas will have fewer and less diverse opportunities, amenities, and industries. This should reduce the percentage of children who later stay in the metro area during their adult working careers. The result is that local economic development benefits would be lower for early childhood programs in smaller metro areas.

For business incentives, the effects of metro area size on economic development benefits are uncertain. Smaller metro areas may attract fewer in-migrants. On the other hand, smaller metro areas may have more trouble matching their current workforce to new job opportunities. In addition, a typical small metro area may have more close substitute locations than a typical large metro area. This may increase the responsiveness of area employment to business incentives in small metro areas. On the other hand, some small metro areas may be dominated by less-footloose industries, those having strong historical or natural resource ties to the area. This would tend to reduce the response of area employment to incentives.

Metro Area Growth Trend

Metro areas differ in their usual growth rates. The previous metro growth trend matters to economic development benefits because this growth trend will affect the baseline ratio of job opportunities to labor supply. If the previous metro growth trend was slow, the metro area will have a lower ratio of job opportunities to labor supply. We would expect this to discourage persons from staying in the metropolitan area. This would lower the local economic development benefits from early childhood programs.

Slower growth in a metro area means there are greater economic development benefits to adding jobs through business incentives. The previous slow growth means there is more local nonemployed population available to fill newly created jobs. In addition, the newly created jobs will be less attractive to in-migrants because the local labor market still has higher unemployment.

EMPIRICAL EVIDENCE ON VARIATION ACROSS STATES

Across states, there is some variation in what percentage of childhood residents stay during adulthood. However, this variation is insufficient to dramatically alter the economic development benefits of early childhood programs.

The variation in out-of-state mobility can be illustrated by considering what percentage of persons born in a state still live in the state. Based on the 2000 Census, on average 68 percent of all Americans born in a state still live there. But the percentage living in their birth state varies across states. At one extreme, only 43 percent of those born in Wyoming still lived there in 2000, and 45 percent of those born in North Dakota still lived in that state. At the other extreme, 80 percent of those born in Texas were still living there in 2000, and 77 percent of those born in California. Thirty-seven states had a percentage of "birthright" state residents still living there of 60 percent or greater as of 2000 (Table 9.1).

These variations in out-of-state mobility can be used to estimate how economic development benefits of early childhood programs vary across states. Consider the case of pre-K programs. For the typical state, the economic development benefits per dollar of program costs are 2.78. Across states, economic development benefits per dollar of program costs vary from a high of 3.15 in Texas to a low of 1.96 in Wyoming. However, in 38 states this ratio is 2.50 or above (Table 9.2).[2]

The bottom line is that the economic development benefits-to-cost ratio of early childhood programs does not differ dramatically for most states. Even for states that have more out-migration of former child participants, a sufficient number of former child participants will stay to yield economic development benefits that exceed program costs.

EMPIRICAL EVIDENCE ON METROPOLITAN AREAS VERSUS STATES

The empirical evidence suggests that persons are only modestly less likely to spend their career in their childhood metropolitan area than in their childhood state. Therefore, *metropolitan* economic development benefits of early childhood programs are only modestly less than *state* economic development benefits. (This statement is for a typical state and a typical metropolitan area. We consider metropolitan areas of different size and growth later in this chapter.)

The available evidence suggests that the percentage of four-year-olds who still live in the same metropolitan area at age 31 and above is a little less than four-fifths of the percentage of four-year-olds who reside in the same state at age 31 and above. This finding is based in part upon research of mine that uses data from the Panel Survey of Income

Table 9.1 Percentage of Persons Living in Birth State

State of birth	% living in state of birth	State of birth	% living in state of birth	State of birth	% living in state of birth
Alabama	68.2	Louisiana	71.6	Ohio	70.9
Alaska	53.5	Maine	66.3	Oklahoma	60.3
Arizona	69.9	Maryland	68.5	Oregon	66.0
Arkansas	58.8	Massachusetts	66.2	Pennsylvania	69.1
California	76.9	Michigan	73.7	Rhode Island	60.4
Colorado	62.0	Minnesota	71.1	South Carolina	69.8
Connecticut	65.0	Mississippi	60.3	South Dakota	49.6
Delaware	62.3	Missouri	66.0	Tennessee	70.2
Florida	73.6	Montana	53.3	Texas	79.8
Georgia	73.4	Nebraska	56.0	Utah	70.7
Hawaii	63.0	Nevada	62.9	Vermont	59.1
Idaho	55.4	New Hampshire	61.1	Virginia	67.3
Illinois	65.7	New Jersey	64.5	Washington	70.4
Indiana	69.1	New Mexico	59.9	West Virginia	52.2
Iowa	59.0	New York	63.2	Wisconsin	73.3
Kansas	55.9	North Carolina	74.8	Wyoming	42.8
Kentucky	65.8	North Dakota	44.8	U.S. average	68.4

NOTE: This is derived from a special tabulation by the U.S. Census Bureau from the 2000 U.S. census, released on the Internet on January 31, 2005, and available at http://www.census.gov/population/www/cen2000/phct38.html (accessed June 28, 2010). This includes all U.S. residents in 2000 born in the United States. The percentage simply reflects what percentage of native-born citizens are living in the same state they were born in, broken down by state of birth. For example, the 68.2% for Alabama means that 68.2% of persons born in Alabama still live in Alabama, and should not be interpreted as meaning that 68.2% of current residents of Alabama were born in Alabama.

Table 9.2 Ratio of Economic Development Benefits to Costs of Universal Pre-K, by State

State	Ratio	State	Ratio	State	Ratio
Alabama	2.77	Louisiana	2.88	Ohio	2.86
Alaska	2.31	Maine	2.71	Oklahoma	2.52
Arizona	2.83	Maryland	2.78	Oregon	2.71
Arkansas	2.47	Massachusetts	2.71	Pennsylvania	2.80
California	3.05	Michigan	2.95	Rhode Island	2.53
Colorado	2.58	Minnesota	2.87	South Carolina	2.83
Connecticut	2.67	Mississippi	2.52	South Dakota	2.18
Delaware	2.59	Missouri	2.71	Tennessee	2.84
Florida	2.95	Montana	2.30	Texas	3.15
Georgia	2.94	Nebraska	2.38	Utah	2.85
Hawaii	2.61	Nevada	2.61	Vermont	2.48
Idaho	2.37	New Hampshire	2.55	Virginia	2.75
Illinois	2.69	New Jersey	2.65	Washington	2.84
Indiana	2.80	New Mexico	2.51	West Virginia	2.26
Iowa	2.48	New York	2.62	Wisconsin	2.94
Kansas	2.38	North Carolina	2.98	Wyoming	1.96
Kentucky	2.70	North Dakota	2.03	U.S. average	2.78

NOTE: These state-specific ratios of economic development benefits to costs are generated by adjusting for differential out-migration. This is based on the percentage of those born in the state that still live there. I extrapolate to different states based on how benefits are altered from the United States to the typical state by out-migration. The benefits to pre-K participants in the typical state are a ratio of 2.65 to costs. (There are also balanced-budget multiplier benefits and benefits to parents. These benefits are assumed to be unaltered by state migration, as these benefits are more immediate. There are also benefits from social spillover effects of more education. These are also assumed to be unaltered, as these may be larger if there is more mobility.) The benefits to pre-K participants in the United States are 3.66. To extrapolate this to other states, I multiply 3.66 by the following ratio: $(1 - [(3.66 - 2.65) / 3.66] \times [100 - \% \text{ born in state that remain}] / [100 - 68.4])$. The figure 68.4 is the percentage of those born in a typical state that are still living there in the 2000 Census. This calculation generates a figure of 3.66 for the United States and 2.65 for the typical state. After this figure is calculated for some other state, using figures from Table 9.1, I add 0.13 to reflect benefits of more spending, benefits to parents, and social spillover benefits of education.
SOURCE: Author's calculations.

Dynamics (PSID) to follow the same four-year-olds for up to 31 years. (Thirty-one years is the maximum number of years for which we can follow a sufficiently large sample using the PSID to obtain reasonably precise estimates.) The percentage of four-year-olds who live in the same state at ages 31–35 as they lived in at age four averages 72.2 percent. The percentage of four-year-olds who live in the same metropolitan area at ages 31–35 as they lived in at age four averages 56.2 percent. Other evidence suggests that the percentage living in the same area at ages 31–35 does not change much at later ages (Bartik 2009b). (Figure 9.1 presents the data from the PSID on the percentage of four-year-olds living in the same state or metropolitan area at later ages.)

Because the percentage staying in a typical metro area is about four-fifths of the percentage staying in a typical state, the economic development benefits of early childhood programs for the typical metro area will be about four-fifths of the economic development benefits for the

Figure 9.1 Percentage of Four-Year-Olds Living in Same State or Metro Area at Later Ages

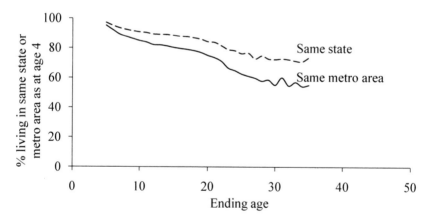

NOTE: Data are from the Geocode version of the Panel Survey of Income Dynamics (PSID), 1970 to 2005. Estimated percentages pool data over all year pairs. All estimated percentages use appropriate individual weights in the PSID. All metro area definitions for all year pairs are based on year 2008 metro area definitions. Percentage living in same state or metro area includes returnees—that is, the person does not need to have stayed continuously in the same state or metro area; rather, the question is whether at some later age they are living in the state they were in at age four.

typical state.[3] Consider universal pre-K programs. I estimate that for the typical metropolitan area, economic development benefits per dollar of costs will be 2.20, compared to 2.78 for the typical state. Economic development benefits are modestly lower for the typical metropolitan area. However, the economic development benefits still considerably exceed the costs.[4]

For business incentives, there is no clear evidence on whether the economic development benefits of increasing employment growth differ at the metropolitan level compared to the state level. In the absence of clear evidence, I assume the benefits are the same.[5] There also is no clear evidence on whether incentives are more effective in causing business growth at the metro area level than they are at the state level. I assume that incentives have the same growth effects in the typical metro area as in the typical state.[6] If incentives affect growth similarly in the typical metro area and in the typical state, and if growth affects real earnings similarly in the typical metro area and in the typical state, then incentives will have similar economic development benefits in the typical metro area as in the typical state. The ratio of economic development benefits to costs for the typical metro area will then be 3.14, as it is for the typical state.

EMPIRICAL EVIDENCE ON METROPOLITAN AREA SIZE

Empirical evidence suggests that the percentage of children in a metro area who stay as adults only varies significantly from the all-metro-area average for the smallest metro areas (Bartik 2009b). These smallest metro areas have a population of less than 330,000. For these smallest metro areas, the percentage of four-year-olds who as adults live in the same metro area is about one-fifth lower than for the average metro area.[7]

This lower percentage staying should lower the economic development benefits of early childhood programs in the smallest metro areas. The adjustment should be to lower benefits by about one-fifth compared to the average metro area. For example, I estimate that for universal pre-K programs in the smallest metro areas, the ratio of economic development benefits to costs is 1.74. This is modestly smaller than the all-metro-area average ratio of 2.20, which in turn is modestly smaller than the state ratio of 2.78. However, even though this ratio is smaller in the smallest metro areas, economic development benefits still exceed costs. Even in metro areas with less than 330,000 in population, the local economic development benefits from universal pre-K are sufficient to justify the costs. Similar results are obtained for other early childhood programs.[8]

For business incentives, the empirical evidence suggests that the effects of local growth on real earnings might be larger for the smallest metro areas (Bartik 2009c). Growth has larger effects on real earnings for metro areas below about 800,000 in population. However, growth effects do not vary significantly among larger metro areas.[9] This empirical evidence is only suggestive because we do not have good measures of local prices for smaller metro areas. However, at least part of the differential higher growth effects in smaller metro areas seems to be due to greater effects on labor force participation rates, which are not biased by problems in measuring local prices.

The estimates suggest that smaller metro areas, compared to the average metro area, may have growth effects on real earnings that are about one-sixth greater in magnitude.[10] Much of this greater effect is due to the greater effects on labor force participation. Newly created jobs in smaller metro areas are more effective at increasing the labor force participation rates of the original residents, as opposed to attracting in-migrants.

These one-sixth-greater effects on real earnings suggest that economic development benefits will be increased by a similar amount. For business incentives in these smallest metro areas, I estimate that the ratio of economic development benefits to incentive costs will be 3.66. This compares favorably with the baseline estimates for the average metro area or average state of 3.14.[11]

EMPIRICAL EVIDENCE ON METRO AREA GROWTH

The empirical evidence suggests that the percentage of adults living in the same metro area as they did when children only differs significantly with metro growth for the slowest-growing one-fifth of metro areas (Bartik 2009b). These are metro areas whose annual population growth is less than 0.2 percent. For these slowest-growing metro areas, the percentage of four-year-olds who live in the same metro area as adults is a little more than one-tenth lower than for the average metro area.[12]

As a result, for the slowest-growing metro areas, the economic development benefits of early childhood programs will be about one-tenth lower. For universal pre-K, I estimate that for the slowest growth metro areas, the ratio of economic development benefits to program costs is 1.96. This can be compared with 2.20 for the average metro area and 2.78 for the average state. However, although economic development benefits are lower, they still exceed costs. Even for slow-growing metro areas, a sufficient number of child participants in early childhood programs will remain in the metro area for these programs to produce economic development benefits that exceed costs.[13]

For business incentives, the empirical evidence suggests that the effect of additional jobs on real earnings only differs significantly for metro areas with the highest previous growth trends (Bartik 2009b). These high-growth metro areas are metro areas whose growth rates are ranked in the highest two quintiles, or the highest 40 percent of all metro areas. In the time period examined, these metro areas had annual employment growth rates exceeding 1.9 percent. For these high-growth metro areas, the real earnings effects of additional jobs are considerably lower than for the average metro area. Real earnings effects of additional jobs in these high-growth metro areas are only one-seventh of effects in the average metro area.[14]

The lesser effects of additional jobs on real earnings in high-growth metro areas are due in part to the lesser effects on local labor force participation rates. In a metro area that is already experiencing high growth, additional jobs are less likely to find untapped local labor supply. Additional jobs are more likely to attract in-migrants. The original residents benefit less from additional jobs in these high-growth metro areas.

Based on these estimates, we would expect the economic development benefits of business incentives to be considerably lower than average in high-growth metro areas. I estimate that in the highest-growth metro areas, the ratio of local economic development benefits to incentive costs is only 0.42, as compared to the baseline estimate for the

Figure 9.2 How Ratios of Economic Development Benefits to Costs Vary in Different Types of Local Economies, for Universal Pre-K Programs and Business Incentives

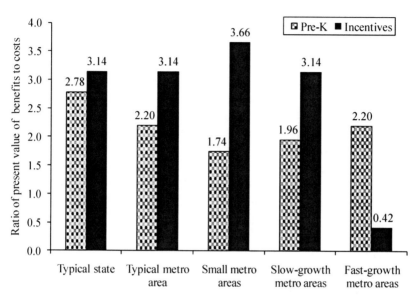

NOTE: Each ratio is the ratio of the present value of economic development benefits to the present value of program costs for either a permanent universal pre-K program or a permanent business incentive program. Each pair of bars shows these ratios for a particular type of local economy.

SOURCE: Author calculations, as discussed in chapter text and endnotes, and in Appendix 9B.

average metro area of 3.14. In the highest-growth metro areas, adding additional jobs through business incentives does not yield sufficient local economic development benefits to justify the incentive costs.

CONCLUSION

Figure 9.2 provides a summary of this chapter's results.[15] The local economic development benefits of early childhood programs are somewhat lower for metro areas than they are for states. This is particularly true for smaller metro areas or slower-growing metro areas.

However, even in small and slow-growing metro areas, early childhood programs yield local economic development benefits that considerably exceed costs. Such programs can effectively promote local economic development even if they are totally paid for by local government.

For average-growth or slow-growth metro areas, the economic development return to early childhood programs is somewhat reduced relative to business incentives. In such metro areas, which need additional jobs, a comprehensive economic development strategy should consider including high-quality business incentives that directly target employer job creation.

However, in high-growth metro areas, the benefits of creating new jobs through business incentives are much lower. In high-growth areas, which already are creating many new jobs, economic development strategies should focus more on improving the skills of the local labor force. Early childhood programs are one effective way of increasing local skills.

The current chapter, like the preceding ones, has focused on the state or local perspective on economic development benefits. The next chapter reconsiders the economic development benefits of early childhood programs and business incentives from a national perspective.

Notes

1. We might also expect state characteristics, such as the average health of state labor markets, to matter for the economic development benefits of business incentives. The rationale would be the same as what is given below for metropolitan areas: states with faster growth of labor demand are less likely to benefit from even faster growth. However, it is difficult to empirically measure these effects, given that there is a limited sample of 50 states. It is much easier to detect such effects for the larger numbers of metropolitan areas. I therefore focus in this chapter on exploring how metro area characteristics affect the returns to business incentives. Furthermore, one could argue that metropolitan areas are local economies, whereas states are at best some collection of local economies. Therefore, the returns to business incentives at a state level should depend not only on the average characteristics of the local economies that make up the state, but also on the distribution of such characteristics.

2. Similar calculations can be done for other early childhood programs. See Appendix 9A for calculations. Appendix 9A, like all appendices in this book, is available from the Upjohn Institute.
3. The actual calculation is more complicated because I extrapolate from how benefits are reduced from the national level to the state level. Furthermore, I use the percentage leaving the local area, rather than the percentage staying, to center the extrapolation.
4. Similar results occur for other early childhood programs. See Appendix 9B.
5. There is actually some evidence, cited in Bartik (2001, p. 419) that the earnings effects of employment growth shocks might be somewhat greater at the metropolitan level than they are at the state level. However, these estimates do not control for prices. We don't know whether the price impact of growth is greater at the metropolitan level or at the state level. It could be argued that housing supply is likely to be less elastic at the metropolitan level than at the state level, which may offset the greater effects of growth on nominal earnings at the metropolitan level. Furthermore, I note that the baseline estimates of how business incentives affect real earnings at the state level are derived from metropolitan area data. Therefore, if some future research eventually finds that employment growth shocks have greater effects at the metropolitan level than at the state level, the baseline state estimates should be adjusted downward rather than the metropolitan estimates adjusted upward.
6. The research literature that examines the effects of business taxes implicitly assumes this by combining results for states and metropolitan areas. See Bartik (1991a) or Wasylenko (1997).
7. The exact estimate is for metro areas in the lowest quintile of population size, where the quintiles are population-weighted quintiles (i.e., one-fifth of the total metro population lives in each quintile). For this smallest quintile of metro areas, the percentage of four-year-olds who still live there as 30- to 35-year-olds is estimated to be 43.7 percent. This can be compared with a metro area average of 56.3 percent. The ratio of 43.7 percent to 56.3 percent is 0.776.
8. See Appendix 9B.
9. See Bartik (2009c) for more details on the estimates. The estimates actually classify metro areas by employment size, not population size. I assume that the ratio of total population to CPS-defined employment is about two in stating results for population size. These estimates suggest that effects are only significantly different from the all-metro-area average for the lowest employment size quintile, where quintiles are defined as employment-weighted quintiles (i.e., one-fifth of the total employment in this metro area sample is in each quintile).
10. This estimate is based upon comparing the estimated effect on real earnings for this metro-area-size quintile of 0.466 to baseline estimates of 0.4 for the average metro area.
11. This estimate is simply derived by multiplying 3.14 by the ratio of 0.466 to 0.4.
12. These estimates are for the slowest-growth quintile of metro areas, where quintiles are population size–weighted quintiles. The exact estimate is that for ages 30–35,

the percentage of four-year-olds remaining in the same metro area for the slowest-growth quintile is 49.7 percent. The average percentage remaining over all metro areas is 56.3 percent. The ratio of 49.7 percent to 56.3 percent is 0.882.

13. Similar findings apply to other early childhood programs. See Appendix 9B.

14. See Bartik (2009c) for more details on these estimates. These estimates average results for the top two metro area quintiles in prevailing employment growth trends. Effects are 0.0245 for the highest growth rate quintile and 0.0827 for the second-highest growth rate quintile. The average is 0.0536. This is 13.4 percent of the 0.4 baseline effect used in previous calculations. These estimates do not have good local price data for most metro areas. However, a considerable portion of these differential real earnings effects for metro areas with different growth rates is due to the different effects on labor force participation rates.

15. Appendix 9B provides similar information for other early childhood programs.

10
The National Perspective

How Local Business Incentives and Early Childhood Programs Affect the National Economy

Thus far, this book has adopted the perspective of a state or local policymaker. This perspective focuses on what a state or local area's business incentives or early childhood programs can do for that state or local area. Any benefits or costs of this state's policies for other states are irrelevant.

But what about the national perspective? What if a state's business incentives have spillover effects on other states? For example, some of the jobs created by business incentives may have otherwise been created in other states. This loss of jobs in other states is a cost. From a national perspective, this cost should be considered.

And what if a state's early childhood programs have spillover effects on other states? For example, some former child participants in a state's early childhood programs will end up living in other states. The greater skills of these former child participants will increase their employability and wage rates in these other states. This will enhance earnings in these other states. This increase of earnings in other states is a benefit. From a national perspective, this benefit should be considered.

This chapter explores the national perspective on business incentives and early childhood programs. Two issues are of importance. First, what is the magnitude of the spillover benefits or costs for the nation of one state's business incentives or early childhood programs? These spillover benefits or costs are benefits or costs that states probably will not consider. Larger spillover benefits or costs imply that states are less likely on their own to pursue the best policies toward business incentives and early childhood programs.

Second, what would be the national benefits if the nation as a whole adopted large-scale business incentives or early childhood programs?

This chapter's findings on these two issues will lead to a discussion of the federal role toward business incentives and early childhood programs. Should the federal government encourage or discourage these programs? If federal intervention is needed, what form should it take? Should the federal government take over these programs?

According to the data presented in this chapter, a national perspective provides more of a case for federal regulation of state business incentive programs than of early childhood programs. The national perspective provides a cautious case for federal encouragement of early childhood programs. However, such federal intervention should allow for local flexibility.

NATIONAL VERSUS STATE BENEFITS OF BUSINESS INCENTIVES

> The U.S. . . . derives no social benefit when jobs move from Missouri to Mississippi, and any tax dollars spent to fund such a move result in a net loss of social welfare.
>
> —Ev Ehrlich and Tracy Kornblatt (2004, p. 4)

Business incentives are often argued to be against the national interest. As in the above quotation from Ehrlich and Kornblatt, the argument is that business incentives are a "zero-sum game." The jobs gained by one state are lost by other states.

If this argument was completely true, then "economic development benefits" of business incentives would not represent national benefits. The increased earnings of this state's residents would be 100 percent offset by the reduced earnings of other states' residents.

The zero-sum game argument is far-reaching. This argument does not just apply to the effects of business incentives on relocating jobs from one state to another. The argument would also apply to any newly created jobs. This includes jobs created in small businesses. For example, suppose a business incentive encourages the creation of new export-based jobs in small businesses in industry Y and state X. The zero-sum-game argument is that the national market for industry Y would otherwise be served by businesses throughout the nation. The business incentive only determines where industry Y is located. The business incentive does not affect total national activity in industry Y.

My research suggests that the zero-sum-game argument is partly true. To be more precise, the argument is 79.3 percent true, and 20.7 percent untrue. Simulations suggest that each dollar invested in business incentives creates $0.65 in increased present value of national earnings. This $0.65 national "economic development benefit" is 20.7 percent of what investing $1 in business incentives provides in economic development benefits for a state, which was estimated in Chapter 3 to be $3.14.

The logic for this national economic development benefit is as follows.[1] There are four reasons why national effects of business incentives might differ from state effects. First, the cost of creating a new job in an industry might be different at the national level, compared to the state level. Second, the multiplier effects of creating a new job might differ at the national level. Third, the earnings effects might differ at the national level because these earnings effects will include persons who move out of state. Fourth, the labor market might respond differently at the national level to an increase in labor demand.

Estimates of how businesses respond to investment incentives at the national level suggest that there is some national response. However, this response is less per dollar of incentives than is true at the state level. This makes sense because at the state level, businesses can respond to incentives in two ways, only one of which is possible at the national level. At the national level, an incentive may induce new job creation. At the state level, an incentive can induce new job creation, or it can cause the location of jobs to be different. This makes it easier to create a new state job than a new national job. Estimates suggest that per dollar of incentives, the job effect at the national level in assisted businesses is only 14 percent of the effect found at the state level (or more precisely, 13.7 percent). To put it another way, the cost of creating a job through business incentives at the national level is seven times as great as it is at the state level ($7.299 = 1 \div 0.137$).

But multiplier effects of the additional jobs in assisted businesses will be greater at the national level than at the state level. Multiplier effects of additional jobs in assisted businesses will in part occur in suppliers to assisted businesses. Some suppliers will be located in the same state, and some in other states. Therefore, more supplier jobs will be created in the nation than in the state. Multiplier effects also occur because of additional retail demand from workers at assisted businesses and suppliers. Only a portion of this increased retail demand will increase jobs in the same state as the assisted business. Increased retail demand will also increase jobs outside the state. Estimates suggest that multiplier effects at the national level will be about 40 percent greater than at the state level (or to be more precise, 40.7 percent greater).

At the national level, earnings effects will include residents of all states. At the state level, earnings benefits exclude out-migrants. Including residents of all states increases earnings benefits by about 7 percent (more precisely, 7.3 percent).

Finally, there is the issue of how earnings will respond to an increase in labor demand. Increased labor demand does not mean that the quantity of labor supplied will fully match that increase. An increase in labor demand will affect wages, unemployment, and labor force participation. This will in turn affect the quantities of labor supplied and demanded. This will feed back into further equilibrium effects on wages, unemployment, and labor force participation. There will be some final resulting equilibrium effect on earnings. I assume that the earnings response to a labor demand increase is similar at the national and state levels.[2]

These four factors combine to yield national effects on the present value of earnings, per dollar of incentives, of $0.65. Net earnings effects at the national level versus the state level will equal the product of the following:

- The ratio of effects on assisted businesses at the national level to those effects at the state level, or 0.137;

- The ratio of the multiplier effect at the national level to the multiplier effect at the state level, or 1.407;

- The ratio of total earnings effects considering residents of all states to effects including only residents who stay in a particular state, or 1.073;

- The ratio of net earnings effects at the national level to net earnings effects at the state level from a shock to labor demand, assumed to be 1.000.

This combines in the following calculation: $0.65 = 3.14 \times (0.137 \times 1.407 \times 1.073 \times 1.000)$.

This calculation of only 65 cents in earnings benefits per dollar of business incentives applies to typical business incentives of reasonable quality, as detailed in Chapters 3 and 5. National benefits would be lower for lower quality incentive designs. National benefits would be higher for higher quality incentive designs.

For example, as discussed in Chapter 5, some customized job training programs have been estimated to be at least 10 times as effective as average financial incentives to business. This implies that a high-quality customized job training program might yield $6.50 in national benefits per dollar of incentives (= a 0.65 effect of typical incentives × 10). As another example, manufacturing extension services have been estimated to be nine times as effective as financial incentives. A high-quality manufacturing extension program might have nine times the national economic development benefits per dollar of program cost, or $5.85 (= 0.65 × 9).

Financial incentives could also be redesigned to increase the $0.65 return to over a dollar. For example, calculations suggest that financial incentive returns would have national benefits of more than a dollar, for each dollar of incentives, if the created jobs paid an average wage premium of 20 percent or more. As another example, increasing the multiplier effects of assisted businesses by 54 percent would also increase the national benefit to more than one dollar per dollar of incentives.

However, the business incentives considered in the baseline simulations are business incentives of reasonable quality. These are the kind of business incentives that are commonly used. Therefore, the findings suggest that commonly used business incentives return considerably less than $1 in national economic development benefits per dollar invested. This in turn suggests the need for drastic reforms to current business incentive practice.

The $0.65 in benefits at the national level, versus $3.14 in benefits at the state level, suggests that state policymakers' perspective on business incentives is distorted. It appears that state policymakers' pursuit of state interests will lead them to use incentives more than is good for the nation. Federal policy to discourage such business incentives would seem warranted. As suggested by Arthur Rolnick and Melvin Burstein of the Federal Reserve Bank of Minneapolis, federal taxes and grants could discourage business incentives (Rolnick and Burstein 1994). The federal government could tax businesses receiving incentives at higher rates. The federal government could deny some federal aid to states providing large business incentives.

In addition, it would appear that the typical incentive does not make any sense for the federal government to pursue. National economic development benefits are less than two-thirds of the cost of a typical business incentive. It would seem that federal business incentive programs can only be justified if they are significantly above average in quality.

These conclusions about the need for a federal policy stance against business incentives will be analyzed further below.

NATIONAL VERSUS STATE BENEFITS OF EARLY CHILDHOOD PROGRAMS

> To sustain America's economic strength, community leaders, business leaders, policymakers, and parents must make providing access to high-quality early childhood education a top priority across the country.
>
> —Jim Rohr (2009), chairman and CEO of PNC Bank

Thus far, this book has focused on the benefits of early childhood programs from a state perspective. But is there also a national stake in early childhood programs, as Jim Rohr contends in the above quotation?

For early childhood programs, focusing on the state level means only including earnings effects for former child participants who remain in the state financing the programs. Obviously some former child participants will leave the state. Their participation in high-quality early childhood programs will raise their earnings. From a national perspective, the earnings benefits for those who leave the state should also be included in economic development benefits.

I resimulated economic development benefits including the earnings benefits of former child participants who leave the state. I also included any earnings benefits for parents who leave the state.

This resimulation leads to significant increases in economic development benefits. Compared to state economic development benefits, national economic development benefits for early childhood programs are increased by more than one-third. Benefits from a national perspective compared to a state perspective increase by the following percentages: pre-K, 36 percent; the Abecedarian program, 35 percent; and the Nurse-Family Partnership program, 34 percent.

The percentage increase in benefits due to considering out-migrants is greater for early childhood programs than for business incentives. In the previous section, including out-migrants only increased the benefits of business incentives by about 7 percent.

Why does including out-migrants make more of a difference for early childhood programs than for business incentives? There are two reasons. First, early childhood programs' effects compared to business incentives are delayed. There is more time for former early childhood program participants to move out of state before most of the earnings effects occur. Second, early childhood affects earnings over the entire work career, whereas business incentives affect earners at a wide range of different ages. The older workers affected by business incentives are less mobile than the younger workers affected by early childhood programs. Cross-state mobility tends to be highest for individuals from their late teens until their late twenties. This high mobility age period intervenes between early childhood programs and their earnings effects for former child participants.

Figure 10.1 shows national versus state economic development benefits for these three early childhood programs. For the sake of comparison, I also show national versus state economic development benefits for business incentives. For each program, I calculate the ratio of the present value effects on earnings to the present value of costs.

As the figure shows, high-quality business incentives are quite competitive with high-quality early childhood programs in providing state benefits. But early childhood programs do far better in providing national benefits.

The higher rate of return to early childhood programs from a national perspective than from a state perspective would seem to argue for a federal role. State policymakers fail to recognize about one-quarter or more of the total benefits of these programs. Some federal subsidy for these programs would seem warranted. Whether federal subsidies make sense will be further discussed later in this chapter.

The spillover benefits of early childhood programs for the national economy mean there would be net national benefits from adopting these programs at full scale in all states. These net benefits are sometimes sizable.

Figure 10.2 shows gross earnings benefits, costs, and net benefits from full-scale national implementation of each of these three early

**Figure 10.1 Ratio of Economic Development Benefits to Costs, State
versus National Perspective**

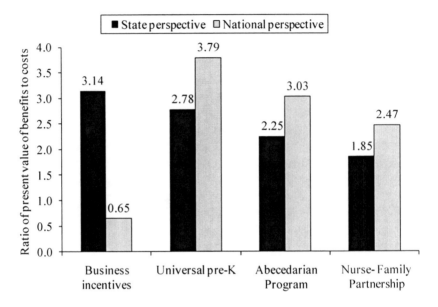

NOTE: This figure shows the ratio of the present value of economic development benefits to the present value of program costs. For each program, this ratio is shown both
from a state perspective and from a national perspective. See text for details.
SOURCE: Author's calculations, as detailed in text.

childhood programs. Net national benefits are positive for all three programs. Net national benefits are only truly sizable, however, for universal pre-K and the Abecedarian program. These two programs would
have net national benefits in the range of three-quarters of 1 percent to
1½ percent of national earnings. In contrast, the Nurse-Family Partnership has net national benefits of only around one-tenth of 1 percent of
earnings.

The NFP simply isn't large enough or intense enough to have large
net benefits, although the NFP has quite healthy rates of return per dollar invested. Universal pre-K and the Abecedarian program are large
enough and intense enough to have sizable net benefits. On the other
hand, the costs of these programs are considerably greater. This is particularly true of the Abecedarian program, which has costs of about

Figure 10.2 National Economic Development Benefits and Costs for Full-Scale National Implementation of Three Early Childhood Programs

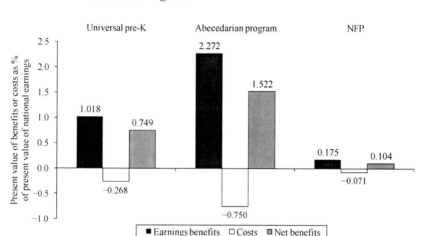

NOTE: The figure shows the effects of full-scale national implementation of each of these three early childhood programs. Effects are measured from a national perspective. Effects are measured as effects on present value of benefits or costs as a percentage of the present value of national earnings. Net benefits are simply earnings benefits minus program costs.
SOURCE: Author's calculations.

0.75 percent of earnings. Universal pre-K costs about one-third as much as the Abecedarian program. The Nurse-Family Partnership costs less than one-tenth as much.

These results suggest that the national economy would benefit from full national implementation of any one of these three early childhood programs. Should the federal government implement one or more of these three programs at full scale as federal programs?[3] This important issue will also be discussed further below.

MACROECONOMIC BENEFITS OR COSTS FROM REDISTRIBUTING JOBS

The discussion above of business incentives does not consider how redistributing jobs might affect the macro economy. Business incentives in a high unemployment state or local area will redistribute jobs to that high unemployment local economy, and away from low unemployment local economies. Business incentives in a low unemployment state or local area will do the reverse. Redistributing jobs across different local economies may have macroeconomic consequences.

These macroeconomic consequences will occur if the inflationary effects of job creation are different in different local economies. For example, evidence suggests that the effects of 1 percent lower unemployment in increasing wages and prices will be greater in a low-unemployment-rate local economy. If this is so, then redistributing jobs to high unemployment economies, and away from low unemployment local economies, will lower inflation. As a result of this redistribution of jobs, the Federal Reserve and other macroeconomic authorities can expand the economy more, yet keep inflation under control.

Redistributing jobs to low unemployment local economies, and away from high unemployment local economies, will increase inflation. The Federal Reserve and other macroeconomic authorities may need to restrain economic output to control inflation.

I did calculations of the potential macroeconomic benefits and costs of such redistribution of jobs.[4] For the calculations, I used the U.S. economy in 2007. In 2007, average U.S. unemployment was 4.6 percent, and inflation was a concern. (In the U.S. economy as of 2009, when this paragraph was first written, the Federal Reserve might welcome more inflation.) I considered business incentives in a high unemployment state. I used the unemployment rate of the highest unemployment state in 2007—Michigan, at 7.1 percent unemployment. I also considered business incentives in a low unemployment state. I used the unemployment rate of the lowest unemployment state in 2007, Utah, which had 2.7 percent unemployment.

These simulations suggest a modest macroeconomic benefit from business incentives in high-unemployment-rate states: these business incentives do reduce inflationary pressures. Lower inflationary pressure allows macro policymakers to be more aggressive in lowering overall U.S. unemployment. Aggregate U.S. earnings are increased. However, the effects are modest. The present value of the additional earnings from these macroeconomic effects is only 0.09 of the overall costs of the business incentives. If national benefits of the business incentives were 0.65 of costs, they would be increased to 0.74 of costs.

The effects are so modest for several reasons. Business incentives only affect unemployment rates for a few years in this model. Michigan's business incentives only slightly increase unemployment rates in the rest of the United States, and therefore only slightly reduce inflationary pressures.

The simulations suggest significant macroeconomic costs from business incentives in low-unemployment-rate states such as Utah. These business incentives increase inflationary pressures, and the resulting need for macroeconomic restraint is estimated to reduce U.S. earnings. This reduction is equal to 0.98 of the costs of the business incentives. If national benefits of the business incentives were 0.65 of costs, they would be reduced to −0.33 of costs. Business incentives in a low-unemployment-rate state reduce total U.S. earnings, once macro policy responses are taken into account.

These effects are larger because the business incentives are lowering unemployment by a great deal in a low unemployment state. In the model, the effects of lower unemployment on wage and price inflation go up quite a bit in low-unemployment local economies. Therefore, the macroeconomic consequences of allowing business incentives in a low unemployment state are large.

It appears that at times of low unemployment, business incentives in low unemployment states may be problematic. The gains for the state are more than outweighed by the macroeconomic costs for the United States as a whole.

SOCIAL BENEFITS FROM MORE JOBS: GREATER IN HIGH-UNEMPLOYMENT LOCAL ECONOMIES?

Thus far, this discussion has assumed that earnings effects measure social benefits. Business incentives are close to a zero-sum game because most of the earnings benefits in the state adopting the incentives are offset by lower earnings in other states.

However, earnings effects are only an indicator of economic development benefits. Social benefits will be higher with more earnings effects, all else being equal. However, other factors may affect the economic development benefits from more jobs. It is theoretically plausible that the economic development benefits associated with more jobs are greater in high-unemployment local economies. If this is so, then redistributing jobs to high-unemployment local economies would increase social benefits, even if the total number of national jobs is little affected. However, although this is theoretically plausible, there is scant empirical evidence that bears on this hypothesis.

As discussed in Chapter 2, there are several reasons why more jobs might provide social benefits. Based on these reasons, it is plausible that social benefits will be higher in high-unemployment local economies.

One reason that jobs might provide social benefits is that there is involuntary unemployment. Wages may be above the wages that would clear the labor market. As a result, not all of those willing to work at the market wage or below will find a job. Some of the unemployed may have reservation wages—the lowest wage at which the unemployed person will accept a job—that are considerably below the market wage. In such a reservation wage model, the social benefits of hiring an unemployed person are equal to the market wage minus that person's reservation wage.

It seems likely that the average reservation wages of the unemployed will be lower in a high-unemployment local labor market than in a low-unemployment local labor market. In a low-unemployment local labor market, it is relatively easy to find a job. Persons with low reservation wages have high benefits from getting a job. Therefore, they are likely to have already obtained one. The remaining unemployed will be those whose reservation wages are close to the market wage.

In contrast, in a high-unemployment local labor market, even persons with low reservation wages will have great trouble finding a job. The pool of unemployed will include many persons whose social benefits from obtaining a job are large.

Another social benefit from lower unemployment is the value of lowering the risk posed by local unemployment. This social value may partly be a matter of self-interest. Each individual may be concerned with how the overall local unemployment rate affects his or her risk of losing a job or finding a job. Individuals may also be concerned about how the overall unemployment rate affects the jobs prospects of their friends, family, and neighbors.

It is plausible that this social benefit from additional jobs may be higher in high-unemployment local labor markets than in low-unemployment local labor markets. For many an individual, lowering the overall local unemployment rate from 4 percent to 3 percent would not be perceived as significantly affecting his or her own job prospects, or those persons he or she knows. When the overall local unemployment rate is high, a much larger proportion of the population will consider the unemployment rate to be a serious problem. A higher percentage of individuals will perceive their own job prospects to be at risk, or perceive the job prospects of their family and friends as being at risk. The perceived social benefits from lowering local unemployment from 10 percent to 9 percent are likely to be great for a relatively high proportion of the population.

On the other hand, for the unemployed, the social benefits of lowering unemployment may actually be greater in low-unemployment local labor markets. There is some evidence that the social stigma effects of unemployment for the unemployed are higher when unemployment is low (Clark 2003). If one's unemployment is not shared by others he or she knows, then it may lead to greater feelings of shame and greater doubts about self-worth. However, as there are more employed than unemployed, the employed's perception of social benefits may dominate the overall social valuation. The social value of lowering unemployment sums its monetary valuation across the entire population, so the numbers of people in various groups matter, not just the intensity of effects on individuals.[5]

Although these arguments are plausible, there is little evidence available from empirical research. For example, there is no research showing how the effects of a 1 percent lower local unemployment rate on overall happiness varies at different starting levels for the local unemployment rate.[6]

With respect to reservation wages, the evidence is mixed. One study finds that each 1 point rise in the local unemployment rate reduces reservation wages by 1.2 to 1.6 percent (Jones 1989). Another study finds no effects of local unemployment rates on reservation wages (Haurin and Sridhar 2003). Several studies find that longer unemployment duration reduces reservation wages (Fishe 1982; Kasper 1969; Kiefer and Neumann 1979; Stephenson 1976). Higher local unemployment rates would increase unemployment duration. This suggests that higher local unemployment rates should reduce reservation wages.

Where does this leave policymakers? Redistributing jobs to high-unemployment local labor markets may raise social benefits. However, empirical evidence on this hypothesis is not definitive. We certainly have no agreement on the magnitude of increased social benefits from such job redistribution.

Perhaps this should leave national policymakers somewhat hesitant to denounce business incentives in high unemployment states or high unemployment local areas as a zero-sum game. It is possible that such incentives may produce net national social benefits. On the other hand, this argument does nothing to advance the case for business incentives in average-unemployment or low-unemployment local economies.

There also is the issue of whether business incentives tend to be higher in high unemployment areas. I will consider this issue below.

FEDERALISM AND BUSINESS INCENTIVES: A POLICY WONK'S PERSPECTIVE

What does this imply for the appropriate federal role in business incentives and early childhood programs? I will first consider the appropriate federal role in business incentives, before going on to early childhood programs. In considering the appropriate federal role, I will first imagine the perspective of a policy wonk. This policy wonk is assumed to have absolute power to design the perfect federal and state policy to advance economic efficiency and equity. I will then imagine a more realistic perspective on what to do given what is politically feasible.

It might seem that typical business incentives are inefficient from a national perspective: national benefits are $0.65 per dollar of program costs. But state policymakers perceive higher benefits of $3.14 per dollar of costs. Economic efficiency would seem to demand federal efforts to abolish or curtail typical business incentives, which are dominated by tax and other financial incentives. Only business incentives with significantly above-average efficiency, such as customized job training and manufacturing extension services, would seem to pass a national benefit-cost test.

However, from the perspective of a policy wonk who can always perfectly implement the ideal policy, it is not obvious that federal intervention is needed. If all states perfectly pursue their own self-interest, competition among states through business incentives may be efficient. Furthermore, any adverse effects on the income distribution from this competition can be offset through other policies.

To explain this somewhat startling conclusion, I first note that the cost of business tax incentives is, from an economist's perspective, largely not a true resource cost. Business tax incentives are mostly a transfer payment from the general taxpayer to businesses. Few real resources are used up in business tax incentives. There are some labor costs and materials costs in administering business tax incentives. But the tax incentive itself is a transfer from the general taxpayer to the assisted businesses.

Business tax incentives have a corresponding financial benefit to the assisted business. In an economic efficiency analysis, we must count equally the benefits and costs to everyone, with no discrimination. The benefit to assisted businesses is equal to the cost to the general taxpayer. The net cost is zero.

Business incentives that are services, such as customized job training and manufacturing extension services, do have real resource costs. These programs require significant use of labor and material resources. However, if these services are efficient, they have benefits to the assisted businesses that exceed their resource costs.

Thus, our analysis up to now has been incomplete. We have acted as if benefits to assisted businesses count for nothing. But from an economic efficiency perspective, these benefits should be fully counted. If the benefits to assisted businesses are counted, this changes our perspective on the net efficiency benefits of business incentives.

Consider an extreme case. Suppose there is some business tax incentive that has zero effects on location decisions. Suppose that this incentive has zero administrative costs. Then the net benefits of this business incentive are zero. The costs of this business incentive to the general taxpayer are exactly offset by the benefits to the assisted businesses.

Who benefits from providing business incentives to the assisted businesses? If nothing else changes, the owners of the assisted businesses get extra profits. If many businesses throughout the United States are provided with these incentives, this may have effects on overall prices or wages. Some of the initial extra profits for assisted businesses may be transferred to consumers through lower prices, or to workers through higher wages. How much will be so transferred? We don't know. Economists have never fully agreed on who bears the burden of the corporate income tax among shareholders, workers, and consumers. A general system of business incentives is similar to having reduced corporate income taxes. It is unlikely that economists will fully agree on the true economic incidence of widespread business incentives.

So far, this analysis suggests that business incentives may have zero efficiency benefits (tax incentives) or positive efficiency benefits (services to businesses whose value is greater than costs). However, this analysis so far has assumed that business incentives have no effect upon business location decisions. As discussed in Chapter 3, that assumption seems to be empirically incorrect. Business incentives do have significant effects on where businesses locate. These location effects are not as big as some economic developers like to claim, but the location effects are not zero.

If business location decisions are affected by business incentives, then an efficiency analysis needs to consider whether a system of business incentives will make the pattern of business locations more or less efficient. If there are no "social benefits" of business location decisions—that is, no benefits to parties other than the business itself—then business incentives can only make location decisions worse from an efficiency perspective. This argument has often been made by opponents of business incentives. For example, economist Art Rolnick, director of research at the Minneapolis Federal Reserve Bank, has told the following story for why business incentives will lead to inefficiency:

> Let us suppose a company chooses to relocate its manufacturing plant from a warm climate state, like Louisiana, to Alaska, even though its operating costs are substantially higher in a cold weather climate. I will assume that the company is more than fully compensated by Alaska for the move and for the additional operating costs. However, it now takes more resources for this company to produce the same quantity of output in Alaska than it did in Louisiana. (Rolnick 2007)[7]

But his argument assumes that there are no social benefits of business location decisions. One of the key arguments of this book is that business location decisions, by affecting employment, do create social benefits for the local unemployed population and local workers. If there are such social benefits, then it can be potentially economically efficient to induce different location decisions. Consider a world with all-powerful policy wonks in complete control of each state's policy. These policy wonks have perfect knowledge of their states' social benefits. Accordingly, these policy wonks will tend to adopt business incentives that will match these social benefits. The system of business incentives will induce more efficient business location decisions.

The example given by Rolnick is illustrative. Suppose that there are no social benefits of extra employment in Louisiana. Perhaps Louisiana has enough jobs for everyone who wants one. But suppose there are such social benefits in Alaska. Alaska is assumed to not have enough jobs. Both the unemployed and the working force in Alaska will benefit from creating additional jobs in that state to lower Alaska's unemployment rate. As long as the incentives offered by Alaska are equal to or less than these social benefits of job creation, the relocation of jobs from Louisiana to Alaska is economically efficient. Yes, production costs are higher. But the extra social benefits more than outweigh these higher production costs.

If all-powerful and all-knowing policy wonks are in charge of business incentives in each state, they will always offer business incentives that are equal to or less than the social benefits from additional jobs. Offering higher incentives than social benefits would not be in the state's individual interest. The resulting competition for businesses will drive up business incentives to be equal to whatever the social benefits are from additional jobs in each state. Businesses will make location decisions based on the combination of business incentives and their own private costs. Because business incentives perfectly reflect social benefits, this relocation will be economically efficient. Businesses will not relocate from state X to state Y unless the social benefits from so doing outweigh the extra production costs.

This system of all-out state competition for businesses via business incentives will tend to transfer resources from the general taxpayer to the business sector. Net business taxes after incentives will be lower than they otherwise would be. As mentioned above, it is uncertain what the incidence will be of lower net business taxes. To the extent that lower net business taxes result in higher profits for owners of businesses, the benefits from this incentive competition will have a regressive effect on the income distribution. Ownership of stock in businesses is highly concentrated in upper income groups.

However, in our perfect policy-wonk world, all-powerful and all-knowing policymakers at the federal level can offset any regressive effects of business incentive competition on the income distribution. For example, federal policymakers could choose to make the personal income tax more progressive. A surcharge for high income groups could offset the extra profits accruing to corporate shareholders. In this perfect world, this income tax redistribution is preferable to trying to prevent incentive competition among the states. The incentive competition leads to businesses taking the social benefits of employment into account in making location choices. It is economically efficient to take such social benefits into account. Therefore, business incentive competition should not be prohibited.

FEDERALISM AND BUSINESS INCENTIVES: A PRACTICAL POLITICAL PERSPECTIVE

A practical politician would regard the policy wonk's perspective as unrealistic. Practical politicians must take distributional effects into account. In an imperfect world, incentives are unlikely to match social benefits.

State and local policymakers cannot count on any regressive effects of business incentives being offset by more progressive federal taxes. In addition, from a state perspective, the "benefits" of business incentives for business owners largely flow to out-of-state residents. There are good reasons for state and local policymakers to heavily discount benefits to wealthy out-of-state business owners. It is reasonable for state and local policymakers to consider business incentives to be largely a cost. The social benefits from payments to business owners should be heavily discounted.

Even from a national perspective, federal policymakers cannot assume that incentive reforms will be offset by tax policy. Expanding or contracting business incentives will in part expand or contract the incomes of business owners. Because business owners are a very upper-income group, the benefits of incentives to business owners should be heavily discounted. Business incentives should be regarded as largely a cost, with social benefits (if any) coming in terms of increased earnings.

Competition among states in offering business incentives has not led to some ideal pattern of net tax rates. Net business tax rates after incentives are not lowest in state or local areas with the highest unemployment. The best empirical exploration of how incentives affect the spatial pattern of investment returns is by Fisher and Peters (1998). They do find that "explicit development incentives," such as "state tax credits and . . . local taxes and tax incentives . . . tend to be more favorable in states and cities with higher unemployment" (p. 200). However, these development incentives mostly serve to offset the effects of overall state tax systems. Basic state business taxes tend to be higher in states with high unemployment. Basic state tax systems "exhibit a strong tendency to skew returns on new industrial investment in a perverse direction, producing higher after-tax returns in states with lower unemployment rates . . . The end result [of the combined effect of the basic state and local tax system plus incentives] is a spatial pattern of returns on new investment that has little or no bearing to the spatial pattern of unemployment among cities" (p. 200). The best that we can say of incentives is that "incentive competition has produced a neutral (or random) spatial distribution of returns, which at least is better than what would have prevailed in the absence of incentives" (p. 200). Furthermore, it is possible that the basic state and local business tax system would adjust if business financial incentives were reduced. Perhaps the basic state and local business tax system would adjust toward a more "neutral" pattern, one that would show similar average tax rates in local economies that have different unemployment rates.

Therefore, at most it is only possible to give a weak endorsement of business incentives as helping high-unemployment local economies. Perhaps business incentives even the playing field a bit. But business incentives do not clearly favor high unemployment areas.

It is possible to make a practical political case for federal action to restrict business financial incentives. The case is particularly strong for restricting business financial incentives offered by low unemployment states or local economies. The social benefits of such incentives are particularly low. They sometimes have adverse effects upon inflation. And encouragement of business financial incentives tends to worsen the U.S. income distribution, which has already become more unequal over the past 30 years.

There is not as strong a case for federal action to restrict business incentives that provide services to business such as customized job training or manufacturing extension services. Well-run programs of customized job training or manufacturing extension probably have sufficient national economic development benefits to justify their costs.

Federal control of business incentives might be modeled after the procedures used by the European Union to regulate "state aid" (Sinnaeve 2007; Thomas 2000, 2007). State aid is broadly defined by the European Union as including "all advantages [to business] selectively granted by the state or through state resources that distort competition or threaten to distort it and affect trade between member states, e.g., grants, loans at nonmarket conditions, state guarantees, all types of tax advantages, and the sale of land at nonmarket conditions" (Sinnaeve 2007, p. 88). The basic principle of the EU's regulation of state aid is that state aid is outlawed unless "it promotes other EU objectives, such as regional development [of distressed regions], R&D, employment, etc. which outweigh the distortion in a proportional way" (p. 89). The EU then goes on to define "the conditions under which aid projects can be authorized for different types of aid, specifically aid for regional development, promotion of SME [small and medium-sized enterprises], employment, R&D, environmental protection, training of workers, restructuring of enterprises in difficulties, and provision of risk capital . . ." (p. 90). Even for the state aid that is allowed, the EU applies rules for how great the aid can be relative to the project's overall costs. The state aid is administered by requiring advance EU approval of state aid for specific projects. However, EU member states can apply for blanket approval of some program of state aid (for example, a program to aid small and medium-sized businesses, or to provide job training to employees). If the EU has not given prior approval to a particular state aid project, the EU may then subsequently investigate the legality of the project, with such an investigation being initiated either by the EU or in response to complaints by other member states or competing businesses. If the state aid is found to violate EU rules—i.e., the aid is excessive relative to the aid's overall benefits for the EU—the European Commission can order that the state aid be repaid by the assisted business, with interest.

The U.S. Constitution would seem to authorize Congress to understate such regulation of business incentives. The Constitution specifically authorizes Congress to "regulate Commerce . . . among the several States" (Article I, Section 8). As argued by Rolnick (2007), this provision was adopted in response to problems under the Articles of Confederation: "Under the Articles, the states had freely engaged in destructive economic warfare by imposing all types of trade barriers against one another. To address this, James Madison, the recognized father of the Constitution, added the Commerce Clause to the Constitution, to help promote an economic union of the states."

Of course, wrongheaded federal regulation of business incentives could do more harm than good. Federal regulation should not discourage cost-effective business incentives such as customized job training and manufacturing extension programs. Federal regulation should not discourage states from using business incentives to help distressed local labor markets.

It would be politically difficult to enact federal regulatory authority over state and local business incentives. For example, a federal appeals court in 2004 struck down an Ohio tax incentive as unduly interfering with interstate commerce. Soon after, several bills were introduced to get around the court's ruling. Legislation to negate the court's ruling was endorsed by the National Association of Manufacturers, the National Governors Association, and the U.S. Conference of Mayors (Mazerov 2005). The court ruling was eventually overturned by the U.S. Supreme Court on the grounds that the plaintiffs lacked standing.

If a political coalition is powerful enough to enact federal regulatory authority over business incentives, then it might be powerful enough to increase the progressivity of federal income taxes. Suppose the primary national concern about unregulated business incentives is their redistribution to business interests. Then it could be argued that this redistributional issue should be more directly addressed. However, the regulation of business incentives may attract political support beyond those persons concerned about income distribution. For example, there are economists such as Rolnick who are concerned that business incentives may distort market competition. Furthermore, the general public may be more supportive of restraining business incentives than of redistributing income.

If federal regulation of business incentives proves too politically difficult, an alternative is to appeal to state policymakers' own self-interest. As was reviewed in Chapter 6, there is sufficient uncertainty about the effectiveness of business financial incentives that policymakers may decide that reining in incentives is in their state's self-interest. For example, most business tax incentives could be made nondiscretionary and incorporated into the regular business tax system. Incorporating incentives into the overall business tax system is likely to encourage greater discussion of their overall revenue cost. In contrast, discretionary business tax incentives are sometimes promoted as self-financing, from the increased business activity. Discretionary business tax incentives are also promoted as being limited to a few cases. However, in practice, once tax incentives are given to a few businesses, the political pressure to help other businesses is difficult to resist. And, as was discussed in Chapter 3, the effects of business tax incentives are too low for the incentives to be self-financing.

The self-interest of states also is promoted by more efficient incentives. The empirical evidence suggests that customized job training and manufacturing extension services are more cost-effective than business tax incentives.

In fast-growing localities, as was shown in Chapter 9, the benefits from business incentives are lower than costs from the locality's perspective. These fast-growing localities are also likely to have low unemployment rates. It is in the self-interest of booming localities to cut back on the business incentives that also impose national macroeconomic costs.

Advocates of restraining business incentives believe that reform must start with greater transparency (Bartik 2005; LeRoy 2007; Markusen and Nesse 2007). Transparency includes specific information on what incentives have been offered to what businesses. Such information will increase political pressure to rein in business incentives. According to LeRoy (2007, p. 185), "Twelve states have already enacted some sort of economic development subsidy disclosure (Connecticut, Illinois, Louisiana, Maine, Minnesota, Nebraska, North Carolina, North Dakota, Ohio, Texas, Washington State, and West Virginia)."

Another useful reform is more and better evaluation. Even if it is hard to determine whether a particular tax incentive was decisive, it is quite feasible to evaluate the likely labor market effects of a particular business's location or expansion decision. Such evaluation can even be required prospectively, as is done, for example, in Michigan's MEGA program. Such evaluation puts pressure on business incentives to be used more in businesses that have higher wages or multiplier effects.

As was discussed in Chapter 6, more rigorous ex-post evaluation of business incentive programs that provide services to individual businesses can also be done. Such evaluations can be done by matching assisted to unassisted businesses and comparing their relative performance. Past research suggests that such services to businesses are in many cases more cost-effective than financial incentives. Therefore, good evaluations are likely to increase political pressure for reforming business incentives toward more services and less financial incentives.

Moving the mix of business incentives toward services rather than tax incentives is likely to be advantageous for three reasons. First, as was discussed in Chapter 5, the available empirical evidence suggests such incentives are more cost-effective. Second, business incentives that are services are likely to be more strictly monitored, because they are subject to an annual appropriations process. Business tax incentives are not reviewed through an annual appropriations process. Third, business demand for such services will only materialize if the services are useful to businesses. Business tax incentives will be demanded by businesses even if they have no effect upon location or expansion decisions. Tax incentives increase profits even if they do not change business behavior.

Improved evaluation of business incentives may be encouraged from the bottom up. Grassroots political pressure may lead state legislatures to enact evaluation requirements or legislative audit requirements.

Encouraging better evaluation of business incentives may also be an important federal role. The federal government could fund such evaluations; such funding is an appropriate federal role. High-quality evaluations of one state's business incentives provide useful knowledge for all states.

FEDERALISM AND EARLY CHILDHOOD PROGRAMS:
A POLICY WONK'S PERSPECTIVE

A policy wonk's analysis of optimal federal policy toward early childhood programs is simpler. Three conclusions seem warranted.

First, the spillover effects of early childhood programs are large enough to justify a considerable federal subsidy. This subsidy in some cases may be larger than the cost of these programs.

For example, the calculations reported in Figure 10.1 suggest that the present value for universal pre-K of national economic development benefits is $3.79 per dollar of program costs, compared to state economic development benefits of $2.78. This means that the spillover benefits of universal pre-K that accrue in other states are $1.01 (3.79 − 2.78) per dollar of program costs. Other states should be willing to subsidize the program's entire costs based on these spillover benefits.

Similar calculations based on Figure 10.1 can be made for other early childhood programs. The resulting spillover benefits, per dollar of early program costs, are $0.78 for the Abecedarian program and $0.62 for the Nurse-Family Partnership program. Spillover benefits can justify a federal subsidy of a considerable portion of these programs' costs.

Second, as was argued in Chapter 4, these programs produce benefits greater than costs from a state perspective. Therefore, if state policymakers are perfectly rational and are maximizing the present value of benefits, state policymakers should adopt these programs. No federal subsidy should be needed to get states to adopt these programs.

Third, if, despite their self-interest, states choose not to adopt these programs, it is in the national interest for the federal government to pay for these programs. The present value of the national economic development benefits of all these programs considerably exceeds their costs.

FEDERALISM AND EARLY CHILDHOOD PROGRAMS:
A PRACTICAL POLITICAL PERSPECTIVE

What political problems might there be with a heavy federal subsidy, or even a federal takeover, of early childhood programs? As discussed in Chapter 6, one major issue is that our knowledge of what constitutes quality in these programs is uncertain. We need to encourage innovation and creativity in early childhood programs. The concern is that too great a federal role may inhibit the needed innovation and creativity.

As discussed in Chapter 5, Head Start on average seems to be somewhat less effective than some of the better state pre-K programs. Some analysts have expressed concern that Head Start's effectiveness may have been reduced by the way the program has been managed by the federal government. For example, Rolnick has expressed the following concerns about Head Start: "Another disappointing example of a large-scale program is Head Start. It is not getting the kind of returns that we saw in the Perry–High Scope study. I would argue that the disappointing results are partly because Head Start is underfunded relative to Perry–High Scope. More fundamentally, I think that Head Start [has] performed well below expectations because [it] approaches the problem of early childhood development from the top down" (Haskins and Rolnick 2006).

In Head Start's case, as mentioned in Chapter 5, the problem may not be too much federal regulation, but rather the wrong kind of federal regulation. For example, Head Start traditionally has not had strong educational requirements for lead teachers. This may reflect political pressure to use the program as a community jobs program.

One possible compromise is to try to circumscribe the federal role. The federal role should be shaped so that it helps support high quality in early childhood programs without dictating 100 percent of program content. For example, one option would be to have heavy federal subsidies for some of the crucial physical capital, human capital, information, and support infrastructure of early childhood programs. The federal government could support building costs, curriculum materials and instructional supplies costs, costs for testing of children and evaluation of these programs, costs of staff training, transportation costs, and special student support services costs. The remainder of regular operating costs would be paid for at the state and local level.

Such a division of federal versus state responsibilities might encourage programs to be of higher quality by encouraging better staff training, curriculum, and evaluation. Better data and evaluation of these programs would have particularly high spillover benefits for other states. All states can learn from the development of better program models.

The hope is that because federal aid would not pay for regular operating costs, the federal government would not seek to control all program design and content. Of course, it is possible for the federal government to use its control of these support costs to try to dictate programs. For example, the federal government could seek to only fund a very limited number of curriculum approaches. Federally paid-for training could be restricted to particular training approaches. For this model of federal support to still encourage innovation and creativity, there would have to be an understanding that new and different curricula and staff training approaches could be considered and tested.

Federal support for this physical capital, human capital, and information infrastructure would support a considerable percentage of the costs of high-quality early childhood programs. For example, for a three-hour-per-day school year pre-K program, with a class-size ratio of 20 to 2, the Institute for Women's Policy Research estimates the following percentages of costs in some of these categories: 11.5 percent for infrastructure costs, which is mostly the cost of facilities but also includes quality monitoring and evaluation costs; 16.9 percent for student support services and staff training; 6.5 percent for instructional supplies; and 4.5 percent for transportation. The total is almost 40 percent of overall costs. Implementing universal pre-K in all states is estimated to cost $14 billion per year. If all states implemented universal pre-K, and the 40 percent federal cost share was applied to all pre-K expenditures, then the federal government would pay about $6 billion for universal pre-K. State and local governments would pay the remaining $8 billion.

Federal support for uniform measurement of quality might be particularly important. As discussed in Chapter 7, good comparable measures of early childhood program quality across state and local areas might encourage capitalization of these programs' benefits into housing values. Such capitalization would provide greater up-front benefits for early childhood programs. These greater up-front benefits would encourage state adoption of these programs. More voter awareness of program quality relative to national norms might also increase pressure by voters for higher program quality.

But federal operating support may also be needed. Without a federal operating subsidy, many states' investments in early childhood programs may be inadequate. As John Donahue has argued in his book on the role of American states, *Disunited States*, states may skimp on human capital investments because their benefits are mainly long-term. I made a similar argument in Chapter 7. The possibility of capitalization may only be a partial solution to this problem. Donahue (1997, p. 158) also argues that states may be reluctant to make human capital investments because "education and training policy has a distributional element—an element that becomes more important as economic inequality deepens . . . The political tension inherent in taxing the mobile, the well-off, and the childless to pay for education spending that matters most to the less skilled, the less affluent, and those with large families could quite plausibly lead states to scale back their overall commitment to human-capital development."

Just because the federal government is sometimes overly rigid does not mean that state and local governments will be willing to make needed investments. We should not naively assume that state and local policymakers will always be wise and far-sighted.

A larger federal role could certainly be justified *if* this larger federal role allowed for needed local flexibility. As mentioned, the spillover benefits justify full federal funding of universal pre-K. If the federal government could be induced to allow creativity and experimentation in early childhood programs, then federal funding for regular operating costs might be encouraged. Federal funding might be particularly helpful in helping overcome possible bias by state and local governments against early childhood investments that only pay off in the long run.

One possible model for federal operating funding is as follows. The federal government could agree to provide states with a certain amount of early childhood funding for each low or middle income household. For example, the federal government could agree to provide 80 percent of early childhood education funding up to a $10,000 cap per low or middle income household. I am here defining low or middle income households as those belonging to the lower three quintiles in the household income distribution—i.e., up to $62,000 in annual household income (DeNava-Walt, Proctor, and Smith 2008). This approach would be a compromise between the advocates of targeting and universalism. (See Chapter 8 for more discussion of this issue.) The targeting advocates would be pleased that the federal funding did not include the upper two income quintiles, which are thought to have lower benefits from early childhood programs. The universalism advocates would be pleased that the federal funding included 60 percent of all households, and probably about half of all children.[8] The universalism advocates would argue that these children from middle income households would gain considerably from early childhood programs.

To reduce stigma and administrative costs, the funding system might want to avoid collecting income data from every household participating in these federally funded early childhood programs. It would be quite feasible to base federal funding on the incomes found in a random sample of participating households in each state.

The $10,000 cap would be for total funding per child under age five. For example, the federal government would be willing to pay up to $10,000 for a one-year program for a child from a low or middle income household, or $5,000 per year for a two-year program, or $2,000 per year for a five-year program. How exactly to allocate these funds across different ages from birth to age five, or across different types of programs, would be left to state discretion.

The funding process should allow for considerable state discretion. Some type of state process to monitor and measure program quality would be required. And, as mentioned above, full federal funding would be provided for any quality monitoring and staff training. Federal funding would also be provided for a variety of experimental or other rigorous evaluations of these state programs.

Because a wide variety of early childhood programs would be eligible, this would make it more difficult for the federal government to micromanage the program. In contrast, if the federal government only funded one type of early childhood program, there would be some temptation for federal program managers to only fund the "ideal" pre-K program or "ideal" nurse home visitation program.

With reasonable assumptions about participation, such a program might cost about $15 billion per year. About half of this funding would be sufficient to provide funding for about half the participants in an age-four universal pre-K program. The other half could support other early childhood programs.[9]

For a variety of reasons, significant new federal funding support for early childhood programs may be hard to come by. (Among other things, looming budget deficits and the cost of health care programs pose barriers. The federal government has a lot on its plate.) Furthermore, it is by no means obvious that any federal support for early childhood programs would be enlightened enough to support local flexibility. Advocates for early childhood programs may need to rely on states taking the lead.[10] As pointed out in this chapter and throughout this book, high-quality early childhood programs cost a state less than what the state gets back in economic development benefits. But a calculus of benefits exceeding costs means nothing unless accompanied by political pressure. Better information and awareness by the voting and home-buying public of the benefits of high-quality early childhood programs, and the quality of their states' current early childhood programs, may help create the needed state-level political pressures. This book's concluding chapter, Chapter 13, further considers the potential for state and local activism to expand early childhood programs.

CONCLUSION

A national perspective on business incentives and early childhood programs suggests the potential for federal intervention to improve outcomes for these programs. But wrongheaded federal intervention could also make matters worse.

Federal intervention is particularly needed for business incentives. The state perspective on the benefits of these programs differs greatly from the national perspective. Although state and local governments have some self-interested reasons to improve business incentive policies on their own, these reasons are likely insufficient to motivate the needed reforms. The negative national spillovers of wrongheaded state business incentive policies are potentially large, compared to these policies' benefits for states.

Federal intervention should discourage business financial incentives in low unemployment areas, as these lack sufficient national benefits. But federal intervention should not discourage creative new programs that effectively promote economic development. Customized job training or manufacturing extension programs should not be discouraged.

In contrast, for early childhood programs, state and local governments have more reason to pursue constructive policies on their own, without federal intervention. High-quality early childhood programs have benefits that are considerably greater than costs from a state and local perspective. These programs have some national spillover benefits, but these benefits are more modest in size compared to the state's own benefits.

Federal support for early childhood programs should encourage states to make needed investments while encouraging creativity and experimentation in program delivery. Early childhood programs have sufficient spillovers and national benefits to justify considerable federal support. But there is enough uncertainty about the best program approaches that we also need plenty of state and local discretion.

If federal support is provided for operating spending for early childhood programs, a wide variety of state and local program approaches should be funded. Funding should not be restricted to one supposedly ideal program design, as this overstates our current knowledge.

Federal support for evaluation and data collection for early childhood programs can provide national benefits for all states. Better information on quality may cause voters and the housing market to put more pressure on state and local policymakers to make quality improvements. Federal support for staff training can increase the odds that early childhood programs will be research-based and of high quality.

This policy advice assumes the possible legitimacy of government intervention in business incentives and early childhood education. The next chapter will consider the ethical issues raised by such government intervention.

Notes

1. Appendix 10A presents more detail. This appendix, like all the appendices in this book, is available from the Upjohn Institute.
2. Appendix 10B discusses why this is a reasonable assumption.
3. This ignores the issue of whether the benefits of each of these three early childhood programs are independent of each other. It is possible that implementing one of these programs (e.g., the Abecedarian program) may decrease or increase the net benefits of the other programs (e.g., Universal pre-K).
4. The model details are reported in Appendix 10C.
5. For example, in DiTella, MacCulloch, and Oswald's (2001) evaluation of the social cost of unemployment, 90 percent of the loss in happiness due to higher unemployment is that of the employed. In Blanchflower's (2007) estimates, three-fourths of the loss in happiness due to higher unemployment is that of the employed. When one person becomes unemployed, the monetary value of that individual's loss of happiness is higher than the monetary value of the resulting

loss of happiness (due to a higher unemployment rate) of an individual employed person. But the sum of the monetary value of the loss of happiness of all the employed is greater than the monetary value of the loss of happiness to the individual who becomes unemployed.

6. DiTella, MacCulloch, and Oswald's (2001) research found no significant influence of national unemployment squared in regressions explaining differences in happiness for a particular country and year in a panel data analysis. If the nation is considered the relevant labor market, this implies that the marginal benefits of lowering unemployment do not vary significantly with the unemployment rate. However, trying to detect nonlinearities in a limited number of countries and years is quite difficult.

7. Rolnick's testimony also makes two other arguments for the inefficiency of business incentives. One argument is that competing via business incentives erodes the local tax base and leads to economically inefficient underproduction of public goods. This argument is only valid if state and local governments are forced to rely on business capital taxes for all or a fixed percentage of public good costs. If other taxes are available, this result does not hold (Oates and Schwab 1988). A second argument is that business incentives lead to variations across businesses in tax rates that inefficiently reallocate capital. However, as argued in the text of this chapter, if these business incentive differentials are related to the social benefits provided by the business, then this capital reallocation will not be inefficient.

8. The assertion that the bottom 60 percent of all households include about half of all children is consistent with the calculations in Appendix 8A. It is also consistent with the on-line statistic, from the Census Bureau's data files for the 2008 Annual Social and Economic Supplement to the CPS, that the bottom three income quintiles include 49.7 percent of all family households (U.S. Census Bureau 2008).

9. I base this calculation on year 2008 data on persons by age in the United States from the Census Bureau. I update these data to 2011 by assuming 0.3 percent growth per year at all age levels. I assume that 49.7 percent of all children are eligible for this federal funding. Among those eligible, I assume 70 percent participation. The funded program is assumed to provide $5,000 in funding for an age four program. This federal support would be 80 percent of total spending, with total spending at $6,250 per four-year-old. Such funding would be sufficient to support a high-quality pre-K program, based on data from the Institute for Women's Policy Research (2008). The remaining $5,000 in federal funding would arbitrarily be allocated at $1,250 per year across the four years from age zero to age three. Again, since this funding is at 80 percent, it would support spending $1,563 per year for these four years. Alternatively, the $5,000 would be sufficient to fund about half the cost of the Nurse-Family Partnership for each child. (The funding would still be only a tiny percentage of the total cost of an Abecedarian program for each child, which would cost over $60,000 per child.)

10. One point to note is that state and local governments face incentives, due to capitalization effects, to value the long-run effects of universal pre-K. At the national level, universal pre-K is unlikely to lead to capitalization effects, as capitalization

effects depend upon the attractiveness of a local area affecting in-migration and out-migration. Therefore, the federal government does not have incentives from capitalization to value the long-run effects of universal pre-K. We are depending upon the federal government deciding to expand early childhood programs in the right way because it is the right thing to do.

11
The Ethics of Early Childhood Programs and Business Incentives

Early childhood education and business incentives can be discussed from many perspectives. Thus far, I have focused on these programs' consequences. Empirical evidence has been presented on these programs' benefits and costs.

But early childhood education and business incentives can also be discussed from a philosophical perspective. Do these programs violate or promote any ethical principles? Do these programs violate any principles about the appropriate role of government? An ethical perspective would also include a consideration of these programs' consequences. But do ethical principles suggest that these programs are likely to promote or detract from what is best for our society? Do ethical principles suggest worrying about additional consequences of these programs? Ethical principles can provide a useful guide amidst conflicting empirical evidence.

In this chapter, I first consider philosophical arguments against early childhood education programs. I then consider philosophical arguments against business incentive programs. I discuss some common elements of these arguments.

I then respond to these philosophical arguments. This response is in part that early childhood education and business incentive programs can promote legitimate public purposes. But the response also argues that good program design can avoid transgressing ethical boundaries. The right design of early childhood programs can avoid unduly interfering with the family. The right design of business incentives can avoid unduly interfering in the business marketplace.

315

THE PHILOSOPHICAL ARGUMENT AGAINST EARLY
CHILDHOOD PROGRAMS

Abecedarian and CPC [Chicago Child-Parent Centers] . . . provide pretty good evidence that the right kinds of interventions—
if it's intense enough, if it's done well, in certain situations, with
certain children . . . can change outcomes. That is not surprising.
The Abecedarian program took these children when they were
infants. The average age was four months old, not four years old.
So, you're talking about, in essence [the] creation of a home away
from home. And you can bet that creating a different home away
from home can change a child's outcomes.

The question, then, for policymakers . . . is whether that is a level of
intervention that parents are comfortable with and, certainly, that
is one of the reasons that I believe the state needs to stay far away
from this. It reminds me a little bit of *Brave New World*, where
babies are assigned to different categories and they know they can
produce certain outcomes. You can do that. But that is a level of
social engineering that most people are not comfortable with, and
so participating in these programs voluntarily is important. Making sure that they're not government-directed and government-run
is critically important. You can change outcomes, but who should
be in the position of determining what those outcomes should be
and who need[s] to be changed?

—Darcy Olsen, from Olsen and Rolnick (2005, p. 10)

My progressive friends berate the Bush Administration for their
dictatorial stands on moral issues, telling us all how to live our
lives. But somehow now it's okay for some liberals to tell all parents that early development is about getting three- and four-year-
olds ready for standardized testing.

I urge you to consider what the evidence has to say, and whether
central government should be advancing a one-size-fits-all institution for young children.

—Bruce Fuller (2006a)

The main philosophical argument against early childhood programs
is that they infringe too much on the family. These programs may violate parents' rights. They may take over parental responsibilities.

Effective early childhood programs can be argued to require too much government intrusion. Effective programs may involve the government requiring that children achieve specific standardized outcomes. These standardized outcomes may be defined by centralized government authority. This centralized government authority may dictate outcomes that could be bad for an individual child. Good child development may be more likely if individual families define their own child outcomes and means of achieving those outcomes.

Philosophers have long noted a possible conflict between the family and social justice. Plato outlined a society in *The Republic* in which children were raised communally. In John Rawls's famous 1971 book, *A Theory of Justice*, the late Harvard philosopher noted the following argument against the family: "It seems that even when fair opportunity . . . is satisfied, the family will lead to unequal chances between individuals. . . . Is the family to be abolished then? Taken by itself and given a certain primacy, the idea of equal opportunity inclines in this direction" (Rawls [1971], quoted in Brighouse and Swift [2009, p. 45]).

We know that family environment makes a major difference in child outcomes. For example, Professors Betty Hart and Todd Risley have studied how parents from different socioeconomic backgrounds differ in verbal interactions with their children. They focused on interactions from 7–9 months of age up to three years old. Hart and Risley found that "simply in words heard, the average child on welfare was having half as much experience per hour . . . as the average working-class child . . . and less than one-third that of the average child in a professional family . . ." (Hart and Risley 2003). Hart and Risley found a widening gap from infancy to age three in children's vocabulary. For example, by age three, children from professional families on average used twice as many different words per hour as children from families on welfare. These age three differences are significant predictors of children's school performance at ages nine and ten.

Equal opportunity can be argued to be unattainable without significant interventions in the family. Darcy Olsen, president and CEO of the Goldwater Institute, argues in the quote that led off this section that truly changing child outcomes requires dramatic changes in the child's environment. The Abecedarian program certainly is a major intervention. Full-time, full-year child care, starting at the age of 6 to 12 weeks and continuing to age five, is a major change. Some Americans will hesitate before promoting such interventions.

A weakening of parental relationships with the child can sometimes damage child development. Jane Waldfogel, a professor at Columbia who is a well-known expert in child policy, concludes that "maternal sensitivity [to the child] is the most important predictor of child social and emotional development—more important than parental employment, child care, or other child and family factors" (Waldfogel 2006, p. 62). In addition, Waldfogel concludes that "children do tend to do worse if their mothers work full-time in the first year of life. Negative effects are found on health, cognitive development, and externalizing behavior problems. Part-time work in the first year or [full-time] work in the second and third years does not have the same effects" (pp. 61–62).

It is certainly possible to wonder about the extent to which early childhood programs can substitute for the family. Jennifer Roback Morse, an economist who has promoted traditional marriage and family structures, argues that "we [cannot] replace the family with a series of government programs . . . The government is no substitute for the family" (Morse 2008).

Too much government intrusion into the family may also potentially interfere with parental rights. Philosopher Harry Brighouse has argued that an important part of well-being and meaning for many persons is the right as a parent to raise one's children.

> Even if alternative arrangements (such as state child-rearing institutions) could serve children's interests better (which we doubt), they could not be justified because parents also have an interest in being able to have intimate relationships with their children in which they are the main agents responsible for meeting their children's needs. The institution of the family allows adults to have a relationship of a kind that cannot be substituted for by relationships with other adults; they enjoy an intimate relationship with a dependent who spontaneously loves them, and a good deal of discretion over the specific means by which that relationship develops. Parents have a special duty to promote their children's interests (including the interest most have in becoming eventually someone who has no need of the parent's care), but they also have a non-fiduciary interest in being able to play a fiduciary role; it is valuable for their children that they play it well, but playing it is also valuable for them. The family is justified partly by the fact

that it is the institution for raising children that provides this good to adults. (Brighouse 2007)

An extreme view is that parents have the right to provide their children with advantages. For example, the well-known conservative author Dinesh D'Souza has argued that it is illegitimate for government to provide help to children whose parents have not done as much to help them succeed.

I have a five-year-old daughter. Since she was born—actually, since she was conceived—my wife and I have gone to great lengths in the Great Yuppie Parenting Race . . . Why are we doing these things? We are, of course, trying to develop her abilities so that she can get the most out of life. The practical effect of our actions, however, is that we are working to give our daughter an edge—that is, a better chance to succeed than everybody else's children . . .

Now, to enforce equal opportunity, the government could do one of two things: it could try to pull my daughter down, or it could work to raise other people's children up. The first is clearly destructive and immoral, but the second is also unfair. The government is obliged to treat all citizens equally. Why should it work to undo the benefits that my wife and I have labored so hard to provide? Why should it offer more to children whose parents have not taken the trouble?[1]

Another concern is that early childhood programs run by centralized government authority may be insufficiently responsive to community needs. Bruce Fuller, professor of education and public policy at the University of California, Berkeley, has expressed concern, in the quotation at the beginning of this section and elsewhere, that some universal pre-K proposals give too much power to the public education system. He believes that community-based pre-K education programs may be more responsive to diverse needs. These community-based pre-K programs may use more diverse curricula and employ teachers from more diverse backgrounds. "One reason I became so involved in questioning elements of the Reiner initiative in California [a 2006 ballot initiative for universal pre-K that badly failed] was that his caucus was so eager to win at any cost—including a willingness to risk sacrificing community-based programs, some of which started in the 1920s and many more that sprung up with the community action movement in the 1960s" (Fuller 2006b).[2]

A final philosophical objection is to a strong federal role in early childhood education. To some conservatives, any significant federal role in early childhood education goes beyond the federal government's constitutional powers. For example, Olsen (1999) argues that "the provision or funding for early education programs by the federal government cannot be squared with the notion of a national government whose powers are enumerated and thus limited by the Constitution."

These philosophical arguments are made against a version of early childhood education that is a straw man. I consider later whether early childhood education usually or necessarily leads to excessive intrusion in the family.

THE PHILOSOPHICAL ARGUMENT AGAINST BUSINESS INCENTIVES

The central philosophical argument against business incentives is that the government should not be "picking winners." The government should not be selecting particular businesses for government assistance. This assistance increases these selected businesses' chances of success. Which businesses "win" should be based on the merits of the business, as judged by the market. By picking business winners, the government, it is argued, is unduly intruding on the proper role of the competitive market.

Business incentives to selected businesses use public funds to increase private profits. The "winners" benefit at the expense of the public. William Greider, a well-known left-of-center political journalist, makes the following argument on principle against business incentives: "Here is a simple proposition to consider as we absorb the facts of the scam: public money should be devoted to public purposes . . . The subsidy system in American governance has now become so distorted—actually deranged—that it largely amounts to a corrupt pork barrel of private favors at public expense" (Greider 2005, pp. x, xi).

Aiding "winning" businesses is argued to be unfair to "losing" businesses. The libertarian Cato Institute argues that "by aiding some businesses, corporate subsidies put other businesses without political connections at an unfair disadvantage" (Cato Institute 2009, p. 281).

Tax incentives to businesses have the further problem that they are often not very visible. According to Greg LeRoy of the advocacy group Good Jobs First, which argues against business incentive programs, "The tax breaks . . . granted by states . . . are the least visible, least accountable, and most corrosive means by which states fund job creation" (LeRoy 2005, p. 2). Tax incentives to businesses are typically not regularly reviewed by state legislatures. Agencies that hand out tax incentives in many cases do not provide adequate data on costs and effects of tax incentives. Accountability is more difficult because there are insufficient data on which to judge these programs. Accountability is also more difficult because of the lack of regular review.

Business incentives can be argued to be prone to corruption. This corruption may not take the form of outright bribes. I know of little evidence of explicit bribes. But corruption may also occur by businesses lobbying and making campaign contributions. This political pressure may promote business incentives that increase business profits. Business incentives provide large increases in profits to relatively few businesses. Costs are spread across many taxpayers. As a result, incentive proponents find it easier to politically organize than opponents. Steven Slivinski, former director of budget policy at the Cato Institute, makes the following argument:

> Subsidies are usually given to a few recipients at the expense of many taxpayers. Because there are such a large number of taxpayers—and each corporate subsidy may cost each taxpayer only a few cents or a few dollars—most individual citizens don't have an interest in lobbying against subsidies since the cost of doing so far outweighs simply paying the taxes. However, the recipients of those subsidies have a substantial interest in making sure they protect the flow of money to them. That leads to a great deal of lobbying by special interests but very little lobbying on behalf of taxpayers. (Slivinski 2007, p. 5)

The possibility of business incentives may divert businesses' attention away from improving the quality of their businesses. Instead, businesses may spend more time lobbying for incentives. Slivinski (2007, pp. 5–6) makes the following argument: "Subsidies create a perverse incentive for businesses: if an entrepreneur's competitors are receiving help from the government, it may appear to be in his or her interest to try to get some of that help, too. That incentive serves only to turn many businesspeople into lobbyists, sidetracking them from their role as entrepreneurs. That, in turn, leads to an overallocation of private resources to pursuing and protecting government subsidies."

Business incentives may also divert the attention of government policymakers from policies that would be more effective in creating jobs. LeRoy (2005) argues that policymakers who question incentives are labeled as being "against jobs": "Those [policymakers] who would dare to ask an impertinent question are quickly singled out for ridicule and isolation: they must be against jobs" (p. 4).

Finally, it can be argued that business incentives violate federal and state constitutional standards. At the least, business incentives could be argued to violate these standards' spirit. Slivinski argues that "direct corporate subsidies fall outside the limited enumerated functions of the federal government" (p. 6). As was mentioned in Chapter 10, Art Rolnick of the Minneapolis Federal Reserve Bank has argued that the federal Constitution's Commerce Clause, which gives the U.S. Congress exclusive power to regulate interstate commerce, was enacted to prevent the states from engaging in "destructive economic warfare" against each other. At the time of the U.S. Constitutional Convention, this "economic warfare" was in the form of state trade barriers. State business incentives can be seen as a modern form of such economic warfare.

State constitutions and state court precedents also can be viewed as questioning business incentives. This is a theoretical question, as state courts have rarely overturned business incentives. State constitutions often require that public funds or credit should only be used for "public purposes." According to Ferdinand Schoettle, a law professor at the University of Minnesota, "even if a state constitution does not expressly require that taxes be levied and collected for public purposes only, courts will generally find the public purpose doctrine implicit either in other constitutional provisions or in general doctrines and principles" (Schoettle 2003, p. 33). Many of the state constitutional provisions against use of public funds and credit for private purposes developed in the late nineteenth century. According to Schoettle,

> These doctrines had their development, if not their genesis, in the second half of the nineteenth century when the public became concerned about the activities of governments in financing internal

improvements. As the nation's population expanded westward between 1820 and 1840 . . . the anticipated rewards from such improvements led to partnerships between states and private enterprise through which the states financed the construction of privately or jointly owned canals, railroads, turnpikes and toll roads . . . State officials were particularly inspired by the great success of New York's Erie Canal . . . Other states followed New York's lead in incurring large debts in order to grant aid to private corporations . . . However, other state projects were not as successful as the Erie Canal. By 1837, some internal improvement projects lacked funds to complete their project . . . State residents then began to show displeasure at the state's mismanagement of internal commerce . . . The judiciary also took note of popular discontent with governmental assistance to private industry . . . (pp. 28–29)

It could be argued that today's business incentives have some similarity to this aggressive state government promotion of economic development in the early nineteenth century. Perhaps business incentives too should be subject to greater legal restrictions.

These arguments against business incentives also argue against a straw man. I will consider below whether business incentives necessarily or usually lead to unwarranted interference with the business marketplace.

COMMON ELEMENTS TO THE ARGUMENTS AGAINST THESE GOVERNMENT PROGRAMS

These arguments against early childhood programs and business incentives have many differences. But they also have some elements in common. In both cases, the argument is that some government program is substituting its decision-making for some existing entity or process. For early childhood programs, the existing entity and process is the family. For business incentives, the existing entity and process is the business competing in the marketplace.

The argument is that this substitution of government for the existing entity (the family or business competition) is a bad idea in principle. The existing entity and process will as a general principle do better if left on its own. The existing entity has a right to be left on its own. The presumption is that government interference will be a poor substitute. The burden of proof is argued to be on proponents of government interference to demonstrate its efficacy.

This entire book can be seen as a response to these arguments. The book has offered specific empirical evidence on the benefits and costs of early childhood programs and business incentives. If the benefits exceed the costs from these government programs, then these programs can be argued to have overcome the presumption against government intervention in the family or business marketplace. This empirical evidence suggests that such government intervention is warranted.

But there is a long-standing joke in economics: "So it's true in practice; is it also true in theory?" Are there theoretical or conceptual reasons for thinking that early childhood programs and business incentives might work? A conceptual argument for these programs might augment the specific empirical evidence.

I give a conceptual rationale for each of these two programs below. The conceptual rationales for these two programs have some elements in common. There are some reasons in principle to think that these existing entities (the family or business competition) will fail to bring about socially desirable outcomes. Government interference may help. Government interference may even help strengthen the family or business competition.

As we will see, this debate also suggests some design principles for these programs. Even if concern about government interference in the family or the business marketplace is overstated, undue interference may be undesirable. The right design of these programs may avoid some of the concerns of those opposed to such government intervention.

THE CONCEPTUAL CASE FOR EARLY CHILDHOOD PROGRAMS

The conceptual case for early childhood programs is this: many families on their own may not obtain sufficient services of the type provided by early childhood programs. The services the family obtains on its own may be insufficient from two perspectives. Services may be insufficient from the family's own perspective, in that the family may not obtain services that maximize the overall long-term well-being of all family members. Services may also be insufficient from a social perspective: the services that the family obtains on its own may provide too few social benefits for various groups outside the family.

Even if early childhood programs provide benefits exceeding costs, many families may be unable to afford these services. If a family's resources are scarce, the family may rationally choose to spend more on goods and services that yield short-term returns, squeezing out services that will only yield a return in the long term. This is so even if the long-term return to these early childhood services far exceeds costs.

Some economists might argue that in theory even low-income families may be able to afford early childhood programs by borrowing. Suppose these programs' future earnings benefits for the child exceed their costs. If capital markets were perfect, then a family should be able to borrow against the value of the child's future earnings. In practice, capital markets do not work that way. Lenders are more reluctant to lend when the collateral is harder to repossess and sell. Houses and business machinery can be repossessed. But a person's increased skills as an adult that result from an early childhood program are impossible to repossess. As a result, loans for programs that help enhance human skills are more limited than would be socially desirable.

Another issue is that families may not fully understand the future value of early childhood programs. Markets work more efficiently when consumers have better information. It is easier to have good consumer information on a good or service that is immediately consumed. How much a particular new variety of apple is worth is something a consumer can easily find out by eating that apple. Goods or services whose value only becomes readily apparent in the future are more difficult for consumers to evaluate. Early childhood programs have long-delayed benefits. These delayed benefits may be downweighted by consumers in favor of immediate benefits from other goods and services.

Even if families understand the future benefits of early childhood programs, they may undervalue the future. Families may place a lower value on future benefits now than they later would find to be desirable.

Part of the issue is that parents are making decisions on behalf of their child. From the viewpoint of the future adult that the child could potentially have grown into had there been more early investment, the family may underinvest in child development. There is no effective way that the demand of this potential future adult can be reflected in the family's decision-making today.

Investment in early childhood programs may also have social benefits that spill over outside the child's family. Higher future skills may increase overall social productivity beyond the increase in earnings for the individual. For example, there is significant evidence that an individual's wage rate depends not only on his or her own education, but also is positively affected by higher average education levels (Moretti 2003, 2004). This can be explained in several ways. The productivity of teams may depend on the education of all members. Businesses deciding whether to introduce new technology may believe the success of the innovation depends on the typical education of the workforce. A more educated workforce may also contribute more ideas for innovation.

In addition, increased future earnings of former child participants in early childhood programs will increase future tax revenues. The increased employment and earnings may also reduce involvement in welfare. Both of these effects provide fiscal benefits for the average taxpayer.

Former child participants in early childhood programs may be less likely to become involved in crime. There is some evidence of anti-crime effects from the Perry Preschool program, the Chicago Child-Parent Center program, and the Nurse-Family Partnership program.[3] Many of the benefits of lower crime accrue to taxpayers, who save some costs in the criminal justice system. Other benefits of lower crime go to those who escaped being victims of crime because some crimes were never committed that otherwise would have been.

Early childhood programs may also raise civic participation. For example, we know that more-educated persons are more likely to vote and to volunteer (Baum and Ma 2007).

All these points apply equally well to public schools. The argument is that without public funding for K–12 education, many families would not obtain sufficient quantity or quality of K–12 educational services. The conceptual case for early childhood programs is the same as the conceptual case for public schools.

ARE EARLY CHILDHOOD PROGRAMS REALLY OPPOSED TO FAMILY RIGHTS?

But there still is the issue of whether early childhood programs infringe on the rights and functions of the family. How serious a concern is this in actuality? Are there ways to minimize any unproductive conflict between early childhood programs and the family?

Family rights are not absolute. As argued above, parents have the right to develop a mutually enriching relationship with their child that involves helping shape their child's values. But the right to such a relationship does not extend to denying opportunities for other children. Consider Dinesh D'Souza's comments above. It is unclear how the government is denying his family's rights by helping enhance the future development of some other child. What about children's rights? Aren't they enhanced if more children have greater opportunities?

In practice, it is unclear whether early childhood programs significantly interfere with family rights. Consider Goldwater Institute CEO Darcy Olsen's comments above, comparing early childhood programs to Aldous Huxley's novel *Brave New World*. Early childhood programs have little in common with forcible assignment of children to predetermined social roles—the policy practiced in *Brave New World*. The pre-K program with the highest return appears to be a half-day school-year program at age four. Such a program does not signal the start of a totalitarian society. The Nurse-Family Partnership program has a limited number of nurse visits from the prenatal period to age two. Contrary to Darcy Olsen's comment, we do not need to "creat[e] a different home away from home" to make significant and meaningful improvements in child outcomes.

Even the Abecedarian program does not necessarily weaken the family. The program is full-time, full-year child care from infancy through age five. But many of these parents would have used some type of full-time child care anyway. The issue in many cases is the quality of that care, not child care versus family care.

Many of these programs may strengthen the family. The Nurse-Family Partnership seeks to improve the parent's interactions with the child. High-quality pre-K programs and child care programs include some outreach to parents. More importantly, high-quality pre-K programs and child care programs help promote goals that the parent has for the child. The parent-child relationship is not just an end in itself; it is also a means to better child development.

Program design can minimize infringements on parental and family rights. All of these early childhood programs are voluntary. Parents can opt out.

I have argued previously in this book that we want considerable state and local discretion in how early childhood programs are operated. I argued that state and local flexibility leads to more innovation. It also may allow parents more options for different types of early childhood programs.

Within a given state or local area, early childhood program design can also allow for considerable parental choice. Programs can be designed so that a variety of different program types are available. Programs can be delivered by a variety of institutions. For example, pre-K programs do not need to be delivered or controlled by the public schools; there is an existing infrastructure of private pre-K programs. Many but not all are of high quality. Many of those that are not of high quality could be improved. It seems sensible to work to improve rather than replace that infrastructure. Public policies can honor a diversity of program approaches while encouraging quality improvements. This can be a difficult balancing act, but one that is possible to pull off.

State and local areas in which voters highly value parental choice may opt for a system that funds a variety of public and private providers. Funding a variety of providers may also make sense in state and local areas in which there are many existing private providers of high quality. In other state and local settings, private providers of high quality may not be as widespread. The local political culture may be more supportive of a pre-K system that largely works through the public schools.

THE CONCEPTUAL CASE FOR BUSINESS INCENTIVES

The main argument for business incentives has already been made in Chapter 2. The process of business competition, left to its own devices, does not recognize some social benefits. The pure free market does not recognize the social benefit of greater employment. Business incentives can be justified as a way to promote employment expansions that have large social benefits.[4]

Some of the more effective economic development services also address other failings of a pure private market. Manufacturing extension services and customized job training programs may reflect problems of markets in dealing with imperfect information. Businesses, particularly small and medium-sized businesses, may have imperfect information about what they can do to improve their productivity.

Information can be purchased. But if one lacks information, it is difficult to ascertain whether the information one is buying is accurate, or to ascertain its worth. Therefore, in a pure free market, there may not be sufficient trade in high-quality information and training to improve business productivity.

Manufacturing extension services and customized job training may improve matters by providing more reliably high-quality information and services to improve productivity. Some evidence that these services correct a market failure is provided by the estimated high value of these services relative to the costs. If high-quality information and training were already easily and reliably available to businesses, then government programs should find it more difficult to provide valuable services.

If these economic development services have a value to businesses that exceeds their costs, why shouldn't such services be priced at full cost? There are two reasons. First, these services are being provided to promote employment and earnings creation. This is better accomplished by providing services below costs.

Second, many of the small and medium-sized businesses being helped may be insufficiently financed because of financial market failures. Financial markets may not always optimally finance different activities. As we have seen recently, sometimes excessively risky loans and investments are financed. Other times, sound business projects are not financed. There are many small and medium-sized businesses that could viably expand if they could get financing. Free or low-cost extension services or customized job training may be an indirect way of providing financial support.

Thus, economic development services to businesses can be seen as addressing multiple market failures. Providing such services free or at a low price helps overcome the failure of markets to achieve socially beneficial employment and earnings expansions, while also addressing failures in information and financial markets for small and medium-sized businesses.

What about the charge that business incentives are unfair to the business that does not receive incentives? In theory, if business incentive programs are run optimally, this criticism is invalid. Economic development policymakers would not be arbitrarily "picking winners" by providing some businesses with greater incentives. Greater incentives would be provided to businesses whose expansions yielded greater social benefits. For example, greater incentives might be provided to businesses in a more distressed local labor market. Or greater incentives might be provided to businesses that paid a higher wage premium. The differentials in incentives would be related to social benefits. If incentive differentials are related to social benefits, the charge of unfairness loses force.

So in theory, optimal business incentives can be seen as correcting for market failures. But is this true in practice? As discussed in Chapter 10, there is some sign that business incentives are quite large even in low-unemployment areas, where the social benefits of incentives are lower. This suggests that politics may play a role in business incentive policy: even when social benefits are low, the business beneficiaries will lobby for continued large incentives. As discussed previously in this chapter, it may be easy for businesses that benefit from incentives to politically out-organize the opponents to incentives.

As mentioned in Chapter 10, one way to control such political pressures is to incorporate business tax incentives into the regular tax code. Currently, business tax incentives are often handed out in a discretionary manner. Making such incentives part of the regular tax code would provide greater potential for control and monitoring. Legislative agencies and administrative agencies would cost out the implications of these tax incentives for state and local revenues, so that there would be more of a potential for a balanced discussion of these tax incentives' benefits and costs.

Economic development services are more under control, because they are politically overseen as part of the legislative authorization and appropriations process. In addition, the demand for economic development services is more politically limited. There is no limit to the business demand for cash. Once state and local governments start handing out business incentives as tax reductions or other types of cash, there is unlimited business demand for expanding such assistance. However, services are only demanded by businesses that need such services, and only if the services are of some significant value.

Therefore, another way to encourage more efficient use of business incentives is to shift more incentives from tax and financial incentives toward services. Such a shift of emphasis may limit the potential for political pressure to inordinately expand incentives.

As mentioned in Chapter 10, transparency and federal regulation of incentives may also promote greater efficiency. Full public awareness of the magnitude and effects of incentives may restrain the worst abuses. Federal regulation may restrain incentives that do not promote overall national purposes.

If business incentives are run reasonably well, they may enhance the process of market competition. Business employment may expand to provide greater social benefits. Services that increase business productivity may enhance business competition.

CONCLUSION

There are philosophical reasons to be concerned about early childhood programs and business incentives. However, well-run and high-quality versions of early childhood programs and business incentives can deal with these concerns. The purposes of the family and of business competition can be enhanced rather than diminished by the right program design.

The next chapter turns to extending the economic development analysis of early childhood programs to other human capital improvements.

Notes

1. This quotation from Dinesh D'Souza is from a discussion by Slate writer Timothy Noah of D'Souza's 2000 book, *The Virtue of Prosperity* (Noah 2000).
2. See also Fuller's more extended discussion of these issues in his 2007 book, *Standardized Childhood*, coauthored with Margaret Bridges and Seeta Pai.
3. For a good recent review, see Julia Isaacs's 2008 paper for First Focus and Brookings.
4. A more extensive discussion of market failures justifying economic development is in my 1990 paper on market failures and economic development.

12
Extending Economic Development Analysis to Other Human Development Programs

Education, Public Health, Crime Reduction

Early childhood programs are just one type of human development program. The economic development analysis that I have applied to early childhood programs can be applied to other programs than enhance human capital. Any program that increases the quantity or quality of human capital will stimulate earnings creation in a state economy.

In this chapter, I illustrate how this economic development analysis can be extended to other human development programs. I consider the following types of human development policies:

- Policies to improve K–12 test scores;

- Policies to improve educational attainment (high school graduation, college graduation);

- Policies to improve public health; and

- Policies to reduce crime rates.

This book does not consider the details of additional policies—beyond early childhood programs—that could improve human capital in these policy areas. Instead, I estimate the economic development benefits for state economies of improving key human development outcomes. These outcomes include education test scores, educational attainment, crime, and public health indicators. Future studies could match up these estimates with estimates of the costs of achieving these outcomes. This matching would allow comparing economic development benefits to costs of human development policies.

Previous studies have considered the economic effects of improving these human development outcomes. For example, there are many studies by research organizations, interest groups, and academics of the economic effects of improving K–12 education (Belfield and Levin 2007a; Hungerford and Wassmer 2004; Levin and Belfield 2007; McKinsey and Company 2009; National Education Association 2007). For postsecondary education, studies by the College Board, individual universities, and academics have considered the economic effects of improving college education (Bartik and Erickcek 2008; Baum and Ma 2007; Siegfried, Sanderson, and McHenry 2006). Studies by think tanks and academics have considered the economic benefits of reducing crime (Greenwood et al. 1998; Holzer, Offner, and Sorensen 2005; Raphael 2007). Studies have estimated the economic effects of improvements to public health and medical care (Aos et al. 2006; Bartik and Erickcek 2008; Currie et al. 2009).

Such economic analysis is sometimes meant to promote more funding for these human development programs. For example, in recent years, the National Education Association (NEA) has supported an initiative with the acronym TEF (Tax Structures, Economic Development, and Funding for Education). Under TEF, NEA and its state affiliates present information on the high costs of tax incentives for promoting economic development, and the potential economic development benefits of better K–12 education. According to NEA (2007), the TEF initiative is meant to promote the following argument: "Investing in education pays—always. But now more than ever . . . in the new knowledge-based global economy, investing in public education—in our human capital—provides a greater return to our economic prosperity investment than tax cuts and subsidies."

What this book does differently is to focus on how these human development outcomes offer economic development benefits at the state level. This focus on state-level effects means that I adjust downward for participants in these programs who move out-of-state. The focus on economic development benefits means that I adjust downward for displacement effects. I want to estimate the net effects of human development programs on state economies, not just effects on individuals.

Policies targeting human development have been justified on the basis of economic development benefits. For example, the "Kalamazoo Promise" program was apparently intended by its anonymous donors to promote the economic development of Kalamazoo (Miller-Adams 2009). The Kalamazoo Promise, begun in 2005, provides graduates of Kalamazoo Public Schools with up to 100 percent subsidies for college tuition. The Kalamazoo Promise is in part intended to increase high school and college graduation rates. But in so doing, the donors apparently believe that the Promise will attract households and businesses to Kalamazoo. Households will be attracted by the tuition benefit for their children. Businesses will be attracted because households are attracted, and because of the Promise's effects on educational attainment.

The focus of this chapter is somewhat different from Richard Florida's well-known focus on the role of the so-called creative class in regional development (Florida 2002). Florida's work has focused on how overall regional growth is affected by attracting or retaining highly creative persons. Thus, Florida's focus is on growth in the size of the overall local economy, whereas I focus on the earnings per capita of the original local residents. In other words, Florida focuses more (although not exclusively) on affecting the geographic migration of talent, whereas I focus on the effects of a local economy's developing its own talent.

METHODOLOGY

My estimates of the state-level economic development benefits of better human development outcomes follow a similar methodology. I summarize this methodology here.[1] The discussion of estimates of specific outcomes indicates exceptions to this methodology.

For each outcome, I derive from various sources estimates of the effects of some changes in human development outcomes on earnings for an individual at different ages. The program initiating the changes in human development outcomes is assumed to occur at some earlier age.

From these gross effects on some individual's earnings, I calculate net effects on state earnings. This is done by adjusting the gross earnings downward to account for mortality, out-migration from the state, and displacement effects.

For some human development interventions, as indicated below, I also adjust upward for positive peer effects. These positive peer effects are assumed to occur in elementary school. Higher human development outcomes for one individual or group are assumed to help improve academic achievement in elementary school for that person's or group's classroom peers. These positive peer effects are restricted to human development interventions that intervene at early enough ages to affect elementary school acheivement.

I then calculate the present value of these state earnings effects from improving human development outcomes for one individual. This represents the economic development benefits for the state from a program that would make such an improvement for one individual. These benefits could be compared with costs: what does it cost to improve human development outcomes by this amount for one individual? Of course, this is not a complete benefit-cost analysis. However, it does indicate whether the state economic development benefits would justify the intervention's costs.

I also then calculate the effects on earnings from a permanent program that will make this change in human development outcomes for many individuals in the state. For each human development outcome below, I present my assumption about whether this change in human development outcomes takes place for the entire population or some smaller group. Such assumptions about how the program is scaled are arbitrary. Without cost figures for achieving these human development outcomes, the scaling of these various human development outcomes cannot be compared.

I then calculate the net percentage effect on state earnings from this permanent program. This permanent program is assumed to be initiated in the year 2011. I calculate the percentage effect of this program from 2011 until the percentage effect stabilizes. The percentage effect stabilizes when all cohorts in the labor market have been affected by the permanent program.

I report the peak percentage effect on state earnings from the program. I also calculate the net present value of the earnings effect of the permanent program, as a percentage of the net present value of future state earnings. This percentage net present value calculation averages in early years of program effects with later years. In the early years, the program has few or no effects because few cohorts affected by the program are yet in the labor market.

K–12 TEST SCORES

For K–12 education quality, I analyze the state economic development benefits of improvements in early elementary test scores and secondary test scores. Improving such test scores is a key goal of school reformers.

For these test score improvements, I consider the economic development benefits from improving that outcome, along with subsequent educational attainment increases associated with that outcome. For example, the economic development benefits of improving elementary or secondary test scores include the higher high school graduation rates and college graduation rates that may result from these higher test scores. Higher test scores do have effects beyond their effects upon educational attainment. For example, research by Murnane et al. (2000) concludes that for men, only one-third of the effects of higher secondary test scores are due to the effects of these higher test scores on educational attainment.[2]

Elementary Test Scores

To estimate the economic development effects of higher elementary test scores, I use techniques similar to what I used to estimate the effects of lower K–3 class size in Chapter 7. I used evidence on how test scores affected employment rates and wage rates at ages 23 and 33 to extrapolate earnings effects to other ages.[3]

I assumed the change in early elementary test scores was initiated at age seven. I assumed that this change in outcomes for one individual or a group has positive peer effects.

For these estimates, I considered the economic development effects of increasing early elementary test scores in both reading and math by an "effect size" of 0.1. An effect size of 0.1 is defined as one-tenth of the standard deviation in test scores among the students in early elementary school. Such an increase in test scores is a relatively small effect. It corresponds to moving a student up from 50 percent to 54 percent in his or her percentile ranking on reading and math test scores. A one-tenth effect-size increase in test scores in early elementary school is equal to what students in early elementary school typically learn in about one month of school (Hill et al. 2007).

For comparison's sake, Camilli et al.'s (2010) meta-analysis of early childhood education studies suggests that the "average-quality" intervention increases elementary test scores by an effect size of 0.18. More effective early childhood education programs increase elementary test scores by an effect size of up to 0.58.[4] Of course, pre-K education may have effects on adult earnings and other outcomes beyond those predicted by its effects on elementary test scores. Based on the Tennessee Class Size Study, lowering class sizes in grades K–3 by 7 or 8 students (from averages of 22–24 students to 15–16 students) is estimated to increase early elementary test scores by effect sizes that range from 0.14 to 0.19 (Schanzenbach 2007).

Consider the economic development effects of increasing by a 0.1 effect size the early elementary test scores of one student. I estimate that the state economic development benefits of doing so have a present value of $8,312.[5, 6]

Eight thousand dollars is a considerable economic development benefit from such a modest educational improvement for one student. From a state economic development perspective, such a large benefit could justify considerable efforts in summer school or tutoring for that student.

What if we succeeded in improving early elementary test scores by an effect size of 0.1 for all students in a state? In the long run, this improvement in early elementary test scores would boost state residents' income by a little over 1 percent (to be exact, the long-run boost is 1.08 percent). The present value of the future boost in state earnings, as a percentage of the present value of total future state earnings, is estimated to be about three-fifths of 1 percent (0.63 percent).[7]

Why does such a small improvement in early elementary test scores have such large state economic development benefits? These large benefits reflect in part the large effects of educational achievement on the earnings potential of individuals throughout their future work lives. These large benefits also reflect the assumption that the state achieves these higher outcomes for all students.

It should be kept in mind that these economic development benefits of higher elementary test scores include the effects of all the improvements these higher test scores bring about. This includes later educational improvements such as higher secondary test scores and higher high school graduation rates. These early education improvements are valued in part because these early improvements lead to higher secondary test scores and higher graduation rates.

Secondary Test Scores

To estimate the economic development benefits of improving secondary test scores, I rely on a recent literature survey by Brooks-Gunn, Magnuson, and Waldfogel (2009) on how secondary test scores affect later earnings.[8]

I again considered the economic development benefits from an improvement in test scores of 0.1 in effect-size units. This is a much larger improvement at the secondary level than it is at the elementary level. Children vary more in academic achievement levels in secondary school than they do in elementary school. Therefore, a given effect-size change in secondary school describes a much bigger improvement in academic achievement than it does in elementary school. For example, at age 17, an improvement in test scores of 0.1 effect-size units is equivalent to about how much the average student learns in half an academic year, or five months. At age seven, an improvement in test scores of 0.1 effect-size units corresponds to what a student learns in one month. The same change in effect-size units corresponds to about five times as much of a gain in academic achievement at the secondary level as at the elementary level. Is it therefore five times as difficult or costly to make such a change at the secondary level? We don't know. However, it does seem likely that improving secondary test scores by 0.1 effect-size units will be more difficult.

I estimate the state economic development benefits from a 0.1 effect-size improvement in secondary test scores for one student. I estimate that the present value of the economic development benefits from this improvement is $7,050. This is the net increase in state residents' earnings from this one student's test score improvement.

I also estimate the state economic development benefits of a 0.1 increase in secondary test scores for all the state's students.[9] These economic development benefits occur sooner than they do for improvements in all students' elementary test scores. Secondary students enter the labor market sooner than elementary students. However, the long-run economic development benefits are slightly less for secondary students than for the previously considered improvement in elementary test scores. The long-run economic development benefit for state residents' earnings is estimated to max out at a little more than four-fifths of 1 percent (more precisely, 0.83 percent). However, the present value of the economic development benefits as a percentage of earnings is about the same, at around three-fifths of 1 percent (or more precisely, 0.57 percent), because the benefits occur sooner.

The improvement in secondary test scores has about the same economic development benefits as the improvement in elementary test scores. However, the secondary improvement is probably harder to accomplish and corresponds to a greater improvement in months of achievement. What explains this pattern of effects? In part, this pattern reflects my assumption that elementary test score improvements have peer-effect spillovers, whereas secondary test score improvements do not. But this pattern also reflects the estimates I use that relate test scores to earnings. I use estimates that find similar correlations of elementary and secondary test scores with adult earnings. Because the improvements in early elementary test scores are probably easier to make, this provides an argument for earlier investments in K–12 quality.[10]

EDUCATIONAL ATTAINMENT

I now consider increases in educational attainment. Specifically, I consider the effects of increasing the numbers of persons with a high school degree, a four-year college degree, and an associate's degree.

In interpreting the below results, the following should be kept in mind: inducing one person to get any one of these degrees is a much more difficult improvement than increasing either elementary or secondary test scores by an effect size of 0.1. A program might increase the average test scores of some group of students by an effect size of 0.1. But even the best of programs is highly unlikely to be able to take a group of persons, all of whom would not have obtained a degree but for the intervention, and induce 100 percent of that group to obtain a particular degree.

Reducing High School Dropouts

To analyze the economic development benefits from reducing high school dropouts, I use data on the earnings of high school dropouts versus those who get a high school degree. I assume that the marginal student whom we convert from a dropout to a high school graduate is less likely than the average high school graduate to complete postsecondary education. Based on estimates by Belfield and Levin (2007b), I assume that this additional high school graduate will have the following postsecondary experience: four-fifths will have no further education, 14 percent will attend college but will not get a bachelor's degree, and 6 percent will get a bachelor's degree.[11]

Based on these procedures, I estimate that converting one high school dropout to a high school graduate will have economic development benefits for a state's economy with a present value of $175,234.[12]

I also estimate the effects of reducing the high school dropout rate by 1 percentage point out of all students. (A 1-percentage-point reduction would mean a change from the average national high school dropout rate of 23 percent [Heckman and LaFontaine 2007] to 22 percent.) Such a change in educational outcomes begins to have some economic effects almost immediately. The long-run estimated effect is to boost state earnings by 0.21 percent. The net present value of the earnings benefits for the state, as a percentage of the present value of state earnings, is 0.14 percent.[13]

Bachelor's Degree

I do analysis similar to the high school dropout analysis for college graduation. First, I consider the economic development benefits if we succeeded in switching one person from being a high school graduate without a bachelor's degree to one having a bachelor's degree.

This analysis is based on comparing earnings of persons with a bachelor's or higher degree to the earnings of persons with a high school degree but without a bachelor's degree. The group of persons with a high school degree but without a bachelor's degree includes persons with some college or with an associate's degree.[14]

Based on this analysis, I estimate that the state economic development benefits from one additional bachelor's degree have a present value of $375,912.[15] Economic development benefits justify a significant investment to increase the number of bachelor's degree holders even by one person.

I also consider the state economic development benefits of increasing the percentage of a state's population with a bachelor's degree by 1 percent of the population. As of March 2008, among 25- to 29-year-olds, 30.8 percent had a bachelor's degree (*Digest of Education Statistics* 2010). This 1-percentage-point increase would increase this percentage to 31.8 percent. I estimate that a 1-percentage-point increase in the college graduation rate would in the long run provide state economic development benefits of 0.45 percent of state earnings. The net present value of these economic development benefits, divided by the net present value of expected future state earnings, is 0.31 percent.

Associate's Degree

I also considered the economic development benefits from having more community college graduates. Estimates are based on comparing the earnings of those persons having an associate's degree, but not a bachelor's degree, to the earnings of high school graduates who did not have any postsecondary degree but might have some college.[16]

This analysis is similar to the high-school-degree and bachelor's-degree analyses, with one exception: inducing an associate's degree is assumed to not lead to any subsequent changes in educational attainment, whereas inducing a high school degree or bachelor's degree is allowed to lead to subsequent degrees. I judged it unclear what effect should reasonably be assumed for how an associate's degree affects subsequent educational attainment. If a reader believes that an associate's degree increases the probability of obtaining a bachelor's degree by x percent, then x percent of the estimated bachelor's degree effects can be added to the below effects for an associate's degree alone.

Based on this analysis, getting a single person to earn an associate's degree provides state economic development benefits whose present value is $126,995.

I also consider increasing the percentage of a state's population with an associate's degree by 1 percent of the population. As of 2008, the percentage of 25- to 29-year-olds with an associate's degree but no higher degree is 9.0 percent (*Digest of Education Statistics* 2010).

An increase of 1 percentage point would move this percentage to 10 percent. I estimate that the long-run state economic development benefits from this change would be 0.15 percent of state earnings. The net present value of the state earnings benefits from a 1-percentage-point increase in associate's degree holders, as a percentage of the present value of expected future state earnings, is 0.10 percent.

PUBLIC HEALTH

In the area of public health, I estimate the state economic development benefits of improving child health and adult health. The child health outcomes considered are a reduction in the incidence of low birth weight among babies and a reduction in attention deficit hyperactivity disorder and related conduct disorders (ADHD). The adult health outcomes considered are a reduction in the severity of mental illness and drug and alcohol abuse.

In interpreting the below per-person estimates, it should be kept in mind that eliminating these problems for one person is a large change. In general, interventions would reduce the probability of these problems' occurring, but would not take that probability from 100 percent all the way down to 0 percent. In other words, interventions would not change the probability of persons' having these problems from being certain to being nonexistent.

Reducing Low Birth Weight

Low birth weight is thought to lower adult earnings in two ways. First, low birth weight lowers educational attainment. Second, low birth weight has direct effects on cognitive ability beyond its effects on educational attainment.

I estimate the state economic development benefits of turning one low-weight birth into a normal-weight birth. I also estimate the economic development benefits of reducing the incidence of low birth weight by 1 percent of overall births. The current percentage of low-birth-weight babies in the United States is 8.3 percent (Martin et al. 2009).

Estimated economic development benefits from reducing low-birth-weight incidence are based on research by Rucker Johnson and Robert Schoeni. Johnson and Schoeni (2007) compare the earnings of brothers in families where one or more brothers fall into both the low-birth-weight and normal-birth-weight groups.[17] I assume these percentage earnings penalties apply to both men and women over their working lives.[18]

Based on this analysis, the state economic development benefits from switching one low-weight birth to a normal-weight birth have a net present value of $135,631.[19] This justifies considerable costs in converting one low-weight birth to a normal-weight birth. The state economic development benefits of reducing the incidence of low birth weights by 1 percent of all births would in the long run increase state earnings by 0.17 percent. The net present value of the state economic development benefits from this reduction in low-birth-weight incidence, as a percentage of the net present value of state earnings, is 0.09 percent.

Reducing Recurrence of ADHD/Conduct Disorders

Attention deficit hyperactivity disorders (ADHD) and related conduct disorders during youth may affect state economic development by affecting adult earnings capacity. These effects on adult earnings capacity may take place directly or through affecting educational attainment.

I base my estimated economic development effects on research by Currie et al. (2009). They examine how occurrences of ADHD/conduct disorders at various ages affect secondary test scores. I combine these estimates with estimates of how secondary test scores affect adult earnings, as described previously in this chapter. Thus, the estimated effects of child ADHD on adult earnings are only the effects that are manifested in secondary test scores. There probably are additional effects of child ADHD on adult earnings that are not manifested in secondary test scores. Therefore, the estimates here probably understate the effects of child ADHD on adult earnings.

In Currie et al.'s research, they have data on whether ADHD/conduct disorders occur for a young person during each of four age periods: 0–3, 4–8, 9–13, and 14–18. Their model explains secondary test scores as a function of ADHD/conduct disorders occurring during just one of these age periods, and of ADHD/conduct disorders occurring during more than one of these age periods. These estimates control for whether the birth was low weight, as well as for other factors.

For my estimates, I focused on the effects of reducing the incidence of multiple-period ADHD/conduct disorders. This seems more feasible to do than reducing the incidence of single-period ADHD/conduct disorders. After ADHD/conduct disorders have been diagnosed during a given age period, interventions might reduce future incidence of ADHD.[20]

I estimate that reducing one case of multiple-age-period ADHD has state economic development benefits with a present value of $31,123.

I also consider reducing the incidence of multiple-age-period ADHD by 1 percent of the overall population. In Currie et al.'s sample, the overall incidence of multiple-age-period ADHD is 2.7 percent. The incidence of ADHD during any of these age periods is 10.2 percent. Therefore, about one quarter of children diagnosed with ADHD during one period are diagnosed with ADHD for more than one period (Currie et al. 2009, Table 2). I estimate that a 1-percentage-point reduction in children with multiple-period ADHD would have economic development benefits that in the long run exceed 0.04 percent of state earnings. The net present value of these economic development benefits, as a percentage of the net present value of state earnings, is 0.03 percent.

Reducing Problems with Severe Mental Illness, Alcohol Abuse, and Drug Abuse

I base estimates of the economic development benefits from reducing these problems on a meta-analysis by Aos et al. (2006). They estimate that about 3.8 percent of the adult population has a serious mental illness. About 7.6 percent of the adult population has a clinically significant alcohol or drug disorder. Their summary of the research literature suggests that each one of these disorders has similar effects on earnings: about a 15 percent reduction in earnings.

In estimating state economic development benefits from reducing these adult health problems, I followed a somewhat different procedure than for the other human development outcomes. In the case of adult mental illness, or drug or alcohol problems, it is unclear when the intervention will take place. Therefore, in doing these calculations,

I assume that we are reducing these problems for state residents at all ages. Therefore, I do not adjust for out-migration or survival. I do adjust downward for displacement effects in the state economy. Better mental health treatment or alcohol or drug treatment will add labor supply to the state economy. This added labor supply will have some displacement effects.

I estimate the state economic development benefits from eliminating the 15 percent earnings penalty for one person suffering from serious mental illness or alcohol or drug problems. I assume this person lives from ages 16 to 79 and stays in the state. These state economic development benefits have a net present value of $91,394.

I also estimate the state economic development benefits if we can reduce the incidence of mental illness or alcohol or drug problems by 1 percent of the entire population. This could be due to totally eliminating this earnings penalty for 1 percent of the population. Alternatively, this could be from some reduction in severity of problems that is equivalent to totally eliminating the earnings penalty for 1 percent of the population. (For example, we could cut the earnings penalty in half for 2 percent of the population.) The estimated state economic developments are 0.10 percent of state earnings.[21]

REDUCING CRIME

I also estimate the state economic development benefits from policies to reduce crime rates. Specifically, I estimate the state economic development benefits from some policy that could intervene with one or all 16-year-olds in a state and lower all future crimes they commit by 10 percent.

Reduced crime has economic development benefits through several avenues. First, it reduces the population in prison or jail at any time. Because prisoners are not part of the regular labor force, a reduction in prison population will increase state labor supply.

Second, lower crime reduces the number of state residents with a criminal record. A criminal record has been shown to reduce employment rates and wage rates (Holzer, Offner, and Sorensen 2005; Western 2002). These lower employment rates and wages are due in part to employers' reluctance to hire ex-offenders. In addition, time spent in prison means that ex-offenders have accumulated less job experience. To determine the potential earnings benefits of lower crime, I consider data on earnings that are weighted to reflect the typical educational mix of prisoners. Prisoners tend on average to have lower educational attainment. This lowers somewhat the potential earnings benefits of reducing crime.[22]

To estimate the forgone earnings from being imprisoned, I used data on the proportion of persons of each gender in prison or jail at different ages.[23] I also obtained estimates of the proportion of each gender at different ages that will have a prison record if current trends in first incarceration rates continue.[24]

Being in prison is assumed to lower the employment rate to zero. Having a prison record is assumed to reduce the person's subsequent employment rate by 21 percent, based on research by Holzer, Offner, and Sorensen (2005).[25] Having a prison record is assumed to lower wages by 16 percent, based on research by Western (2002).

I then simulate what happens if we intervene with 16-year-olds to lower their future crime by 10 percent. This will lower the number of prisoners at each age by 10 percent. It will also lower the number of persons with a prison record at each age by 10 percent. In addition to aggregate impacts, we can consider the effects for a single 16-year-old. We lower the probabilities of this 16-year-old's engaging in future criminal activity by 10 percent. This lowers the probability that this person will be in prison or have a prison record at each age by 10 percent.

I estimate that lowering a single person's propensity to engage in crime by 10 percent has state economic development benefits of $1,189. Lowering crime overall by 10 percent would in the long run have state economic development benefits equal to 0.124 of state earnings. The present value of the state economic development benefits of 10 percent lower crime, as a percentage of the present value of state earnings, is 0.10 percent.

These state economic development benefits justify considerable efforts in crime prevention. However, these benefits are modest enough that major anticrime spending would require also considering other benefits, such as benefits to crime victims or lower justice system costs.

Why aren't these economic development benefits greater? First, only a small percentage of the population, 0.7 percent, is in prison at any point in time. Second, although eventually 6.6 percent of the population is expected to have a prison record, this percentage is lower at earlier ages (Bonczar 2003). Furthermore, a prison record does not lower employment rates to zero. Third, although a reduction in crime adds to the labor force, the added labor force is predominantly persons with low educational attainment. This means potential earnings effects are smaller.

CONCLUSION

Table 12.1 summarizes this chapter's estimates. Without cost information for achieving these outcomes, this table should not be used to rank the desirability of achieving these outcomes. Some outcomes with modest effects may be sufficiently cheap to offer higher net benefits.

The main point of this chapter is that state economic development benefits can be calculated for many outcomes of human development programs. Early childhood programs happen to have some of the best estimates of the costs of achieving human development outcomes.

The chapter also suggests that many human capital improvements can have large economic development benefits. Sizable and costly programs can be justified to achieve some of these improvements in the quality of a state's human capital.

Chapter 13 summarizes the importance of the local economic development argument for early childhood programs.

Notes

1. This methodology is detailed in Appendix 12A, which, like all of this book's appendices, is available from the Upjohn Institute.
2. For women, the proportion of the effects of higher secondary test scores that were due to higher educational attainment varied from 40 to 80 percent in different specifications (Murnane et al. 2000).
3. The estimated earnings effects at ages 23 and 33 were based on a study by Currie and Thomas (1999). I assumed no effects before age 23. I interpolated between ages 23 and 33 to get in-between effects. Beyond age 33, I assumed that percentage effect on male or female employment rates and wage rates stayed the same for the remainder of their lives. The estimated effects derived from this procedure are

Table 12.1 Summary of State Economic Development Benefits of Possible Outcomes of Human Development Programs

Area	Change considered for one person	Present value of effect on earnings (in dollars)	Societal change considered	Long-run effects as % of state earnings
Elementary test scores	Increase by 0.1 effect size	8,312	All students increase by 0.1 effect size	1.08
Secondary test scores	Increase by 0.1 effect size	7,050	All students increase by 0.1 effect size	0.83
High school dropout	HS dropout to grad	175,234	Increase HS grads by 1% of population	0.21
Bachelor's degree	HS grad to bachelor's degree	375,912	Increase bachelor's degrees by 1% of population	0.45
Associate's degree	HS grad to associate's degree	126,995	Increase associate's degrees by 1% of population	0.15
Low birth weight	Improve one low-birth-weight baby to normal weight	135,631	Reduce incidence of low-birth-weight babies by 1% of population	0.17
ADHD	Prevent one case of multiple-age-period ADHD	31,123	Reduce incidence of multiple-age-period ADHD by 1% of population	0.04
Mental illness, drug or alcohol problems	Prevent negative earnings effects from one case of severe mental illness, or serious alcohol and drug problems	91,394	Reduce negative earnings effects of mental illness, or serious alcohol or drug problems, by 1% of population	0.10
Crime	Reduce probability of crime and imprisonment by 10%	1,189	Reduce crime and imprisonment by 10%	0.14

NOTE: This table focuses on state economic development benefits of specific changes in different human development outcomes, either for one person or for the aggregate population. All estimates are net effects on state residents' earnings. The dollar effects of changes for one person are the resulting net increase in earnings in this state associated with that one person's changed outcomes, calculated in present value terms using a discount rate of 3%, and discounted back to the age at which the change was initiated. The percentage effects of a society-wide change in outcomes are long-run percentage effects on state residents' earnings. All estimates adjust for mortality, out-migration, and displacement effects. Where plausible, estimates also adjust for positive peer effects.

quite similar to those estimated in a recent study by Chetty et al. (2010). Chetty et al. estimate that a one standard deviation increase in kindergarten test scores will increase earnings by 14.8 percent when individuals are around age 27. I am considering a test score increase of one-tenth as much, an increase of 0.1 in "effect size units." At age 27, the estimates used from Currie and Thomas imply an earnings increase of 0.9 percent for men and 1.6 percent for women. These age 27 effects then increase until age 33, after which the percentage effects are assumed to remain stable. These long-run effects are 1.5 percent for men and 1.7 percent for women.

4. These estimates use the nonlinear specification for scenarios 4 and 6 in their Table 7.

5. This is in 2007 dollars, as are all figures in this book unless otherwise indicated.

6. This represents the net increase in state residents' earnings, after considering out-migration and displacement, of this improvement in early elementary education quality for one student.

7. Appendix 12A presents the detailed economic development benefits by year.

8. Specifically, I rely on Brooks-Gunn, Magnuson, and Waldfogel's (2009) estimate that a one standard deviation increase in test scores during late adolescence in high school increased earnings by 10 to 20 percent. I used the midpoint of the range they estimated, 15 percent. I used the same percentage figure for both men and women because the studies seem to get various results for whether effects are higher for men or women (Cawley, Heckman, and Vytlacil 2001; Murnane et al. 2000; Neal and Johnson 1996).

9. Appendix 12A shows the year-by-year state economic development benefits.

10. My results are similar to estimates of Brooks-Gunn, Magnuson, and Waldfogel (2009) when they don't assume much tail-off in early elementary test scores. But their results are quite different when they require that all the effects of early elementary test scores occur through secondary test scores. I agree with them that early elementary test score improvements tail off at the secondary level. However, I think it likely that early elementary test scores affect earnings through mechanisms other than secondary test scores. Higher elementary test scores may be correlated with other changes in the student's behavior and self-confidence.

11. More specifically, I used estimates from the 2007 CPS-ORG on employment rates, wage rates, and weekly hours for high school dropouts and for the three high school graduate groups (high school education only, some college but no BA, and BA and above), weighted based on Belfield and Levin's (2007b) assumptions. Calculations are done separately for males and females. The actual weights also are somewhat different for men and women, based on Levin and Belfield. I take Levin and Belfield's figures on different ethnic groups and use weights for each ethnic group to calculate overall average percentages in each educational category for men and women separately.

12. Age 17 is assumed to be the age that future earnings benefits are discounted back to. The intervention is initiated in 2011.

13. Appendix 12A presents the detailed year-by-year numbers.

14. Unlike the high school dropout analysis, I restrict the bachelor's versus non-

bachelor's comparison to being zero for ages prior to age 22. There are some observed positive differentials prior to age 22, but obtaining such earnings benefits would not be typical for the average bachelor's degree recipient. I should also note that I do not include any local economy spillover benefits of having more college graduates. These spillover benefits were included in my pre-K analysis. However, the spillover effects of college graduates proved to be very small in this analysis.

15. Present value is calculated as of age 18.

16. Persons with an associate's degree included both those with an occupational vocational associate's degree and those with an academic program associate's degree. I set earnings differences between associate's degree holders and nonholders to zero prior to age 21, even though there were some positive differentials before then.

17. My estimates are based upon the raw differences Johnson and Schoeni (2007) report in their Table 3. Using their figures, I calculate the percentage earnings penalty, as a percentage of non-low-birth-weight earnings, for men in three age brackets: ages 18–26, 27–36, and 37–52. I assume that these percentage changes apply to the midpoints of these three age brackets. I interpolate the percentage effects to individual years of age from 16 to 52. Percentage effects beyond age 52 are assumed to be the same as at age 52. Johnson and Schoeni's figures imply a percentage earnings penalty of 10 percent for ages 18–26, 25 percent for ages 27–36, and 26 percent for ages 37–52. The estimated numbers imply a percentage effect of close to zero at age 16. This grows fairly steadily to 25 percent at age 32 and doesn't change much thereafter. Johnson and Schoeni also do some multivariate analysis. This multivariate analysis seems roughly consistent overall with this simple comparison. However, the functional forms chosen for how age alters the effects of low birth weights imply implausible earnings effects at older and younger ages.

18. I adjust upward for positive peer effects during school of reduced incidence of low birth weight. Positive peer effects seem plausible, as there is evidence that birth weight affects school performance (Johnson and Schoeni 2007).

19. This present value is calculated as of birth.

20. Perhaps some prior interventions would reduce the incidence of ADHD in any period. But these interventions might be interventions in prenatal care rather than interventions providing public health treatment directly for ADHD.

21. These benefits are 1 percent of the 15 percent per person penalty, reduced by one-third because of displacement effects.

22. Based on Harlow (2003, Table 1), I assumed that the educational mix of prisoners was 41 percent high school dropouts, 46 percent high school graduates but no college (this includes GEDs), 10 percent some college but not a bachelor's degree, and 3 percent a bachelor's degree. I used these weights to estimate annual earnings by age for males and females separately.

23. West and Sabol (2009), Table 19. West and Sabol only give data on certain age ranges. To get other ages, I interpolated and extrapolated based on their data.

24. Bonczar (2003). I used the Excel spreadsheets that back up Figures 4 and 5 in Bonczar's paper.

25. I took Holzer's estimate that having a criminal record lowered the employment

rate of black males by 17.5 percent. I assumed that this estimate applied to black males at age 40. The 21 percent is the proportion that 17.5 percentage points is of the black male age 40 employment rate. I assumed this downward effect on the employment rate was the same percentage of baseline employment rates for all groups.

13
Thinking and Acting Locally

What Potential Is There for Local Support for High-Quality Early Childhood Programs?

While working on this book, I have also been involved in efforts to implement universal pre-K education in my home community, Kalamazoo, Michigan. A local interfaith community organizing group, ISAAC, adopted early childhood education as an issue. (ISAAC is affiliated with the Gamaliel Foundation, whose most famous former community organizer is Barack Obama.) ISAAC members decided on universal pre-K education as a key "ask" for which they would solicit the support of community leaders. The ISAAC effort led to formation of a Kalamazoo County committee, with representation from United Way, local school superintendents, many pre-K programs and child care centers, parents, local political leaders, and local business leaders. This committee has been drawing up a plan for universal pre-K education in Kalamazoo County: how many additional slots would be needed, how many years and hours of pre-K education would be provided to children under the program, who would provide pre-K education, the role of existing providers, how quality would be determined, and other aspects. The plan is now (2010) at the early stages of seeking funding from various sources. If it is funded, it will not be fully implemented until at least 2013–2014.[1]

Such local efforts face a fundamental issue: Do they make any sense? Does it make sense to think of early childhood education as a policy that can be locally pursued? Does universal pre-K really provide any "local" benefits? The answer this book has given is "Yes." Universal pre-K, and other early childhood programs, can provide significant local economic development benefits. Local benefits justify the potential for local activism.

The remainder of this chapter gives more context for both the potential for and the need for local activism for early childhood programs. In the process of providing the context, I emphasize some of the important findings of this book.

EARLY CHILDHOOD PROGRAMS AND LOCAL ECONOMIC
DEVELOPMENT: HOW DO THEY FIT INTO THE BIG ISSUES?

Is the effect of early childhood programs on local economic development a big issue? Obviously the United States and the world face many major challenges. There are major environmental challenges such as climate change. There are problems with lagging development in much of the Third World. There are issues of improving global financial regulation and macroeconomic stability. There is religious and cultural strife. There are issues of the quality of culture and family life around the world.

Within the United States, a major issue is how to make sure the gains from economic growth are shared more fully with the bottom and middle of the income distribution. Over the last three decades, real earnings have grown sluggishly for most U.S. households. For example, in calculations I did with my colleague Susan Houseman, we found that from 1979 to 2006, real wage growth for 90 percent of all U.S. workers lagged behind the growth in labor productivity of the U.S. economy. If wages below the ninetieth percentile had grown as fast as overall U.S. productivity growth from 1979 to 2006, earnings for these workers would have been over $700 billion higher in 2006. These higher earnings would equal about 12 percent of all U.S. wage and salary income (Bartik and Houseman 2008).

Sluggish earnings growth for most U.S. households has many costs. The economic costs are the most obvious. But, as Harvard economics professor Benjamin Friedman (2005) argues in his book *The Moral Consequences of Economic Growth*, a U.S. society with sluggish growth for most households is likely to be mean-spirited in many ways. Sluggish growth reduces support for stronger environmental protection. It reduces support for engaging generously with the rest of the world. Sluggish growth increases the appeal of simple answers, even authoritarian answers. Global progress as well as U.S. progress is likely to be impeded by a United States in which the broad middle class fears it is losing ground.[2]

We need to figure out how to increase the earnings of the lower and middle portions of the U.S. income distribution. As this book has argued in Chapter 2, these earnings gains are particularly valuable if they are provided in one's home region. Such higher earnings in a home region, which I have labeled "local economic development benefits," are of great importance to many U.S. households.

Many policies must be addressed to deal with this U.S. labor market problem. Better access to affordable health care for all Americans will help. (The 2010 passage of a health care reform bill is just a first step in a long process.) Better assistance for workers displaced because of increases in imports or other economic changes would also help.

But responses to sluggish U.S. earnings growth for most workers must include efforts to improve the human capital development of all U.S. workers. As this book has argued, consistent with most labor economists' views, the labor market will respond to a greater supply of more productive workers by creating additional job slots and additional earnings. "If you supply the labor, the jobs will come" is not perfectly true. But it is true to a large extent.

Among human capital development programs, perhaps the most rigorous empirical evidence for effectiveness is for high-quality early childhood programs. K–12 reforms, changes in higher education financing and design, and a better job training system are also needed. But how to expand early childhood programs, while ensuring high quality, is a key component of any overall U.S. human capital development strategy.

WHAT CAN AND SHOULD BE DONE LOCALLY?

To what extent can and should these various issues be dealt with at the state and local level, versus the federal or international level? For many of these issues, state and local governments cannot lead, but must follow. Climate change policy must be set at a global and national level. Financial regulation is largely a national and global issue.

Even as regards U.S. living standards for typical households, many of the policies must be instituted at the national level. For example, health care reform is clearly a national issue.

But early childhood education is one issue where a strong state and local role makes sense. Consider Harvard professor John Donahue's criteria for when governmental authority and responsibility should

devolve from the federal government to U.S. states: "Do Devolve—
Where It Makes Sense . . . Where states vary greatly in circumstances or
goals, where external impacts are minor or manageable, where the payoff from innovation exceeds the advantages of uniformity, and where
competition boosts efficiency instead of inspiring destructive strategies,
the central government should stand clear" (Donahue 1997, p. 165).

As discussed throughout this book, these criteria are to a large
extent met by early childhood programs.

"Where states vary greatly in circumstances or goals . . . " Early
childhood education can be delivered in a quality way through a variety of institutions, including public schools and private pre-K programs
(Chapter 5). State and local areas may differ in the extent and quality
of such institutions. The culture of different states or local areas may
demand more or less parental choice in pre-K programs (Chapter 11).

" . . . where external impacts are minor or manageable . . . " The
state-level economic development benefits of early childhood programs
are two-thirds to three-quarters of their national economic development
benefits (Chapter 10). Local economic development benefits are not
much below state economic development benefits (Chapter 9). One can
argue that the glass is one-quarter to one-third empty. The spillover economic development benefits of early childhood programs are sufficient
to rationalize very large federal subsidies for the costs of these programs (Chapter 10). But one can also argue that the glass is two-thirds
to three-quarters full. The state or local economic development benefits
of high-quality early childhood programs are more than enough to rationalize vigorous state or local support for these programs. In this they
contrast with, for example, policies to control global warming, in which
spillover benefits are so large compared to local benefits that state or
local efforts to control global warming can only be justified as a way to
encourage more effective global action.

**" . . . where the payoff from innovation exceeds the advantages
of uniformity . . . "** We know something about what policies lead to
higher-quality pre-K programs, such as smaller class sizes (Chapter 5).
But there are many uncertainties (Chapter 6). We need more knowledge
about what early childhood programs and program designs will be most

effective for what children. State and local flexibility in program design is one way to encourage early childhood programs to be innovative (Chapter 10).

" . . . where competition boosts efficiency instead of inspiring destructive strategies . . . " When offering financial incentives to businesses, state and local governments engage in competition that leads to incentive levels that excessively redistribute income toward the rich and produces only limited national economic development benefits (Chapter 10). But for early childhood programs, competition may provide an incentive to come up with better program approaches. For example, the prospect of higher property values may spur state and local competition to improve pre-K access and quality (Chapter 7).

There is a strong need for federal involvement to evaluate the results of early childhood programs. Innovation's benefits accrue throughout the nation, and perhaps even to other countries. Innovation without evaluation has no proof of effectiveness. Because most of the benefits of evaluating innovations spill over into other states around the nation, state and local areas have an incentive to underinvest in evaluating innovations. Federal funding can increase evaluation to a more socially beneficial level.

States were famously referred to by Supreme Court Justice Louis Brandeis as "laboratories of democracy." However, if no one bothers to rigorously measure results in these laboratories, the learning from such laboratories will be too limited.

There is also a strong need for federal involvement to measure early childhood program quality. State and local political leaders and bureaucrats may have some incentive to claim success regardless of reality. Voters and home buyers would benefit from outside objective information on program quality. The availability of such outside objective information may even be essential in allowing property value effects to occur from better program quality (Chapter 7). The possible capitalization of better program quality provides incentives for state and local competition to promote higher program quality.

There is also a more pragmatic political case for federal involvement in early childhood education. There are both local and national economic development benefits from fostering more and better-quality early childhood programs. If state and local governments fail to act, for whatever reason, there is still a rationale for federal involvement. The national interest is served by expanding high-quality early childhood programs. Such federal involvement should respect the need for innovation and flexibility in early childhood programs (Chapter 10).

IS LOCAL ACTION REALLY POLITICALLY FEASIBLE?

Of course, there are barriers to the efforts of local activists to expand high-quality early childhood programs. These programs' short-run costs are high relative to their benefits (Chapters 4 and 7). (This assumes that there is no capitalization of greater access to higher-quality early childhood programs into higher property values, and that early childhood programs are not coupled with complementary programs of adult training that have short-term benefits. See Chapter 7 for discussion of these possibilities.) Short-sighted local political leaders may be hesitant to incur short-term costs whose largest benefits are long-term.

The distribution of benefits from early childhood programs may also be a political problem. For example, pre-K's dollar benefits per household in the lowest income quintile are three times the dollar benefits for the median income household (Chapter 8). Tax costs of universal pre-K or targeted pre-K exceed benefits for the upper two income quintiles (Chapter 8). If upper income households have disproportionately large political influence compared to lower income households in state and local politics, then the tax costs of upper income households may politically outweigh the benefits for lower income households.

However, one common critique of state and local action on human capital investments does not seem to be sufficiently empirically valid. For example, John Donahue (1997), in his book on U.S. states, makes the following argument for why states may inadequately invest in education: "Mobility . . . dilutes the incentives of states to invest in education. Workers educated at the expense of one state can move away and apply their productive skills elsewhere . . . The mobility of human capital clouds confident predictions that development-minded states will emphasize education" (p. 158). Donahue's argument would seem to apply with even more force to early childhood programs, which take place earlier, with more time for persons to move out of state.

However, the empirical evidence suggests that there is considerably less out-of-state mobility from one's childhood state than some might expect (Chapter 2). Over three-fifths of Americans spend the bulk of their working career in their childhood state. Out-of-state mobility does reduce the state-level economic development benefits of early childhood programs. But the remaining state-level economic development benefits of early childhood programs still far exceed costs, by ratios of two to one and more (Chapter 4).

Transferring the debate over early childhood programs to the federal level does not solve the problems of politicians' favoring a short-term perspective or favoring the rich. The U.S. Congress's actions on budget deficits or climate change legislation do not suggest an enthusiasm for a long-term perspective. Furthermore, as political scientist Larry Bartels contends in his book *Unequal Democracy*, U.S. senators are much less responsive to the political views of their low income constituents than they are to the views of their middle income and upper income constituents (Bartels 2008, Chap. 9).

If the problem is that state and local leaders, as well as federal leaders, do not pay attention to the long-term or the needs of the poor, then the most direct solution would seem to be political pressure. Organizations and campaigns should pressure political leaders to adopt a long-term perspective that considers the needs of all households. Effective political pressure on behalf of the poor is certainly a goal of community organizing. Sometimes such community organizing groups are quite politically effective. (See, for example, Paul Osterman's [2003] description of the many successful organizing efforts of the Industrial Areas Foundation, the community organizing group founded by Saul Alinsky.) The efforts of Pew Charitable Trusts and its affiliated organizations to build a business case for pre-K education also can be seen as an effort to change the political climate.

Successful grassroots efforts to expand education have U.S. historical precedents. The common school movement of the nineteenth century successfully advocated for free public elementary education through grade eight. The high school movement of the early twentieth century dramatically expanded public high schools and public high school enrollment from 1910 to 1940.

These successful education expansions seem to have stemmed from grassroots pressure as well as pressure from business groups and educated elites. For example, according to Harvard professors Claudia Goldin and Lawrence Katz in their book *The Race between Education and Technology*, the common school movement of the nineteenth century benefited from a wide range of supporters.

> Across much of America, mass education was a truly grassroots movement. Its popular base is clear from the referenda in many states that led to the passage of constitutional amendments, constitutions, and legislative statutes providing for taxation and free public education. It is also clear from the role of migration of New Englanders into the western lands and the institutions they brought with them. Yet it is also the case that public education was championed by energetic and persuasive school men such as Horace Mann, and that some manufacturers and property owners, particularly in the wake of the large migration of the Irish to New England, wanted to create Protestant Americans out of newly arrived Catholics . . . (Goldin and Katz 2008, p. 148)

In the early twentieth century, in Goldin and Katz's view, the high school movement was also a "grassroots movement. It sprung from the people and was not forced upon them by a top-down campaign" (p. 245).

As an example of how these movements promoted educational investments, consider the following statement from the Iowa Department of Public Instruction in 1914:

> The landlord who lives in town . . . may well be reminded that when he offers his farm for sale it will be to his advantage to advertise, "free transportation to a good graded school." Those who have no children to attend school . . . should be interested in securing to the children of the whole community the best educational advantages possible . . . if they live out their years with no children to depend upon in old age, they must of necessity rely upon someone, they know not whom, who is today in the public schools. Their only safeguard lies in giving the best advantages possible to all. (Quoted in Goldin and Katz [2008], p. 193)

The case made in 1914 by the Iowa Department of Public Instruction for "a good graded school" is similar in spirit to today's "business case" for high-quality early childhood programs. Both make an appeal to economic self-interest as well as the broad public interest.

A key point is that the common school movement and the high school movement were not federal initiatives. These dramatic increases in educational access were won by state and local activism.

It is certainly conceivable that a new national norm of universal access to high quality early childhood programs might be established by grassroots campaigns at the state and local level. Whether this occurs is up to political choices and the political activism of many groups, from citizen activists to business groups.

NEW THINKING ABOUT EARLY CHILDHOOD PROGRAMS AND LOCAL ECONOMIC DEVELOPMENT

Like most economists, and perhaps most academics interested in government policy, I would like to believe (but often doubt!) that John Maynard Keynes was right when he famously stated, at the end of *The General Theory*, his confidence in the power of ideas: "The ideas of economists and political philosophers, both when they are right and when they are wrong, are more powerful than is commonly understood. Indeed the world is ruled by little else . . . Soon or late, it is ideas, not vested interests, which are dangerous for good or evil" (Keynes 1936, p. 383).

Local economic development policy does not have the national prominence of macroeconomics. But it is the preeminent goal of state and local governments in the United States. Achieving better state and local economic development is the direct goal of many state and local programs. All other state and local policies are influenced by their per-ceived effects on local economic development.

As this book has argued, we need to rethink local economic devel-opment. Local economic development should not be thought of as simply growth in local output or employment. Rather, local economic development should be thought of as growth in employment and earn-ings per capita.

When thought of in this way, local economic development gains social significance. It provides the great social benefit of helping per-sons to obtain a good job while allowing them to retain valuable ties to their home region.

If local economic development increases local earnings per capita, then it becomes an important class of labor market benefit. It then becomes apparent that such labor market benefits can be affected by labor market policies on both sides of the labor market: the demand side and the supply side.

The labor demand side, incentives to business, has traditionally been emphasized by state and local economic development policy. But this tradition is not backed up by empirical evidence. At least as important to local economic development is what state and local public policies do on the labor supply side, in enhancing the quantity and quality of the human capital of local residents.

Early childhood programs can play a key role in such local human capital policies. We know enough to say that such programs, if run in a high-quality way at sufficient scale, can play a significant role in enhancing local economic development. We also know enough to say that we need to continue learning how to more effectively design and implement these programs. Continued public as well as private innovation is an important part of local economic development.

The idea of early childhood programs as a spur to state and local economic development is a powerful idea. The empirical evidence supports this idea. Will this idea become accepted by the public, the business community, and political leaders? If so, this new way of thinking about economic development may encourage the political support needed to make early childhood programs more broadly available to American children.

Notes

1. Among other activities, I have written a paper that applies some of this book's analysis to the particular case of universal pre-K in Kalamazoo County (Bartik 2009a).
2. I hasten to add that for environmental reasons, policies to promote growth need to be accompanied by policies that will over time sufficiently reduce CO_2 emissions (and other environmental damage) per dollar of global output, and control population, so that total CO_2 emissions and other environmental damage will decline even as global output per person expands.

References

Administration for Children and Families. 2010. *HHS Announces National Effort to Raise Quality in Head Start Programs.* Washington, DC: Administration for Children and Families. http://eclkc.ohs.acf.hhs.gov/hslc/ Head Start Program/roadmap/ (accessed October 7, 2010).

Agee, Mark D., and Thomas D. Crocker. 1996. "Parents' Discount Rates for Child Quality." *Southern Economic Journal* 63(1): 36–50.

Akerlof, George, and Janet Yellen, eds. 1986. *Efficiency Wage Models of the Labor Market.* New York: Cambridge University Press.

Anderson, Michael L. 2008. "Multiple Inference and Gender Differences in the Effects of Early Intervention: A Reevaluation of the Abecedarian, Perry Preschool, and Early Training Projects." *Journal of the American Statistical Association* 103(484): 1481–1495.

Anderson, Patricia M., and Phillip B. Levine. 2000. "Child Care and Mothers' Employment Decisions." In *Finding Jobs: Work and Welfare Reform*, David Card and Rebecca M. Blank, eds. New York: Russell Sage Foundation, pp. 420–462.

Aos, Steve, Roxanne Lieb, Jim Mayfield, Marna Miller, and Annie Pennucci. 2004. *Benefits and Costs of Prevention and Early Intervention Programs for Youth: Technical Appendix.* Olympia: Washington State Institute for Public Policy.

Aos, Steve, Jim Mayfield, Marna Miller, and Wei Yen. 2006. *Evidence-Based Treatment of Alcohol, Drug, and Mental Health Disorders: Potential Benefits, Costs, and Fiscal Impacts for Washington State.* Olympia: Washington State Institute for Public Policy.

Bania, Neil, Jo Anna Gray, and Joe Stone. 2007. "Growth, Taxes, and Government Expenditures: Growth Hills for U.S. States." *National Tax Journal* 60(2): 193–204.

Bania, Neil, and Joe Stone. 2007. "Ranking State Fiscal Structures Using Theory and Evidence." Working paper. Eugene: University of Oregon.

Barnett, W. Steven. 1993. "Benefit-Cost Analysis of Preschool Education: Findings from a 25-Year Follow-Up." *American Journal of Orthopsychiatry* 63(4): 500–508.

———. 2004. "Maximizing Returns from Prekindergarten Education." Federal Reserve Bank of Cleveland *Proceedings* (2005): 5–18.

———. 2006. *Universal or Targeted Preschool? The Case for Universal Preschool.* Education Sector Debates. Washington, DC: Education Sector.

———. 2007. "Revving Up Head Start." *Journal of Policy Analysis and Management* 26(3): 674–677.

————. 2008. *Preschool Education and Its Lasting Effects: Research and Policy Implications*. Boulder, CO: Education and the Public Interest Center; Tempe, AZ: Education Policy Research Unit. http://epicpolicy.org/publication/ preschooleducation (accessed September 2, 2009).

Barnett, W. Steven, Dale J. Epstein, Allison H. Friedman, Judi Stevenson Boyd, and Jason T. Hustedt. 2008. *The State of Preschool 2008: State Preschool Yearbook*. New Brunswick, NJ: National Institute for Early Education Research, Rutgers University.

Barnett, W. Steven, and Ellen Frede. 2009. "Federal Early Childhood Policy Guide for the First 100 Days." NIEER Policy Brief. New Brunswick, NJ: National Institute for Early Education Research, Rutgers University.

Barrow, Lisa, and Cecilia Elena Rouse. 2004. "Using Market Valuation to Assess Public School Spending." *Journal of Public Economics* 88(9–10): 1747–1769.

Bartels, Larry M. 2008. *Unequal Democracy: The Political Economy of the New Gilded Age*. New York: Russell Sage Foundation; Princeton, NJ: Princeton University Press.

Bartik, Timothy J. 1989. "Small Business Start-Ups in the United States: Estimates of the Effects of Characteristics of States." *Southern Economic Journal* 55(4): 1004–1018.

————. 1990. "The Market Failure Approach to Regional Economic Development Policy." *Economic Development Quarterly* 4(4): 361–370.

————. 1991a. *Who Benefits from State and Local Economic Development Policies?* Kalamazoo, MI: W.E. Upjohn Institute for Employment Research.

————. 1991b. "The Effects of Metropolitan Job Growth on the Size Distribution of Family Income." Upjohn Institute Working Paper 91-06. Kalamazoo, MI: W.E. Upjohn Institute for Employment Research.

————. 1993a. "Who Benefits from Local Job Growth, Migrants or the Original Residents?" *Regional Studies* 27(4): 297–311.

————. 1993b. *Economic Development and Black Economic Success*. Report to U.S. Economic Development Administration. Upjohn Institute Technical Report 93-001. Kalamazoo, MI: W.E. Upjohn Institute for Employment Research.

————. 1994a. "What Should the Federal Government Be Doing about Urban Economic Development?" *Cityscape* 1(1): 267–292.

————. 1994b. "The Effects of Metropolitan Job Growth on the Size Distribution of Family Income." *Journal of Regional Science* 34(4): 483–502.

————. 1999. "Growing State Economies: How Taxes and Public Services Affect Private-Sector Performance." In *The End of Welfare: Consequences of Federal Devolution for the Nation*, Max B. Sawicky, ed. Washington, DC: Economic Policy Institute, pp. 95–126.

———. 2001. *Jobs for the Poor: Can Labor Demand Policies Help?* New York: Russell Sage Foundation; Kalamazoo, MI: W.E. Upjohn Institute for Employment Research.

———. 2002. "Spillover Effects of Welfare Reforms in State Labor Markets." *Journal of Regional Science* 42(4): 667–701.

———. 2004a. "Economic Development." In *Management Policies in Local Government Finance*, 5th ed., J. Richard Aronson and Eli Schwartz, eds. Washington, DC: International City/County Management Association, pp. 355–390.

———. 2004b. "Thinking about Local Living Wage Requirements." *Urban Affairs Review* 40(2): 269–299.

———. 2005. "Solving the Problems of Economic Development Incentives." *Growth and Change* 36(2): 138–166.

———. 2006. *Taking Preschool Education Seriously as an Economic Development Program: Effects on Jobs and Earnings of State Residents Compared to Traditional Economic Development Programs.* Report to the Committee for Economic Development and Pew Charitable Trusts. Kalamazoo, MI: W.E. Upjohn Institute for Employment Research. http://www.upjohn .org/preschool/full_report.pdf (accessed July 15, 2010).

———. 2008. *The Economic Development Effects of Early Childhood Programs.* Issue Paper 6. Washington, DC: Partnership for America's Economic Success. http://www.partnershipforsuccess.org/uploads/20080723 _Bartikformatted.pdf (accessed July 16, 2010).

———. 2009a. "Economic Development Benefits of Preschool Expansion in Kalamazoo County." Upjohn Institute Working Paper 09-147. Kalamazoo, MI: W.E. Upjohn Institute for Employment Research.

———. 2009b. "What Proportion of Children Stay in the Same Location as Adults, and How Does This Vary across Location and Groups?" Upjohn Institute Working Paper 09-145. Kalamazoo, MI: W.E. Upjohn Institute for Employment Research.

———. 2009c. "How Do the Effects of Local Growth on Employment Rates Vary with Initial Labor Market Conditions?" Upjohn Institute Working Paper 09-148. Kalamazoo, MI: W.E. Upjohn Institute for Employment Research.

———. 2009d. "What Should Michigan Be Doing to Promote Long-Run Economic Development?" Upjohn Institute Working Paper 09-160. Kalamazoo, MI: W.E. Upjohn Institute for Employment Research.

Bartik, Timothy J., Peter Eisinger, and George Erickcek. 2003. "Economic Development Policy in Michigan." In *Michigan at the Millennium*, Charles Ballard, Paul Courant, Doug Drake, Ron Fisher, and Elizabeth Gerber, eds. East Lansing: Michigan State University Press, pp. 279–298.

Bartik, Timothy J., and George Erickcek. 2003. *Economic Impact of Various Budgetary Policy Options for the State of Michigan to Resolve Its Budget Deficit for FY 2004.* Upjohn Institute report. http://www.upjohninstitute .org/michigan_budget_study.pdf (accessed July 15, 2010).

———. 2008. "'Eds and Meds' and Metropolitan Economic Development." In *Urban and Regional Policy and Its Effects*, Margery Austin Turner, Howard Wial, and Harold Wolman, eds. Washington, DC: Brookings Institution Press, pp. 21–59.

———. 2010. "The Employment and Fiscal Effects of Michigan's MEGA Tax Credit Program." Upjohn Institute Working Paper 10-164. Kalamazoo, MI: W.E. Upjohn Institute for Employment Research.

Bartik, Timothy J., George Erickcek, Wei-Jang Huang, and Brad Watts. 2006. "Michigan's Economic Competitiveness and Public Policy." *State Tax Notes* 42(5): 297–319.

Bartik, Timothy J., and Susan N. Houseman. 2008. "Introduction and Overview." In *A Future of Good Jobs? America's Challenge in the Global Economy*, Timothy J. Bartik and Susan N. Houseman, eds. Kalamazoo, MI: W.E. Upjohn Institute for Employment Research, pp. 1–16.

Bartik, Timothy J., and V. Kerry Smith. 1987. "Urban Amenities and Public Policy." In *Handbook of Regional and Urban Economics*, Vol. 2, Edwin S. Mills, ed. Amsterdam and New York: North-Holland, pp. 1207–1254.

Baum, Sandra, and Jennifer Ma. 2007. *Education Pays: The Benefits of Higher Education for Individuals and Society.* Washington, DC: College Board.

Bayer, Patrick, Fernando Ferreira, and Robert McMillan. 2007. "A Unified Framework for Measuring Preferences for Schools and Neighborhoods." *Journal of Political Economy* 115(4): 588–638.

Belfield, Clive R., and Henry M. Levin, eds. 2007a. *The Price We Pay: Economic and Social Consequences of Inadequate Education.* Washington, DC: Brookings Institution Press.

Belfield, Clive R., and Henry M. Levin. 2007b. "The Education Attainment Gap: Who's Affected, How Much, and Why It Matters." In *The Price We Pay: Economic and Social Consequences of Inadequate Education*, Clive R. Belfield and Henry M. Levin, eds. Washington, DC: Brookings Institution Press, pp. 1–17.

Benus, Jacob M., Michelle L. Wood, and Neelima Grover. 1994. *A Comparative Analysis of the Washington and Massachusetts UI Self-Employment Demonstrations.* Report to the U.S. Department of Labor, Employment and Training Administration, Unemployment Insurance Service. Cambridge, MA: Abt Associates.

Besharov, Douglas. 2007. *Investing in Young Children Pays Dividends: The Economic Case for Early Care and Education.* Hearing before the Joint Economic Committee, Senate, U.S. Congress. 110th Cong., 1st sess.

Besharov, Douglas J., and Caeli A. Higney. 2007. "Head Start: Mend It, Don't Expand It (Yet)." *Journal of Policy Analysis and Management* 26(3): 678–681.

Besharov, Douglas J., Caeli A. Higney, and Justus A. Myers. 2007. *Federal and State Child Care and Early Education Expenditures (1997–2005): Child Care Spending Falls as Pre-K Spending Rises.* Report to the Administration on Children, Youth, and Families, Administration for Children and Families, U.S. Department of Health and Human Services. Washington, DC: American Enterprise Institute for Public Policy Research; College Park: Welfare Reform Academy, University of Maryland.

Besley, Timothy, and Ravi Kanbur. 1990. "The Principles of Targeting." Policy, Research, and External Affairs Working Paper 385. Washington, DC: World Bank.

Black, Sandra E. 1999. "Do Better Schools Matter? Parental Valuation of Elementary Education." *Quarterly Journal of Economics* 114(2): 577–599.

Blair, John P., and David W. Swindell. 1997. "Sports, Politics, and Economics: The Cincinnati Story." In *Sports, Jobs and Taxes: The Economic Impact of Sports Teams and Stadiums*, Roger G. Noll and Andrew Zimbalist, eds. Washington, DC: Brookings Institution Press, pp. 282–323.

Blanchard, Olivier Jean, and Lawrence F. Katz. 1992. "Regional Evolutions." *Brookings Papers on Economic Activity* 1992(1): 1–75.

Blanchflower, David G. 2007. "Is Unemployment More Costly than Inflation?" NBER Working Paper 13505. Cambridge, MA: National Bureau of Economic Research.

Blanchflower, David G., and Andrew J. Oswald. 1994. *The Wage Curve.* Cambridge, MA: MIT Press.

———. 2004. "Well-Being over Time in Britain and the USA." *Journal of Public Economics* 88(7–8): 1359–1386.

Blau, David M. 1997. "The Production of Quality in Child Care Centers." *Journal of Human Resources* 32(2): 354–387.

———. 2000. "The Production of Quality in Child Care Centers: Another Look." *Applied Developmental Science* 4(3): 136–148.

———. 2001. *The Child Care Problem: An Economic Analysis.* New York: Russell Sage Foundation.

Blau, David M., and Janet Currie. 2006. "Pre-School, Day Care, and After-School Care: Who's Minding the Kids?" In *Handbook of the Economics of Education*, Vol. 2, Eric Hanushek and Finis Welch, eds. Amsterdam: North-Holland, pp. 1163–1278.

Blau, David M., and Alison P. Hagy. 1998. "The Demand for Quality in Child Care." *Journal of Political Economy* 106(1): 104–146.

Bloom, Howard. 2006. "The Nature and Pitfalls of the Effect Size." PowerPoint presentation to Institute of Education Sciences, U.S. Department of Edu-

cation. Washington, DC: Institute of Education Sciences. http://ies.ed.gov/
director/conferences/06ies_conference/plenary/index.asp (accessed July 23,
2010).

Bolton, Roger. 1992. "'Place Prosperity vs. People Prosperity' Revisited: An
Old Issue with a New Angle." *Urban Studies* 29(2): 185–203.

Bonczar, Thomas P. 2003. *Prevalence of Imprisonment in the U.S. Population,
1974–2001*. Bureau of Justic Statistics Special Report NCJ 197976. Washington, DC: U.S. Department of Justice, Bureau of Justice Statistics.

Bound, John, Jeffrey Groen, G. Gabor Kezdi, and Sarah Turner. 2004. "Trade
in University Training: Cross-State Variation in the Production and Stock
of College-Educated Labor." *Journal of Econometrics* 121(1–2): 143–173.

Brighouse, Harry. 2007. "What's So Great about the Family Anyway?" Paper
presented in a talk at the Center for the Humanities, University of Wisconsin–
Madison, December. http://crookedtimber.org/2008/09/16/whats-so-great-
about-the-family-anyway (accessed July 15, 2010).

Brighouse, Harry, and Adam Swift. 2009. "Legitimate Parental Partiality."
Philosophy and Public Affairs 37(1): 43–80.

Brooks-Gunn, Jeanne, Katherine Magnuson, and Jane Waldfogel. 2009. "Long-
Run Economic Effects of Early Childhood Programs on Adult Earnings."
Issue Paper 12. Washington, DC: Partnership for America's Economic
Success.

Bueno, Marisa, Linda Darling-Hammond, and Danielle Gonzales. 2010. *A
Matter of Degrees: Preparing Teachers for the Pre-K Classroom*. Education Reform Series. Washington, DC: Pew Center on the States.

Bureau of Labor Statistics (BLS). 2008. *Employer Costs for Employee Compensation*. Data series. Washington, DC: Bureau of Labor Statistics. http://
www.bls.gov/ncs/ect/ (accessed July 22, 2010).

Burwell, David, and Robert Puentes. 2009. *Innovative State Transportation
Funding and Financing: Policy Options for States*. Washington, DC: NGA
Center for Best Practices, National Governors Association. http://www.nga
.org/Files/pdf/0901transportationfunding.pdf (accessed July 15, 2010).

Camilli, Gregory, Sadako Vargas, Sharon Ryan, and W. Steven Barnett. 2010.
"Meta-Analysis of the Effects of Early Education Interventions on Cognitive and Social Development." *Teachers College Record* 112(3). http://
www.tcrecord.org (accessed March 19, 2010).

Card, David. 1995. "Using Geographic Variation in College Proximity to Es-
timate the Return to Schooling." In *Aspects of Labour Market Behaviour:
Essays in Honour of John Vanderkamp*, Louis N. Christofides, E. Kenneth
Grant, and Robert Swidinsky, eds. Toronto, Canada: University of Toronto
Press, pp. 201–222.

Cato Institute. 2009. *Cato Handbook for Policymakers*, 7th ed. Washington, DC: Cato Institute.

Cawley, John, James Heckman, and Edward Vytlacil. 2001. "Three Observations on Wages and Measured Cognitive Ability." *Labour Economics* 8(4): 419–442.

Chetty, Raj, John N. Friedman, Nathaniel Hilger, Emmanuel Saez, Diane Schanzenbach, and Danny Yagan. 2010. "How Does Your Kindergarten Classroom Affect Your Earnings? Evidence from Project STAR." Power-Point presentation. http://obs.rc.fas.harvard.edu/chetty/STAR_slides.pdf (accessed July 28, 2010).

Clark, Andrew E. 2003. "Unemployment as a Social Norm: Psychological Evidence from Panel Data." *Journal of Labor Economics* 21(2): 323–351.

Cline, Robert J., and Thomas S. Neubig. 1999. *Masters of Complexity and Bearers of Great Burden: The Sales Tax System and Compliance Costs for Multistate Retailers*. Report prepared for the eCommerce Coalition. Washington, DC: Ernst and Young.

Corporation for Enterprise Development. 2007. *Assets and Opportunity Scorecard, 2007–2008*. Tax Expenditure Report Policy Brief. Washington, DC: Corporation for Enterprise Development. http://cfed.org/assets/pdfs/2007_Scorecard.pdf (accessed July 30, 2010).

Courant, Paul N. 1994. "How Would You Know a Good Economic Development Policy if You Tripped over One? Hint: Don't Just Count Jobs." *National Tax Journal* 47(4): 863–881.

Currie, Janet. 2007. "Response to Besharov/Higney and Barnett." *Journal of Policy Analysis and Management* 26(3): 688–689.

Currie, Janet, and Matthew Neidell. 2007. "Getting Inside the 'Black Box' of Head Start Quality: What Matters and What Doesn't." *Economics of Education Review* 26(1): 83–99.

Currie, Janet, Mark Stabile, Phongsack Manivong, and Leslie L. Roos. 2009. *Child Health and Young Adult Outcomes*. Issue Paper 9. Washington, DC: Partnership for America's Economic Success.

Currie, Janet, and Duncan Thomas. 1999. "Early Test Scores, Socioeconomic Status, and Future Outcomes." NBER Working Paper 6943. Cambridge, MA: National Bureau of Economic Research.

Daniel-Echols, Marijata, and Larry Schweinhart. 2007. "Lessons from the Evaluation of the Michigan School Readiness Program." Paper presented at the National Invitational Conference of the Early Childhood Research Collaborative, held in Minneapolis, MN, December 7–8.

Davidson, Carl. 1990. *Recent Developments in the Theory of Involuntary Unemployment*. Kalamazoo, MI: W.E. Upjohn Institute for Employment Research.

DeNava-Walt, Carmen, Bernadette D. Proctor, and Jessica C. Smith. 2008. *Income, Poverty, and Health Insurance Coverage in the United States: 2007.* U.S. Census Bureau Current Population Reports P60-235. Washington, DC: U.S. Government Printing Office.

Diamond, Adele, W. Steven Barnett, Jessica Thomas, and Sarah Munro. 2007. "Preschool Program Improves Cognitive Control." *Science* 318(5855): 1387–1388. http://www.devcogneuro.com/Publications/Science%20article%20-%20 Diamond%20et%20al.pdf (accessed July 23, 2010).

Dickens, William T., and Charles Baschnagel. 2008. *Dynamic Estimates of the Fiscal Effects of Investing in Early Childhood Programs.* Report to the Partnership for America's Economic Success. Issue Paper 5. http://www .partnershipforsuccess.org/docs/researchproject_dickens_200802_paper .pdf (accessed July 26, 2010).

Dickens, William T., Isabel Sawhill, and Jeffrey Tebbs. 2006. *The Effects of Investing in Early Education on Economic Growth.* Brookings Institution Policy Brief 153. Washington, DC: Brookings Institution.

Digest of Education Statistics. 2010. Various editions, prepared by the National Center for Education Statistics, Institute of Education Sciences, U.S. Department of Education. http://nces.ed.gov/Programs/digest (accessed July 15, 2010).

DiTella, Rafael, Robert J. MacCulloch, and Andrew J. Oswald. 2001. "Preferences over Inflation and Unemployment: Evidence from Surveys of Happiness." *American Economic Review* 91(1): 335–341.

Donahue, John D. 1997. *Disunited States.* New York: Basic Books.

Dresser, Laura, and Joel Rogers. 1997. "Rebuilding Job Access and Career Advancement Systems in the New Economy." Center on Wisconsin Strategy Briefing Paper. Madison, WI: University of Wisconsin–Madison.

Duncan, Greg J., Ariel Kalil, and Kathleen Ziol-Guest. 2008. "Economic Costs of Early Childhood Poverty." Partnership for America's Economic Success Issue Paper 4. Washington, DC: Partnership for America's Economic Success.

Dye, Richard F., and David F. Merriman. 2006. "Tax Increment Financing: A Tool for Local Economic Development." *Land Lines* 18(1): 2–7. http:// www.lincolninst.edu/pubs/PubDetail.aspx?pubid=1078 (accessed July 15, 2010).

Early, Diane M., Kelly L. Maxwell, Margaret Burchinal, Soumya Alva, Randall H. Bender, Donna Bryant, Karen Cai, Richard M. Clifford, Caroline Ebanks, James A. Griffin, Gary T. Henry, Carollee Howes, Jeniffer Iriondo-Perez, Hyun-Joo Jeon, Andrew J. Mashburn, Ellen Peisner-Feinberg, Robert C. Pianta, Nathan Vandergrift, and Nicholas Zill. 2007. "Teachers' Education, Classroom Quality, and Young Children's Academic Skills: Results from Seven Studies of Preschool programs." *Child Development* 78(2): 558–580.

Ehlen, Mark. 2001. "The Economic Impact of Manufacturing Extension Centers." *Economic Development Quarterly* 15(1): 36–44.

Ehrlich, Ev, and Tracy Kornblatt. 2004. "Developmental Education: The Value of High Quality Preschool Investments as Economic Tools." Working paper. New York: Committee for Economic Development.

Federal Reserve Board. 2009. *Balance Sheet Tables, Flow of Funds Accounts of the United States.* Based on March 12, 2009, release of data for fourth quarter of 2008. http://www.federalreserve.gov/releases/z1/20090312/z1r-5 .pdf (accessed July 26, 2010).

Fishe, Raymond P.H. 1982. "Unemployment Insurance and the Reservation Wage of the Unemployed." *Review of Economics and Statistics* 64(1): 12–17.

Fisher, Peter S., and Alan H. Peters. 1998. *Industrial Incentives: Competition among American States and Cities.* Kalamazoo, MI: W.E. Upjohn Institute for Employment Research.

———. 2004. "The Failures of Economic Development Incentives." *Journal of the American Planning Association* 70(1): 27–38.

Fisher, Ronald C. 1996. *State and Local Public Finance.* Chicago: Irwin.

Florida, Richard. 2002. *The Rise of the Creative Class, and How It's Transforming Work, Leisure, Community, and Everyday Life.* New York: Basic Books.

Frey, Bruno, and Alois Stutzer. 2002. "What Can Economists Learn from Happiness Research?" *Journal of Economic Literature* 40(2): 402–435.

Friedlander, Daniel, David H. Greenberg, and Philip K. Robins. 1997. "Evaluating Government Training Programs for the Economically Disadvantaged." *Journal of Economic Literature* 35(4): 1809–1855.

Friedman, Benjamin M. 2005. *The Moral Consequences of Economic Growth.* New York: Alfred A. Knopf.

Friedman, Dana E. 2004. *The New Economics of Preschool: New Findings, Methods, and Strategies for Increasing Economic Investments in Early Care and Education.* Prepared for the Early Childhood Funders' Collaborative. Silver Spring, MD: Grantmakers for Children, Youth, and Families. http:// www.earlychildhoodfinance.org/handouts/FriedmanArticle.doc (accessed July 15, 2010).

Fuller, Bruce. 2006a. "The Arguments for Targeting." In *Education Sector Debates: Universal or Targeted Preschool?* Washington, DC: Education Sector.

———. 2006b. "Response to Steve Barnett." In *Education Sector Debates: Universal or Targeted Preschool?* Washington, DC: Education Sector.

Fuller, Bruce, with Margaret Bridges and Seeta Pai. 2007. *Standardized Childhood: The Political and Cultural Struggle over Early Education.* Palo Alto, CA: Stanford University Press.

Gabaix, Xavier. 2008. "Power Laws in Economics and Finance." NBER Working Paper 14299. Cambridge, MA: National Bureau of Economic Research.

Galbraith, James. 2008. *The Predator State.* New York: Free Press.

Galinsky, Ellen. 2006. *The Economic Benefits of High-Quality Early Childhood Programs: What Makes the Difference?* Washington, DC: Committee for Economic Development.

Garces, Eliana, Duncan Thomas, and Janet Currie. 2002. "Longer-Term Effects of Head Start." *American Economic Review* 92(4): 999–1012.

Gault, Barbara, Anne W. Mitchell, and Erica Williams, with Judy Dey and Olga Sorokina. 2008. *Meaningful Investments in Pre-K: Estimating the Per-Child Costs of Quality Programs.* Washington, DC: Institute for Women's Policy Research.

General Accounting Office (GAO). 1996. *Job Training Partnership Act: Long-Term Earnings and Employment Outcomes.* Report to Congressional Requesters. GAO/HEHS-96-40. Washington, DC: General Accounting Office.

Goffin, Stacie. 2010. "Promoting Children's School Readiness: Rethinking the Levers for Change." *NCRECE In Focus* 1(1): 1–2. http://ncrece.org/wordpress/wp-content/uploads/2010/03/NCRECEInFocus_v1n1.pdf (accessed July 22, 2010).

Goldin, Claudia, and Lawrence Katz. 2008. *The Race between Education and Technology.* Cambridge, MA: Belknap Press of Harvard University Press.

Gomby, Deanna S. 2005. "Home Visitation in 2005: Outcomes for Children and Parents." Working Paper 7. Washington, DC: Invest in Kids Working Group.

Gordon, Robert J. 2009. "Rising American Inequality: New Facts and Interpretations." PowerPoint presentation presented at ASSA Meetings, held in San Francisco, January 3. http://faculty-web.at.northwestern.edu/economics/Gordon (accessed July 14, 2010).

Gordon, Robert J., Thomas J. Kane, and Douglas O. Staiger. 2006. "Identifying Effective Teachers Using Performance on the Job." Hamilton Project Discussion Paper 2006-01. Washington, DC: Brookings Institution. http://www.brookings.edu/papers/2006/04education_gordon.aspx?p=1 (accessed July 22, 2010).

Gormley, William T. Jr. 2007a. "Early Childhood Care and Education: Lessons and Puzzles." *Journal of Policy Analysis and Management* 26(3): 651–689.

———. 2007b. "Small Miracles in Tulsa: The Effects of Universal Pre-K on Cognitive Development." Paper presented at the National Conference of the Early Childhood Research Collaborative, sponsored by the Federal Reserve Bank of Minneapolis and the University of Minnesota, held in Minneapolis, December 7.

Gormley, William T. Jr., Ted Gayer, Deborah Phillips, and Brittany Dawson.

2004. *The Effects of Oklahoma's Universal Pre-K Program on School Readiness: An Executive Summary*. Washington, DC: Center for Research on Children in the United States, Georgetown University.

———. 2005. "The Effects of Universal Pre-K on Cognitive Development." *Developmental Psychology* 41(6): 872–884.

Gormley, William T. Jr., Deborah Phillips, Shirley Adelstein, and Catherine Shaw. 2009. "Head Start's Comparative Advantage: Myth or Reality?" Paper presented at the Annual Meeting of the Association for Public Policy Analysis and Management (APPAM), held in Washington, D.C., November 6. http://www.crocus.georgetown.edu/reports/hscompad.pdf (accessed July 22, 2010).

Greenberg, David H., Charles Michalopoulos, and Philip K. Robins. 2003. "A Meta-Analysis of Government-Sponsored Training Programs." *Industrial and Labor Relations Review* 57(1): 31–53.

Greenstein, Robert. 1991. "Universal and Targeted Approaches to Relieving Poverty: An Alternative View." In *The Urban Underclass*, Christopher Jencks and Paul E. Peterson, eds. Washington, DC: Brookings Institution, pp. 437–458.

Greenwood, Michael J., and Gary L. Hunt. 1995. "Economic Effects of Immigrants on Native and Foreign-Born Workers: Complementarity, Substitutability, and Other Channels of Influence." *Southern Economic Journal* 61(4): 1076–1097.

Greenwood, Peter W., Karyn Model, C. Peter Rydell, and James Chiesa. 1998. *Diverting Children from a Life of Crime: Measuring Costs and Benefits*. Santa Monica, CA: RAND Corporation.

Greider, William. 2005. "Foreword." In *The Great American Jobs Scam: Corporate Tax Dodging and the Myth of Job Creation*, by Greg Leroy. San Francisco: Berrett-Koehler Publishers.

Groshen, Erica L. 1991. "Five Reasons Why Wages Vary among Employers." *Industrial Relations* 30(3): 350–381.

Hanushek, Eric A. 2002. "Evidence, Politics, and the Class Size Debate." In *The Class Size Debate*, Lawrence Mishel and Richard Rothstein, eds. Washington, DC: Economic Policy Institute, pp. 37–65.

Harlow, Caroline Wolf. 2003. *Education and Correctional Populations*. Bureau of Justice Statistics Special Report NCJ 195670. Washington, DC: U.S. Department of Justice, Bureau of Justice Statistics.

Hart, Betty, and Todd R. Risley. 2003. "The Early Catastrophe: The 30 Million Word Gap by Age 3." *American Educator* 27(1): 4–9.

Haskins, Ron, and Art Rolnick. 2006. "Early Childhood Education: Do Enthusiasts Exaggerate What It Can Do?" Transcript of presentations, debate, and response to questions at a forum presented by the Center for the American Experiment. Minneapolis, MN: Center for the American Experiment.

Haurin, Donald S., and Kala S. Sridhar. 2003. "The Impact of Local Unemployment Rates on Reservation Wages and the Duration of Search for a Job." *Applied Economics* 35(13): 1469–1476.

Heckman, James J. 2005. "Interview." *Region* 19(2): 18–29.

Heckman, James J., and Paul LaFontaine. 2007. "The American High School Graduation Rate: Trends and Levels." IZA Discussion Paper 3216. Bonn, Germany: Institute for the Study of Labor. http://papers.ssrn.com/sol3/papers.cfm?abstract_id=1136378 (accessed July 15, 2010).

Helms, L. Jay. 1985. "The Effect of State and Local Taxes on Economic Growth: A Time Series–Cross Section Approach." *Review of Economics and Statistics* 67(4): 574–582.

Henry, Gary T., and Dana K. Rickman. 2007. "Do Peers Influence Children's Skill Development in Preschool?" *Economics of Education Review* 26(1): 100–112.

Hill, Carolyn J., Howard S. Bloom, Alison Rebeck Black, and Mark W. Lipsey. 2007. "Empirical Benchmarks for Interpreting Effect Sizes in Research." MDRC Working Papers on Research Methodology. New York: MDRC.

Hines, James R. Jr. 1996. "Altered States: Taxes and the Location of Foreign Direct Investment in America." *American Economic Review* 86(5): 1076–1094.

Hollenbeck, Kevin. 2008. "Is There a Role for Public Support of Incumbent Worker On-the-Job Training?" Upjohn Institute Working Paper 08-138. Kalamazoo, MI: W.E. Upjohn Institute for Employment Research.

Hollenbeck, Kevin, and Wei-Jang Huang. 2006. *Net Impact and Benefit-Cost Estimates of the Workforce Development System in Washington State.* Upjohn Institute Technical Report TR06-020. Kalamazoo, MI: W.E. Upjohn Institute for Employment Research.

———. 2008. *Workforce Program Performance Indicators for the Commonwealth of Virginia.* Upjohn Institute Technical Report TR08-024. Kalamazoo, MI: W.E. Upjohn Institute for Employment Research.

Holtz-Eakin, Douglas. 2005. "The Future of Social Security: Statement of Douglas Holtz-Eakin, Director." CBO Testimony before the Special Committee on Aging, United States Senate. Washington, DC: Congressional Budget Office.

Holzer, Harry J., Paul Offner, and Elaine Sorensen. 2005. "Declining Employment among Young Black Less-Educated Men: The Role of Incarceration and Child Support." *Journal of Policy Analysis and Management* 24(2): 329–350.

Hoyt, William H., Christopher Jepsen, and Kenneth R. Troske. 2008. "Business Incentives and Employment: What Incentives Work and Where?" Working Paper 2009-02. Lexington, KY: University of Kentucky, Institute for Federalism and Intergovernmental Relations.

Hungerford, Thomas, and Robert Wassmer. 2004. *K–12 Education in the U.S. Economy: Its Impact on Economic Development, Earnings, and Housing Values*. Washington, DC: National Education Association.

Hussar, William J., and Tabitha M. Bailey. 2008. *Projections of Education Statistics to 2017*. Washington, DC: National Center for Education Statistics, U.S. Department of Education. http://nces.ed.gov/pubsearch/pubsinfo .asp?pubid=2008078 (accessed July 15, 2010).

Inman, Robert P. 1979. "The Fiscal Performance of Local Governments: An Interpretative Review." In *Current Issues in Urban Economics,* Peter Mieszkowski and Mahlon Straszheim, eds. Baltimore: Johns Hopkins University Press, pp. 270–321.

Institute for the Study of Knowledge Management in Education. 2008. *The Governors Speak—2008: A Report on the State-of-the-State Addresses of the Nation's and U.S. Territories' Governors*. Report prepared for National Governors Association. Washington, DC: National Governors Association. http://www.nga.org/Files/pdf/GOVSPEAK0804.pdf (accessed July 15, 2010).

Institute for Women's Policy Research. 2008. *Meaningful Investments in Pre-K: Estimating the Per-Child Costs of Quality Programs*. Washington, DC: Institute for Women's Policy Research.

Isaacs, Julia B. 2007. *Cost-Effective Investments in Children*. Report for Budgeting for National Priorities Project. Washington, DC: Brookings Institution.

———. 2008. *Impacts of Early Childhood Programs*. Washington, DC: First Focus and Brookings Institution.

Jackson, Russell, Ann McCoy, Carol Pistorino, Anna Wilkinson, John Burghardt, Melissa Clark, Christine Ross, Peter Schochet, and Paul Swank. 2007. *National Evaluation of Early Reading First: Final Report*. Report to the Institute of Education Sciences, U.S. Department of Education. Washington, DC: U.S. Government Printing Office.

Jacobson, Linda. 2007. "Early-Education Advocates Face Tougher Sell: Economic Benefits Still Remote and Intangible, Business Skeptics Warn." *Education Week* 27(4): 16.

Jarmin, Ronald S. 1999. "Evaluating the Impact of Manufacturing Extension on Productivity Growth." *Journal of Policy Analysis and Management* 18(1): 99–119.

Johnson, Julia Overturf. 2005. *Who's Minding the Kids? Child Care Arrangements: Winter 2002*. Current Population Report P70-101. Washington, DC: U.S. Census Bureau.

Johnson, Rucker C., and Robert F. Schoeni. 2007. "The Influence of Early-Life Events on Human Capital, Health Status, and Labor Market Outcomes over the Life Course." Institute for Research on Labor and Employment Working Paper IIRWPS-140-07. Berkeley: University of California, Berkeley.

Jones, Stephen R.G. 1989. "Reservation Wages and the Cost of Unemployment." *Economica* 56(222): 225–246.

Kahlenberg, Richard D. 2001. *All Together Now: Creating Middle-Class Schools through Public School Choice.* Washington, DC: Brookings Institution Press.

Kane, Thomas J., Stephanie K. Riegg, and Douglas O. Staiger. 2006. "School Quality, Neighborhoods, and Housing Prices." *American Law and Economics Review* 8(2): 183–212.

Karoly, Lynn A., and James H. Bigelow. 2005. *The Economics of Investing in Universal Preschool Education in California.* Santa Monica, CA: RAND Corporation.

Karoly, Lynn A., Peter W. Greenwood, Susan S. Everingham, Jill Hoube, M. Rebecca Kilburn, C. Peter Rydell, Matthew Sanders, and James Chiesa. 1998. *Investing in Our Children: What We Know and Don't Know about the Costs and Benefits of Early Childhood Interventions.* Santa Monica, CA: RAND Corporation.

Kasper, Hirschel. 1967. "The Asking Price of Labor and the Duration of Unemployment." *Review of Economics and Statistics* 49(2): 165–172.

Kelley, Pamela, and Gregory Camilli. 2007. "The Impact of Teacher Education on Outcomes in Center-Based Early Childhood Education Programs: A Meta-Analysis." NIEER Working Paper. New Brunswick, NJ: Rutgers University, National Institute for Early Education Research.

Kenworthy, Lane. 2008. *Jobs with Equality.* Oxford and New York: Oxford University Press.

Kesselman, Jonathan R. 1982. "Taxpayer Behavior and the Design of a Credit Income Tax." In *Income-Tested Transfer Programs: The Case For and Against,* Irwin Garfinkel, ed. New York: Academic Press, pp. 215–281.

Keynes, John Maynard. 1936. *The General Theory of Employment, Interest, and Money.* London: Palgrave Macmillan.

Kiefer, Nicholas M., and George R. Neumann. 1979. "An Empirical Job-Search Model, with a Test of the Constant Reservation-Wage Hypothesis." *Journal of Political Economy* 87(11): 89–107.

Kirp, David L. 2007. *The Sandbox Investment: The Preschool Movement and Kids-First Politics.* Cambridge, MA: Harvard University Press.

Kitzman, Harriett, David L. Olds, Kimberly Sidora, Charles R. Henderson Jr., Carole Hanks, Robert Cole, Dennis W. Luckey, Jessica Bondy, Kimberly Cole, and Judith Glazner. 2000. "Enduring Effects of Nurse Home Visitation on Maternal Life Course: A 3-Year Follow-up of a Randomized Trial." *Journal of the American Medical Association* 283(15): 1983–1989.

Krueger, Alan B. 2002. "Understanding the Magnitude and Effect of Class Size on Student Achievement." In *The Class Size Debate*, Lawrence Mishel and Richard Rothstein, eds. Washington, DC: Economic Policy Institute, pp. 7–35.

———. 2003. "Economic Considerations and Class Size." *Economic Journal* 113(485): F34–F63.

Lamy, Cynthia Esposito, Ellen Frede, Holly Seplocha, Janis Strasser, Saigeetha Jambunathan, Jo Anne Juncker, and Ellen Wolock. 2005. *Giant Steps for the Littlest Children: Progress in the Sixth Year of the Abbott Preschool Program.* Year Three Initial Update, 2004–2005, Early Learning Improvement Consortium. Trenton: New Jersey Department of Education.

Layard, Richard, Stephen Nickell, and Richard Jackman. 1991. *Unemployment: Macroeconomic Performance and the Labor Market.* New York: Oxford University Press.

Layzer, Jean I., Carolyn J. Layzer, Barbara D. Goodson, and Cristofer Price. 2007. *Evaluation of Child Care Subsidy Strategies: Findings from Project Upgrade in Miami–Dade County.* Report to U.S. Department of Health and Human Services. Cambridge, MA: Abt Associates.

Lee, David, and Thomas Lemieux. 2009. "Regression Discontinuity Designs in Economics." NBER Working Paper 14723. Cambridge, MA: National Bureau of Economic Research.

Lerman, Robert I., and Caroline Ratcliffe. 2001. "Are Single Mothers Finding Jobs without Displacing Other Workers?" *Monthly Labor Review* 124(7): 3–12.

LeRoy, Greg. 2005. *The Great American Jobs Scam: Corporate Tax Dodging and the Myth of Job Creation.* San Francisco: Berrett-Koehler Publishers.

———. 2007. "Nine Concrete Ways to Curtail the Economic War among the States." In *Reining in the Competition for Capital*, Ann Markusen, ed. Kalamazoo, MI: W.E. Upjohn Institute for Employment Research, pp. 183–198.

Levin, Henry M., and Clive R. Belfield. 2007. "Educational Interventions to Raise High School Graduation Rates." In *The Price We Pay: Economic and Social Consequences of Inadequate Education*, Clive Belfield and Henry Levin, eds. Washington, DC: Brookings Institution Press, pp. 177–199.

Levin, Henry M., and Heather L. Schwartz. 2007. "Educational Vouchers for Universal Pre-Schools." *Economics of Education Review* 26(1): 3–16.

Lipsey, Mark W. 2009. PowerPoint presentation on "Generalizability: The Role of Meta-Analysis." Presented at the Workshop on Strengthening Benefit-Cost Methodology for the Evaluation of Early Childhood Interventions,

Board on Children, Youth, and Families, the National Academies, held in Washington, DC, March 4–5.

Logan, John, and Harvey Molotch. 1987. *Urban Fortunes: The Political Economy of Place.* Berkeley: University of California Press.

Lubotsky, Darren. 2004. "The Labor Market Effects of Welfare Reform." *Industrial and Labor Relations Review* 57(2): 249–266.

Ludwig, Jens, and Douglas L. Miller. 2007. "Does Head Start Improve Children's Life Chances? Evidence from a Regression Discontinuity Design." *Quarterly Journal of Economics* 122(1): 159–208.

Ludwig, Jens, and Deborah A. Phillips. 2007. "The Benefits and Costs of Head Start." NBER Working Paper 12973. Cambridge, MA: National Bureau of Economic Research.

Ludwig, Jens, and Isabel Sawhill. 2007. "Success by Ten: Intervening Early, Often, and Effectively in the Education of Young Children." Hamilton Project Discussion Paper 2007-02. Washington, DC: Brookings Institution.

Luria, Daniel, and Joel Rogers. 1999. *Metro Futures: Economic Solutions for Cities and Their Suburbs.* Boston: Beacon Press.

———. 2008. "Manufacturing, Regional Prosperity, and Public Policy." In *Retooling for Growth: Building a 21st Century Economy in America's Older Industrial Areas*, Richard M. McGahey and Jennifer S. Vey, eds. Washington, DC: Brookings Institution Press, pp. 249–274.

Lynch, Robert G. 2004. *Rethinking Growth Strategies: How Local Taxes and Services Affect Economic Development.* Washington, DC: Economic Policy Institute.

———. 2007. *Enriching Children, Enriching the Nation: Public Investment in High-Quality Prekindergarten.* Washington, DC: Economic Policy Institute.

Markusen, Ann, and Katherine Nesse. 2007. "Institutional and Political Determinants of Incentive Competition." In *Reining in the Competition for Capital*, Ann Markusen, ed. Kalamazoo, MI: W.E. Upjohn Institute for Employment Research, pp. 1–41.

Marston, Stephen T. 1985. "Two Views of the Geographic Distribution of Unemployment." *Quarterly Journal of Economics* 100(1): 57–79.

Martin, Joyce A., Brady E. Hamilton, Paul D. Sutton, Stephanie J. Ventura, Fay Menacker, Sharon Kirmeyer, and T.J. Mathews. 2009. "Births: Final Data for 2006." *National Vital Statistics Report* 57(7): 1–102.

Mashburn, Andrew J., Robert C. Pianta, Bridget K. Hamre, Jason T. Downer, Oscar A. Barbarin, Donna Bryant, Margaret Burchinal, Diane M. Early, and Carollee Howes. 2008. "Measures of Classroom Quality in Prekindergarten and Children's Development of Academic, Language, and Social Skills." *Child Development* 79(3): 732–749.

Masse, Leonard N., and W. Steven Barnett. 2002. "A Benefit-Cost Analysis of the Abecedarian Early Childhood Intervention." In *Cost-Effectiveness and Educational Policy*, Henry M. Levin and Patrick J. McEwan, eds. Larchmont, NY: Eye on Education Press, pp. 157–173.

Mazerov, Michael. 2005. *Should Congress Authorize States to Continue Giving Tax Breaks to Business?* Washington, DC: Center for Budget and Policy Priorities. http://www.cbpp.org/archiveSite/2-18-05sfp.pdf (accessed July 22, 2010).

McGuire, Therese. 1992. "Review of *Who Benefits from State and Local Economic Development Policies?* by Timothy J. Bartik." *National Tax Journal* 45(4): 457–459.

McIntyre, Robert S., Robert Denk, Norton Francis, Matthew Gardner, Will Gomaa, Fiona Hsu, and Richard Sims. 2003. *Who Pays? A Distributional Analysis of the Tax Systems in All 50 States.* 2d ed. Washington, DC: Institute on Taxation and Economic Policy.

McKinsey and Company. 2009. *The Economic Impact of the Achievement Gap in America's Schools*. New York: McKinsey and Company, Social Sector Office.

M Cubed Consulting Group. 2002. *The National Economic Impacts of the Child Care Sector*. Report to the National Child Care Association. Conyers, GA: National Child Care Association.

Michigan Manufacturing Technology Center. 2008. *Annual Report*. Ann Arbor, MI: Michigan Manufacturing Technology Center.

Miller-Adams, Michelle. 2009. *The Power of a Promise: Education and Economic Renewal in Kalamazoo*. Kalamazoo, MI: W.E. Upjohn Institute for Employment Research.

Molina, Frieda. 1998. *Making Connections: A Study of Employment Linkage Programs*. Washington, DC: Center for Community Change.

Molotch, Harvey. 1976. "The City as a Growth Machine: Toward a Political Economy of Place." *American Journal of Sociology* 82(2): 309–332.

Moore, Mark A., Anthony E. Boardman, Aidan R. Vining, David L. Weimar, and David H. Greenberg. 2004. "Just Give Me a Number! Practical Values for the Social Discount Rate." *Journal of Policy Analysis and Management* 23(4): 789–812.

Moretti, Enrico. 2003. "Human Capital Externalities in Cities." NBER Working Paper 9641. Cambridge, MA: National Bureau of Economic Research.

———. 2004. "Estimating the Social Return to Higher Education: Evidence from Longitudinal and Repeated Cross-Sectional Data." *Journal of Econometrics* 121(1–2): 175–212.

Morse, Jennifer Roback. 2008. "It Takes a Family." *Mercatornet* (blog), March

17. http://www.mercatornet.com/articles/view/it_takes_a_family/ (accessed July 30, 2010).

Munnell, Alicia H. 1990. "How Does Public Infrastructure Affect Regional Economic Performance?" *New England Economic Review* 1990(September/October): 11–33.

Murnane, Richard J., John B. Willett, Yves Duhaldeborde, and John H. Tyler. 2000. "How Important Are the Cognitive Skills of Teenagers in Predicting Subsequent Earnings?" *Journal of Policy Analysis and Management* 19(4): 547–568.

National Center on Education and the Economy. 2006. *Tough Choices or Tough Times: The Report of the New Commission on the Skills of the American Workforce.* Hoboken, NJ: Jossey-Bass.

National Center for Health Statistics. 2005. *U.S. Life Tables, 2003.* Washington, DC: National Center for Health Statistics. http://www.cdc.gov/nchs/products/life_tables.htm (accessed July 22, 2010).

National Education Association (NEA). 2007. *What is TEF?* TEF Series, Vol. 1. Washington, DC: National Education Association. http://www.mea.org/tef/pdf/1whatistef.pdf (accessed July 22, 2010).

Neal, Derek A., and William R. Johnson. 1996. "The Role of Premarket Factors in Black-White Wage Differences." *Journal of Political Economy* 104(5): 869–895.

Noah, Timothy. 2000. "Dinesh D'Souza vs. 'Equal Opportunity.'" Slate magazine on-line, October 10. http://www.slate.com/id/1006238 (accessed July 22, 2010).

Noll, Roger G., and Andrew Zimbalist. 1997. "Sports, Jobs, and Taxes: The Real Connection." In *Sports, Jobs and Taxes: The Economic Impact of Sports Teams and Stadiums,* Roger G. Noll and Andrew Zimbalist, eds. Washington, DC: Brookings Institution Press, pp. 494–508.

Nordhaus, William D. 2007. "A Review of *The Stern Review on the Economics of Climate Change.*" *Journal of Economic Literature* 45(3): 686–702.

Nurse-Family Partnership. 2010. *Nurse-Family Partnership Snapshot.* Denver: Nurse-Family Partnership. http://www.nursefamilypartnership.org/assets/PDF/Fact-sheets/NFP_Snapshot (accessed September 27, 2010).

Oates, Wallace E., and Robert M. Schwab. 1988. "Economic Competition among Jurisdictions: Efficiency Enhancing or Distortion Inducing?" *Journal of Public Economics* 35(3): 333–354.

Old-Age and Survivors Insurance and Disability Insurance Trust Funds Board of Trustees (OASDI). 2005. *The 2005 Annual Report of the Board of Trustees of the Federal Old-Age and Survivors Insurance and Disability Insurance Trust Funds.* Washington, DC: U.S. Government Printing Office.

Olds, David L. 2002. "Prenatal and Infancy Home Visiting by Nurses: From Randomized Trials to Community Replication." *Prevention Science* 3(3): 153–172.

———. 2005. *Presentation to Invest in Kids Working Group.* Washington, DC: Committee for Economic Development.

Olds, David L., John Eckenrode, Charles R. Henderson Jr., Harriet Kitzman, Jane Powers, Robert Cole, Kimberly Sidora, Pamela Morris, Lisa M. Pettitt, and Dennis Luckey. 1997. "Long-Term Effects of Home Visitation on Maternal Life Course and Child Abuse and Neglect: Fifteen-Year Follow-Up of a Randomized Trial." *Journal of the American Medical Association* 278(8): 637–643.

Olds, David L., Charles R. Henderson Jr., Robert Cole, John Eckenrode, Harriet Kitzman, Dennis W. Luckey, Lisa M. Pettitt, Kimberly Sidora, Pamela Morris, and Jane Powers. 1998. "Long-Term Effects of Nurse Home Visitation on Children's Criminal and Antisocial Behavior: 15-Year Follow-Up of a Randomized Controlled Trial." *Journal of the American Medical Association* 280(14): 1238–1244.

Olds, David L., Harriet Kitzman, Robert Cole, JoAnn Robinson, Kimberly Sidora, Dennis W. Luckey, Charles R. Henderson Jr., Carole Hanks, Jessica Bondy, and John Holmberg. 2004. "Effects of Nurse Home-Visiting on Maternal Life Course and Child Development: Age 6 Follow-Up Results of a Randomized Trial." *Pediatrics* 114(6): 1550–1559.

Olds, David L., JoAnn Robinson, Ruth O'Brien, Dennis W. Luckey, Lisa M. Pettitt, Charles R. Henderson Jr., Rosanna K. Ng, Karen L. Sheff, Jon Korfmacher, Susan Hiatt, and Ayelet Talmi. 2002. "Home Visiting by Paraprofessionals and by Nurses: A Randomized, Controlled Trial." *Pediatrics* 110(3): 486–496.

Olds, David L., JoAnn Robinson, Lisa M. Pettitt, Dennis W. Luckey, John Holmberg, Rosanna K. Ng, Kathy Isacks, Karen L. Sheff, and Charles R. Henderson Jr. 2004. "Effects of Home Visits by Paraprofessionals and by Nurses: Age 4 Follow-Up Results of a Randomized Trial." *Pediatrics* 114(6): 1560–1568.

Oldsman, Eric, and Jack Russell. 1999. "The Industrial Resource Center Program: Assessing the Record and Charting the Future." Unpublished report prepared for the state of Pennsylvania.

Olsen, Darcy. 1999. *Universal Preschool Is No Golden Ticket: Why Government Should Not Enter the Preschool Business.* Cato Institute Policy Analysis 333. Washington, DC: Cato Institute.

Olsen, Darcy, and Arthur Rolnick. 2005. "Early Childhood Education: A Conversation with Art Rolnick and Darcy Olsen." *American Experiment*

Quarterly 8(1): 1–16. http://www.americanexperiment.org/uploaded/files/ aeq2005springrolnickolsen.pdf (accessed July 22, 2010).

Olsen, Darcy, and Lisa Snell. 2006. *Assessing Proposals for Preschool and Kindergarten: Essential Information for Parents, Taxpayers, and Policymakers.* Los Angeles: Reason Foundation. http://reason.org/newsshow/127450 .html (accessed July 22, 2010).

Orszag, Peter, and Joseph Stiglitz. 2001. *Budget Cuts versus Tax Increases at the State Level: Is One More Counterproductive than the Other during a Recession?* Washington, DC: Center on Budget and Policy Priorities. http:// www.fiscalpolicy.org/10-30-01sfp.pdf (accessed July 22, 2010).

Osterman, Paul. 2003. *Gathering Power: The Future of Progressive Politics in America.* Boston: Beacon Press.

Parrish, Thomas, Jenifer Harr, Jean Wolman, Jennifer Anthony, Amy Merickel, and Phil Esra. 2004. *State Special Education Finance Systems, 1999–2000, Part II: Special Education Revenues and Expenditures.* Palo Alto, CA: American Institutes for Research, Center for Special Education Finance.

Partridge, Mark D., and Dan S. Rickman. 2006. "An SVAR Model of Fluctuations in U.S. Migration Flows and State Labor Market Dynamics." *Southern Economic Journal* 72(4): 958–980.

Passell, Peter. 1992. "50 Different Economies; Workers Who Follow the Jobs Are the Keys to Economic Health." *New York Times,* July 5, A1.

Pechman, Joseph. 1985. *Who Paid the Taxes, 1966–1985?* Washington, DC: Brookings Institution Press.

Persky, Joseph, Daniel Felsenstein, and Virginia Carlson. 2004. *Does "Trickle Down" Work? Economic Development Strategies and Job Chains in Local Labor Markets.* Kalamazoo, MI: W.E. Upjohn Institute for Employment Research.

Peters, Alan H., and Peter S. Fisher. 2002. *State Enterprise Zone Programs: Have They Worked?* Kalamazoo, MI: W.E. Upjohn Institute for Employment Research.

Peterson, Paul. 1981. *City Limits.* Chicago: University of Chicago Press.

Phelps, Edmund. 1972. *Inflation Policy and Unemployment Theory.* New York: Norton.

Pindus, Nancy M., Carolyn T. O'Brien, Maureen Conway, Conaway Haskins, and Ida Rademacher. 2004. *Evaluation of the Sectoral Employment Demonstration Program.* Washington, DC: Urban Institute.

Pollin, Robert, and Stephanie Luce. 2000. *The Living Wage: Building a Fair Economy.* New York: New Press.

Poterba, James, and Lawrence Summers. 1995. "Time Horizons of American Firms: New Evidence from a Survey of CEOs." In *Capital Choices: Chang-*

ing the Way America Invests in Industry, Michael Porter, ed. Boston: Harvard Business School Press.

Preschool Curriculum Evaluation Research Consortium. 2008. *Effects of Preschool Curriculum Programs on School Readiness: Report from the Preschool Curriculum Evaluation Research Initiative*. Washington, DC: U.S. Department of Education, National Center for Education Research, Institute of Education Sciences. http://ies.ed.gov/ncer/pubs/20082009/pdf/20082009_rev.pdf (accessed July 22, 2010).

Puma, Michael, Stephen Bell, Ronna Cook, and Camilla Heid. 2010. *Head Start Impact Study: Final Report*. Washington, DC: Office of Planning, Research, and Evaluation, Administration for Children and Families, U.S. Department of Health and Human Services.

Ramey, Craig T., and Frances A. Campbell. 1991. "Poverty, Early Childhood Education, and Academic Competence: The Abecedarian Experiment." In *Children in Poverty: Child Development and Public Policy*, Aletha C. Huston, ed. Cambridge: Cambridge University Press, pp. 190–221.

Ramey, Craig T., Frances A. Campbell, Margaret Burchinal, Martie L. Skinner, David M. Gardner, and Sharon L. Ramey. 2000. "Persistent Effects of Early Childhood Education on High-Risk Children and Their Mothers." *Applied Developmental Science* 4(1): 2–14.

Raphael, Steven. 2007. "Understanding the Causes and Labor Market Consequences of the Steep Increase in U.S. Incarceration Rates." Working paper. Berkeley: Goldman School of Public Policy, University of California, Berkeley.

Rawls, John. 1971. *A Theory of Justice*. Cambridge, MA: Belknap Press of Harvard University.

Reed, Lawrence. 1996. *Time to End the Economic War between the States*. Washington, DC: Cato Institute.

Reschovsky, Andrew. 1998. "The Progressivity of State Tax Systems." In *The Future of State Tax Systems*, David Bruori, ed. Washington, DC: Urban Institute Press.

Reynolds, Arthur J. 1995. "One Year of Preschool Intervention or Two: Does It Matter?" *Early Childhood Research Quarterly* 10(1): 1–31.

Reynolds, Arthur J., Judy A. Temple, Dylan L. Robertson, and Emily A. Mann. 2002. "Age 21 Cost-Benefit Analysis of the Title I Chicago Child-Parent Centers." *Educational Evaluation and Policy Analysis* 24(4): 267–303.

Roback, Jennifer. 1982. "Wages, Rents, and the Quality of Life." *Journal of Political Economy* 90(6): 1257–1278.

Robin, Kenneth B., Ellen C. Frede, and W. Steven Barnett. 2006. *Is More Better? The Effects of Full-Day vs. Half-Day Preschool on Early School Achievement*. Report to the National Institute for Early Education Research,

Rutgers University. New Brunswick, NJ: National Institute for Early Education Research.

Rohr, Jim. 2009. *Testimonials*. A testimonial on the value of pre-K education. Washington, DC: Pre-K Now. http://www.preknow.org/community/testimonials.cfm (accessed October 8, 2010).

Rolnick, Arthur J. 2007. "Congress Should End the Economic War among the States." October 10, 2007, Testimony before Domestic Policy Subcommittee, Oversight and Government Reform Committee, U.S. House of Representatives. 110th Cong., 1st sess. http://www.minneapolisfed.org/publications _papers/studies/econwar/rolnick_testimony_2007.cfm (accessed July 22, 2010).

———. 2008. *Interview Conducted by David Boulton*. Children of the Code Project. Washington, DC: Children of the Code. http://www.children ofthecode.org/interviews/rolnick.htm (accessed July 22, 2010).

Rolnick, Arthur J., and Melvin L. Burstein. 1994. *Congress Should End the Economic War among the States*. Annual Report Essay. Minneapolis: Federal Reserve Bank of Minneapolis.

Rolnick, Arthur J., and Rob Grunewald. 2003. "Early Childhood Development: Economic Development with a High Public Return." *Fedgazette* 15(2). Minneapolis: Federal Reserve Bank of Minneapolis. http://minneapolisfed .org/pubs/fedgaz/03-03/earlychild.cfm (accessed October 8, 2010).

Rowthorn, Robert, and Andrew J. Glyn. 2006. "Convergence and Stability in U.S. Employment Rates." *Contributions to Macroeconomics* 6(1): 1–42.

Rubin, Herbert J. 1988. "Shoot Anything That Flies; Claim Anything That Falls: Conversations with Economic Development Practitioners." *Economic Development Quarterly* 2(3): 236–251.

Schaeffer, Adam. 2008. *Pre-K Pushers Peddling Patent Prevarications*. Cato@ Liberty blog, July 14. Washington, DC: Cato Institute. http://www.cato-at-liberty.org/2008/07/14/pre-k-pushers-peddling-patent-prevarications/ (accessed June 15, 2010).

Schanzenbach, Diane Whitmore. 2007. "What Have Researchers Learned from Project STAR?" *Brookings Papers on Education Policy* 9(2006/2007): 205–228.

Schechter, Carlota, and Beth Bye. 2007. "Preliminary Evidence for the Impact of Mixed-Income Preschools on Low-Income Children's Language Growth." *Early Childhood Research Quarterly* 22(1): 137–146.

Scheppach, Ray. 2003. "Testimony by NGA (National Governors Association) Executive Director Ray Scheppach before the Senate Committee on Commerce, Science, and Transportation on State Use of Tobacco Settlement Funds." 108th Cong., 1st sess.

Schoettle, Ferdinand P. 2003. "What Public Finance Do State Constitutions Allow?" In *Financing Economic Development in the 21st Century*, Sammis B. White, Richard D. Bingham, and Edward W. Hill, eds. Armonk, New York, and London: M.E. Sharpe, pp. 27–50.

Schweinhart, Lawrence J., Jeanne Montie, Zongping Xiang, W. Steven Barnett, Clive R. Belfield, and Milagros Nores. 2005. *Lifetime Effects: The High/Scope Perry Preschool Study through Age 40*. Ypsilanti, MI: High/Scope Press. See also errata-corrected tables at http://www.highscope.org/file/Research/PerryProject/Errata_3Final.pdf (accessed October 8, 2010).

Sheldon, Paul. 2006. "Issues in Financing Early Education." PowerPoint presentation to Partnership for America's Economic Success/Invest in Kids working group. http://www.partnershipforsuccess.org/docs/ivk/iikmeeting_slides200610sheldon.pdf (accessed July 22, 2010).

Siegfried, John J., Allen R. Sanderson, and Peter McHenry. 2006. "The Economic Impact of Colleges and Universities." Working Paper 06-W12. Nashville, TN: Vanderbilt University, Department of Economics.

Sindelar, Jody, and Tracy Falba. 2004. "Securitization of Tobacco Settlement Payments to Reduce States' Conflict of Interest." *Health Affairs* 23(5): 188–193.

Sinnaeve, Adinda. 2007. "How the EU Manages Subsidy Competition." In *Reining in the Competition for Capital*, Ann Markusen, ed. Kalamazoo, MI: W.E. Upjohn Institute for Employment Research, pp. 87–102.

Skocpol, Theda. 1991. "Targeting within Universalism: Politically Viable Policies to Combat Poverty in the United States." In *The Urban Underclass*, Christopher Jencks and Paul E. Peterson, eds. Washington, DC: Brookings Institution, pp. 250–274.

Slivinski, Steven. 2007. *The Corporate Welfare State: How the Federal Government Subsidizes U.S. Businesses*. Policy Analysis 592. Washington, DC: Cato Institute.

Smith, Kristin E. 2002. *Who's Minding the Kids? Child Care Arrangements, Spring 1997*. Washington, DC: U.S. Census Bureau.

Solow, Robert M. 1990. *The Labor Market as a Social Institution*. Cambridge, MA: Basil Blackwell.

Stephenson, Stanley P. Jr. 1976. "The Economics of Youth Job Search Behavior." *Review of Economics and Statistics* 58(February): 104–111.

Stern, Nicholas. 2007. *The Economics of Climate Change: The Stern Review.* Cambridge and New York: Cambridge University Press.

Tella, Rafael Di, Robert J. MacCulloch, and Andrew J. Oswald. 2001. "Preferences over Inflation and Unemployment: Evidence from Surveys of Happiness." *American Economic Review* 91(1): 335–341.

Temple, Judy A., and Arthur J. Reynolds. 2007. "Benefits and Costs of Investments in Preschool Education: Evidence from the Child-Parent Centers and

Related Programs." *Economics of Education Review* 26(1): 126–144.

Thomas, Kenneth. 2000. *Competing for Capital: Europe and North America in a Global Era.* Washington, DC: Georgetown University Press.

———. 2007. "The Sources and Processes of Tax and Subsidy Competition." In *Reining in the Competition for Capital,* Ann Markusen, ed. Kalamazoo, MI: W.E. Upjohn Institute for Employment Research, pp. 43–55.

Tocqueville, Alexis de. 2000. *Democracy in America.* Trans. and ed. by Harvey Mansfield and Delba Winthrop. Chicago: University of Chicago Press.

Travers, Jeffrey, and Barbara Dillon Goodson. 1980. *Research Results of the National Day Care Study, Vol. 2.* Prepared for the Department of Health, Education, and Welfare. Cambridge, MA: Abt Associates.

Treyz, George. 1993. *Regional Economic Modeling: A Systematic Approach to Economic Forecasting and Policy Analysis.* Boston: Kluwer Academic Publishers.

Urahn, Susan K., and Sara Watson. 2006. "The Trusts' Advancing Quality Pre-K for All Initiatives: Building on Four Years of Progress." *Preschool Matters* 4(1): 7–10.

U.S. Census Bureau. 2007. *2007 Census of Governments.* Washington, DC: U.S. Census Bureau. http://www.census.gov/govs/cog/ (accessed October 7, 2010).

———. 2008. *Table HINC-05. Percent Distribution of Households, by Selected Characteristics within Income Quintile and Top 5 Percent in 2007.* Washington, DC: U.S. Census Bureau. http://www.census.gov/hhes/www/macro/032008/hhinc/new05_000.htm (accessed July 1, 2010).

———. 2009. *Geographic Mobility, 2007 to 2008.* Data from the Annual Social and Economic Supplement to the Current Population Survey, 2008. Washington, DC: U.S. Census Bureau. http://www.census.gov/population/www/socdemo/migrate/cps2008.html (accessed July 22, 2010).

U.S. Department of Education. 2008. *Digest of Education Statistics.* Washington, DC: U.S. Department of Education. http://nces.ed.gov/programs/digest/ (accessed July 22, 2010).

Waldfogel, Jane. 2006. *What Children Need.* Cambridge, MA: Harvard University Press.

Wallis, John J. 2000. "American Government Finance in the Long Run: 1790 to 1990." *Journal of Economic Perspectives* 14(1): 61–82.

Warner, Mildred E. 2005. "Using Economic Development Policy to Strengthen Quality Child Care." Summary of conference call, May 24. Washington, DC: Smart Start National Technical Assistance Center.

Warner, Mildred E., and Zhilin Liu. 2006. "The Importance of Child Care in Economic Development: A Comparative Analysis of Regional Economic

Linkage." *Economic Development Quarterly* 20(1): 97–103.

Wasylenko, Michael. 1997. "Taxation and Economic Development: The State of the Economic Literature." *New England Economic Review* (March/April): 37–52.

Weber, Rachel. 2002. "Do Better Contracts Make Better Economic Development Incentives?" *Journal of the American Planning Association* 68(1): 43–55.

———. 2007. "Negotiating the Ideal Deal: Which Local Governments Have the Most Bargaining Leverage?" In *Reining in the Competition for Capital*, Ann Markusen, ed. Kalamazoo, MI: W.E. Upjohn Institute for Employment Research, pp. 141–160.

Weitzman, Martin L. 2007. "A Review of *The Stern Review on the Economics of Climate Change*." *Journal of Economic Literature* 45(3): 703–724.

West, Heather C., and William J. Sabol. 2009. *Prison Inmates at Midyear 2008—Statistical Tables*. March report, NCJ 225619. Washington, DC: U.S. Department of Justice, Bureau of Justice Statistics.

Western, Bruce. 2002. "The Impact of Incarceration on Wage Mobility and Inequality." *American Sociological Review* 67(4): 526–546.

Wong, Vivian D., Thomas D. Cook, W. Steven Barnett, and Kwanghee Jung. 2008. "An Effectiveness-Based Evaluation of Five State Pre-Kindergarten Programs." *Journal of Policy Analysis and Management* 27(1): 122–154.

Yilmaz, Yesim, Sonya Hoo, Matthew Nagowski, Kim Rueben, and Robert Tannenwald. 2006. *Measuring Fiscal Disparities across the U.S. States: A Representative Revenue System/Representative Expenditure System Approach, Fiscal Year 2002*. Assessing the New Federalism Occasional Paper 74. Washington, DC: Urban Institute.

The Author

Timothy J. Bartik is a senior economist at the W.E. Upjohn Institute for Employment Research. His research focuses on state and local economic development and local labor markets, including research in the following areas: evaluating economic development programs, the effects of taxes and public services on economic development, the benefits and costs of local economic development, and alternative policies for increasing labor demand for the poor.

Bartik is recognized as a leading scholar on state and local economic development policies in the United States. His 1991 book *Who Benefits from State and Local Economic Development Policies?* is widely cited as an important and influential review of the evidence on how local policies affect economic development. Bartik is coeditor of *Economic Development Quarterly*, the only journal focused on local economic development in the United States, and also serves on the editorial board of other regional economics journals.

National dialogues concerning the recent economic recession and recovery have included the policy option of job creation tax credits. Such job creation programs were analyzed and proposed in Bartik's 2001 book *Jobs for the Poor: Can Labor Demand Policies Help?*, published by the Russell Sage Foundation and the Upjohn Institute. Bartik's work has been extensively cited in the ongoing debate during 2009 and 2010 over job creation policies by administration officials, Congress, various Washington think tanks, and the media.

Bartik's *Jobs for the Poor: Can Labor Demand Policies Help?* in 2001 was named a "Noteworthy Book in Industrial Relations and Labor Economics" by Princeton University's Industrial Relations Section. Other recent research includes the following works: "Bringing Jobs to People: How Federal Policy Can Target Job Creation for Economically Distressed Areas," Washington, D.C., Hamilton Project, Brookings Institution, 2010; "The Revitalization of Older Industrial Cities," *Growth and Change*, 2009; "The Job Creation Tax Credit," Washington, D.C., Economic Policy Institute, 2009 (with John Bishop); "'Eds and Meds' and Metropolitan Economic Development," in *Urban and Regional Policy and Its Effects*, Howard Wial, Hal Wolman, and Margery Turner, editors, Washington, DC, Brookings Institution, 2008 (with George Erickcek); and *A Future of Good Jobs? America's Challenge in the Global Economy*, coedited with Susan Houseman, Kalamazoo, Michigan, Upjohn Institute, 2008.

Bartik received both his PhD and his MS in economics from the University of Wisconsin–Madison in 1982. He earned a BA from Yale University in political philosophy in 1975. Prior to joining the Upjohn Institute in 1989, he was an assistant professor of economics at Vanderbilt University. From 2000 to 2008, Bartik served on the Kalamazoo School Board.

Index

The italic letters *n*, *f,* and *t* following a page number indicate that the subject information of the heading is within a note, figure, or table, respectively, on that page. Double italics indicate multiple but consecutive elements.

Community colleges, *cont.*
(*see also above subentry,* JTPA
programs at)
Community Development Block Grants,
uses, 59, 61*t*, 173*n*10
Community life, 14, 17, 319, 355
leaders of, and universal pre-K
planning, 353, 362*n*1
local economic development benefits
on residents and, 18–19, 53
Community organizers, political
effectiveness of, 359
Competition
business and, 321, 323, 328–329
effect of, between states, 297, 299–
300, 301
enhance *vs.* diminish, with program
design, 331, 357
localities in, to attract capital and
quality labor force, 17–18, 357
parental right to, on behalf of child's
advantage, 319
Connecticut
benefit-cost ratio for universal pre-K
in, 274*t*
business incentives disclosure
required in, 304
economic impact of child care studied
in, 105
resident stability in, 273*t*
Consumption, value of, 177–178,
325–326
Cornell University, economic
development centers at, 5, 105
Corporation for Enterprise Development,
150*n*13
Cost-effectiveness
business incentives design and, 9, 73
customized services and, 127, 150–
151*n*15
early childhood programs design and,
9, 83*f*, 137, 152–153*n*25
See also Benefit-cost ratios
Cost reduction of early childhood
programs, 175–176, 182–194, 210
borrowing as short-term, 182–184

K–12 school budgets in the short
term, 188–194, 192*f*
special education offsets as short-
term, 184–188, 186*f*, 187*f*
Costs, 162, 172–173*n*3
child care and, 95, 97, 108, 222,
266*n*21
child-welfare system, and NFP, 185
class size and, 137, 151–152*n*23
dollar value of business incentives,
16–17, 49–50*n*2, 53, 59, 60*t*–61*t*,
70, 73, 73*n*1, 74*n*5, 75–76*n*16,
113, 118, 149*n*5, 260*n*2
early childhood education programs
and, 79–82, 81*f*, 84, 86*t*, 93, 96,
99, 110–111*n*3, 213*n*9, 216–
217*n*29, 260*n*2, 265–266*n*20, 310,
313*n*9
health care, 310, 355
high, of economic development, 334
job creation, and uncertainty, 64–65,
74*n*9
job creation, in assisted businesses,
63–65, 70, 72, 73, 74*nn*5–8,
76*n*17, 126–127, 127, 150–
151*n*15, 160, 162, 172–173*n*3
job training, 205, 297
labor supply as, 23, 162, 172–173*n*3
time as, in research, 167–168
CPC. *See* Child-Parent Center program,
Chicago
CPS. *See* Current Population Survey
Creative class, regional development and
the, 335
Crime reduction, 14, 70
estimating economic development
benefits of, 10, 333–334, 346–348,
349*t*
as long-term side-effect of early
childhood programs, 2–3, 4, 11*n*5,
100, 185, 326
Current Population Survey (CPS)
families with pre-K children, 111*n*7
supplement to, and household income
quintiles, 260–261*n*3, 313*nn*8–9

Job creation, *cont.*
   new, and effects, 67–68, 69*f,* 103,
      120, 128–129, 149–150*n*7,
      151*n*16, 285
Job growth, 88*t*
   as an economic impact, 107, 355
   hysteresis and, 21–22
   local/state effects of, 28–30, 50*n*6,
      68–69, 69*f,* 71
   occupational upgrading and, 32,
      51*n*11, 128
   property values and, 30–32, 50*n*7
Job redistribution
   macroeconomic effects from, 292–
      293, 312*n*4, 355
   social benefits absent from, 284,
      298–299, 313*n*7
Job skills, 67
   acquiring increased, 5, 8, 22, 49, 129,
      280
   investment in, 123, 326
   (*see also* Workforce Investment
      Act [WIA])
   pre-K participants and, 5, 8
Job training, 206, 210, 355
   government funding for, 16, 57, 58,
      60*t,* 125, 126–127, 150*n*12,
      216*n*22
Job Training Partnership Act (JTPA)
   programs, 203–209, 217*n*31
   benefit-cost ratios of, 207*f,* 208*f,*
      216*n*24, 216*nn*25–28,
      216–217*n*29, 217*n*32
JTPA programs. *See* Job Training
   Partnership Act (JTPA) programs

Kalamazoo County, Michigan, universal
   pre-K plan in, 353, 362*n*1
Kalamazoo Promise, as public-private
   partnership, 183, 334–335
Kansas, data on, 273*t,* 274*t*
Karoly, Lynn, pre-K design and, 92–94,
   95
Katz, Lawrence, coauthor, 33–36, 51*n*14,
   51–52*n*15, 360

Kentucky
   benefit-cost ratio for universal pre-K
      in, 274*t*
   customized job training compared to
      tax incentives in, 127
   resident stability in, 273*t*
Keynes, John Maynard, on power of
   ideas, 361
Kirp, David, on pre-K expansion, 1
Kornblatt, Tracy, on job redistribution,
   284

Labor demand, 102
   business incentives and, 6, 7, 8,
      51*n*10, 280*n*1
   change in local, and national
      variables, 36, 52*n*19
   effects of increased local, 30–33,
      50*nn*7–8, 50–51*n*9, 52*nn*10–12,
      286
   Galbraith oriented toward, 45–47, 48
   occupational upgrading and, 24, 32,
      51*n*11, 53, 69, 73*n*2, 75*n*15
Labor force participation
   change in labor supply and, 34, 40,
      51*n*13, 52*n*17, 75–76*n*16
   employer response to increase in,
      45–48, 52*nn*19–20
   job creation and, 68–69, 69*f*
   low wage standards and, 67–68
   mothers and, 95, 99, 318
   national response to, 48, 52*n*21,
      293–296
   work as a social norm and, 25–26,
      295
Labor supply, 39, 355
   change in, 21–22, 34, 46–48, 51*n*13,
      52*nn*20–21, 165, 346, 348
   costs of, 23, 162, 172–173*n*3
   growth in local earnings per capita
      and, 13, 362
   programs for, that affect local
      economic development benefits,
      40–42
   quality of, 5, 6, 8, 40, 49, 52*n*17, 114,
      175

Wages, *cont.*
   low, for retail and service jobs,
      122–123
   newly created jobs at assisted
      businesses and, 67, 120–121,
      149n6, 149–150n7, 150n8
   property values and, 214n14
   unemployment and, 20, 21–22, 23–
      24, 50n4, 50n5, 294–296
Warner, Mildred, research of, 5, 104, 105
Washington, D.C. *See* District of
      Columbia
Washington (state)
   benefit-cost ratio for universal pre-K
      in, 274t
   business incentives disclosure
      required in, 304
   community college programs for job
      prep in, 205, 216n25
   economic impact of child care studied
      in, 105
   resident stability in, 273t
W.E. Upjohn Institute for Employment
      Research. *See* Upjohn Institute
Weitzman, Martin, on discount rates,
      178–179, 179t
Welfare programs, 78, 266n22
   reduced need for, 29, 99, 185
   See also under Costs, child-welfare
      system
West Virginia
   benefit-cost ratio for universal pre-K
      in, 274t
   business incentives disclosure
      required in, 304
   economic impact of child care studied
      in, 105
   resident stability in, 273t
WIA. *See* Workforce Investment Act
Wisconsin, data on, 273t, 274t
Woodcock-Johnson III Test of
      Achievement, effects of CLASS-
      IS on, 155–156n35
Workforce Investment Act (WIA), 204,
      205

Wyoming, 274t
   resident stability in, 272, 273t

Youth, crime reduction programs and, 3,
      100, 347

Zero-sum-game argument, local
      economic development policies
      and national benefits, 36–38,
      284–285, 293–294, 296

About the Institute

The W.E. Upjohn Institute for Employment Research is a nonprofit research organization devoted to finding and promoting solutions to employment-related problems at the national, state, and local levels. It is an activity of the W.E. Upjohn Unemployment Trustee Corporation, which was established in 1932 to administer a fund set aside by Dr. W.E. Upjohn, founder of The Upjohn Company, to seek ways to counteract the loss of employment income during economic downturns.

The Institute is funded largely by income from the W.E. Upjohn Unemployment Trust, supplemented by outside grants, contracts, and sales of publications. Activities of the Institute comprise the following elements: 1) a research program conducted by a resident staff of professional social scientists; 2) a competitive grant program, which expands and complements the internal research program by providing financial support to researchers outside the Institute; 3) a publications program, which provides the major vehicle for disseminating the research of staff and grantees, as well as other selected works in the field; and 4) an Employment Management Services division, which manages most of the publicly funded employment and training programs in the local area.

The broad objectives of the Institute's research, grant, and publication programs are to 1) promote scholarship and experimentation on issues of public and private employment and unemployment policy, and 2) make knowledge and scholarship relevant and useful to policymakers in their pursuit of solutions to employment and unemployment problems.

Current areas of concentration for these programs include causes, consequences, and measures to alleviate unemployment; social insurance and income maintenance programs; compensation; workforce quality; work arrangements; family labor issues; labor-management relations; and regional economic development and local labor markets.

CPSIA information can be obtained at www.ICGtesting.com
Printed in the USA
BVOW011726030213

312225BV00004B/8/P